DICTIONARY OF WORD AND PHRASE ORIGINS

By WILLIAM MORRIS:

It's Easy to Increase Your Vocabulary

By WILLIAM and MARY MORRIS:

The Word Game Book

DICTIONARY
OF WORD
AND PHRASE
ORIGINS

By William and Mary Morris

HARPER & ROW, PUBLISHERS
NEW YORK, EVANSTON and LONDON

E-R

Library of Congress catalog card number: 61-10842

AUTHOR'S NOTE

During the past quarter-century I have had the good fortune to be associated with several of America's foremost reference book publishers, first as a member of the educational department of the G. & C. Merriam Co., publishers of the Merriam-Webster Dictionaries. During the late 1940's I was editor-in-chief of *Words: The New Dictionary,* published jointly by Grosset & Dunlap and Henry Holt, Inc. In the past decade I have been successively advisory editor of the Funk & Wagnalls Standard Dictionaries and, currently, executive editor of a major encyclopedia-in-progress for the Grolier Society.

In each of these professional capacities I have garnered many of the facts that have gone into this book. Much more to the point, from my associations both within the companies named and with our friendly competitors, I have developed knowledge of and respect for the technical disciplines required in compiling a book of this nature.

Among my professional associates to whom I feel most obligated—not for any specific items, rather for the encouragement that has led me along the twenty-five-year road to this book—I should like to mention John P. Bethel, late editor-in-chief of the Merriam-Webster Dictionaries; Clarence Barnhart, creator of the famous Thorndike-Barnhart Dictionaries and many other great reference books; Jess Stein, editor-in-chief of the *American College Dictionary;* Charles F. Berlitz, editor-in-chief of the many Berlitz language books; William Roulet, executive vice president of Funk & Wagnalls; Henry L. Mencken and S. I. Hayakawa, whose enthusiasm for my early venture into lexicography, *Words: The New Dictionary,* was most gratifying; Harold L. Wentworth, author of the *American Dialect Dictionary* and co-author of *Dictionary of American Slang,* an old and valued friend whose books have been very nearly indispensable to me; and Joseph Vergara, my editor at Harper & Row, without whose appreciative and very practical encouragement this volume would not have seen print.

A few major contributions should also be noted. To the editors of *Holiday* magazine go thanks for much of adman's jargon; to Mitch Miller and Norman Paris for jazzmen's slang; to Joseph Kaselow, peerless advertising columnist of the New York *Herald Tribune,* for help in rounding up the language of Madison Avenue; to Charlie Rice and Stewart Beach of

This Week magazine for frequent, if frequently unwitting, contributions over the course of many conversations; to unnumbered government servants for examples of what has variously been called governmentese, pentagonese and gobbledegook; to William W. Vosburgh, Jr. of the Waterbury *American* for new light on the humor of our grandparents, Little Willie's "grues"; to Elmer Roessner, faithful and ever-helpful editor at Bell Syndicate, who, among many other leads, first touted us onto those confused and depressed beetles; lastly to Mimi and Evan, the youngest of the Morris offspring, who, though they seldom appear by name on these pages, left their imprint on virtually every one of them. If you don't believe that, just you try concentrating with two brilliant and highly vocal teenagers in the same house!

Most of all, of course, my gratitude goes to my wife and co-author, who has not only contributed at very least the inspiration and very often the content for many items, but has performed the far more onerous task of collating thousands of random items, indexing them assiduously, and editing them brilliantly.

WILLIAM MORRIS

INTRODUCTION

This *Dictionary of Word and Phrase Origins* is quite unlike any similar work. For one thing, it derives directly from research done over the past ten years at the behest of some twelve million readers of my daily column carried by more than fifty newspapers in the United States, Canada and Mexico. You would be surprised—as we have frequently been—at the difference between the real word-origin interests of people and what ivory-tower experts think should interest them. Many thousands of queries, suggestions and contributions have come from readers during the past decade —far too many to be acknowledged here.

Committing to print the result of years of research should be a serious business indeed. Yet we find a puzzlingly light-hearted mood upon us as we near the end of the long journey through the by-ways and back roads of the American and British Languages.

Perhaps the reason is that the task itself, though arduous, has been so rewarding. It's fun, believe us, to engage an old circus hand in conversation and learn, among other delightful things, that the bottom man of a human pyramid is called, with superb logic, the "understander." Or to quote Christopher Morley's word for one who sympathizes with the under-dog, "infracaninophile"—and receive a spate of learned and witty letters proving that it should have been "infracanophile." Or to learn that beetles may be either confused or depressed, but never both at the same time.

In the pages ahead you will find an unbelievable variety of language— from the "hush puppies" of Southern dialect to the "fine Italian hand" of papal secretaries, from the "ax" of hip musicians to the "sluggh-ghairm" (today's "slogan") of Highland chieftains. Without exception, these entries represent a query, interest in, or contribution to our language on the part of readers or associates, plus careful research on our part. Although the text in this volume is, for the most part, quite informal, we believe that you will find on close scrutiny that this careful research underlies every item.

Here, then, is your *Dictionary of Word and Phrase Origins*. Dip in and savor for yourself the wondrous varieties of the languages we call English and American.

WILLIAM AND MARY MORRIS

A

abacus

This word comes from the Greek *abax,* a tablet for writing or ciphering. The bead-and-frame gadget that we call an *abacus* was originated by the Chinese and called *suan pan.* Amazingly fast and intricate computations can be made by skillful users of the instrument. All authorities agree that the correct pronunciation places the stress on the first syllable: AB-uh-kus.

aboard. *See* baseball jargon.

A.B.S. marks. *See* Plimsoll mark.

according to Hoyle. *See* Hoyle, according to.

acronym

Probably the most interesting and widespread recent development in our changing language has been the vast popularity of acronyms.

Acronym (pronounced AK-roh-nim) is the name for a word formed by combining the initial letters or syllables of a series of words, for example, *Jato* (Jet Assisted Take-off) or *Basic* (British-American Scientific International Commercial) English. It comes from the Greek *akros* (tip) and *onym* (name).

The earliest acronyms are not known, though some scholars claim to have located examples in ancient Hebrew scriptures. Acronyms are found among nineteenth-century British and American word coinages but their appearance in profusion dates from World War I, when *Anzac* (Australian–New Zealand Army Corps) and *WAAC* (Women's Army Auxiliary Corps) were coined.

The full tide of popularity of acronyms in America, however, came with the advent of the New Deal and World War II. The custom of referring to the "alphabet agencies," such as *WPA* and *NLRB,* by their initials undoubtedly accelerated the trend toward naming organizations and offices by pronounceable combinations of letters. The U.S. Navy was especially prolific in coining acronyms, such as *Bupers* (Bureau of Personnel) and the ill-chosen *Cincus* (Commander in Chief, U.S. Fleet), which was abruptly changed after the disaster at Pearl Harbor.

During World War II, acronyms ranging from technical labels like *Radar* (Radio Detection and Ranging) to slang terms like *Snafu* (Situation Normal; All Fouled Up) became commonplace. During the years since World War II no single classification of word coinages has proliferated so rapidly.

Here is a list of the acronyms most commonly met today, together with a few (*Nabisco,* for example) that all of us will remember from our earliest childhood.

Alcoa   Aluminum Company of America
Anzac   Australia–New Zealand Army Corps
Anzus   Australia–New Zealand–United States Treaty
ASCAP   American Society of Composers, Authors and Publishers
AWOL   Absent Without Official Leave
Babs   Blind Approach Beacon System (flying)
Bad   Berlin Airlift Device (military)
Basic   (English) British-American Scientific International Commercial
      English
Benelux   Belgium, Netherlands, Luxembourg
Binac   Binary Automatic Computer
Biowar   Biological Warfare
BIPAD   Bureau of Independent Publishers and Distributors
BOMCOM   Bomber Command
Bosox   Boston Red Sox (baseball team)
Budocks   Bureau of Yards and Docks (Navy)
Bupers   Bureau of Personnel (Navy)
Caltech   California Institute of Technology
Cats   Civil Affairs Training School (Navy)
Cebar   Chemical, Biological, Radiological Warfare
Cermet   Ceramic Material Bonded to Metal
Chacom   Chain of Command (military)
Chisox   Chicago White Sox (baseball team)
Comintern   Communist International
Comseafron   Commander Sea Frontier (Navy)
CONAD   Continental Air Defense Command (military)
Contrail   Condensation Trail (flying)
Convair   Consolidated-Vultee Aircraft
COPE   Committee on Political Education (AFL-CIO)
CORE   Congress of Racial Equality
Dynasoar   Dynamic Soaring (space flight)

ENIAC   Electronic Numerical Integrator and Computer
Esso   Standard Oil
Eurailpass   European Railway Passenger (ticket)
EURATOM   European Atomic Energy Community
EUROMART   European Common Market
Fannie Mae   Federal National Mortgage Association
Fido   Fog, Intensive Dispersal of (military)
Flak   *Fliegerabwehrkanone* (German for "antiaircraft cannon")
Fubar   Fouled Up Beyond All Recognition
Fubb   Fouled Up Beyond Belief
Fumtu   Fouled Up More Than Usual
Jato   Jet Assisted Take-Off (flying)
Laser   Light Amplification through Simulated Emission of Radiation
Maser   Microwave Amplification through Simulated Emission of Radiation
MATS   Military Air Transport Service (Air Force)
Motel   Motor Hotel
Mouse   Minimum Orbital Unmanned Satellite of the Earth
Nabisco   National Biscuit Company
NANA   North American Newspaper Alliance
NASA   National Aeronautics and Space Administration
NATO   North Atlantic Treaty Organization
Nazi   National Socialist (German: *National-Sozialist*)
NICE   National Institute of Ceramic Engineers
OAFIE   Office of Armed Forces Information and Education
Panagra   Pan American–Grace Airways
Pan-Am   Pan American World Airways System
Paradrop   Airdrop by Parachute
Positron   Positive Electron
Radar   Radio Detection and Ranging
Radiac   Radiation Detection, Identification and Computation
Reo   Ransom E. Olds Co. (automobile)
Rif   Reduction in Force
SAC   Strategic Air Command
SACEUR   Supreme Commander Allied, Europe
SCAT   Service Command Air Transportation (Navy)
Scoop   Scientific Computation of Optimum Procurement
Score   Signal Communications by Orbiting Relay Equipment
Scuba   Self-Contained Underwater Breathing Apparatus
SEATO   Southeast Asia Treaty Organization
Slim   Submarine-Launched Inertial Missile
Smart   Supersonic Military Air Research Track
Smog   Smoke and Fog

Snafu   Situation Normal; All Fouled Up (military slang)
Snort   Supersonic Naval Ordnance Research Track
Socony   Standard Oil Company of New York
Stanvac   Standard Vacuum Oil Company
Tarfu   Things Are Really Fouled Up (military slang)

acrophobia

One of the most common phobias, *acrophobia,* meaning fear of heights, is derived from the Greek *akros* (at the point, end or top) and *phobos* (fear).

adamant

Adamant, a word that has been part of our language since Chaucer's time, has quite an interesting background. It was originally coined by the ancients from the Greek words *a* (not) and *damao* (I tame) to describe a mineral of incomparable hardness. For many centuries it was regarded as synonymous with "diamond"—the hardest of gems. The two words, indeed, come from precisely the same Greek root.

adman's jargon

In my column I have been known, from time to time, to view with stern and reproving eye some of the wilder excesses of the advertising gentry. The excessive and unsubstantiated claim of excellence, the open-end comparative ("Laboratory tests prove hot-shots *better*") and the calculated bad grammar designed to appeal to the "common man"—all these have drawn my fire on occasion.

But one aspect of life among the Madison Avenue cliff dwellers never ceases to excite my somewhat rueful admiration. That is the shop talk used by members of the advertising fraternity. As would be expected of craftsmen who deal daily in superlatives, it is characterized by fanciful, freewheeling metaphor. "What this account needs is men who can plug the holes in the dike without getting their thumbs wet" is a sample. Or "Take it to the lab and see if it's a mushroom or a toadstool."

The problems besetting an agency copywriter are not really much different from those faced by thousands of other modestly creative people working at desks in other industries. But the language he uses to describe each predicament bears little resemblance to the triter observations of lay folk.

Situation: A program into which much thought and planning has gone is rejected by management. Adman's comment: "Bigdome just exploded our lotus blossom."

Situation: First client reaction to a new campaign is less than enthusiastic. Adman's comment: "Let's throw a blanket on this and keep it warm" or "We'll have to put this in a traction splint and hope it knits."

Situation: The hour is late and a crisis impends. Adman's comment: "Let's not open *that* can of peas."

And always there is the realization that man is seldom the master of his fate in today's business world. As the agency man says, "When you've got a bear by the tail, you have to go where the bear goes." Why? Because "that's the way the banana peels!"

The first presentation of a new campaign to the client might well call forth the tentative "Let's run up the flag and see who salutes." Or a cautious account executive—and who among them, behind the self-confident exterior, isn't pretty cautious?—might counsel: "Let's leave it in deep water overnight and see if it springs any leaks." Another version of this runs: "Let's drive it into the parking lot and see if we dent any fenders."

"Compound fracture" translates to "five account executives laughing at one client's joke."

A first attempt at copy for a campaign might well get this comment from the copy chief: "I see pinfeathers on this, but you're not flying yet"—or, in the common patois: "Nice try."

The era of "think big" is still with us, of course, but the boys on the Avenue phrase it differently: "If you're going to build a bridge across the Mississippi, do it lengthwise."

Admirable Crichton, the

Actually there were two "Admirable Crichtons"—one fictional and one real and it's hard to tell which was the more fascinating. One is the hero of James M. Barrie's play of the same name, first performed in 1902 and revived many times since. In it, Crichton, the very model of the typical British butler, serves in the household of Lord Loam, who likes to believe that class distinctions are silly stuff. To prove his point he insists, one day each year, on serving Crichton and the other servants at tea, an eccentricity that horrifies Crichton.

Later the household is shipwrecked on a desert island and Crichton, as the man best qualified to manage things, takes over and becomes the unquestioned leader of the group. He even proposes to marry his former lord's daughter. A rescue party comes to the island, however, and Crichton —again the very model of a proper British manservant—reverts to his former menial status.

The earlier, real-life Crichton was born in 1560 and was the outstanding physical and mental prodigy of his age. By the time he reached fifteen he had taken his Master of Arts degree and at twenty was reported to have mastered a dozen languages and to be knowledgeable in all the then-known sciences.

The British Isles were obviously too small a theater for a lad of his gifts, so he went first to France where he dazzled the best brains of the Sorbonne, served a year or two with the French Army, then went on to Italy. There he became tutor to sons of dukes and princes, dazzling everyone with his beauty, brilliance and ability as a swordsman. While still in his early twenties, he was rash enough to steal the love of a prince's lady and was treacherously assaulted by three masked men. Thus he died—not wholly admirably, perhaps—one of history's most fabled prodigies.

adroit. See gauche.

aestheticism. See ascetic.

affluent

Affluent (pronounced AF-loo-ent) today usually means "rich." Thus, "The mink-upholstered Cadillac belongs to an *affluent* newcomer from Texas." Derived from the Latin *ad* (to) and *fluere* (flow), it literally means flowing abundantly—like the *affluent* oil wells which may well have made our Texas newcomer financially *affluent*.

affront

Affront (pronounced uh-FRUNT) means to insult or to offend by disrespect. It is perhaps more commonly met in the passive than the active voice, in sentences like, "The Congressman was *affronted* by the lobbyist's lack of respect." *Affront* comes from the Latin words *ad* (to) and *frons* (forehead). Its original meaning was to confront a person face to face. Nowadays, however, it has the special meaning of to insult a person openly and deliberately. You may insult or offend another person in private, but you can *affront* him only in public. *Affront* is also a noun, in such a sentence as "Your action in snubbing me at the dance constituted an *affront.*"

afghan

It's curious but the way the name *afghan* came to be applied to the familiar knitted woolen blanket has not previously been documented in any standard reference book. That it is derived from "Afghan," a native or product of Afghanistan, is obvious, of course. But it does seem odd that a name coming from such a faraway corner of the world, deep in Asia, should have been used for so long for such a homely item typically found in the American cedar chest.

One characteristic of the *afghan* is that, in the words of the *Modern Textile Dictionary,* it is "made with a series of stripes, zigzag effects, or squares, varying in size and vivid colorings." This characteristic is shared, of course, with *afghan* rugs, which also feature geometric patterns and vivid colors. So the likelihood is that the *afghan* blanket was named for its resemblance to these Oriental rugs which enjoyed such a great vogue in America during the latter part of the Victorian era.

aficionado

Aficionado (pronounced ah-fee-shuh-NAH-doh) is a Spanish word, much affected in recent years by people who want to add a little highfalutin tone to their talk or writing. It simply means "devotee," especially an enthusiastic, amateur follower of an art form.

After me, the flood. *See* Après moi le déluge.

ailurophile

A lover of cats is an *ailurophile,* from the Greek *ailouros,* meaning "cat," and *philos,* meaning "loving" or "fond of."

airplane jargon

Here is a brief look at the private language of two phases of our newest industry, aviation. First, a few of the words current in the daily talk of our jet aircraft pilots.

"The jet was making mach 1.2 at twenty-two angels when the fly boy, all hunched up, made the break and, for a second, thought he'd have to hit the panic rack to avoid blackout."

This extraordinary gibberish, which sounds rather like something out of a twenty-fifth-century science-fiction story, actually is made up of slang and technical terms used by today's jet airplane pilots and engineers.

Mach 1.2 refers to the speed of the plane. Reference to the speed of a supersonic airplane in conventional "miles per hour" terms grates on the ears of a jet pilot just as much as the phrase "knots per hour" irritates a sea captain. Indeed, to a modern aviator "miles per hour" is nearly a meaningless term. He is interested in the ratio of his speed in the air to the speed of sound and this he expresses by a *mach number* (see SPACE JARGON). For example, a plane flying at precisely the speed of sound is flying at *mach 1.* Speeds faster or slower than the speed of sound are expressed thus: *mach 1.1* (or higher) and *mach .9* (or lower).

Twenty-two angels tells the altitude at which the plane is flying, an *angel* being a unit of 1,000 feet. This plane, therefore, is at 22,000 feet.

The *fly boy* is the pilot, though any member of the crew in a large plane can be so designated.

All hunched up means extremely nervous and the *break* is a sharp turn.

The *panic rack* is the special seat designed for jet pilots which, when a release lever is hit, ejects the pilot—parachute and all—into space. And *blackout,* of course, is loss of consciousness due to speed, air pressure, centrifugal force and other factors acting upon the pilot under such circumstances.

Thus the sentence in layman's language goes something like this: "The jet plane was going approximately 900 miles per hour at 22,000 feet when the pilot, nervous about the maneuver, made a sharp turn and momentarily thought he might have to eject himself from the plane to avoid loss of consciousness."

Now let's take a look at the behind-the-scenes language of commercial aviation. Do you know the difference between a *go-sho* and a *no-sho?* Can you translate *check rez, no-op* and *mechanical?*

The *no-sho* is the archvillain of the airlines. He holds a reservation, neglects to cancel it when he changes his plans and permits a plane to depart with an empty seat.

A *go-sho,* it follows, is a person who stands by at the airport—with ticket but without confirmed reservation—in hopes that a passenger on a flight booked to capacity will prove to be a *no-sho* and, by thus defaulting, supply a seat for the *go-sho.*

A typical response to a customer's query about a flight to San Francisco might sound like this, if phrased in the jargon the airline agents themselves use: "Now let's see. I could book you on Two-Six but it's unable out of Shy. Four-Six is no-op on Tuesday, so that's out. Seven-Three has a mechanical. Sorry, the only thing I see is a go-sho." All this after he has *checked rez,* that is, checked reservation control.

Translated into everyday English, the agent's remarks run something like this: "I could get space for you on Flight 26, but it terminates at Cheyenne. Flight 46 does not operate on Tuesday. Flight 73 is grounded because of mechanical difficulties. The only thing I can recommend is that you go out to the airport and stand by in case a reservation is canceled or a reservation holder fails to appear at flight time."

alibi

In law an *alibi*—technically "being elsewhere"—is the plea that a person accused of a crime could not have committed it because he was someplace other than at the scene of the crime when it was committted.

In popular usage, *alibi* usually carries with it the implication that there is something spurious about the explanation given. We speak of a person trying to alibi his way out of an embarrassing situation. *Alibi* also, as

Webster's *Dictionary of Synonyms* puts it, "implies a desire to shift blame or avoid punishment."

Of course a person can give an "excuse" in his desire to shift blame or avoid punishment, and we often do exactly that. When, for instance, a child brings to school an "excuse" from his parents for an absence from school, he is surely doing so to avoid punishment.

But because *alibi* has been so long and so widely used in its legal sense and since it carries with it an odor of wrongdoing that does not normally attach to "excuse," there is a valid distinction between the two words.

Alibi Ike

Every outfit in the military services has its "operators"—the fellows who are just a little sharper, just a little smoother, just a little more glib than the ordinary GI.

Apparently the streamlined "new Army" is no different from the old, judging by this letter from a soldier. "We have a fellow in our outfit," he wrote, "who is always high man in poker and low man when any physical effort is involved. In fact he has managed to dodge duty so often, with such a brilliant variety of excuses, that he is known around our barracks as *Alibi Ike*. But he doesn't mind the nickname. In fact, he rather enjoys it. He says if we knew what *alibi* meant, we wouldn't use it for him. He claims it has some sort of perfectly good legal meaning, but to us an *alibi* is a phony excuse. What do you say?"

As it happens, they're both right. The company's "operator" is referring to the technical legal meaning of *alibi,* the plea that a person accused of a crime was actually at some distance from the scene of the crime when it was committed. When such an alibi is supported by appropriate evidence, it establishes the innocence of the accused. So, in this technical sense, there is nothing derogatory about the word *alibi,* and the *Alibi Ike* interpreted his nickname as an unconscious tribute to his ability to be occupied elsewhere when there was heavy work to be done.

In everyday speech, of course, *alibi* means simply an excuse—especially one which won't stand close scrutiny. And *Alibi Ike*—a nickname which Ring Lardner coined, by the way—would not normally be regarded as at all flattering.

alligator. *See* crocodile tears.

alumnus, alumna

Alumnus and *alumna* are simply the Latin words for "foster son" and "foster daughter." Though used in Great Britain to mean "pupil," in America they describe only graduates of a school or college.

Incidentally, the unusual plurals of these two words often cause trouble. They retain the original Latin endings, but the accepted American pronunciations of these endings happen to be precisely transposed from the classical Latin sounds. Thus, *alumni* (men graduates) in Latin was pronounced uh-LUM-nee and *alumnae* (women graduates) was uh-LUM-nye. However, present-day pronunciation throughout the English-speaking world is uh-LUM-nye for *alumni* and uh-LUM-nee for *alumnae*.

-ama (suffix)

Foodorama, Bowlerama, Pizzarama—the *"ama*-addicts" have gotten completely out of hand. As Wolcott Gibbs once wrote in another connection, "Where it all will end, knows God."

But if no one can predict when the craze for such "nonce words" (words coined and used for a single occasion) will end, we can tell pretty well where it started. Specifically, though the coinage was in imitation of *panorama,* the first such word was *Wonderama,* a trade-marked name devised by the General Motors people to describe their "World of Tomorrow" exhibit in the New York World's Fair of 1939.

Perhaps because most of us were too busy with the war to be bothered coining grandiose names, the suffix *ama* went into temporary eclipse for a few years, only to be revived in 1952 by Lowell Thomas when he coined the name *Cinerama* for one of the more spectacular wide-screen movie techniques. After that the deluge: *sporteramas, bowleramas, chickeneramas* (where "bar-b-q" chicken is sold, of course) and countless others, each a trifle more distressing to lovers of language.

amateur

An *amateur* is—or was originally—a person who loves a game or subject. The word comes from the Latin *amare* (to love). Thus a painter like Sir Winston Churchill may properly be called an *"amateur* painter" for, though his works may indeed have genuine artistic merit, he paints them primarily for the sheer love of painting.

Love in tennis and other racket games is directly derived from this idea of amateurism. A person who "plays for love," in the age-old expression, is literally playing for nothing—at least nothing in the form of a tangible reward. Thus the figure "O" has for more than two centuries been called *love*—and the person who remains on the *love* end of many sets of tennis must truly be called *amateur* in all the senses of that much abused word.

ambiguous

Ambiguous (pronounced am-BIG-yoo-us), an adjective, and the noun *ambiguity* (pronounced am-big-YOO-ih-tee) both come from the Latin words *ambi-* (around) and *ago* (to go) and have the meaning of evasion or "going around" an issue. If you say that a person's answer to a question is *ambiguous,* you mean that he has been evasive and that his answer has two or more possible meanings. He has been guilty of *ambiguity* in his reply to your question.

ambulance

Through most of mankind's wars, men injured in battle were allowed to lie where they fell until, under cover of night, doctors or medical aid men could reach them. During Napoleon's campaigns, medical men devised a quicker means of bringing help to the wounded—a light, readily portable, covered litter, fitted out with bandages, tourniquets and other first-aid equipment. This was called an *hôpital ambulant,* literally a "walking hospital." Because of the speed with which it functioned—by comparison with earlier methods, at least—these portable aid stations became known as *ambulances volantes* (flying travelers). When the British Army adopted the system, the name of the vehicles was shortened to *ambulance.*

ameliorate

Coming directly from the Latin *ad* (to) and *melior* (better), *ameliorate* means to make better, to improve. See also UNUSUAL WORDS.

ampere. *See* volt.

ampersand

The sign *&* is called the *ampersand,* from the phrase "and per se and" or *"& by itself means *and*."* The character is believed to have originated as an abbreviation of the Latin *et* meaning "and." It is pronounced AM-persand.

anchor, weigh. *See* weigh anchor, to.

anemophobia

Derived from the Greek *anemos* (the wind) and *phobos* (fear), *anemophobia* is the dread of hurricanes and cyclones. See also PHOBIAS.

animosity

Animosity (pronounced an-ih-MOSS-ih-tee) means intense dislike, amounting sometimes to open hostility. It comes from the Latin word *animus,* which originally meant "soul" or "driving force" and came in time to mean "passion." Nowadays only one kind of passion is represented in *animosity*—the passion of hatred.

animus

Animus (pronounced AN-ih-mus) comes, of course, from the same Latin root as *animosity.* Although *animus* retains some of the original idea of the soul as a driving force, even here the more common interpretation today is of *animus* in the sense of "ill-will" or "dislike."

ankh

Pronounced like "tank" without the "t," *ankh* is an ancient Egyptian symbol of life, a cross with a loop at the top. See also WEIRD WORDS.

antic. *See* frantic.

antimacassar

A century ago, long before today's greaseless hair tonics had been devised, it was the fashion for dandies to slick down their locks with fragrant pomades and oils, the better to charm their fair ladies. One of the favorite lotions contained a large percentage of macassar oil. In England, indeed, the word "Macassar" was trade-marked as the name of a proprietary brand of hair oil.

Here enters the practicality of women. Wishing neither to blight the vanity of their gentlemen callers nor to spend hours trying to remove hair oil from their upholstered furniture, they devised attractive yet practical lace coverlets and pinned them on the furniture to absorb the Macassar oil. Hence the name, *anti-* (against) *Macassar* (hair oil).

anzac. *See* acronyms.

A-O.K.

A-O.K. is one of the oddest terms in the history of language. Perhaps it's indicative of how fast things move today, even linguistically, when we reflect on the fact that our space efforts have resulted in the creation of a phrase that died before it was born, a term which—except in the mind of a public relations officer—never existed at all.

In giving the oral report to newsmen and on radio of the first (Shepard) suborbital flight, Colonel "Shorty" Powers, NASA public relations officer, misunderstood Shepard and mistook a routine "O.K." for *A-O.K.* He fancied the term so much that he repeated it several times, and it caught on with headline writers, if not with the astronauts themselves. According to reliable reports, no astronaut has ever used the term *A-O.K.* It's Powers' term and his alone. Judging by its absence from the account of the Glenn flight, Powers has decided to forget it, too.

apartheid

Apartheid (pronounced uh-PAR-thide) is a South African Dutch word descriptive of the policy of segregation of white and colored races promulgated by former Prime Minister Daniel F. Malan (pronounced, incidentally, Muh-LAN) of the Union of South Africa. It is derived from two Dutch words *apart* and *heid* (hood). Thus it literally means the state of being apart or segregated.

The first recorded appearance of the word in print was in 1949 and to date its use seems to have been limited to that government's policy of segregation administered by Malan. It has not, I believe, been used as yet in reference to segregation in any other part of the world.

apocryphal, apocrypha

Apochryphal (pronounced uh-POK-ruh-ful) is an adjective derived from the Greek words *apo* (from) and *kryptein* (to hide). Thus it meant originally "hidden from" but today it means "of doubtful authenticity" or even counterfeit. The most famous *apochryphal* writings, of course, are the fourteen books of the Septuagint Bible which were not found in the Hebrew Old Testament. Regarded by some scholars as of doubtful authenticity, they are called the Apochrypha.

apple-pie order

Apple-pie order has little to do with the culinary arts. It is, in fact, a corruption of the French phrase *nappe plié,* meaning "folded linen." It is applied to dinner napkins, and perhaps the transition from the dining room to the kitchen is not so very far, after all.

The expression *apple-pie bed,* meaning one in which prankish bunkmates have folded the sheets so that a person cannot stretch his legs full length, likewise comes from this French phrase.

One widely held theory is that *apple-pie order* comes to us from our historic past, from the early days of New England. One of the Colonial housewives was in the habit of baking seven pies ahead for the new week just starting. When she had her pies all baked and cooled, she then placed them on her pantry shelves just so; the pie that was to be eaten on Monday was set on the first shelf, the one for Tuesday right next to it, and so on.

Being a meticulous housekeeper, she always checked to make sure they were lined up just right, hence the phrase *apple-pie order*.

Well, that's a nice little story and I don't suppose it will do anyone any harm to believe it. The only trouble with it is that there isn't a shred of truth in it, since the one point that all authorities agree on is that the term *apple-pie order* was commonly used in England long before it appeared in this country.

And anyway, wouldn't that seventh pie have been pretty stale after sitting on the shelf for a week? If only our Colonial housewife had been equipped with a food freezer, the story would be more credible—and the pie more edible!

Après moi le déluge.

Après moi le déluge means literally "After me, the flood." The popularity of the phrase stems from its use by Madame de Pompadour, celebrated beauty and intimate of King Louis XV of France. The French court at the time was famed for its lavish and wasteful extravagances. When Pompadour, whose philosophy was "Live for the minute—who cares what happens when we're gone?" was reproved for these excesses, she replied, *"Après nous le déluge."*

Incidentally, the pompadour hair-do in which the hair is brushed straight up from the forehead—a style which has been in and out of fashion a hundred times since her day—was, of course, named after this celebrated court favorite.

April Fool's Day

April Fool's Day is the day for childish pranks, the day when the gullible and unwary are fair game for the inventive and enterprising among us.

Just where did this custom begin? Well, there seem to be almost as many theories about the origin of All Fool's Day, as the British call it, as there are pranks to be played. One account traces it back to Roman mythology. It seems that Proserpina, daughter of Ceres, the goddess of agriculture, was playing happily in the Elysian fields and had just plucked a lapful of daffodils when she was seized by Pluto, king of Hades, and carried off to rule as his queen. Her mother heard the echo of her screams and went in search of Proserpina but, of course, it was a fruitless errand. Thus, say some, began the custom of sending gullible people on fool's errands.

Perhaps the soundest theory of the day's origin traces it back to the time when the Gregorian calendar (the one we now use) replaced the Julian calendar which had been in use since Roman times. During the Middle Ages most Christian countries celebrated the start of the new year with a festival beginning March 25 and ending April 1. Traditionally, the last day of this period was devoted to the bearing of gifts to one's friends and neighbors. When the Gregorian calendar was finally adopted by England in 1752, New Year's Day was moved back, of course, to January 1. But some practical jokers continued to make calls and give mock gifts on April 1 and thus, so the story goes, April Fool's Day was born.

The Scots have an amusing phrase to describe the chap sent to fetch a left-handed monkey wrench or a can of cold steam. He's said to be *hunting the gowk*—and *gowk* is the cuckoo bird. In France, the victim of such pranks is called *poisson d'Avril* (fish of April). The April fish, of course, is newly hatched and thus naïve and easily trapped.

aqua

Aqua, when used as the name of a color, is merely a shortened form of "aquamarine" and means, in the words of Webster, a "color, green-blue in hue, of low saturation and medium brilliance." Since aquamarine is pronounced ak-wuh-muh-REEN, it logically follows that the proper pronunciation of the abbreviated form is AK-wuh. The only exception is the predominately British pronunciation AY-kwuh.

arbitrary

This is a rather difficult word to pin down, since synonyms for it in standard dictionaries run the gamut from "absolute" and "autocratic" to "capricious" and "uncertain." An *arbiter,* of course, is one who has the authority to decide between two conflicting points of view. Thus, there is a discretionary element in any *arbitrary* decision. But the fact that the decision is final and conclusive accounts for the "absolute" element in the word's meaning. Hence, *arbitrary* in current usage has come to mean "conclusive but based on the judgment or whim of an individual."

Around New York's famed club, The Players, they still tell a story about one of their members, Oliver Herford, that illustrates pretty well the meaning of *arbitrary*. Herford, "the humorist's humorist," was known as an inveterate cigar smoker. In some thirty years of daily attendance at the club he had never been seen without a fine Havana jauntily set in the corner of his mouth. It was a matter of some concern to his fellow clubmates, therefore, when it was noticed that he had appeared two days in succession without his cigar.

Pressed for an explanation, he told his old friend, Franklin P. Adams, that he had given up the weed because his wife had suddenly decided she couldn't stand cigar smoke. "Heavens, man," F.P.A. remonstrated. "You mean that you're giving up cigars after thirty years, just because of a whim of your wife?"

"You don't know my wife, Frank," Herford replied gently. "She has a whim of iron!"

arcane

Arcane (pronounced ar-KANE) is derived from the Latin word *arcanum* which meant anything hidden from the masses of men, especially any of the great secrets of nature. In medieval times alchemists tried to discover such great *arcana* as the means by which base metals could be transformed into gold.

architectural jargon

In the complex language of the professional architect there are root words from every tongue, ancient and modern, which has contributed to today's English, but it is somehow comforting to recognize the large number of them that had a familiar ring to Chaucer's ear.

Arris—The angle formed by the meeting of two surfaces, as in the outer corner of a mitered joint.

Batten—A thin strip of wood.

Bib—A faucet, usually threaded to receive a hose.

Clerestory—The part of a structure that rises above the main roof line.

Gambrel—A roof with five-sided gables.

Joggle—A notched or doweled joint.

Mullion—A slender vertical bar between the "lights" in windows.

Purlins—Pieces of timber used to support rafters.

Putlog—A short timber, one end inserted in the masonry, to hold scaffolding.

Stringers—The sides of a flight of stairs which run diagonally from one floor to the next.

Weepers—An outlet in masonry walls for drainage.

army slang. *See* Old Army slang.

arraign, arrange

Arraign (pronounced uh-RAYN) comes from the Latin *ad* (to) and *ratio* (judgment) and means the summoning before the bar of justice of a person accused of crime. At the *arraignment* (uh-RAYN-ment) a prisoner may plead guilty or not guilty.

Arrange comes from the old French word *arangier* and literally means to place in order or rank. This meaning still is common as in such phrases as "to arrange flowers."

So, although *arraign* and *arrange* look alike, their meanings differ and their origins are totally unrelated.

Ars Gratia Artis

Since Metro-Goldwyn-Mayer has released its backlog of motion pictures to television, Leo the Lion is becoming a fairly regular visitor in our living room. If you're blessed with 20-20 vision, you can barely make out the Latin motto that appears on the screen at the beginning of each MGM picture. It reads *"Ars Gratia Artis,"* "Art for Art's Sake"—a motto which seems wildly irrelevant when you think of the millions of dollars paid for this "art" by the television sponsors.

artesian well

This well gets its name from Artois, formerly a province in northern France, where such wells were first drilled. Actually the spelling *artesian* comes from the Old French name of the province, "Arteis." An *artesian well* is, of course, one which is drilled through one or more impermeable strata until water or oil is reached, whereupon the fluid spurts up spontaneously, forced by underground pressure.

artillery pie. *See* Old Army slang.

ascetic, asceticism, aestheticism

Ascetic (pronounced uh-SET-ik) is an adjective meaning self-denying, rigorous and austere. Interestingly enough, it came from the Greek word *askein,* meaning "exercise," and originally referred to the rigorous self-denial practiced by an athlete when in training. In the early days of the church, an *ascetic* was a person who removed himself from all worldly temptations and devoted himself to a life of contemplation and austerity. The religious doctrine followed by those sects who hold that a closer approach to divine grace is achieved by self-denial and abstinence from worldly things is called *asceticism.*

Asceticism (pronounced uh-SET-uh-siz'm) should not, by the way, be confused with *aestheticism* (sometimes spelled *estheticism*), which means devotion to beauty and good taste in the arts. *Aestheticism* (pronounced es-THET-uh-siz'm) comes from the Greek *aisthetikos,* meaning "sensitive," and an *aesthetic* person is one whom we consider especially sensitive in matters of beauty and art.

assault and battery

This phrase is a technical one as used in courts of law. It is not redundant or repetitious, though much legal language is. There is a fine distinction in law between *assault* and *battery*. You can *assault* a person without actually touching him. In the eyes of the law, *assault* is committed if you merely offer or threaten to do bodily injury to a person.

The commission of *battery,* however, involves illegal beating or injury to a person or his personal belongings. Thus the difference between the two is that *assault* is the attempt or threat of bodily violence, while *battery* is the actual striking of another person.

astronaut, cosmonaut

Our word *astronaut,* from the Greek words *astron* (star) and *nautes* (sailor or seaman), aptly labels a person who sails among the stars. But the stars are not the whole of our cosmos (from the Greek *kosmos* meaning "universe"). So it would seem that *cosmonaut* is more all-encompassing than *astronaut.*

Perhaps *cosmonaut* was chosen by the Russians with a thought to its propaganda implications, since cosmos implies not merely the universe but specifically a universe conceived as an orderly, harmonious system.

Funk & Wagnalls' *Standard Dictionary,* International Edition, of which I am advisory editor, entered *astronautics* ("the science and art of space travel") and *astronaut* in their edition published in 1958. This would indicate that the staff editors must have been collecting "citations"— examples of the use of this word in print—at least as early as 1954.

I believe the word appeared with some frequency in science-fiction stories and articles during the 1940's and 1950's—and I should not be at all surprised if that pioneer master of the science-fiction form, Jules Verne, didn't use the French equivalent of *astronaut* back in the nineteenth century. You'll recall that in his *A Trip to the Moon* (1865) he told a story that had several remarkable parallels to the story of Russia's first Sputnik, even to the inclusion of a small dog in the first space ship. Also, of course, the ship carried humans—the first *astronauts.*

atmospherics

What is known as static in American radios becomes *atmospherics* to the British. See also ENGLISH ENGLISH.

auld lang syne

Auld lang syne is a Scottish term meaning literally "old long since." Freely translated, it means "long ago" and thus it lends itself with singular appropriateness to New Year's Eve, when we review the joys and sorrows of the past and prepare to face the challenge of the year to come. Incidentally, the last word should be pronounced as spelled (SYNE) not, as all too often it is, as if it were spelled "zyne."

auntie

Auntie is astronautical slanguage for the antimissile missile. See also SPACE JARGON.

Australian slang

You probably remember *billabong* from the song "Waltzing Matilda," which was the marching favorite of Australian troops during World War II, but do you know what it means? And do you know what a *bonzer bushwhacker* is?

I have recently been occupied with galley proofs for the first Australian edition of a dictionary I edited, and the part which pleased me most was a special section on native Australian slang.

Here I learned that *bonzer* means "very good, likable" and so a *bonzer bushwhacker* is a likable resident of rural areas. That *billabong* of the popular song is a riverside lagoon. A *swagman* is what we would call a "hobo" and when he *humps his bluey* he is hoisting his blanket roll and getting set to hit the road. With a touch of regret I note that *matilda* of the song title is not a delectable female—as most Americans thought—but the same thing as *bluey,* a blanket roll.

Now some of my readers may think that instead of being a *dabster* (expert) I am only a *dag* (humorous fellow) who is *giving a fly* (making an attempt) at talking *fodder* (nonsense), but that is far from the truth. Indeed, I assure you that this is all *square dinkum* (thoroughly trustworthy) or, as we *Yanks* (Americans) say, "The Real McCoy!"

automobile designers' slang

Like every other group of craftsmen, the designers of the nation's automobiles have their own jargon or private trade language. It's refreshingly down to earth and candid—especially in contrast to the high-flown terms concocted by advertising copywriters to describe the results of the designers' efforts.

"Drag out the eyebrows, recess the eggcrate and beef up the blade on the dagmars," reads a summation of plans for the redesign of a car's front end, according to the Ford Motor Company's house organ. Here's what it means:

The *eyebrows* are the front fender edges extending out over the top of the headlights. The leading edge of the engine housing is known as the *creaseline* by analogy to the creases on men's pants. It's also sometimes called the *prow*—a term taken straight from ship designing, of course.

The grill in front of the radiator is the *eggcrate,* so called from the resemblance of its horizontal blades and vertical struts to the common or market variety of eggcrate.

Beefing up the blade means adding emphasis to the vertical forms on the bumper guards. And *dagmars?* Well, here I fear we have an instance of the rapid obsolescence of slang. The young lady whose attributes are likened to the rounded projections on the bumper guards seems already to have slipped into the limbo of forgotten television stars and there must be a whole new generation of young motor enthusiasts to whom this allusion will be meaningless.

automobile slang, British

There's an ocean of difference between British and American automotive jargon. Should an Englishman mention that he has a *strangler in his saloon,* for example, there's no need to summon the bobbies. He merely means that his sedan's engine is equipped with a choke.

Should he say that he's going in to be *decoked,* don't jump to the conclusion that he's suffering from an overdose of a popular soft drink. He's merely taking the car in for a carbon job.

On the sound premise that no one has ever been known to stow gloves in a glove compartment, he labels this space a *cubby locker in the drop head.* The trunk is a *boot* and shock absorbers are *dampers.*

Then, too, an Englishman of the most unsaintly sort may have his *wings* crumpled, for *wings* are to him what "fenders" are to us. And if he promised to "tool around nineish sort of, bringing the *caravan,*" don't look for a colorful troupe of gypsy wagons arriving at breakfast time. To him a *caravan* is simply a trailer.

autopsy, biopsy

Both *autopsy* and *biopsy* refer to the close examination, often by microscope, of body tissues. There are, however, two chief points of difference. First, an *autopsy* is performed on dead tissue, while a *biopsy* is performed on living tissue. Second, the purpose of the *autopsy* is to determine the cause of death, while the *biopsy* is a clinical and diagnostic examination whose chief purpose is to help determine the proper treatment for a diseased organ.

Both words are derived from the Greek root *opsis,* meaning "sight." The prefix *auto* is from the Greek *autos* (self). Thus an *autopsy* is literally "a seeing for oneself." The combining form *bio* in *biopsy* is from the Greek *bios* (life), so that a *biopsy* is literally a "looking at" or study of living flesh.

avant-garde

A literal translation of the French words making up *avant-garde* would be "before the guard." The English modification of it is "vanguard," meaning a group in the leading position in any field.

Today the original French phrase is used to designate leaders in political and intellectual fields. In this use it also usually connotes a deviation from the normal pattern, as in the case of *avant-garde* poetry, *avant-garde* art and so on.

ax. *See* jazzmen's jargon.

B

bachelor

A *bachelor,* in the marital or premarital use of the word, means only one thing: a man who has not been married. Use of this word in place of "widower" or "divorced man" is simply careless or ignorant.

From its earliest origin, *bachelor* has had the connotation of "novice," a sense that is reflected also in the other major use of *bachelor*—in such phrases as "*bachelor* of arts" to designate the first degree awarded by a college or university. Back in the Middle Ages a *bachelor* was a young knight serving a period as vassal to a member of the landed gentry. In fact, the original *bachelor* was little more than a glorified cowhand—*baccalaris* being the Latin term for "one who cares for cows."

back and fill, to

Back and fill is a term from the language of sailing men. It describes a maneuver of tacking when the tide is running with your craft and the wind against it. Obviously not much progress is made under these circumstances. The end result is that there's a good deal of motion fore and aft—much shifting of ground, so to speak—but the boat stays just about where it was. So to *back and fill* has been taken into popular speech as synonymous with "to vacillate" or "to be irresolute."

bacon, to bring home the

As so often happens, there are two theories of the origin of this phrase. The first is that it refers to the fact that the winner of the greased pig contest at country fairs traditionally keeps the pig and thus *brings home the bacon.*

An earlier story of the origin of the phrase goes all the way back to 1111 A.D. and the town of Dunmow in England. A noblewoman, wishing to encourage marital happiness, decreed that "any person from any part of England going to Dunmow and humbly kneeling on two stones at the church door may claim a gammon [side] of bacon, if he can swear that for twelve months and a day he has never had a household brawl or wished himself unmarried."

So the "Dunmow flitch," as the side of bacon was called, became a symbol of domestic felicity and a man *bringing home the bacon* would be a rare and happy fellow. Let cynics make what they will of the record that in a period of five centuries (1244–1772) there were only eight claimants of the prize.

bad ball. *See* baseball jargon.

bagel and lox

Bagel and lox with cream cheese is as popular a breakfast delicacy in America's Jewish community as doughnuts and coffee in the nation as a whole. And, incidentally, many non-Jews have learned to savor this unusual gustatory treat.

The *bagel*—which has been described as "a doughnut with a Jewish education"—is similar to the doughnut in shape but is made of an unsalted yeast dough which is first simmered in water and then baked. It gets its name from the Yiddish word *beigen,* meaning "to bend or twist."

The *bagel* is split before serving, spread well with cream cheese and then topped with *lox.* And what is *lox,* you ask? Simply thin-sliced, salty smoked salmon. Usually the Nova Scotia variety of salmon is served in New York but Alaskan or West Coast salmon may be served in other parts of the country.

Lox, incidentally, comes from another Yiddish-German word, *lachs,* which is closely related to the Anglo-Saxon *leax,* also meaning "salmon."

Bailey Bridge

After the disastrous Connecticut Valley floods a few years ago, a woman from Middletown, Connecticut, wrote me: "Since the flood has struck our Naugatuck Valley, I've been hearing about the Army's *Bailey Bridge*. Several are supposed to be installed in this area, although I haven't seen one due to the ban on sightseeing. For whom and when was this piece of engineering named?"

The *Bailey Bridge* is a portable bridge made of prefabricated steel sections in the form of lattices. It was named for its inventor, Donald Coleman Bailey of the British Ministry of Supply in World War II. So successful was his invention that he was knighted in 1945 for his contribution to the victorious war effort.

bake. *See* jazzmen's jargon.

baker's dozen

There are many theories about the origin of this phrase. The most commonly accepted theory dates back to fifteenth-century England. It seems that bakers had long had a reputation—whether deserved or not—for short-weighting their bread. As a result, very strict laws were passed, regulating the weight of the various breads, muffins and cakes. But, as every cook knows, it's not possible—especially when cooking with the primitive ovens then available—to have the loaves absolutely uniform in weight.

So the practice developed of giving thirteen loaves on every order for twelve, thereby guaranteeing that there would be no penalty for shortages.

Another theory is that the phrase developed by analogy from *printer's* dozen, for in the early days of publishing it was the custom of printers to supply the retailer with thirteen copies of a book on each order of twelve. Since the retailer was billed at list price, the return on the thirteenth book represented his profit on the transaction. As a sidelight on this medieval selling technique, by the way, we may note that today one of the most prevalent practices of the book trade is for the publisher to offer retailers "one-for-ten" or one free book with every ten ordered, thereby increasing the retailer's margin of profit and, of course, the number of books sold by the publisher.

Then there's still another theory. It seems that the bakers of the medieval period had such a bad name that the words *baker* and *devil* were sometimes used interchangeably. Thus, the term *baker's dozen* may have evolved from *devil's dozen,* which was a common folk phrase meaning thirteen. And thirteen was the number of witches usually present at meetings summoned by Old Nick.

balk

The word *balk* comes from the Anglo-Saxon *balca,* a wooden beam, and refers to the huge timbers used to bar outer doors, thus *balking* an enemy's onslaught. See also BILK.

balletomane

This is the name for an enthusiast for ballets. The word, which was coined fairly recently in France, is from the words *ballet* and *manie* (mania). Thus a *balletomane* (pronounced bal-LET-uh-mayn) is one whose devotion to the dance is roughly equal to a Milwaukee baseball fan's enthusiasm for the Braves in mid-August and *fan,* in case you have forgotten is often thought to be a shortened form of *"fanatic."* See also LABANOTATION.

balling the jack

This is a phrase from the jargon of railroadmen and simply means going at top speed. It also has acquired the meaning in gambling circles of risking everything on a single throw of the dice or turn of a card.

ballistophobia

If you suffer from fear of bullets, you are a victim of ballistophobia. Root words for this unusual word are the Latin *ballista* (to throw) and the Greek *phobos* (fear). See also PHOBIAS.

Baltimore chop. *See* baseball jargon.

bankrupt

In medieval Italy moneylenders operated from *bancas*—benches or shelves. When a moneylender was forced to suspend his business from lack of funds, his *banka* was broken up and he was given the name *bancarotto.* From this beginning the word *bankrupt* eventually came to mean any insolvent person, especially anyone who had been legally declared unable to pay his debts.

banns, posting of the

Banns are a series of announcements of the intent of a couple to wed. Today's common meaning of "ban"—to forbid or prohibit—is nowhere involved in the *banns* of marriage. Yet the two words come from the same Anglo-Saxon root, *bannan* (to proclaim or to summon).

What has happened is that the word, which in the times of Robin Hood merely meant to announce, has acquired through the centuries the specialized meaning of to proclaim a prohibition. This probably resulted from the use of *bann* and later *ban* by church authorities to proclaim the excommunication of sinners. This most serious form of ecclesiastical disapproval soon diverted the word from its general meaning to the special sense of prohibition in which it is most commonly used today.

us associate *banshee* with the unearthly wails of a female spirit ...leath in the family. But in the original Gaelic, the *banshee* was ...d as a beautiful woman, not a hag.

...ratively easy matter to trace down *barley duck* and dis-...tangy preserve made of gooseberries or currants, fre-...an accompaniment to the main roast meat course at ...lid the strange name come from? It's what the language ...pted" pronunciation of *Bar-le-Duc* (pronounced bar-...the name of the French town where this preserve is ...ted.

...w almost exclusively a political word meaning to ...country making speeches wherever people will ...eatrical term. It described itinerant stock com-...l talent were not topflight and who in conse-...ond-rate auditoriums and even occasionally in ...as they had were usually hastily improvised, ...*torming* (moving impetuously) around the

...are lawyers who practice in the superior ...re two classes: the simple *barrister*, an ...gher order known as "King's Counsel." ...ppointed "K.C." because they thence-...counsel (barristers) wear gowns of

...embers of the bar and do not plead

baseball jargon

The sport pages are a daily reminder that no American activity has developed so colorful and extensive a vocabulary as baseball. Ever since the days of Abner Doubleday, sports writers and the players themselves have coined graphic and picturesque phrases to describe all aspects of the National Game.

We assume that everyone knows the difference between a base hit and an out, so we'll pass over the standard terms and concentrate on the colorful "slanguage" of baseball reporters and sportscasters.

Aboard—On base. When there are three men on base, the bases loaded and there are *three men aboard.*

Bad ball—A ball pitched well outside of the strike zone. A batter habitually "goes after" such pitches is known as a *"bad ball* hitter."

Baltimore chop—A ball that hits the ground just in front of the and takes a long, high bounce, slow enough to enable the batter to first base. This term is now almost obsolete. In fact, it's so far out soon be "in" again.

Bases loaded—The situation when there are runners on first, and third bases.

Bean ball—A ball pitched directly at the batter's head, to fo back from the plate. Technically illegal, it is resorted to fairly fre though not so often as indignant batters would have you believe.

Bench jockey—A player or coach who taunts members of the team from his place on the bench. Most notable *bench jockey* years has been Leo "The Lip" Durocher.

Bleeder—Kissing cousin of the *blooper* (which see) exce spends most of its time on the ground. Usually it's a weak gro takes a bad bounce just outside the reach of an infielder. It's a *scratch hit.*

Blooper—A weak fly which falls beyond the infield and outfield. It's also called a *banjo hit* and, in the old days, w *Texas leaguer.*

Change-up or *change of pace*—A slow ball pitched after fast balls, but with the same motions of delivery. What used a "slow ball" is now referred to by most sportscasters as even when the pitch is the first one delivered to the batter.

Clutch hitter—The kind of hitter who can be counted on when it is most needed.

Cousin—A pitcher whom a batter finds consistently ea very great pitchers sometimes find an occasional opposition fathom their trickiest deliveries.

Cripple—Ball pitched when the count on the batter i

one strike, so called because the pitcher usually needs to *groove it* for a strike and therefore eliminates trickery from his delivery.

Dust or *duster*—The pitcher's term for the pitch a batter calls a *bean ball*. It's a pitch thrown hard and close to the batter, designed to make him step back from the plate.

Fireman—A relief pitcher who comes in to put out the "fire" caused by the opposing team getting men on bases. Luis Arroyo's pitching in relief of Whitey Ford was a notable example of work by a *fireman*.

Gopher ball—A pitch which the batter hits for a home run.

Grand slam—A term borrowed from bridge; it is, of course, what batters cherish most: a home run with three men on base.

Homer—A home run, of course. Also an umpire whose decisions consistently favor the home team.

Hot corner—Third base.

In the hole—A batter is *in the hole* if the count is two strikes and no balls; a pitcher is *in the hole* if the count is three balls and no strikes.

Keystone sack—Second base.

Life—Another chance. If a batter hits a foul which a fielder should catch, but doesn't, he gets a *life*. Similarly, if he gets on base through an error, he gets a *life*.

Meat hand—The one a player doesn't have a glove on. Except in unusual circumstances—such as the World Series—most players are understandably loath to try catching hard-hit balls with their *meat hands*.

Money player—One who can always be counted upon to perform well when most is at stake. The New York Yankees have been famous for years as the top-ranking group of *money players*.

Mound, rubber or hill—The slightly elevated pitcher's box in the center of the diamond.

No-hitter—A game in which one side fails to make any hits.

Payoff pitch—The pitch delivered when the count is three balls and two strikes. Unless the batter fouls out of play, a *payoff* decision—hit or out—must result from this pitch.

Peg—A throw, especially a long one from an outfielder to a base or home plate in order to trap a base runner.

Platter—Home plate.

Pick-off—A surprise play in which a base runner who has been taking a long lead is caught away from the base by a sudden throw from the pitcher or catcher.

Pick-up—A ball caught immediately after it strikes the ground.

Rhubarb—An argument on the playing field, especially a noisy, vehement one involving an umpire and players from both teams.

Run-down—One of the most exciting plays in the game, when a base runner is caught between bases by two fielders who throw the ball back and forth several times before tagging him for the put-out. Occasionally, of course, the trapped runner outwits the fielders but then the play should not properly be called a *run-down.*

Shut-out—A game in which the losing team fails to score any runs.

Southpaw—A left-handed player, especially a pitcher.

Sun field—That portion of the outfield where the fielder has to face the sun directly.

Switch-hitter—Well, this is Mickey Mantle, the most proficient *switch-hitter* in many years. He can bat with equal ferocity from either side of the plate, batting right-handed against left-handed pitching and left-handed against right-handed pitching, thereby eliminating the theoretical advantage that pitchers have against batters who stand on the same side of the plate that they deliver their pitches from.

Texas leaguer—A fly ball which falls just beyond the infield and results in a base hit. Sometimes called a *blooper.*

Twin bill or double-header—Two games played between the same two teams on the same day.

Twi-night double-header—Two games between the same teams on the same day, the first starting in late afternoon, the second being played under lights at night.

bases loaded. *See* baseball jargon.

bash

A *bash* originally meant a jam session—a gathering of musicians who played together for their own enjoyment. Nowadays it is loosely used to mean any high-spirited social gathering.

baste, to

Baste, in the cooking use, comes from the Old French word *basser* (to moisten), and thus accurately describes the basting process of moistening meat during roastings.

Baste, as used in the sewing room, comes from the Old High German *bastjan,* meaning "to sew with bast"—and bast, in turn, is a heavy fiber used in making ropes. Thus any stitches taken with such fiber would be long and loose.

The two words are what linguists call "homonyms"—words similar in sound and sometimes in spelling, but of different origin and meaning. Incidentally, there's still a third homonym of *baste*—the meaning of "to strike or beat"—and it comes from still another root, this one Old Norse. So is it any wonder that many foreigners, like the King in *The King and I,* find our language a "puzzlement"?

bastion

Bastion (pronounced BASH-chun or BASS-tee-un) means simply "stronghold" or "defensive bulwark." Originally a French word dating back to the great ages of chivalry, castles and knightly warfare, it denoted a projection in the wall of a fort, designed to give the defenders a wider firing range—hence, an improved defense.

bathos

Bathos (pronounced BAY-thos) is not synonymous with pathos, though the two are closely related. Pathos, properly speaking, is the quality in an experience which moves the onlooker to pity or compassion. *Bathos,* by contrast, is a false, synthetic, exaggerated appeal to the emotions. It comes direct from the Greek *bathos,* meaning "depth."

battery

Most familiar as part of the term "assault and battery," *battery* itself comes from the Latin *battuere* (to beat) and means in this connection illegal beating or touching of another person. See also ASSAULT AND BATTERY.

Other definitions of the word *battery* use it in the meaning of a series of objects arranged or used together.

battle royal

A term from the now outlawed sport of cockfighting, *battle royal* refers to a kind of elimination tournament common to the cockpit.

First, sixteen cocks are pitted against one another. The eight victors are similarly matched. Then the four survivors are pitted and finally the two cocks remaining fight it out to find the winner of the *battle royal.*

This same sport has given us at least one other term current in everyday speech. We often speak of two baseball teams being *pitted* against each other in an important series, little realizing that we are using a metaphor from cockfighting where the contestants are literally dropped into a pit to fight out their bloody battle.

bazaar—bizarre

There seems to be no etymological relation between *bazaar* and *bizarre.* *Bazaar,* meaning a marketplace or a shop where a variety of goods is sold, comes from the Persian word *bazar.* *Bizarre,* meaning odd or unusual in appearance or behavior, comes from the Spanish *bizarro* (brave or gallant).

BCU

A *BCU,* in television language, is a "big close-up" of an actor in a picture so greatly magnified that only his face shows. See also TELEVISION LANGUAGE.

beak—beakie

Beak was originally British and Irish underworld slang for magistrate or constable. In American union lingo, *beakie* means the police used to spy secretly upon members of a union.

bean ball. *See* baseball jargon.

beat

Jack Kerouac and other beat novelists and poets claim that the adjective *beat* is somehow derived from "beatified" or "beatitude." To which, if I may borrow a term from H. L. Mencken, there can be only one comment: "Hogwash."

Beat comes from the jargon of jazz musicians and means simply "worn-out," "exhausted"—especially from musical performance. It's a fine, expressive and colorful word—as originally used by Louis Armstrong, Lester Young and Ella Fitzgerald. If the beatniks want to use it, too, they're welcome. But we'll thank them not to go inventing false etymologies for it!

beat around the bush. *See* bush, beat around the.

beatific

Beatific (pronounced be-uh-TIFF-ik), from the Latin words *beatus* (happy) and *facere* (make), literally means "making blissfully happy." It also means rapturously or exaltedly happy and is often used in a religious context, as one might say, "St. Joan's face was wreathed with smiles of *beatific* rapture."

beatnik

Beatnik, meaning an unconventional devotee of the arts—what earlier generations would have called a "Bohemian"—is a fairly recent coinage. It was in October, 1957, that Sputnik flashed across the heavens and, as a very minor side effect to man's entry into space, added the suffix -*nik* to the already well-established *beat.*

Back in the 1930's *beat* in the sense of "exhausted" was part of the jargon of jazz musicians. After a long night of playing or an unusually arduous recording session, a jazz man might say that he was *beat*.

In the late 1940's a group of West Coast, self-styled intellectuals adopted the term *The Beat* to describe themselves and their activities. One of their number, Jack Kerouac, had the audacity to claim that the word *beat* was a contraction of "beatified." This suggestion didn't quite get him laughed out of the lodge but nobody with any understanding of the evolution of language took his pretentious claim seriously.

So *beatnik* owes its origin to jazz musicians, its present meaning to a cult of Bohemians, and its terminal syllable to a Russian sputnik. It's a curious blend—one more proof that, in today's world of lightning-fast communications, language is changing and growing more rapidly than ever before.

bêche-de-mer

In one of Jack London's later novels certain of the characters speak a sort of pidgin English, a blend of the native dialects of the west Pacific islands and English. The name of the language is *bêche-de-mer* and it literally means "worm of the sea." Here's how this lingua franca—or hybrid language—got its name. The *bêche-de-mer,* also called the trapang or sea cucumber, is much prized as an item of food by natives of the islands of the western Pacific. It is a water animal with a leathery skin and a mouth surrounded by tentacles. Doesn't sound very appetizing, does it? However, it is chiefly used as a base for soups—and the Chinese make a highly esteemed soup from birds' nests, so you never can tell.

During the late eighteenth and nineteenth centuries when trading developed between English-speaking colonists and seamen and the Melanesian natives, a language was needed and one gradually developed that combined elements of English and of the various native dialects. Since a prime item of commerce was *bêche-de-mer,* the new hybrid tongue was called by that name—and that's how the language most widely spoken in the far Pacific has the same name as the lowly sea cucumber. See also PIDGIN ENGLISH.

bee

Apparently the busyness of the ordinary honey bee as he works cooperatively with his fellow bees to fill the community hive was the inspiration for such phrases as *sewing bee, husking bee, spelling bee* and *raising bee.* This sort of social gathering where all work for a common, and often charitable, purpose is nothing new. They were well known to the yeomanry of

England during the Middle Ages, but the name *bee* seems to have been an American invention. One reason for the great popularity of such *bees,* especially among young folk, is that they are usually followed by refreshments and dancing and thus are in the nature of a community-wide celebration.

During the rough-and-ready days when our Western frontier was being opened, the word *bee* was used in several less socially commendable combinations. Thus one might have read in Sam Clemens' Virginia City *Enterprise* or Bret Harte's *Overland Monthly* accounts of such community activities as *lynching bees, shooting bees, hanging bees* and even, for variety, *rattlesnake bees.*

beefeater

One widely held theory of the origin of this word runs so: "In 1485 when the Tower of London was one of King Henry's palaces, the corps of the Yeomen of the Guard was formed as the King's bodyguard. Some of these men were used to wait on table, and, being under a certain French influence, these men were called Buffetiers, which the London cockney in due time corrupted into Beefeaters."

But this is a farfetched notion, for this particular theory has been denied by all leading authorities on language. The *Oxford English Dictionery*—and surely there is no higher court of appeal on a word like this —says explicitly that "beefeater [is] not connected with buffet." Brewer's *Dictionary of Phrase and Fable* says: "There is no evidence whatever for the old guess that the word is connected with the French 'buffet,' and signified 'an attendant at the royal buffet.' "

So what does *beefeater* mean? Simply what it says: eater of beef—for substantial portions of beef have regularly been included among the rations of the Yeomen of the Guard except, perhaps, during England's "austerity" years.

beer, small. *See* small beer.

beer and skittles

Skittles is nothing but the old-fashioned game of ninepins. It's not bowling as we know it today, because the "ball" thrown at the pins was not a ball at all, but a thick, flattened disk that was hurled or slid along the grass.

In centuries past, the average British yeoman's idea of paradise on earth was not "a jug of wine, a loaf of bread and thou beside me in the wilderness." Rather, he was content with a mug of beer, a friendly game of skittles with his fellow farmers—and he'd be just as happy, thank you, if "thou" would stay home tending the children.

beetle. *See* confused beetles.

beggar

Beggar is often used, especially by the British, simply to mean "rascal" or "scoundrel" with no direct reference to the act of begging.

In *Beau Geste,* for example, the hero was practically singlehandedly defending a desert camp against hordes of attacking sheiks. At a critical point he called to his aide: "Look at the *beggars* come!"

begonia. *See* flower names.

beguile

Beguile (pronounced be-GILE) is a combination of the Anglo-Saxon prefix *be-* and *guile,* meaning "deceit" or "cunning," which came unchanged from French, probably at the time of the Norman Conquest. *Beguile* still has the meanings of "to cheat or deceive" and even in the fairly common phrase *beguile the time away* retains the meaning of cheating, since the aim is to make time pass unnoticed. The verb *to beguile* and the noun *beguilement* are often used today with the connotation of gay or pleasurable deceit.

behind the eight ball. *See* eight ball, behind the.

Belisha beacon. *See* Hore-Belisha.

bell, book and candle

Bell, book and candle refers to a solemn form of excommunication from the Roman Catholic Church. When the sentence denying further participation in the sacraments or rituals of the church is pronounced, a bell is rung, the book is closed and a candle extinguished—this last to symbolize the spiritual darkness in which the person sentenced must abide in the future.

belling the cat

Belling the cat, meaning to take on a dangerous task for the benefit of others, has been traced back to one of the very earliest English poems, *Piers Plowman.* There you'll find the fable of the mice who held a meeting to decide what to do about a cat that had been killing off too many members of their clan. One sage old mouse suggested that a bell be put around the cat's neck, so that its tinkle would act as a warning to the mice. "Splendid idea," agreed one of the younger mice, "but who's to bell the cat?"

bellwether

This term has been the designation since Anglo-Saxon times of the *wether* or eunuch sheep which carries a bell around its neck and acts as leader of the herd. Recently *bellwether* has enjoyed a vogue in advertising and financial circles in the adjectival form. One frequently hears such expressions as, "We really need a *bellwether* item for the line if we're going to merchandise it successfully." In this use *bellwether* merely means "leader."

belly robber. *See* Old Army slang.

belly-timber

The word *belly* is one of the oldest English words, traceable to Anglo-Saxon and considered perfectly proper for most of the centuries since. However, it fell under the ban of Victorian "nice-nellyism." "Stomach"— which doesn't mean the same thing at all—came to be used as a euphemism for *belly*. To many people *belly* still sounds slightly indelicate.

The phrase *belly-timber,* however, is another dish of tea. Originally a perfectly serious phrase, it is now used only in jest, as a rather pompously facetious synonym for food.

bench jockey. *See* baseball jargon.

benedict

Originally a *benedict* was a perennial bachelor, one sworn to a life of celibacy in the tradition of St. Benedict, the founder of the Benedictine order of monks. But William Shakespeare created in *Much Ado About Nothing* a character who, though an avowed bachelor, is entrapped into matrimony—and Shakespeare, with one of those plays upon words which the Elizabethans dearly loved, named him Benedick. As a result the two words *benedick* and *benedict* have become interchangeable, with the latter spelling much more common today.

So a *benedict* today means not a bachelor but a married man—especially one who has only recently become married.

benny

In the lingo of the jazz musician, a *benny* is a pawnbroker. See also JAZZMEN'S JARGON.

berm

If you see SOFT BERM—KEEP OFF on a sign, it's simply another way of saying "soft shoulder." Most commonly used in the Central and Southern states, it is occasionally encountered in other parts of the country—sometimes with the spelling *berme*. It is not, as you might think, a regional dialect term. Indeed, *berm* has a history dating back to the romantic days of knightly chivalry. A *berm,* in Norman times, was the ridge between the edge of the moat around a castle and the fortress wall itself. Thus its use to designate the shoulder of a road is not at all farfetched.

best bib and tucker

When one puts on his *best bib and tucker,* he dresses his finest. This term originated shortly before 1700. The *bib* was an item of apparel not unlike a child's bib of today—and it served a similar purpose: keeping the clothes clean while eating. The *tucker* was an ornamental item, usually of lace or muslin, which women tucked into the necks of their dresses. It hung long and loose enough to cover the neck and shoulders. Thus a couple dressed in their *best bib* (the man) *and tucker* (the woman) was all spruced up for a fancy occasion.

best foot forward, put. *See* put your best foot forward.

best man

This phrase is of Scottish origin and goes back many centuries to the times when a prospective groom simply kidnaped the woman of his choice and carried her away with him.

Such a venture required courage and audacity as well as a good deal of manpower. So the groom selected the bravest of his friends to accompany him. They were known as "groomsmen"—a term still used in some parts of the country to describe ushers at a wedding. The closest and most valiant of the bridegroom's associates became known as the *best man.*

Similarly the bridesmaids were originally the closest friends of the bride, the ones who helped or pretended to help the bride defend herself against her abductors. Thus the customs of a savage and primitive society are echoed in the names used today for the participants in this most formal and civilized of ceremonies, the church wedding.

bev, ev, mev and cutie pie

Bev, ev, mev, and *cutie pie*—these words sound like items from the jazzed-up jargon of today's teen-agers. Actually they are recent creations of perhaps the most serious-minded and dedicated group of professional workers in America today, the nation's atomic energy researchers.

Just as every trade, industry and profession gradually develops its own special language or jargon, so the workers on the newest and most challenging frontier of science have been creating their own body of language to describe the techniques and materials used in their work. Characteristically, they have in one short decade developed a vocabulary of many hundreds of words. Here are just a handful.

An *ev,* to begin with, is an electron volt, a measurement of the amount of energy gained by an electron when it is acted upon by one volt. An *ev* doesn't really represent much energy—but that's only the beginning. From the *ev* we go to the *mev*—a million electron volts—and beyond that to the *bev,* a billion electron volts. Now we are really cooking with nuclear gas, because an electron possessing one *bev* of energy is traveling almost as fast as the speed of light—186,000 miles per second.

Naturally, when scientists are dealing with power of this magnitude, all sorts of precautions must be observed. So it's perhaps not surprising that the thick-walled lead container in which radioactive materials are transported is called, somewhat morbidly, a *coffin.*

The material carried in the coffin is usually designated *hot*—meaning highly radioactive—and when it reaches its destination it may well be stored in a *pig*—another name for a thick-walled container. The capsule used to carry samples in and out of an atomic reactor is known as the *rabbit.* And *cutie pie?* Well, that's a portable instrument used to determine the level of radiation in an area—mighty important work for a device so flippantly named.

Anyway, it's reassuring to know that these scientists, charged with researches of the utmost significance to the futures of all of us, have not mislaid that most stabilizing of influences—a sense of humor.

bib and tucker. *See* best bib and tucker.

b.i.d.

B.i.d. and *t.i.d.* on prescriptions are abbreviations for the Latin terms *bis in die* (twice a day) and *tres in die* (three times a day).

big brass

Originally a military term, alluding to the gold braid on the hats of officers, *big brass* has carried over into civilian life as referring to top-ranking executives in business. See also BRASS.

bilk

This word might well be found in a headline such as CHARITIES BILKED OF MILLIONS.

Bilk—meaning to cheat or defraud—is a variant form of *to balk*. It was first used in cribbage, meaning to spoil your opponent's score and thus, by sharp play, to defraud him of points he has earned.

During the nineteenth century the term came into wide general use in this country and a *bilker* was once defined by a boardinghouse keeper as a man "who never missed a meal and never paid a cent."

The word *balk*, incidentally, has an interesting history. It comes from the Anglo-Saxon *balca*, a wooden beam, and refers to the huge timbers used to bar outer doors, thus *balking* an enemy's onslaughts.

bill

A *bill* is $100 in thieves' argot—and in show and garment business talk too. So 5,000 *bills* is actually $500,000.

A $100 bill is also called *C-note* or a *yard;* $500 is *five bills, five C's* or *a half a G*—the *G*, obviously, being a *grand*, or $1,000.

Incidentally, the little, old dollar bill has dozens of slang names: *buck, buckeroo, one-spot, shekel, simoleon* and *single*, to name only a few.

billion

In America and France a *billion* is a thousand million. In Great Britain and Germany it is a million million. Moral: If you want to be a billionaire, stay right here in America.

binaural. *See* monaural, binaural.

biopsy. *See* autopsy, biopsy.

birdiebacking

The trucking industry has added at least two bright new terms to the lexicon of business English in recent years—*piggybacking* to describe trailers loaded aboard flatcars and transported by rail to their destination and, more recently, *fishybacking*—the transportation of loaded trailers by boat. Now there is still a third new coinage—*birdiebacking*. That's right— now they plan to load the trailers aboard airplanes and fly them to their destination.

bits, not worth two

Bit was originally British slang for any small coin. In the Southwestern U.S., as long ago as 1730, the term *bit* was applied to the Mexican *real,* a coin then worth about 12½ cents. *Two bits* thus meant 25 cents, from which the expression *not worth two bits,* meaning practically worthless, came into being.

bizarre. *See* bazaar, bizarre.

black sheep. *See* sheep, black.

Black Shirts

Black Shirts was the popular name of the elite corps of the Nazi army, so named because *black shirts* were part of the uniform. Official name of the outfit was *Schutzstaffel* or *SS Corps.*

black shoe Navy. *See* Navy, black shoe.

bladders

In circus jargon, balloons are called *bladders;* the man who sells them, the *rubber man.* See also CIRCUS JARGON.

blarney, a touch of

The Blarney Castle, located a few miles north of Cork, Ireland, is famous for its *Blarney stone,* a triangular piece of limestone very difficult to reach. It is said that anyone brave enough to hang by his heels to kiss the stone is rewarded by the gift of a blandly persuasive manner of speech. A man who has kissed the *Blarney stone* is reputed to be able to charm, coax and cajole his fellow humans so long as he lives.

The legends that have grown up about the stone are legion. One theory is that it was brought from ancient Tyre and Carthage by a band of adventurers centuries before Caesar and his legions invaded the British Isles. More credible is the story about McCarthy Mor, the lord of the castle, who, in 1602, was defeated after a long siege and agreed to surrender to British troops under Sir George Carew.

Day after day poor Carew waited for the terms to be fulfilled; day after day the lord of the castle would put him off with some new, fanciful excuse. At last Carew became the butt of jokes from his fellow members of Queen Elizabeth's court. Finally the Queen herself took a hand in the proceedings, but all she could get was a long, windy and evasive letter, about which she is reported to have said: "This is more of the same *blarney*"—and a word was born.

bleb

A word seldom seen outside a dictionary or a book such as *The Scrabble Word Guide, bleb* comes unchanged from the Middle English *bleb* (the sound produced by forming a bubble with the lips) and now means "blister."

bleeder. *See* baseball jargon.

blend words

Words that are really combinations of two words are generally called *blend words,* though the most illustrious inventor of such words called them *portmanteau words.* He was, of course, Lewis Carroll whose pages sparkled with such inventions as " 'Twas brillig and the slithy toves did gyre and gimble in the wabe," in a language he labeled "Jabberwocky."

In *Through the Looking Glass,* Carroll explains that he chose the word *portmanteau*—a then fashionable term for a kind of suitcase—because there are two meanings "packed up" in such a word. Among his most vivid concoctions were *slithy,* a blend of "lithe" and "slimy," and *mimsy* from "miserable" and "flimsy."

Some of Carroll's other coinages have become part of Standard English. For example, *squawk* from "squeal" and "squall" and *chortle* from "chuckle" and "snort." But the native American genius for creation of blend words has been in evidence at least since 1812, when *gerrymander* (from "Gerry" and "salamander") was coined. The dreadful extremes to which this tendency can be pushed are on display in almost any Broadway column (*cinemactress, hemotion, snoopervise* and so on). Perhaps the moral to all this comes from another of Lewis Carroll's creations, Humpty-Dumpty, who said: "When I use a word, it means just what I choose it to mean—neither more nor less."

bloodhound

Bloodhounds are so called simply because theirs was the first breed whose "blood" or breeding records were maintained. The first chronicles of the genealogy of this breed were maintained by the monks of St. Hubert's Abbey in France in the ninth century.

bloomers

There is a story behind bloomers—a story more than a century old. It was Mrs. Amelia Bloomer, one of New York's earliest and most vehement suffragettes who first tried to get American women to wear trousers. The costume she advocated consisted of loose-fitting trousers, gathered tight at the ankle, with a knee-length outer skirt. The fashion never met with great success but much later, after the turn of the century, the billowing, knee-length pants which most of us remember as *bloomers* were devised for girls to wear while exercising.

A national magazine recently gave several pages to a spread on summer fashions for women in which several items were labeled *bloomers,* but these garments looked remarkably unlike the *bloomers and middies* we recall from the school playgrounds of our youth.

So the present use of *bloomers* in women's fashions actually represents the third time the name has been applied to a different kind of garment. Ironically, Amelia Bloomer insisted to her dying day that she was not the person who invented the first *bloomers.* She always credited the style to a Mrs. Elizabeth Miller, daughter of a New York Congressman. But the public liked the word *bloomers*—and *bloomers* they remain.

blooper

Blooper is a slang term of fairly recent origin meaning "blunder" or "error." It usually has the connotation of an inadvertent error, such as a slip of the tongue, which exposes a prominent or pompous person to ridicule.

The word *blooper* is also used in baseball slang in quite a different sense to mean a weakly hit fly ball which drops just beyond the infield. Years ago this was called a *Texas leaguer.*

blue-chip stock

The phrase *blue-chip stock* comes from the chips used in gambling games like poker. These chips or counters range in value from red (cheapest) through white to blue (most valuable—usually worth ten times the red). So a *blue-chip stock* is one likely to give the greatest return on an investment.

blue jeans

In any contest to select the item of wearing apparel most popular among American youth there's not much question but that *blue jeans* would be the winner. Boys and girls alike wear them at work and play the year around—and many a grownup dons them when heavy chores are in prospect.

In the West, especially among cattlemen, they are usually called *Levis.* In the East the name *dungarees* is common, and everywhere you hear *jeans* and *denims.* Interestingly enough, there is a story behind each of these names—and it's hard to tell which of the four is more unusual.

Take *jeans,* for example. Although thousands of girls named Jean have worn them there is no connection at all between the girl's name and the name of the garment. It's actually an altered form of "Genoa," where the cloth was once woven. Similarly, *denim* comes from the phrase *serge de Nîmes,* after the city of Nîmes, France.

Dungaree is the most exotic of the names, though. The name of this prosaic garment comes to us all the way from fabled Hindustan, where the word *dungri* was used to designate a coarsely woven fabric first used for tents and sails. After a while sailors made up work clothes from the material and, presto, *dungarees* were invented. (See DUNGAREE.)

Levis, of course, are an American improvement on traditional *denims.* They derive their name from Levi Strauss, a San Francisco clothing merchant of Gold Rush days. His great contribution was the addition of rivets to the corners of pockets, so that they would not tear out when miners loaded them with samples of ore. As his fame spread throughout the West, *Levis* became the popular term for these durable work clothes—just as "Stetson" or "John B." (both from the John B. Stetson hat manufacturing company) became the accepted terms for the cowpuncher's ten-gallon hat.

As a melancholy footnote on the direction in which our popular culture seems to be heading, the *Wall Street Journal* reports that the company of Levi Strauss, while still making *Levis,* is branching out with "ranch pants" and "breach pants" for women "stunningly colored in orange, lemon and lime."

blue ribbon

The color blue has traditionally been associated with eminence in all fields of endeavor. Perhaps because the blue skies were thought to be the abode of the gods of ancient times, the color has long been associated with royalty—hence, "royal blue."

In Britain the *blue ribbon* is the badge of the Order of the Garter, the highest honor bestowed by the Crown. In France the *cordon bleu* was once the emblem of the highest order of knighthood, a member of the Order of the Holy Ghost. Today it is also used to designate a chef of the very first order. Throughout the Western world the *blue ribbon* signifies "highest honor."

blues

The matter of just where the term *blues* came from is much in dispute. The most widely held theory is that it is an abbreviation of "blue devils"— hallucinations, like pink elephants, popularly believed to accompany delirium tremens. The mood of acute depression following an attack of the "d.t.'s" would surely be depressing enough to cause the moans of anguish which may first have given birth to the *blues*. At any rate, that's more likely than the popular song's theory about the "breeze in the trees" inspiring the first *blues*.

In some instances, *blues* is correctly construed as singular. It refers, you see, to one specific song created on a special occasion. You would say, for example, "W. C. Handy's 'Memphis Street Blues' is one of the authentic classics of our jazz tradition." Note that we use the singular here because one song is referred to. However, in speaking of the great number of *blues* songs created by our folk singers and composers, you would say "The *blues* have made a great contribution to our musical heritage."

blurb

Originally, *blurb* meant a statement of lavish praise quoted on the dust jacket of a book. More recently, it has come to mean any exaggerated advertising claim. The word was coined by the late great humorist, Gelett Burgess, who also invented *bromide* to describe a person addicted to the use of clichés. See also GOOP.

boat, ship

There's a distinction here which no old salt will ever forget—and no landlubber ever seems able to learn. The dictionary puts it this way: "A ship is a vessel of considerable size navigating deep water and not propelled by oars, paddles or the like—distinguished from 'boat.'" A more up-to-date definition would also note that *boats* may be powered by outboard motors—but the basic distinction remains this: a *ship* is big and travels the sea lanes; a *boat* is relatively small and stays mostly in shallow or sheltered waters.

Bohemian

Bohemian as a designation for raffish nonconformists of an earlier vintage comes logically and directly from the place name "Bohemia."

Before World War I, Bohemia was a part of Austria and many centuries earlier it was mistakenly believed to be the home of the gypsy tribes which roamed through Western Europe as early as the fifteenth century. Actually, gypsies were wandering tribes from the Caucasus and are believed to be of Hindu origin. But popular superstition was stronger than fact—which could not have been easy to determine in any event—so *Bohemian* and "gypsy" became virtually synonymous and the latter's connotations of aimless wandering and disregard for conventions were soon attached to *Bohemian* as well.

Thackeray fixed the label once and for all on *avant-garde* thinkers and others who scorn social proprieties when he called Becky Sharp, his headstrong heroine of *Vanity Fair,* a "*Bohemian* by taste and circumstances . . . of a wild, roving nature."

booby hatch

This term, meaning a wooden hood over a hatch leading to the forepeak of a sailing vessel, was common during the last century and it is probable that its present meaning of "insane asylum" may have derived from the practice of confining deranged sailors in the *booby hatch.*

Certainly credit for the widespread popularity of the phrase must go, however, to famed cartoonist Milt Gross, who, two or three decades back, used to draw one of the most hilarious and meaningful of Sunday strips. Many readers will remember the character who each week was freed from the asylum, spent a day being horrified by the antics of "normal" beings in the outer world, and in the last panel was always to be seen hurrying back to the asylum, saying, "Back to the dear old *booby hatch.*"

boodle, boodlers

Part of the political slang of the nineteenth century, *boodle* was a bribe and a *boodler* one who dealt in bribes, especially in an effort to fix elections. See also POLITICAL SLANG, NINETEENTH CENTURY.

boomerang

The word was coined by the Australian aborigines to describe the unique, fly-back weapon which they created—and which American youngsters are beginning to discover as a plaything. The word may have had some such significance in aboriginal lingo as "weapon that flies through the air and returns to part the thrower's hair"—but that's just a guess.

boondocks

Boondocks originated as the Marine's version of a Tagalog word, *bandok,* meaning "mountain." During the occupation of the Philippines, many terms from the native language, Tagalog (tah-GAH-log), found their way into the slang of our soldiers and Marines and often, as in this case, the meaning became somewhat broader in translation. Whereas the Philippine native meant simply "mountain" when he said *bandok,* the American servicemen used the term to apply to any kind of rough back country, eventually making *boondocks* a rough-and-ready synonym for "sticks."

Boondocks first came into general public knowledge during an investigation of allegedly harsh methods of training employed by some Marine noncoms at Camp Lejeune. According to reports then current, recruits were ordered on night marches into the *boondocks,* which included swamp areas where at least one recruit drowned. So, in current application, it appears that *boondocks* may apply to any back-country area, from the original Philippine mountain to sea-level swamps.

boondoggling

This word, in governmental use, was first applied to the "make-work" projects of the first Franklin Roosevelt administration, which many critics thought were wasteful. The term was reported earlier as a slang expression common in the Ozarks and, in 1929, was used by a scoutmaster as a name for ornamental thongs made by Boy Scouts under his direction.

boot. *See* automobile slang, British.

boot, to

The *boot* in *to boot* has nothing whatever to do with the boots we use on our feet. This other *boot* was originally an Anglo-Saxon word *bote* or *bot,* meaning "advantage" or "profit." The word is now completely obsolete, except in the phrase *to boot.*

However, in Milton's time it was commonly used. "Alas, what *boots* it with uncessant care," he wrote in "Lycidas," meaning, "What profit is there in unceasing worry." And Shakespeare wrote of "*bootless* errands," meaning fruitless or profitless trips.

As recently as in the nineteenth century Matthew Arnold wrote "It *boots* not to look backward" which for some reason reminds us of the famous line of the great pitcher Leroy "Satchel" Paige. "Never look back," quoth Satchel. "They might be gaining on you."

Nowadays, when we say that we give something *to boot,* we mean "in addition." Thus a woman might say that she pays a housemaid "two dollars an hour and luncheon *to boot.*"

bootlegger

The word *bootlegger* originated simply from the fact that the first *bootleggers* carried illicit merchandise in the legs of high boots when making deliveries. In this sense, the word was common in the middle nineteenth century. Since the most easily made and profitably sold commodity was illicit liquor, *bootlegger* gradually became a label applied to distributors of illegal booze.

boots, boot camp and boot training

One cold day in World War II, your etymologist (*q.v.*) found himself a *boot* in a *boot camp*. It didn't occur to me at the time to wonder where the curious designation *boot* came from. As any alumnus of a Navy *boot camp* can tell you, there isn't much time allowed for idle speculation. It's a rough, tough-disciplined program, with little time for dreaming.

Well, my stay was happily not a long one and before long I had moved onward, frankly not giving the word *boot* a thought from that year to this. But then I received a letter from C. E. Reynolds, a retired Navy radio chief, remarking that the origin of *boot* has been much booted about and offering a very plausible explanation of how the lowest rank of naval enlisted men are called *boots*.

"When I entered the Navy in 1911," he wrote, "an old-timer called me a '*rubber-boot* sailor.' When I asked for an explanation, he told me that prior to about 1890 all the men prided themselves on getting out on deck and scrubbing down barefooted in the coldest weather. Then there was an influx of kids from the Midwest. They didn't intend to act foolish, so they went ashore and bought boots to wear when it was cold. The older hands sneered and called them '*rubber-boot* sailors.'

"By the time I came on the scene, they had shortened the nickname for recruits to *rubber boots*. That gradually was shortened and by World War I we just said *boots*. Along in the 1920's the other branches started using the name. It amuses an old-timer to hear every branch of the service using the term *boot training* as glibly as you please. I'll bet not one per cent knows where it started or why."

That's an interesting and plausible yarn. However, I believe only the seagoing arms of the service use *boot training*. In the Air Force, for example, preflight cadets are *kiwis* and I believe *rookie* is still the informal Army designation for new recruits.

booze

A friend of mine has an old whiskey bottle, in the shape of a log cabin, which bears the name "E. S. Booz" as the distiller. He says that's where *booze* came from. Others claim it is a word from the Roaring Twenties.

Both theories are about five centuries away from the right answer. It's true that Mr. Booz's bottles had much to do with popularizing the word during the last century, but the Dutch had been using it many centuries earlier, certainly as early as when they settled New Amsterdam. Moreover, a variant form has been in the language as far back as Edmund

Spenser (1590) and the Oxford Dictionary says "boozy—affected by drinking" was in use in 1529.

borax

Borax is the term used to describe furniture that is cheaply made but flashy and ornate in appearance. It is the stock-in-trade of the ten-dollars-down-and-the-rest-when-we-catch-you type of merchandisers.

"Born with the gift of laughter and a sense that the world was mad"

The origin of this quotation puzzled the wisest savants of Yale University for several years. Here's how it came about. In the 1930's Yale, utilizing a large bequest from the Harkness Foundation, built a series of dormitories which they called "colleges" in the British fashion. Quasi-Gothic in style, the buildings were rather elaborately ornamented with gargoyles and the like. Shortly after one college was dedicated, someone noticed the saying quoted cut into the stone arch over the entrance to the college.

There was no author's name appended to the quote so the best brains of Yale's English department set about the task of determining which of the great minds of the ages first said, "He was born with the gift of laughter and a sense that the world was mad." Try as they would, they could not find this line in any of the works of great writers from Chaucer to even William Lyon Phelps. So the task was passed on to the Romance Languages department, then to the Classics and eventually even to the Egyptologists—but all drew blanks.

Finally, to the consternation of the faculty, an undergraduate who had obviously misspent part of his youth in the reading of trashy literature pointed out that the challenging quote came from the opening chapter of Rafael Sabatini's *Scaramouche*.

How did the writings of so minor a novelist come to be imperishably graven on the walls of Yale? Apparently the lines were written in by a draftsman in the architect's office, merely to indicate that some quotation should be put in that space. By an entirely unbelievable series of blunders the quote found itself immortalized in stone. And what did Yale do when the horrid truth came out? Well, ivy was promptly planted and today, thirty years later, Mr. Sabatini's quotation is presumably restored to obscurity.

Borstal Boy, Teddy Boys

Borstal is the location of the first modern reform school in Britain, established just after the turn of the century. Its theory is that youthful offenders can more readily be prepared for re-entry into society by education and technical training, rather than by mere imprisonment. One of Britain's angry young men, Brendan Behan, named his autobiographical book *Borstal Boy* in reference to the time he spent at this institution.

The *Teddy Boys* are the London equivalent of our leather-jacketed, duck-tailed, teen-age punks. They get their name from the tightly fitted "Edwardian" jackets and trousers they affect.

boss

Boss, derived from the Dutch word *baas,* meaning "master," is equally common today in business and politics.

botanophobia

Meaning an intense dislike of flowers and plants, *botanophobia* stems from the Greek *botane* (a plant or herb) and *phobos* (fear).

bouillon, consommé

Any good cook can tell you that a true *consommé* and a *bouillon* are very similar, though today's *bouillon* is all too often merely hot water and a cube of beef concentrate. Both words originally came from the French and in themselves tell a good deal about the process of cooking soups in years gone by.

A good soup had to be, first of all, the product of long slow boiling. *Bouillon* comes from the French word *bouillir* (to boil), and *consommé* is from the verb *consommer* and literally means "finished." In the word you can almost hear the sigh of relief of a French cook that the long task of preparing the perfect, clear soup is finally finished.

bowdlerize

Thomas Bowdler was an English editor of high reputation and even higher moral principles. Disturbed at what he felt were vulgar influences in the literature of the late eighteenth and early nineteenth centuries, he undertook to edit all "improper" references from the works of William Shakespeare and in 1818, published *The Family Shakespeare.* So radical and extreme were his methods of expurgating the text of the Bard's plays, however, that he was ridiculed by his contemporaries and—well intentioned though his efforts were—he lives in memory only through the word *bowdlerize,* a decidedly deprecatory synonym for "expurgate."

Bowery. *See* Tenderloin.

bowie knife

"Who invented the *bowie knife?*" From the throats of millions of young admirers of one of America's folk heroes, I can hear the answer: "Why, everyone knows it was Davy Crockett's pal, Colonel James Bowie, hero of the Alamo, who invented the *bowie knife.*"

It is my painful duty to say nay to these enthusiastic youngsters. Though there can be no doubt that Jim Bowie often used the knife which bears his family name, the fact seems to be that the first such knife was made by a Louisiana blacksmith working from a design by Colonel Bowie's brother, Rezin Pleasant Bowie.

This, I say, is the fact of the matter. But it's never likely to catch up with the legend that Colonel Bowie invented the knife—a tale which received startling impetus from the astonishing popularity a few years ago of anything and everything connected with Davy Crockett.

bowler. *See* derby.

Boxing Day

The *boxing* in *Boxing Day,* a British holiday, has nothing to do with fighting. It refers to the custom of giving gift boxes to faithful employees on the day after Christmas. In earlier times this was also the day when church almsboxes were opened and the contents distributed to the needy members of the parish.

boycott

A word well known to most Americans is *boycott.* But it was in Ireland's County Mayo less than a century ago that the word was coined.

Captain Charles Cunningham Boycott, a retired English Army officer, was land agent in Mayo for the estate of an absentee owner, the Earl of Erne. Now any son of the Old Sod will tell you that there is no love lost between natives of Ireland and those they would label the "English usurpers." But Boycott seemed bound and determined to bring upon himself the concentrated hatred of the entire populace.

Insisting upon the very letter of the law—despite the fact that crop scarcity had made the natives poor indeed—he refused to reduce rents and attempted to evict any tenants who could not pay in full. As a result, he was completely ostracized, his servants departed en masse, and attempts were even made to cut off his supply of food.

By harvest time, public opinion was so inflamed against him that he had to import several hundred British soldiers to protect the harvesters—who themselves had been brought in from Northern Ireland. The Irish Land

League, an organization of tenants, finally made life so completely miserable that Captain Boycott fled to England—thereby making the first *boycott* a success.

Ever since that day to *boycott* a person has meant to combine with one's neighbors in refusing to deal with him, in order to force him to change a position previously taken. A *boycott* may also, of course, be organized against a business firm or racial group.

brain trust

In the course of an interesting TV discussion of the 1930's by Ben Shahn, the artist, Benny Goodman, the musician, Raymond Moley, the columnist, and several other veterans of those years, Moley twice referred to President Franklin D. Roosevelt's *brains trust*—the unofficial cabinet of advisers he assembled during the early days of the New Deal. Social science textbooks and even the encyclopedia refer to this group as the *brain*(no *s*) *trust*. Which is correct?

Both are correct—but Mr. Morley is a bit "more correct," as befits one of the original members of the group. The name was first coined by a *New York Times* political reporter, James M. Kieran, and its original form was *brains trust* (with *s*). However, popular use and the need for headline writers to economize on the number of letters used in their heads soon reduced the label to *brain trust*.

When the British Broadcasting Corporation some years ago created an egghead radio program along the lines of the lamented *Information Please,* it was named the *Brains Trust*—and it was on television until recently and may return.

branch water

A *branch* in regional usage means a small stream, usually slightly smaller than a creek. Water from a *branch,* according to legend at least, is clearer, cooler and more refreshing than ordinary water. Nowadays the term probably survives because the alliterative phrase "bourbon and *branch*" falls pleasantly on many ears. The truth of the matter is that in almost every instance nowadays the so-called *branch water* is just city water from the tap.

brand-new

Where does the expression *brand-new* come from? People say, "I bought a *brand-new* car." Why do they not just say, "I bought a new car"?

Well, it's true that the simple adjective *new* adequately describes the condition of the car, but there is an extra element of excitement and enthusiasm in the phrase *brand-new* which makes it perhaps more completely descriptive not only of the car but of the owner's pleasure with his new possession.

The phrase has a long and honorable history. It dates, indeed, back to the Middle Ages and earlier, when *brand* meant flame or torch—as it does in the still current phrase, "snatching a *brand* from the burning." The description *brand-new* in those days was applied to products—usually made of metal—newly taken from the flames in which they were molded. They were, literally, "fire-new." See also SPANKING NEW.

brands and trade-marks

The practice of *branding* animals for the purpose of identification is so old that its exact origins are unknown. We do know, however, that *brands* were first used on humans—criminal and slaves.

According to the *Oxford Dictionary,* the practice of *branding* animals to indicate ownership was well established in England before Shakespeare's time and the term *trade-mark* for the word or symbol chosen by a manufacturer to identify and distinguish his product was in use before 1838. Official registration of *trade-marks* by the U.S. Patent Office did not begin, however, until 1870.

brass

Brass is simply a shortened form of *brass hat,* a term originally used in the British Army as long ago as 1890. The allusion is to the gold braid worn on officers' hats as an insignia of rank. During World War I the term *brass hat* was commonplace in American Army circles—usually in the form of contemptuous references by enlisted men to their top-ranking officers.

In World War II the term was shortened to *the brass,* sometimes *the big brass* or *the top brass.* With the return of thousands of ex-servicemen to civilian life, it was inevitable that the term would be carried over and applied to top-ranking executives in business. Incidentally, the actual braid adorning the hats of top-ranking officers is usually called *scrambled eggs,* just as a collection of service and combat ribbons worn on the chest is known as *fruit salad.*

brass tacks, to get down to

There are several theories about the origin of this expression, but the first I found that sounds authentic appeared in the book-magazine *American Heritage.* In an article on the wonders of the old country store, Gerald Carson wrote: "In general, the right side of the store might be called the ladies' department. . . . On the shelves [were] piece goods by the bolt. Brass tacks were driven into the time-smoothed counter to mark an exact yard. 'Don't hold it up and guess. Get down to brass tacks.' "

Here is another explanation from one of my correspondents, Bowman O'Ferrall of Alexandria, Virginia:

"I have a different version—probably just as corny and just as unconvincing. I am 72 years old and my Grandma who lived in Civil War days told me many years ago that in the old days upholstering—especially upholstering chairs—began with brass tacks. They were unseen, hidden as much as possible, but very necessary for a good foundation. Thus when anything went wrong, like a chair or sofa suddenly letting you down, the first thing to do was to get to the foundation of the trouble—and that meant *getting down to the brass tacks.*

"Well, to come right down to brass tacks, I'm not at all sure who's right—but I'm sure there are more brass tacks on chair bottoms than there are on country store counters!"

I can't argue that point. It seems to me that we have here two equally valid theories of the origin of this common expression. As the side show barkers used to say, "You pays your nickel and you takes your choice"—unless, that is, some other long-memoried reader has still a third theory of the origin of *brass tacks.*

brat, army. *See* Old Army slang.

bread

Bread, as a term for money, has been current in popular musicians' slang for nearly a decade. Since much teen-age jargon comes from musicians' argot, it's not surprising that the young people have picked up *bread.*

As a matter of fact, a very closely related sense of *bread,* meaning one's livelihood, has been in accepted usage for many years. In one episode of Sherlock Holmes, for example, Conan Doyle has a blackmailer, Milverton, say: "Here's how I make my humble *bread.*"

break, to get a

The origin of the word *break* in such common phrases as "He *got a good break*" or "The *breaks* are against him" comes from the poolroom. At the start of a game of pool the balls are racked up in triangular formation. The first player then plays the cue ball and, depending on whether he gets a good *break* or a bad one, pockets several balls or none at all. Since this initial play is a very chancy thing, it can be seen how readily the terms *good break* and *bad break* could come to mean good or bad luck.

bridge

Bridge is derived from a Russian game, *biritch,* which was introduced to Western cultures as "Russian whist." The name *biritch* was soon transformed to *bridge* (by a process known to linguists as "folk etymology") and so it has remained.

broadcloth

In case you've wondered where *broadcloth* got its name, the answer is really quite simple. It's made on a loom broader than the standard 29-inch width. *Pima* cotton gets its name from Pima County, Arizona, and *Sea Island* cotton is so called because it's grown only on certain islands of the Caribbean—isolated so it won't crossbreed with more plebeian cottons.

bromide. *See* blurb and goop.

brooch

The name of a lady's dress ornament, *brooch* is pronounced as if it were spelled "broach" because it originally *was* spelled "broach."

This ornament with a clasp—usually worn at the neck of a dress—gets its name from the pin that holds it together. The *broaches* of old were sharp-pointed spits or skewers, similar to but larger than a shish-kebab skewer and used for roasting oxen over huge fires. When milady's jewelry was fashioned, the resemblance between the pin and the broach was obvious, so it was called *broach,* later *brooch.*

brouhaha

Brouhaha was borrowed directly from the French, where it originally meant "noisy chattering" and presently has the same meaning of fuss or argument that it has in English today.

It's a fairly recent borrowing, being recorded by *American Speech* magazine as first appearing in the popular press in 1943. Its current vogue is so recent that it has not yet been included in some general-use dictionaries. Quite probably we may credit it to importation by American soldiers stationed in France during and after World War II.

browse

The original meaning of *browse* had nothing whatever to do with *browsing* in stores, for it came from the Old French word *brouz,* meaning the twigs and leaves an animal could feed on. There is still a very nice distinction between *browsing* and "grazing" in that an animal who *browses* eats only foliage from trees and bushes, while a grazing animal eats grass from the ground.

So *to browse* literally means to nibble at. It also has the related meaning of glancing in casual fashion through a book or the various books in a library—nibbling, so to speak, at learning. Many of our bookstores today carry signs in the window inviting passers-by to "come in and *browse* around." Quite possibly this is where some get the idea that the use of *browse* should be limited to places like libraries and bookstores.

However, this seems to me an unwarranted limitation on the word's use and, providing that it's used in the sense of making a leisurely tour of inspection, I don't see why one can't *browse* through a department store just as well as through a bookstore.

brunch

Brunch, meaning a meal combining elements of breakfast and lunch and customarily eaten about noon, is one of a class of words known to linguists as "portmanteau" or "blend" words. At one time, indeed, *brunch* became so widely popular that some scholars labeled the whole category *"brunch* words." Lewis Carroll's *slithy*—from "slimy" and "lithe"—was probably the first such word.

No one seems to know for sure when *brunch* first attained popularity, though H. L. Mencken reports that it appeared in England around 1900. He adds that "it was thirty years later before it began to make headway on this side of the water." In any event, Merriam-Webster entered it for the first time in their 1934 revision, so Mencken's notion of the date of its first use in America would appear to be fairly well founded.

brush-fire war

A completely accurate definition of *brush-fire war* would have to come from an expert in military science, but the general sense of the phrase is a localized war, especially one in which nuclear weapons are not used.

The phrase has been used on several occasions by spokesmen for the Atomic Energy Commission, who take the position that such small local wars are probably inevitable but that the deterrent threat of nuclear bombs will prevent any of the major powers from allowing these minor actions to develop into world-wide warfare. Needless to say, not all authorities support this relatively optimistic viewpoint.

My records indicate that the phrase *brush-fire war* was first used in 1955, though its widespread use is more recent. A somewhat similar phrase, *proxy war,* has not proven so popular—perhaps because of the implication that in these small localized wars the major powers may be using the lesser nations as pawns in the international struggle.

buck

Buck meaning "dollar" is a slang term from that favorite American indoor sport, poker playing. Originally the *buck* was a marker or counter placed before a player to remind him that his was the next turn to deal. In the gambling dens of the early West, silver dollars were often used as such markers and, in time, the name *buck* came to be applied to both silver and paper dollars. Despite the fact that *buck* has been in our language for upwards of a hundred years, it is still labeled "slang."

buff

BUFFS BARRED FROM BLAZES ran a headline in a leading New York newspaper. The story concerned an order by New York City's Fire Commissioner banishing all unauthorized persons from the immediate scenes of fires. The Commissioner, complaining that "you can't get to the fire because of the *buffs,*" said that the *buffs,* who originally came to fires to dispense coffee and sandwiches to the fire fighters, had become carried away by enthusiasm and had taken to fighting the fires themselves. "They're all over the place, making a nuisance of themselves," the Commissioner continued.

This is not a new problem, especially in New York where the late Fiorello H. LaGuardia ranked as the Number 1 Fire *Buff* throughout his several terms as Mayor. Actually *buffs* have been nearly as much nuisance as help ever since the days when New York had only volunteer fire departments—the days when the *buffs* first got their name.

A fire *buff* is a person who drops everything when he hears the fire whistle or the shriek of sirens outside his place of business and pursues the clanging engines to the scene of the blaze. *Buff,* you see, is short for buffalo robe—favorite cold-weather covering of amateur fire fighters midway through the last century. Also, these early volunteer companies attracted wealthy young men by the dash and danger of the assignment—and their favorite winter coats were made of buffalo skins.

So we can credit to the nearly extinct bison the origin of the word *buff* to describe an enthusiast, especially one who delights in attending fires in a semiofficial capacity. He is by no means to be confused with the fire *bug* who, known to the police by the more formal names of "incendiary" and "pyromaniac," is a person who starts fires for the thrill of seeing buildings burn.

A true fire *buff* prides himself on being the first civilian to arrive at the scene of the blaze and, especially in a small town where a large fire may tax the resources of the regular fire department, he can be of great help to the official firemen. He usually makes it a point to become well acquainted with the fire department officers and with all the complex routine of running a fire department, and is regarded by many chiefs as a welcome amateur assistant.

buffalo

The city of Buffalo did not get its name until 1810 (at first it was called New Amsterdam). Long before that plainsmen had discovered and hunted the buffalo; indeed, buffalo rugs and blankets were probably used by the earliest settlers of the area which came to be the city of Buffalo.

The name *buffalo* is, of course, a misnomer when applied to the American bison. It is, nonetheless, the popular name for the animal. However, the Indians had nothing to do with coining it. *Buffalo* comes from Portuguese (*bufalo*) and can be traced to the Latin *bufalus* (wild ox).

buffoon

Jimmy Durante has often been referred to as "America's most beloved *buffoon.*" This is a remarkably appropriate label for Jimmy, since it comes to us from the land to which the Great Schnozzola traces his ancestry, Italy. In the *commedia dell'arte* of the Middle Ages, one of the most beloved stock characters was *buffone,* whose specialty was puffing out his cheeks, then collapsing them suddenly. The resultant noise was not unlike the raucous Bronx cheer (more elegantly called the "raspberry") which long was a staple of the sort of roughhouse cabaret comedy in which Jimmy himself was reared.

bulkhead. *See* painter.

bull (mistake)

Bull meaning "mistake" comes from the French *boule,* which originally meant a lie, especially when made in the form of a bragging statement. Over the centuries, the meaning changed somewhat, so that a *bull* nowadays—or at least in Dickens' day—means a boastful but unwittingly mistaken statement. Also it's usually one that is so obviously wrong that any listener knows at once that the maker of the *bull* has made an utterly absurd remark.

bull, papal

The *papal bull* is derived from the Latin *bulla* (a knob or seal). Originally it referred to the seal affixed to official documents by a Pope. Now, while retaining the earlier meaning, it is more popularly used to refer to the official edicts or decrees of the Pope.

bulldogging

In the slang of the cowboys, *bulldogging* a steer means to get a grip on its horns and twist its neck until it hits the ground. See also HOOLIHAN.

bull in a chinashop. *See* Chinaman's chance.

bullion

Bullion, meaning bars of gold or silver, comes from a French word *billion,* the name of a small coin, and this word in turn came from *bille,* meaning a stick or bar.

bulls and bears

The *bull* is an investor who purchases stock in anticipation of a rise in its value and a *bull* market is one in which the majority of investors act on the assumption that their stocks will continue to increase in value. Various theories are advanced concerning the origin of the term and the most likely is that it refers to the bull's habit of tossing its head upward.

Bears, conversely, buy in anticipation of a slump in the market. Like its counterpart *bull,* this term has been in use at least since 1700 and no one is quite sure how the term first got its meaning. Most plausible is the theory that it comes from the old axiom about "selling the skin before you've caught the *bear*." A trader who operated in this fashion was once known in England as a *bearskin jobber*.

bumbershoot, parachute

Bumbershoot is late nineteenth-century slang. It's a combination of the *umber* part of umbrella and the *chute* from *parachute*.

For some reason our ancestors seem to have been very umbrella-conscious. Harold Wentworth records in his *American Dialect Dictionary* more than fifteen other variations—*bumbershoot, bumbersell* and *umbershoot* among them.

If you're skeptical—as I was—about parachutes being known in the nineteenth century, here's a surprise. The word *parachute,* in precisely the same meaning it has today, first appeared in print in 1785, before the United States had acquired its first President!

The reason? Well, they needed a way to get out of balloons when trouble loomed—and balloons were commonplace long before the Wright brothers conquered the air in heavier-than-air craft.

bunco

Bunco is generally thought to come from *buncombe,* though its present-day meaning—swindle or confidence game—has much more distasteful connotations than does *bunk.* A *bunco steerer* is a swindler's accomplice who "steers" the unwary to a crooked or fixed game of cards, chance or pool.

Incidentally, though *bunco* was common in the latter part of the nineteenth century and appears often in the works of Bret Harte, O. Henry and other writers of the period, it is still a part of today's underworld jargon.

bunk, bunkum

According to fairly well-authenticated legend, Congressman Felix Walker of Buncombe County, North Carolina, made a speech back in 1820 which was notable—even by the extraordinarily tolerant standards of our House of Representatives—for its windiness and general nonsensicality. As member after member rose to leave the floor of the House, the Honorable Felix became gradually aware of the fact that, in today's theatrical parlance, he was "laying an egg." With remarkable humility for a Congressman, he interrupted his speech to remark, "You're not hurting my feelings, gentlemen. I am not speaking for your ears. I am only talking for Buncombe."

Congressman Walker's candor was so relished by his colleagues that they adopted the phrase "talking for Buncombe" as a synonym for talking nonsense. Over the years the spelling was simplified by popular usage to *Bunkum.* In time, of course, the captial *B* was changed to lower case and the terminal *um* was lost. Thus *bunk,* which we all know so well, is, in reality, an abbreviation of "Buncombe County, North Carolina."

bunk, to do a

To do a bunk is British slang for "to depart in haste," especially under suspicious circumstances. It's roughly equivalent to such American slang expressions as *take it on the lam, hightail it out* or, simply, *scram.*

bush, beat around the

The real meaning of *beat around the bush* is not so much to evade an issue entirely but to approach it cautiously and indirectly.

"Stop *beating around the bush!* Get to the point," goes back many centuries and comes from the language of the huntsman. It was once the custom to hire beaters to beat bushes and arouse game birds for the hunter to shoot at. So the beater stirred up the action, but the hunter got to the point.

busman's holiday

Busman's holiday originated in the close relationship between horse teams and their drivers in the days when London's omnibuses were horse-drawn. Almost invariably the regular driver would report to the starting point on his day off to see to it that proper care was used in harnessing his team. If he had any reason to suspect that the substitute driver was negligent in handling the horses, the regular busman might unobtrusively sit among the passengers to observe the new driver's behavior. These rides—beyond the call of duty and without extra pay—came to be called *busman's holidays*.

by and large

It's difficult to fix a precise meaning for *by and large,* since it means "generally speaking" or "on the whole." But originally the phrase had a very precise meaning in the language of sailors.

In the days of sailing ships, when a vessel was running close-hauled, the man at the helm would usually be given one of two orders, *full and by* or *by and large*. The first command, used with a skillful helmsman, meant "sail as close to the wind as you can." The second, by and large, meant "sail slightly off the wind" and was given to the inexperienced helmsman since this tack would leave him in less danger of being "taken aback."

So the phrase *by and large* has come to indicate imprecise generalities. A person speaking *by and large* about a subject can be considered to be something less than entirely expert on it.

bye-bye

The childish farewell, *"bye-bye,"* has become a television trade term for that point in the program when the star announces, "Now we're going to have to say so long. . . ." See also TELEVISION LANGUAGE.

Byzantine logothete

Theodore Roosevelt once described Woodrow Wilson as a *Byzantine logothete*. Actually a *logothete* was an officer—either treasurer or chancellor—of the Byzantine Empire. What T.R. meant, however, was that in his opinion Wilson was an official who talked a lot but did nothing. If memory serves, he used the expression at a time when T.R. thought we should enter World War I, but Wilson still advocated vigilant neutrality.

C

cabal

A widely held but erroneous notion of the origin of this word for a group of persons working together from somewhat hidden or devious motives is that it comes from the first letters of the names of five cabinet ministers of Charles II. But the word is much older than that. Indeed, it may be traced back to a Hebrew word of similar meaning.

While it's true that the word was popularized during the reign of Charles II, the *Oxford Dictionary* reports its appearance in print as early as 1616, nearly sixty years before the cabinet of Clifford, Arlington, Buckingham, Ashley and Lauderdale.

Thanks to the coincidence that their last initials spell *cabal,* the word came into great vogue and was thought to be one of the earliest acronyms (a word made up of the first letters of a group of words).

In point of fact, however, *cabal* was borrowed directly from the French, where it meant a club or society of intriguers. Eventually it can be traced through Latin to the Hebrew *qabbalah*—the doctrines received from Moses and handed down through the centuries by word of mouth. During the Middle Ages the possessors of these doctrines were believed to possess secrets of magical power, and thus the word *cabal* acquired its implications of stealth and mystery.

cablese. *See* upcoming.

caboose

Caboose sounds like a characteristic bit of American railroad jargon, perhaps derived, like *vamoose* and *hoosegow,* from Spanish by way of Mexico. But that is not the case. *Caboose* was originally a Dutch word, or rather two Dutch words, *kaban huis,* meaning cabin house or ship's galley. In time the two words blended into one, *kabuys,* and even before our Revolutionary War, the term *caboose* was commonly used on British ships to designate the cook's quarters.

The word has been traced back as far as 1862 in its current American meaning of the last or trainmen's car on a freight train. Incidentally, it has never been used by British railroaders. To them a *caboose* is a "brake-van."

cache

Pronounced KASH, this word comes from the French *cacher* and retains its original meaning of "to hide away or conceal." See also STASH.

cachet. *See* philatelic jargon.

caddy

Golf *caddies* were originally "cadets." The word *caddie* has been used in Scotland for centuries to mean an errand boy, so it was entirely logical that it be used to designate the boy who carries the clubs, watches the ball and, generally speaking, runs errrands for the golfers. In America today the usual spelling is *caddy*.

caduceus

The medical symbol of a stick with a pair of snakes wrapped around it is called the *caduceus* (pronounced kuh-DOO-see-us). It has been the symbol of the medical profession since ancient times. Its white staff was originally carried by Roman warriors when they desired to ask the enemy to discuss truce terms—just as the white flag is used by peace negotiators today. It was also carried by Mercury, the wing-footed messenger of the gods.

The snakes come from the tradition that Aesculapius, the Roman god of medicine, appeared during a plague in Rome in the form of a snake. The ancients also believed that snakes had discovered the secret of eternal life, interpreting the snake's seasonal sloughing off of its skin as a return to youth. What's more, they credited snakes with being able to search out health-giving medicinal herbs.

Thus the combination of the snakes as symbols of health and the staff representing both speed and peace adds up to a meaningful emblem for the medical profession.

Caesar, Julius. *See* czar.

Caesarian section. *See* czar.

cafeteria. *See* commons.

Cain, to raise. *See* raise Cain, to.

Cajun

If you remember Longfellow's *Evangeline,* you'll recall that the French settlers of what is now Nova Scotia (then called Acadia) were deported by order of the British in 1755. Many of them settled in Louisiana where the name "Acadian" gradually became corrupted to *Cajun.* In theory, the term is restricted to Louisianans of Acadian French ancestry.

call a spade a spade. *See* spade a spade, to call a.

calumny

Calumny (pronounced KAL-um-nee) comes direct from the Latin *calumnia* and means a false and defamatory accusation, one deliberately intended to hurt another person's reputation. In the course of political campaigns during the nineteenth century, many *calumnies* were freely uttered. President Lincoln notably was the object of many *calumniatory* charges.

camellia

The lovely *camellia* is named after George Joseph Kamel, a Moravian Jesuit missionary who brought back the first of these shrubs from the Orient.

camelopard

The camelopard, famed in medieval folklore, is actually the giraffe— tall as a camel, spotted like a leopard.

Canada

According to the best authority, *canada* was originally a word in the Huron-Iroquois language meaning "a collection of lodges." Thus the first *canada* was an Indian village.

canapé, hors d'oeuvre

According to a leading cookbook, "The phrase *hors d'oeuvre* is used to describe savory little appetizers or relishes other than *canapés.*" *Canapés,* in turn, are defined as "savory appetizers made with a bread, cracker or pastry base, so that they can be picked up with the fingers and eaten in one or two bites." *Hors d'oeuvres,* then, include the whole range of cocktail-time tidbits except *canapés.*

Both terms come, of course, from the French and each has an interesting background. Would you have guessed, for instance, that *canapé* originally meant a canopy of mosquito netting over a couch or bed? In time it came to mean the bed or divan itself—whence it was taken into English with its present meaning of a bit of bread or cracker over which a tasty mixture of cheese, meat or fish is spread.

Hors d'oeuvre—which means literally "outside of the work"—came to its present meaning because the appetizers referred to are almost invariably served outside of and in advance of the main meal.

Both words, incidentally, offer some challenge in the matter of pronunciation. None of us is likely to stray so far from the correct pronunciation as the legendary new-rich oil millionaire who demanded "horses' doovers" but it's worth taking the trouble to be right. Say or-DERV for *hors d'oeuvre* and kan-uh PAY for *canapé*.

candidate

In the course of one of our quadrennial political frenzies, with politicians exchanging charges and countercharges with ever-increasing recklessness, it is almost amusing to reflect on the fact that the word *candidate* originally meant a man clad in spotless raiment, a person immune from tawdry mud-slinging. In Roman days a person *candidatus*—"clothed in white"—was a man seeking elective office. The white toga, of course, was intended to indicate that the candidate's motives were as pure and spotless as the gown he wore.

The politics of ancient Rome have given us other words now heard in daily use among our legislators. A *senator,* for instance, was originally one of the elder wise men, and the body in which they met—the *senate*—took its name from *senex,* the Latin word for "old." A *legislator,* logically enough, was one who brings laws, from the Latin words *lator* (bringer) and *lex* (law). *Congress* is a group which "comes together," from the Latin *congredi,* while a *parliament* is, almost too aptly, a place where people talk—from the French *parlement* (talking).

Not all of our political terms come from ancient sources, however. There's at least one which had its origin no farther away than Massachusetts. It is *gerrymander* and means to reallocate the boundary lines of voting districts in such a way as to benefit the party in power. Every time there is a realignment of Congressional districts because of population changes, the charge of *gerrymandering* is sure to be leveled against the officials making the changes.

The first and most notorious instance of *gerrymandering* took place early in the nineteenth century and the instigator was, as you may have guessed, a man named Gerry. Because his redistricting resulted in a county whose outlines closely resembled the shape of a salamander, the word *gerrymander* was coined to describe the technique he employed.

Incidentally, the hubbub caused by his actions did nothing to impair Elfridge Gerry's political career. Governor of the Commonwealth of Massachusetts at the time of the incident, he was elected Vice President of the United States two years later.

candid camera

Dr. Erich Salomon, using one of the first Leica 35-millimeter cameras, in 1928 took a series of unposed pictures of world-famous statesmen at a League of Nations meeting in Geneva. When published in the London *Graphic,* they created a sensation because they were so unlike the customarily stiff and formal group photographs taken at such assemblies. The word *candid* was used to describe Salomon's photos by the *Graphic* and the word soon came into general use to describe the miniature cameras and photographs taken while the subject was unaware and "off guard."

cannibalize

Cannibalize has been standard mechanic's jargon since World War II. It is entered in most up-to-date dictionaries, with the meaning, of course, of salvaging parts from abandoned vehicles to put others into working order. The *Air Force Dictionary* has still another definition—a bit closer to the original jungle sense of the word: "to obtain personnel from other units to build up an organization's strength."

canoe. *See* paddle your own canoe.

Cantab

Cantab is a shortened form of Cantabrigian, an adjective formed from *Cantabrigia,* the Latin name for the city of Cambridge, England. Since the Massachusetts city, like the one in England, houses one of the nation's most distinguished universities, it's not surprising that the name was adopted—though in abbreviated form—to describe the athletes of Harvard.

Cantab has the added virtue of fitting snugly into a newspaper headline. Incidentally, Boston papers also use *Cantab* to describe undergraduates of the Cambridge High and Latin School. See also LIVERPUDLIAN.

capsule

Capsule seems a remarkable word to assign to the part of a space vehicle which deposits astronauts safely back on earth. There is logic in it, however. The word comes to us from the Latin *capsula* (little chest). That, in a sense, is what the astronauts fly—a little chest separated from the larger chest which contains the booster rockets and other equipment used in the early stages of the flight.

The word *capsule* in the precise meaning of a device for depositing a man safely on earth after flight was first used about 1950 when, with fighter jets exceeding the speed of sound, it became necessary to devise an airtight ejectable cockpit or cabin. In an emergency, the pilot could hit the "eject" lever and drop, cabin and all, through the first perilous phases of his descent. The *capsule* of the Friendship 7 space vehicle was, of course, an infinitely more sophisticated device—a maneuverable vehicle in itself. Nevertheless, *capsule* it is, and *capsule* it will remain.

As to *astronaut,* it first appeared in the learned lexicons in 1956—in the excellent *Air Force Dictionary.* Their definition, in the light of recent feats, needs to be revised. In 1956 the editors could only say that an astronaut was "one who would engage in, or is concerned with, interplanetary flight."

carafe

Carafe was a French word before it came into our language, but even earlier it was the Spanish *garrafa* and the Italian *caraffa.* Most likely it came originally from the Arabic verb *gharafa,* meaning to draw water. Two pronunciations are sanctioned for American use: kuh-RAF and kuh-RAHF.

caravan. *See* automobile slang, British.

cardigan, raglan

The Earl of Cardigan gave his name to the popular knitted woolen, front-buttoning sweater. The Earl of Raglan's fame in menswear circles hangs upon his invention of the raglan overcoat in which the sleeves continue in one piece to the collar, without the shoulder seam found in other outercoats.

It's ironic that their fame should now rest on such homely articles, for in their lifetime they were among the most celebrated—and bumble-headed—of military leaders. It was Cardigan who led the doomed March of the Light Brigade at Balaclava in the Crimea, while Raglan was in supreme command of the British forces during that war. Though praised by Victoria for his services, he was sharply criticized by military experts for his handling of the campaign. The story is superbly told, by the way, in Cecil Woodham-Smith's book *The Reason Why,* one of the finest pieces of historical narrative of our time.

carnival. *See* Pancake Tuesday.

carnival talk

Hurry, hurry, hurry! Step right up and take your pick of the glass pitch, the glider, the girl show or the high-striker. The grinder's in front of each pitch and the bally comes loud and fast. Will you end the day happy or hurt? Will the pitches be gimmicked or gaffed so the marks will be properly taken?

Gibberish? Perhaps. But not to anyone who has lived in the colorful, fast-paced world of side shows and carnivals—*carnies,* as they're known in the trade. For these are all expressions common to the jargon of *carny* workers. Like all private languages, this one exists partly so that members of the trade can converse in the presence of outsiders without being understood by them.

A colorful part of small-town life in the summer months has long been the arrival of the traveling carnival show—though there are signs that the *carnies* may be traveling the same unhappy path to oblivion as minstrel shows and tent circuses. While the carnivals are still with us, though, earnest students of the folkways of American speech have chronicled the rough, savory and colorful language of its performers. Here are some of the words and phrases characteristic of the med shows, mud shows and side shows.

A *med show* is a medicine show, while a *mud show* is a small wagon show playing one-night stands in back country where roads may still be unpaved. A *mud show* is no place for a *dry-weather trouper*—which is the label carny folk use in place of "fine-weather friend."

Improbable though it sometimes must seem to the operators, traveling tent shows are supposed to make money—or *lettuce*—and the boss must keep a sharp eye out for the *O.P.C., "office percentage,"* and make sure it gets a cut of the *H.O.*—"holdout" or the agent's graft from the concessions.

This sometimes necessitates *laying the note*—duping the customer by interchanging bills of different denominations—and an operator specially skilled in this technique is said to be *on the whizz.* Naturally he must use a number of *shills*—confederates in the audience, also called *sticks*—and he must have an ample supply of *cush*—money that the shills are permitted to win in order to stimulate interest among the *marks.* And a *mark,* dear reader, is you—the general public, often referred to less elegantly as *suckers.*

A person who travels with a tent show is *kicking sawdust.* Performers are called *kinkers* and their living quarters are known as *kinkers' row.* The spun cotton candy which every child remembers from his visit to the carnival is known as *floss* while the cheap gimcracks used as prizes at the concessions are *slum*.

The *glass pitch* is the familiar side-show concession where the *mark* tries to win a prize by pitching coins into glassware.

The *glider* is the so-called *chairplane*—miniature planes hung on chains from a revolving tower, which spins the planes upward and outward.

The *girl show* needs no introduction to the men in the audience, at least, and most males, at one time or another, have probably tried to impress their fair companions by belting away with a heavy mallet on the *high-striker*.

The *grinder* is the spieler, barker or come-on man who gives you the "hurry, hurry" spiel in front of the *pitches*—or concessions. *Bally,* of course, is his message—or *ballyhoo*.

"Are you happy or hurt?" is the carny operatives' way of asking, "Did you win or lose?"

A *pitch* that is *gimmicked* or *gaffed* is a game of chance whose wheel or other mechanical device has been so rigged that the *mark* cannot possibly win—and an *ungimmicked* wheel is about as common as a nine-dollar bill.

carpetbagger

Carpetbagger, which has become a lasting symbol of political trickery and venality, is a term first used for unscrupulous Northern politicians who roamed the South after the Civil War, carrying their belongings in carpetbags and taking advantage of impoverished Southerners.

carte blanche

This phrase means giving someone blanket permission to do what he thinks best. In French, the phrase simply means "white card." But *carte blanche* means a rather special kind of white card—specifically, one bearing only the signature of a person in authority. The bearer of such a card can, of course, fill in above the signature whatever instructions or conditions he wishes.

Nowadays in America a home-grown idiom that exactly parallels *carte blanche* is coming into general use. It is, of course, *blank check*—which you will find in such statements as, "Congress today gave the President *blank-check* authority to proceed with his disaster relief program."

cartnaper

A cheerful addition to our store of words—though this doesn't speak too well for the honesty of American housewives—is *cartnaping*. According to a report by managers of supermarkets, more than $25,000,000 worth of shopping carts disappear annually at the hands of *cartnapers*.

cast of hawks. *See* **clowder, kindle and cowardice.**

cat, belling the. *See* **belling the cat.**

catalyst

Catalyst (pronounced KAT-uh-list) comes from the Greek *katalysis* which meant "dissolution." *Catalysis* (kuh-TAL-ih-sis) is a term common in chemistry, meaning the process of starting or speeding up a chemical reaction by the addition of a substance which is not itself changed or affected by the reaction. Both words have come into the general vocabulary in recent years. "Peace is sought throughout the world," a statesman might say, "but it will not become a reality until we use our untold wealth as the *catalyst* bringing peace between warring nations."

catawampus. *See* **cater-corner.**

cater-corner, cater-cornered

The correct spelling of this term is either *cater-corner* or *cater-cornered,* though two variant forms, *kitty-corner* and *katty-corner,* are often heard in our various regional dialects. Actually the word *cater* comes from the French *quatre* and thus the term originally meant "four-cornered." But, by a process known to language students as "folk etymology," the ordinary users of the term thought they detected an analogy to the ordinate domestic feline. Hence *cater* soon became *catty* and eventually even *kitty*.

Actually the variations on this phrase are too many to list, but my favorite has long been *catawampus* or *cattywampus,* a dialect term heard throughout the South, from the Carolinas to Texas. You'll often hear the expression "He walked *cattywampus* across the street," and down in Tennessee a college professor of mathematics was once heard to say, "You might call a rhombus a *catawampus* square."

cat on a hot tin roof

As nervous as a cat on a hot tin roof is a phrase common in the popular idiom for at least half a century—probably since tin roofs were invented. It derives originally from a British expression, *like a cat on hot bricks* meaning very ill at ease.

Caucasian

One of the earliest anthropologists, Johann Blumenbach, divided all mankind into five races: Caucasian, Mongolian, Ethiopian, American and Malayan. The best-proportioned skull in his collection was from the Caucasus, so he chose the name *Caucasian* as symbolizing the finest type of the white race.

Blumenbach also thought that the Caucasus was the original home of the hypothetical race known as "Indo-Europeans," to whom most Western and some Eastern cultures trace their language origin. These theories of Blumenbach are, in the words of the *World Webster Dictionary,* "now not scientific and often tinged with racism; however the word [*Caucasian*] is used in default of a better."

caucus

The first *caucus* was probably held before this land of ours was discovered—certainly before it was colonized. The word comes from an Algonquin Indian word *cau-cau-a-su,* meaning "adviser." John Smith in 1624 reported that the word was used in connection with powwows of Indian tribal leaders.

In the early 1700's a back-stage political action group (involving Sam Adams' father) was organized in Boston and known, at least informally, as "The Boston Caucus-club." By the time of the Revolution, the idea of political factions meeting *in caucus* to decide on candidates and campaign issues was well established and *caucus* remains a favorite political device to this day.

The British borrowed this word early in the nineteenth century but, as the *Oxford Dictionary* says, it was "grossly misapplied." Instead of referring to a small group of leaders meeting to chart a program, the British use *caucus* to designate the controlling organization of a party—something rather like the Republican and Democratic National Committees in America.

caveat

Caveat has a rather precise and technical meaning in legal language but in a sentence, such as "Let me enter a *caveat* on that," it merely means a warning or a caution. It's derived direct from the Latin *caveat,* meaning "Let him beware."

The best known *caveat* is certainly *Caveat emptor*—"Let the buyer beware"—which was common business advice in the years before Better Business Bureaus and the Federal Trade Commission stepped in to protect buyers from their own folly.

Cerberus, sop to. *See* sop to Cerberus, give a.

cete of badgers. *See* clowder, kindle and cowardice.

chacun à son gout. *See* **everyone to his own liking.**

chaise longue

Chaise longue is a direct borrowing from French and means, literally, "long chair." The correct pronunciation is "shays long," but the vast majority of people misread the second word, as if it were "lounge." As a result, the pronunciation "shays lounge" is very common, especially in the furniture industry. Partly to avoid confusion, you'll find that this now fairly uncommon item of furniture is usually advertised simply as a *chaise*.

changes, ringing the. *See* **ringing the changes.**

change-up. *See* **baseball jargon.**

Charge of the Light Brigade. *See* **Light Brigade, The Charge of the.**

Charley Noble

Sometime in the shrouded reaches of early maritime history there was a notable ship's cook named Charley Noble. At any rate, so the story goes. What we know for sure is that the smokepipe on a ship's galley is called the *Charley Noble*.

chauvinism

Most of us dream of making so lasting an impression on our fellow human beings that we will be remembered long after our passing. Not many of us ever achieve this high ambition and among those who do attain lasting fame, there is always a handful who "sought not fame but had it thrust upon them." So it is with the people whose names have been immortalized in our language by becoming common nouns and verbs.

Take Nicolas Chauvin, for instance. He was a gallant soldier of Napoleon I, wounded in battle and everlastingly devoted to his peerless leader. By his own standards, he was one of the few true patriots remaining in France after his hero's exile and he was not shy about expressing his continuing high regard for Napoleon. It is ironic that his excessive zeal in behalf of a cause most of his fellow countrymen thought well lost resulted in his becoming an object of ridicule.

Perhaps, though, Nicolas Chauvin has the last laugh for, though all those who mocked him are long-forgotten, his name remains a part not only of his native French but of other languages, including our own. So blind and unreasoning was this patriot's devotion to the lost imperial cause

that the word *chauvinism* was coined to describe his fanaticism—and
it remains in our language today as the one best word to indicate mili-
tant, boastful and wholly unreasoning devotion to one's country or
race.

chaw

Chaw has been a part of our tongue at least since 1530, according to
the *Oxford Dictionary*. It means "to chew," especially to chew some substance which is not to be swallowed, such as tobacco. It also appears as
a noun in such phrases as "a *chaw* of tobacco." The dictionaries variously
label *chaw* as "inelegant" or "vulgar," but not "slang."

cheesecake

There are nearly as many theories of the origin of this term as there
are pretty girls photographed every day in our fair country. Obviously not
all the theories can be correct, but the one most sanctified by time holds
that the word was first uttered by James Kane, photographer for the New
York *Journal* in 1912.

The story runs that Kane was a notable enthusiast for cheesecake,
a delicacy which many New Yorkers regard as the most delectable of
desserts. On a gusty summer afternoon, Kane was posing a toothsome
actress in the conventional railside pose on an incoming ocean liner. Just
as he shot the picture a gust of wind ruffled her skirts with the result that
—as H. L. Mencken put it—the final picture "included more of her person
than either he or she suspected."

Developing the plate later in the dark room, Kane was pleasantly
surprised at the exposure and, searching for the utmost in superlatives to
express his delight, exclaimed: "That's real *cheesecake!*"

Well, that's one theory and, as we have noted before, the one of earliest
origin. However, I theorize that the term may actually have developed
without any reference to the bakery *cheesecake*. Note for the moment that
photographers for years have instructed their models to say "Cheese!" just
as the exposure is being made, in order to force the lips into an attractive
smile. In fact, the standard instruction, once the positioning of model and
lights is completed, is: "Wet your lips and say 'Cheese!' "

Consider further that slang words like *cupcake* and *cookie* were popular
terms of endearment at the time *cheesecake* allegedly was first used for the
fair sex, and *cake-eater* was the virtually standard epithet for "ladies' man."
Thus we have a logical explanation for *cheesecake* being used to describe
the sort of *cupcake* any photographer worth his salt would be sure to have
say "Cheese!" before taking the picture.

chesterfield

The *chesterfield,* a single-breasted, velvet-collared topcoat worn on formal occasions, is named after the fourth Earl of Chesterfield, whose *Letters to His Son* remains a literary classic after nearly two centuries.

chicane

Ever hear the word *chicane?* No, not "chicanery"—which means trickery—but simply *chicane.* Well, the chances are your grandmother, if she was the whist-playing sort, knew it well. *Chicane* is the seldom-used bridge whist name for a hand without trumps. Most present-day bridge players have never heard the term, and, on the unhappy occasions when *chicane* would accurately describe their hands, they're more likely to say they are "void" or have "drawn a blank" in trumps.

chicken tetrazzini. *See* food from the opera.

chimera

Chimera (pronounced kuh-MEER-uh or ky-MEER-uh) comes direct from the Greek *chimaira,* and originally meant a fire-breathing monster with a lion's head and a goat's body. Nowadays it means any wild and foolish fancy. The adjective *chimerical* means visionary, fantastic or wildly improbable. In the space world of today we know that many of the inventions of Jules Verne, which were thought to be *chimerical* in their day, have proven to be practical realities.

Chinaman's chance

A person with only a *Chinaman's chance* is one with practically no chance at all. The history of this phrase is indeed a curious one, since it seems probable that originally the word *Chinaman* did not mean a Chinese person or a native of China at all!

Back in the sixteenth century, traders with the Far East brought back to Europe the first examples of the fine porcelain ware we call *china.* The first merchants to deal in this merchandise were called *chinamen* and their stores were called *chinashops.* So you see, the phrase *a Chinaman's chance* accurately describes the odds against a merchant of china if he were to find *a bull in his chinashop!*

Chinese home run

One of the more colorful phrases from the slang of America's national game is *Chinese home run*—meaning a hit that in most parks would be an easy out but, because of a short fence or some other peculiarity of the field, scores as a homer.

The scandalouly short 250-foot left-field foul line in the Los Angeles Coliseum was the reason for the vogue of the term *Chinese home run* and it set the editors of *Sporting News* to work trying to learn where and when the term originated. As is most often the case, no final verdict can be rendered but, fittingly enough, it appears that the phrase may well have originated in California.

It is the theory of Garry Schumacher, San Francisco Giants' publicity man, that the late, great cartoonist T. A. Dorgan, better known as "Tad," brought the phrase east with him from the California of an earlier day when Chinese coolie labor was a subject of great controversy. Since the word *Chinese* was then synonymous with "cheap," the label *Chinese home run* was self-explanatory.

Other amateur etymologists responding to the *Sporting News* survey credit the coining of *Chinese home run* and its derivative *Shanghai slam* to writers on early Philadelphia papers where the right-field wall was even closer (239 feet) than the much-discussed left-field fence in the Dodgers' new playground. So short was this Philadelphia fence, reports sportswriter Dan Parker, that the club eventually had to build a forty-foot screen atop it. Characteristically, though, the club owners of that day showed little regard for public opinion. The screen, it seems, was not erected to assuage the feelings of fans offended by the spate of *Chinese home runs.* No, it went up only after the club began to get bills for damages from owners of autos hit by balls flying over the low, short fence.

Sportswriters have coined a number of fanciful synonyms for *Chinese home run: homer foo young, chow mein smash* and *eggroll bingle* among them. One has even nicknamed the New York Polo Grounds the *Harlem joss house* because of its notoriously short fences.

chiropody, podiatry

Just as undertakers have long tried to get their future clients to call them "morticians"—with no noticeable success—and real estate agents labor manfully to force the label "realtor" down our throats, so the foot doctors have seemingly decided that now is the time to change to a more lofty label.

Chiropody—which was itself labeled a "barbarism" by H. W. Fowler as recently as the 1920's—is made from the Greek words *cheir* (hand) and *podos* (foot). As you might guess, it originally meant one who treated both hands and feet. However, in the somewhat condescending words of the *Oxford English Dictionary,* a *chiropodist* is "now usually one who treats corns and bunions."

In a sense, therefore, *podiatry* from *podos* and *iatros,* the Greek word for "physician," is more accurate than *chiropody,* since it indicates the treatment of the feet alone, not of the feet and hands. Whichever the label, though, the betting in this corner is that John Q. Public will continue to call the bunion-parers "foot doctors."

chit

Chit is the clubman's favorite phrase for the voucher or *tab* to be signed after the service of drinks. It's a word borrowed from Hindustani, believe it or not. The Hindi word for note or letter is *citthi.* This, in the vocabulary of British colonial officers, soon became *chitty* and finally *chit.* Your host, probably unconsciously, is emulating the founders of Queen Victoria's colonial empire when he calls for his *chit.*

chitlins, chitterlings

What are *chitlins?* Well, most dictionaries insist that the word should be spelled *chitterlings,* but all agree that they are hog's innards, fried or boiled. Popular chiefly in the Southeastern part of the country, they are also known as far west as Missouri and Arkansas and may be bought in markets in the Negro section of Northern cities.

A simple, Southern dialect word, to all intents and appearances, is *chitlins.* Yet to language students it is a word which can readily be traced back to Middle English, where it was used to describe similar organs in the human body. Moreover, it can be ultimately traced to the German *kutteln,* of the same meaning, and is probably related to the Danish *kuit,* meaning "fish roe."

Nor is that all. At least one etymologist suggests that the lowly *chitterlings* can be traced back through Anglo-Saxon to the Indo-European base *geu-,* meaning "to bend, curve or be rounded." All of which adds up to a rather impressive history for such a modest little word.

chorine

A girl who sings or dances in a chorus at a theater, cabaret, etc., is a *chorine.* It's a word that has been in common use since the 1920's at least. Though originally listed in dictionaries as "slang," most authorities now label it "colloquial"—meaning that it is perfectly suitable for use in informal writing or conversation.

chortle. *See* blend words.

chowderhead

The *chowder* in *chowderhead* is neither fish nor clam, not Boston nor

Manhattan. Indeed, it's simply not that kind of chowder at all. Actually, this *chowderhead* is a variation of *cholterhead,* which in turn was originally *jolterhead*—a term much used in Shakespeare's time but now completely obsolete. A *jolterhead,* as you might guess, was simply a stupid dolt, a blockhead.

The method by which an unfamiliar spelling becomes changed into the form of another unrelated but more familiar word (*cholter* to *chowder* in the example above) is known as "folk etymology" or "popular etymology." Examples of this are especially common in folk dialect—*sparrow grass* for asparagus, *very coarse veins* for varicose veins, *crick sand* for quicksand and, more commonly, *cold slaw* for cole slaw.

Christmas words

Every year, as Christmas Day comes around, we find ourselves using a whole splendid galaxy of words for which we have no conceivable use during other seasons of the year. Let's look at a few of these "Christmasy" words and see what special meanings make them appropriate for this season of the year.

Yuletide for "Christmastime" is a term derived from the yule log, which in olden days was a huge log used as the foundation of the holiday fire. *Bringing the yule log in* was, as recently as the nineteenth century, as much a part of the pre-Christmas festivities as putting up an evergreen tree today. Indeed, one authority reports that it was Queen Victoria's consort, Albert, who was responsible for the substitution, in English-speaking countries, of the German Christmas tree custom for the hitherto traditional yule log.

Yule itself can be traced back to the Middle English *yollen* (cry aloud) and is thought to date from early Anglo-Saxon revels in celebration of the discovery (after the winter solstice, December 22) that nights were becoming shorter and thus that Satan's eternal darkness had been averted for yet another year.

Santa Claus, you may be surprised to learn, is austerely labeled by the dictionaries a "corruption" of the Dutch "Sant Nikolaas." But bear in mind that our learned dictionary editors—generally a humorless lot—are here using "corruption" in a purely technical, linguistic sense and are by no means traducing that splendid figure of folklore, *Santa.*

Behind the word *mistletoe* lie the Anglo-Saxon words for "bird dropping" and "twig." In spite of its somewhat drab word history, the mistletoe was highly respected by the Druids and Celts as a bearer of magical health-bringing powers. This belief carries down to the present-day in the romantic custom of kissing under the mistletoe.

So, if your spouse complains about the amount of time you spend with those glamorous guests under the mistletoe, remember it's only mistletoe's "health-bringing powers" that interest you.

chunnel, the

If all goes as planned, you'll be hearing a lot in the next few years about a fabulous construction project called the *chunnel.* It's the long-planned tunnel under the English Channel from England to France. First projected in the mid-nineteenth century, its construction was deferred at the insistence of military leaders on both sides of the Channel, all of whom feared that it would be used as an avenue of invasion in case of war.

Now that nuclear weapons have made obsolete such concepts of defense against aggression, both high commands have agreed that the tunnel no longer represents a threat to security. With the evolution of the European Common Market, Wall Street has taken a lively interest in revived talk of the sub-Channel tunnel and reports are that many of the millions of dollars required to finance it will come from American sources.

cinco. *See* Old Army slang.

circumstance, pomp and

The phrase *pomp and circumstance,* which Elgar used as the title of his composition so often heard at high school graduations, comes from the line in *Othello:* "pride, pomp and circumstance of glorious war."

Circumstance comes from two Latin words, *circum* and *stare,* and originally meant "standing around." Then it came to mean an event at which large numbers of people were standing around. By Shakespeare's day, it meant any formal show or ceremony. This meaning is now archaic.

circus jargon

No craft or trade has a more colorful and interesting private language than the world of circus and carnival. Many words and phrases which originated here have come into wide general use. *Pitchman,* for example, originally meant the hawker who stood on a platform outside a tent and made the "spiel" to induce passers-by to enter. Nowadays, a *pitchman* may be any kind of extravagant or boastful salesman, including those television announcers noted within the industry for their "persuasive pitch."

But the best of circus and carnival jargon remains almost impossible for outsiders to understand—and that's the way the troupers want to keep it. In their world, for instance, a contortionist or acrobat is a *kinker,* and that chap who winds up on top of the human pyramid is, logically enough, the *high man* or *top mounter.*

Members of that admirable institution, the circus band, are known irreverently as *windjammers,* and the beautiful girls who ride horses and elephants in the grand spectacular finale are, simply, *spec girls.*

Believe it or not, you might find *convicts* in a *dog and pony show,* for to circus people a *convict* is a zebra and a *dog and pony show* is any small circus. A show *gone Sunday school* is one from which all gambling concessions have been eliminated, so there would presumably be less need for a *grouch bag*—a money bag concealed inside one's clothes.

Lot lice are townspeople who hang around the lot while the big top is being set up. *Lumber* are loads of seats and poles. And the *main guy* is not the circus owner, but the guy rope which holds up the center pole in the big top.

Hey, Rube! traditionally is the rallying cry of circus people when a fight breaks out with townies—only circus folk don't have fights, they call them *clems.* And a *clem* usually develops only when the *luck boys* (gamblers) have *kifed* (swindled) too many *suckers* (circusgoers).

The come-on man who entices the suckers into the games of chance is, of course, the *shill.* The *rubber man,* though, isn't part of the side show. He's the fellow who sells balloons—which are always called *bladders,* by the way.

The circus clown is always called *Joey* backstage, in honor of the first great modern clown, Joseph Grimaldi, who flourished about 150 years ago in England. The life of the first *Joey,* appropriately enough, had its years of triumph and ended in bitter tragedy.

Joeys are divided into three main groups. The *Auguste* is the garden variety of a clown, the one with the brightly painted face, any of a wide variety of costumes and a bent for slapstick humor. He's the fellow who gets laughs by pretending to hit other clowns with a baseball bat. Next higher on the scale is the *Grotesque* who wears weirdly padded or inflated costumes, ridiculous hats and often carries an incongruously small parasol. The elite among clowns are the *Characters*—of whom Emmet Kelly is the most famous. These are the sad, Chaplinesque hoboes, perpetually frustrated in their efforts to impress the audience.

Of all the words in the colorful jargon of the circus, one is my own special favorite. Can you guess what circus folk call the fellow who stands at the bottom of the human pyramid—that formation so traditional with generations of acrobats? Well, with perfect logic and wonderful directness, they call him *the understander.*

cisatlantic

Anyone who slaved, as high school students did of yore, through Caesar's *Gallic Wars* would not have to guess at the meaning of this word, for nearly every page of that exhausting epic carried a reference to *cisalpine* Gaul. The prefix *cis,* which we take direct from Latin, means "on this side of." Thus *cisatlantic* merely means on this side of the Atlantic.

Occasionally, though rarely, the prefix is used to express a relationship in time, as well as in space. Thus *cis-Elizabethan times* would be the centuries since the end of the reign of Britain's earlier Elizabeth.

claptrap

Claptrap is literally a device to trap claps—handclaps, that is. It was originally a theatrical term and referred to a showy trick designed solely to secure applause. Because the trickery had nothing to do with the main action of the show, the word *claptrap* came (about 1700) into general language to mean any showy, artificial gesture designed, with an utter lack of sincerity, to gain applause.

claustrophobia

Based on the Latin *claustrum* (enclosed place) and the Greek *phobos* (fear), *claustrophobia* is the abnormal fear of being confined.

cleanliness is next to godliness

This expression is often thought to be a saying created by Benjamin Franklin in his *Poor Richard's Almanac.* But if this adage did appear in *Poor Richard,* it certainly was not original with Franklin. The earliest written record of it in English is in a sermon by John Wesley, the great British clergyman of the eighteenth century who founded Methodism. Significantly, Wesley put quotation marks around the phrase when he used it, indicating that it was already a well-known saying.

There is evidence, indeed, that the idea of cleanliness being next to godliness—although not, of course, phrased in those precise English words —is just about as old as civilization. In any event, we find in the Talmud, the collection of writings that forms the foundation of Jewish civil and religious law, the following: "The doctrines of religion are resolved into carefulness; carefulness into vigorousness; vigorousness into guiltlessness; guiltlessness into abstemiousness; abstemiousness into cleanliness; cleanliness into godliness." Thus, you see that, in this formulation of doctrine, cleanliness is quite literally next to godliness.

clem

When a fight breaks out at a circus because the *luck boys* (gamblers) have *kifed* (swindled) too many *suckers* (circusgoers), it's not a fight, it's a *clem!* See also CIRCUS JARGON.

clew, clue

A word with dual spelling is *clew,* which usually appears in mystery stories as *clue.* This has a fascinating history for originally *clewe* was a Middle English word meaning "ball." In time it came to mean specifically a ball of thread or yarn—and then, even more specifically, the ball of yarn used to guide one's way out of a labyrinth. So we come to today's meaning of *clue*—anything which gives an indication of how to solve a puzzle or mystery.

cliché

Not long ago a book on American usage appeared from the typewriters of a pair of self-styled experts on the subject. On page after page—sometimes five or six times on a single page—they would say, "It is pure *cliché,*" or "Should be avoided as a *cliché.*" In fact, I hadn't read more than five or six pages before it struck me that the author's use of the word *cliché* had become in itself a *cliché.*

Perhaps we should define what we mean by a *cliché* (klee-SHAY). The word is borrowed from the French, where it means a stereotype plate. Thus its basic meaning is the same as that of our word "stereotype" when used to describe an expression everlastingly repeated in the same form.

We have all listened to dull, *cliché*-ridden speeches—bored nearly to tears (there's a *cliché* for you) by the everlasting repetition of trite expressions. So I should be the last to attempt a defense of the *cliché.* But this is worth remembering: most *clichés* became popular over the years because they express a thought aptly and concisely. Often a speaker or writer laboring to avoid a *cliché* winds up using many more words than he needs and, sometimes at least, missing the point of what he wants to say.

The advice from here, then, is to avoid trite and threadbare expressions whenever possible. But if the right word or phrase comes to mind—the expression that says precisely what you want it to say—don't avoid it merely because thousands of others have used it before. Remember what Mark Twain said—and this, too, is near to becoming a *cliché* by now: "The difference between the right word and the almost right word is the difference between lightning and the lightning bug."

clinic

Clinicus, the Latin word from which our *clinic* comes, originally meant a person confined to bed by illness. Then it came to mean a doctor whose practice was largely made up of visiting bedridden patients. In time it acquired the meaning of a technique of teaching medicine by examining and treating patients in the presence of medical students. A further refinement of meaning was the development of *clinics* as places where groups of doctors practiced—either each in his own specialty, as at the *Mayo Clinic,* or a group specializing on a single disease, as a *cancer clinic.*

Thus far all the meanings of *clinic* are rather closely related to the original sense of a bedridden patient. But in the past two or three decades, it has moved into broader areas of popular speech and acquired the meaning of any institution or organization offering treatment or advice —such as a *sales promotion clinic, job-finding clinic* or *domestic relations clinic.* By now this broader application of the word *clinic* has earned the approval of leading language authorities.

clinophobia

If you find yourself still sitting in front of the television set long after everyone else is abed, you may be a victim of horrid fascination or of *clino- phobia,* the fear of going to bed (from the Greek *kline,* meaning bed, and *phobos,* meaning fear).

clowder, kindle and cowardice

Among the more delightful and amusing classifications of words is the category made up of the special names given to groups of birds and animals. Everyone has heard, of course, of a *herd* of cattle and a *flock* of sheep. But did you know that cats, moles, coots and leopards all have special and remarkable group labels?

A herd of lions, for example, is referred to by the cognoscenti as a *pride* of lions. Similarly, hunters speak of a *gaggle* of geese, a *cast* of hawks and a *covey* of partridges or quail.

Nearly every country dweller has had the experience of running from a *swarm* of bees, but only the very widely traveled adventurer has come upon a *skulk* of foxes, a *sloth* of bears and a *troop* of monkeys—to say nothing of a *cete* of badgers, a *down* of hares or a *fall* of woodcocks.

Most of these group labels are, of course, obsolete or used only in regional dialects today. In a day when the object of hunting was food rather than recreation, such distinctions in the labeling of animal groups were carefully observed. Nowadays the collection and preservation of phrases like a *sord* of mallard, a *wisp* of snipe and a *drove* of kine are chiefly the work of connoisseurs of words like Mordaunt Hall, of the Bell Syndicate, from whose collection, indeed, many of these words come.

Elk, for instance—and this refers to the animal, rather than the human variety—travel not in herds but in *gangs.* A bird-watcher should speak of a *nye* of pheasants, a *cast* of hawks and a *watch* of nightingales. Peacocks, appropriately enough, assemble in a *muster,* coots in a *covert* and larks in an *exaltation.*

Back in the animal kingdom, one finds a *shrewdness* of apes, a *labor* of moles, a *clowder* of cats, a *rout* of wolves and a *sounder* of boars.

Kittens, we're told, come in *kindles,* although around our house they arrive in "litters." But when the group label for mongrel dogs is given as a *cowardice of curs,* the time has come when your editor feels improvisation has been substituted for research.

For the true collectors, however, here are three recent and notable additions to this list. When a famous actress left the hospital, one news-paper headlined that she exited with a *crush* of admirers. In her newest novel, B. J. Chute speaks of a woman being followed by a *taggle* of chil-dren. And columnist Charlie Rice recently sent from Paris a postcard showing four nuns deep in contemplation in front of Notre Dame. "I have seen *gaggles* of geese, *bevies* of quail, and *prides* of lions," wrote Rice, "but I never expected to see a *hush* of nuns."

clue. *See* clew.

clutch hitter. *See* baseball jargon.

coaches, railroad and football

There is a connection between an athletic *coach* and a railroad *coach,* but the most remarkable thing of all about this common word is that it came to English from Hungarian. A less likely source would be hard to imagine, but here's how it came about. In the city of Kocs, Hungary, not far from present-day Budapest, the first *coaches*—large carriages for the conveyance of several passengers—were invented. First called *kocsi* or *kotczi,* their name spread throughout Europe and by 1550 had been Anglicized to *coach.*

During the 1840's the nickname *coach* was applied to university tutors in England, perhaps from the idea that with their guidance the students were "carried" along. Then—about 1880—the word came into general use to describe a person who trains athletes. And so your school football *coach,* in one sense at least, is strictly from Hungary!

cobweb

Originally this word was *copweb* from the Anglo-Saxon word *coppe* meaning "spider." The change from *p* to *b* evolved over the centuries, resulting in the form we use now: *cobweb.* Maybe it's some consolation, as you sweep the last of the webs from the rafters, to realize that your problem is at least as old as the earliest record of the English lan-guage!

-cock (suffix)

The *-cock* in such names as *Hancock* and *Adcock* merely means "descendant of." Specifically, *Hancock* means "descendant of little Hane, a pet form of John" and *Adcock* means "a descendant of little Ad," which, in turn, was a pet form of "Adam."

The science of classification and formation of names is called "onomatology." There are many thousands of Americans interested in the study of names—so many, indeed, that a professional society, the American Name Society, was formed some years ago. One of its distinguished members, Elsdon C. Smith has compiled two books *The Story of Our Names* and *Dictionary of American Family Names* and I most warmly recommend them to anyone interested in this fascinating hobby.

cock-and-bull story

The origin of this phrase, meaning a rambling, fanciful tale, probably goes back at least as far as Aesop's fables. From the earliest days of recorded history, man has used talking animals in his fables. The folk literature of all lands is full of stories in which animals walk and talk and act like humans. Indeed, in medieval times throughout Europe these tales were collected into tomes called "bestiaries."

The French have a phrase *coq à l'âne* (cock to donkey) to describe such rambling yarns, and it is likely that the English form was influenced by it, the bull being substituted for the donkey. In any event, the phrase was fixed once and for all in our language by one of the most imaginative and surely the most disconnected novel ever written in English, *Tristram Shandy* by Laurence Sterne, whose last lines read: "What is all this story about? —A cock and bull, said Yorick—and one of the best of its kind I ever heard."

cocker spaniel

The *cock* in *cocker spaniel* comes from "woodcock," a small European game bird related to the snipe. This particular breed of spaniel was widely used for hunting the woodcock because its ability to start and retrieve such small game is almost unparalleled.

Spaniel itself, incidentally, means *Spanish dog*—and not because the breed was first developed in Spain, either. During the Middle Ages Spaniards, justly or unjustly, were widely regarded by their enemies as servile, fawning and "meanly submissive." The long silky, drooping ears of the spaniel and his gentle soulful eyes apparently led to the label *Spanish dog* —though anyone familiar with the breed knows that there's nothing "meanly submissive" about spaniels.

Incidentally, spaniels were popular in England as early as Chaucer's time. In the *Canterbury Tales,* he writes: "For as a spaynel, she wol on hym lepe"—"For like a spaniel she would on him leap."

cockles of the heart

You have often heard the phrase *warm the cockles of one's heart,* but these cockles have nothing to do with the cockles and mussels Sweet Molly Malone used to sell.

The cockles of the old ballad are what the dictionaries call "edible bivalve mollusks"—shellfish, to you and me. In appearance they are not unlike our scallops, having a somewhat heart-shaped, ribbed shell.

The *cockles of your heart,* on the other hand, are its ventricles and thus, by extension, the innermost depths of one's heart or emotions. The word comes from the Latin phrase *cochleae cordis,* meaning "ventricles of the heart," while the shellfish *cockle* comes from the Latin *conchylium,* meaning "conch shell."

cockpit

Originally, this word meant only the pit in which fighting cocks did battle. Then it came to mean any small place where many battles have been waged—as in the old saying, "Belgium is the *cockpit* of Europe." By obvious analogy, World War I aviators began calling the pilot's cramped quarters the plane's *cockpit,* and now it has come to mean any space on plane or boat used by the steersman. See also BATTLE ROYAL.

cocktail

One of the less momentous questions facing the nation is just how it happens that two boroughs of New York City have cocktails named after them and the other three do not. There seem to be almost as many theories about the origin of the word *cocktail* as there are varieties of the drink. Nobody knows for sure where this word came from. Henry L. Mencken, who claimed to have invented eleven cocktails and had nine named after him, reported and analyzed no fewer than eight theories of the word's origin in his book *The American Language.*

The most plausible theory is that the word comes from the French *coquetier*—a double-ended eggcup. Antoine Peychaud, who also invented Peychaud's bitters, is reported to have served short, powerful drinks in eggcups to New Orleans tipplers about 1800. The pronunciation *cocktail* is supposed to have come from non-French-speaking enthusiasts for the drink.

A second theory is that French soldiers stationed here during the

Revolution introduced a mixed drink *coquetel,* long know in the Bordeaux region of France. Still a third theory is that it comes from the English phrase "cock-ale," meaning either a mixture of spirits fed to fighting cocks or a mixture of odds and ends of liquors thrown together in public houses and sold at low prices.

None of these explanations, of course, tells us why both Manhattan and the Bronx have cocktails named after them, while no one ever gave a thought to a Staten Island, Queens or Brooklyn cocktail. That last seems a particularly unlikely oversight, especially in light of the ease with which cocktails can be invented. Again I quote the late, great Henry Mencken: "A friend and I once employed a mathematician to figure out how many cocktails could be fashioned of the *materia bibulica* ordinarily available at a first-class bar. He reported that the number was 17,864,392,788. We tried 273 at random and found them all good, though some, of course, were better than others."

C.O.D.

If you think the meaning of the common abbreviation *C.O.D.* is "Cash On Delivery," take a seat at the back of the class. According to the *American College Dictionary, World Webster Dictionary* and Mencken's *American Language,* "Cash On Delivery" is the British interpretation. In America the initials properly stand for "Collect On Delivery"!

coffin

Coffin, a word which stems from the Greek *kophinus* (basket) and which has long meant a box for burial, has acquired a new meaning among the nation's atomic energy researchers. No less grim than its original meaning, the term is now used to designate the thick-walled lead container in which radioactive materials are transported. See also BEV, EV, MEV AND CUTIE PIE.

coffin varnish

Here is one of the seemingly infinite coinages that are substituted for the word "liquor" in American slang. See also SHEETS IN THE WIND.

cold deck

The expression *cold deck* goes back at least to Gold Rush days. It worked this way. The card game got under way with a standard deck (pack) of cards. This was known, especially after play had run on for a bit, as the *warm deck.* Secreted nearby, though, was a previously "stacked" deck, known as the *cold deck.* On signal, the victim's attention was distracted long enough for the *cold deck* to be substituted—and our pigeon was plucked.

colloquial

All too many people think that a word labeled *colloquial* by the dictionary is somehow substandard, common, even vulgar. This is not true. *Colloquial* means simply "conversational." Quite literally, *colloquial* comes from the Latin words *con* and *loquor,* meaning "talk together."

All of us use in conversation a somewhat more casual, easygoing language than we do in formal writing, but the unpretentiousness of ordinary speech does not make it any less "correct" than the carefully formal language we would use, say, in a course report or a sermon.

colonel

The explanation of how *colonel* came to be pronounced KER-nel is a complicated one and involves at least four centuries of British military history. Back in the sixteenth century the word was spelled *coronel* and pronounced with three syllables, pretty much as spelled. Gradually, thanks to the British talent for streamlining pronunciations (with them *Cholmondoley* is pronounced Chumly) the word *coronel* acquired a two-syllable pronunciation: KOR-nel and eventually KER-nel. The spelling was later altered to what we know today, but the pronunciation has remained the same.

Colonel Bogey and his march

During the First World War, according to one British authority, "Troops on the march were forbidden to sing a catchy song called 'Colonel Bogey' as the words they substituted for the real ones were not considered edifying." The same spirited march served as the theme music of the film *Bridge on the River Kwai.*

Who is the Colonel Bogey immortalized in this tune? Well, he's a wholly mythical character from the world of sports. He's the average game player —originally in golf—who never quite makes par but whose score is a fair gauge of the ordinary player's ability. A committee sets for each hole the score that is the lowest a good average player can make it in, usually one above par. Thereafter to *beat Bogey* or *beat the colonel* you must play it in a fewer number of strokes.

combo

Combo is a shortened form of "combination" and means a musical unit of not more than six players. Often a *combo* consists of three instrumentalists who by "doubling" (playing more than one instrument apiece) manage the variety of tone colors of a larger dance band.

come a cropper

Come a cropper is a term from the jargon of horse racing and polo playing and means a head-over-heels tumble from a horse. The phrase *neck and crop,* meaning "completely" or "entirely," has long been a common term in British slang and it is thought that *come a cropper* is probably a variation on that phrase.

comeuppance

This is in fairly general colloquial use, though its first recorded appearance—according to the *Dictionary of American English*—was in 1859. It generally means "merited punishment" or "just desserts." One authority reports that it is occasionally used to mean "due reward" but I have never encountered it except in the sense of deserved punishment or retribution. It sometimes appears in such dialect versions as *comings* and *come-uppings* in different parts of the country.

commencement. *See* graduation and commencement.

commensurate

Commensurate (pronounced kuh-MEN-shoor-it) is an adjective derived from the Latin *com-* (with) and *mensurare* (to measure). It has two distinct but related meanings. The original meaning, and one which is still used in the sciences, was to describe two or more items which could be measured by the same standard or in common units. A more popular current meaning is that of being equal or at least proportionate in extent or value. "The salary offered was not *commensurate* to the work involved."

commentary

Originally *commentary,* from the Latin *commentum* (a commentary), meant a written memoir or record of events—especially one hastily written as a sort of memorandum for future reference. Recently, of course, it has come into wide use as the term for the spoken narration that accompanies films, television shows and so on. In this sense it has even spawned a new verb, *to commentate* and one of our major newspapers recently shocked the purists among its readers by noting that a famed fashion stylist was going to *commentate* his new models at a fashion show.

That particular use of the word is still regarded as a barbarism, but the use of *commentary* as roughly synonymous with "example" is quite acceptable. It could be said, for instance, that the failure of our first attempt to launch a satellite into space "was a sad *commentary* on the state of our missile program."

Webster includes among its definitions of *commentary:* "a thing serving for illustration," and Funk & Wagnalls says: "Anything explanatory or illustrative."

commons, cafeteria

The name *commons* is appropriate for the traditional college or university dining hall, where students sit together at identical tables and are served the same—"common"—meal. However, the label sounds incongruous when applied to the self-service eating places found in many American colleges.

Admittedly the word *cafeteria* lacks the quiet elegance of *the commons,* but it seems much more appropriate for college restaurants which do not serve the same food to all, nor charge all at the same price.

Cafeteria has its origin in the American Spanish spoken in early California. The first *cafeterias* were retail coffee stores, from which evolved the uniquely American self-service restaurants we know today.

complected

Complected in such phrases as "dark-*complected*" is simply illiterate. The correct phrase, of course, is "dark-*complexioned.*" However, *complected* is a perfectly good word in its formal meaning of "woven together." It is quite correct to speak of a "tightly *complected* rug," for instance.

compunction

Compunction (pronounced k'm-PUNK-sh'n) is a noun from the Latin, its origin being *compunctus,* past participle of *compungere,* the intensified form of the verb for "to prick or sting." Used only to apply to the conscience, it has the meaning of uneasiness of conscience and, thus, scruple or remorse. Hence, if you have *compunctions* about certain deeds, these *compunctions* may prevent you from committing the deed or may only bother you after it is done.

con

MAYOR WAGNER SAYS CITY WAS CONNED ON MANHATTANTOWN DEAL, ran the headline on a newspaper clipping sent in by a New York City reader. The story dealt with an elaborate slum-clearance project in New York City which, when completed, was to result in a development roughly comparable to a residential version of Radio City. It all sounded fine on paper—and on paper is just where it remained for more than five years.

At long last, the city canceled its agreement with the dilatory developers and decided to turn the project over to others who would move it along at something faster than a snail's pace. But that's not what interested my correspondent. "What," she asks, "is the meaning of this word *conned* in the headline? My dictionary says that the verb *to con* means to study or commit to memory. If this is true, the headline doesn't seem to make sense. Will you straighten this out for me?"

The answer is that there are two verbs *to con*—identical in spelling and conjugation, but completely different in meaning. The one to which my correspondent referred is the older of the two, being derived from the Middle English word *cunnen* meaning "to try." This is also the root, by the way, of the common word "can."

The second *con* is a slang term derived from the phrase "confidence man"—a swindler who preys upon people whose confidence he has first gained. Thus *to con* a person is to swindle him after first gaining his confidence. What the New York Mayor meant was that he and his associates were taken in by the lavish promises of a group of blue-sky operators and had only just realized that they were the victims of a swindle.

This adds up to a remarkably candid admission on the part of Mr. Wagner and perhaps deserves to rank alongside the all-time high in candid utterances by a politician—the rueful remark of another New York Mayor, Fiorello H. LaGuardia: "I don't often make a mistake—but when I do, it's a beaut!"

conch. *See* conk.

condign punishment

Condign punishment is a penalty suitable to the crime committed, the sort of treatment Gilbert and Sullivan had in mind when their Mikado announced: "My object all sublime, I shall achieve in time—to let the punishment fit the crime."

Condign (pronounced kun-DINE) comes from the Latin *condignus,* meaning "worthy or well deserved."

condone

Condone (pronounced kun-DOHN) is a verb meaning "to pardon" or "to forgive." It can also mean "to overlook" and by so doing to act as though no offense had been committed. It is derived from the Latin *con donare,* whose root word *donare* (to give) has been combined with the intensifier *con-*.

Generally used in such statements as "We cannot *condone* such actions on his part," the word is used most often in the sense of "overlooking" except in legal usage, where it seems to keep its meaning of forgiveness.

Coney Island

Throughout the Midwest you will see signs advertising *Coney Islands*. These, for the benefit of the uninitiated, are frankfurters in rolls on which are heaped successively mustard, relish, raw onions and catsup—a rare feat of culinary ingenuity and very possibly one reason why the American ulcer rate per capita is the world's highest. Don't ever try to buy a *Coney Island* at Coney Island, New York, though! They never heard of such a mixture. The thought of catsup on a hot dog would make a Brooklyn native blanch with horror—mustard or, at most, mustard and relish will serve him nicely, thanks.

confidence

Made up from two Latin words, *con-* (with) and *fidere* (faith), *confidence* means literally "faith in oneself."

confused beetles

Did you know that beetles may be—in fact, are—officially labeled *confused* and *depressed?* I didn't either until one fine day when Elmer Roessner, my editor, sent me a note about the matter. "Last January," he wrote, "the U.S. Department of Agriculture sent out a release mentioning the *confused flour beetle*. As a confused editor, I sought the name in dictionaries and, while I found the *depressed flour beetle,* I could not find the confused beetle, even though I thought confusing was depressing. I wrote the USDA for an explanation—and now I have the answer and the interesting derivation of the names of the two beetles."

Mr. Roessner enclosed a letter from James Reynolds, information specialist for the USDA, shedding light on this confusing topic: "The red flour beetle (*Tribolium castaneum*) and the confused flour beetle (*Tribolium confusum*) look very nearly alike. The only visible difference is in the shape of the area around the eye. Back in the nineteenth century when the red flour beetle was first described, the description was a mixture of the two beetles. When it was discovered that they were two distinct species, someone began calling one species the *confused flour beetle* because of the earlier confusion in identifying it. The *depressed flour beetle* gets it name from its appearance; to a layman certain areas appear to be flattened or depressed."

Is all confusion now clarified and all depression relieved?

congress. *See* **candidate.**

conk, conch

An intriguing example of how words change meaning as they move from British to American English is found when we look into the various meanings of the slang word *conk*. To most Americans *conk* is most familiar as a verb in one of two senses. If you *conk* a person, you hit him on the head. If you *conk out,* you fall asleep or unconscious. Similarly, if an airplane's motor *conks out,* it suddenly fails to operate.

But this is only part of a change in word meanings which led to the creation of an amusing but not quite accurate account of how *conk* got one of its present American meanings. This theory—that Florida Indians used to put conch shells on their hands before engaging in fisticuffs (sort of super brass knuckles) is very interesting, and I surely wouldn't want to be *conked* by an Indian or anyone else using conch shells as brass knuckles. The only trouble with the theory is that *conk*—originally as a slang term for nose and later for the whole head—has been common in England since about 1800. The word's use as a verb, meaning to hit a person on the head, dates back almost as long, certainly long before the Everglades Indians had any need to *conk* invading white men with conch shells. So, though most authorities agree that *conk* in the sense of head or nose originally was a variant spelling of "conch," the direct connection to Florida Indians is fanciful but inaccurate.

The other sense of the word—as when a motor *conks out*—is entirely unrelated to "conch." It was coined in World War I by military aviators in imitation of the coughing noise their engines made just before stopping completely.

connoisseur

Connoisseur comes direct from French and indirectly from the Latin *cognoscere* (to know). A *connoisseur* (and that's a word that belongs in every spelling bee) is a knowledgeable chap, a good judge of quality, especially in the arts.

consommé. *See* **bouillon, consommé.**

contrail

Here's a word that hasn't yet been listed in most general-use dictionaries, since the phenomenon it describes is as recent as jet flights into the stratosphere. *Contrail* is a contraction of "condensation trail" and describes the vapor trail left in the sky by certain airplanes, notably jets. In the words of the *U.S. Air Force Dictionary,* a "contrail" is "vapor formed in supercooled air when disturbed by the passing of an airplane. It also forms from the water content of the exhaust in cold air."

contrite

Contrite (pronounced kun-TRITE) is an adjective made up from the Latin *com-* (together) and *terere* (to rub), and has the meaning of being remorseful. The conscience is "rubbed" by a sense of guilt and remorse sets in.

cook their goose

There is a legend that the burghers of a besieged town in the Middle Ages decided to show their contempt for the attackers by hanging a goose from a tower—the goose having long been a symbol of stupidity and futility. This time, however, the taunt backfired. The attacking force was so enraged at the insult that they burnt the whole town—cooking the goose in the process, of course.

That's an interesting story—but, alas, no more than that. In truth the expression seems not to have appeared in English until 1851 when in a London street ballad referring to charges of "Papal Aggression" appeared these lines:

> If they come here we'll cook their goose,
> The Pope and Cardinal Wiseman.

coony, to play it

Coony is a dialect term meaning "sly or cunning, like a coon." In colloquial speech *to play it coony* is roughly synonymous with "to play it cozy or clever or crafty."

cop

The word *cop* long was a source of irritation to J. Edgar Hoover, and the nickname *nation's top cop* must have proved especially galling because of the frequency with which it turned up in newspaper and magazine articles. All of us know, of course, that any policeman responds more agreeably to the title "officer" than to *cop,* but some people ask whether this attitude on the lawmen's part is justified. Is it the result of inherited prejudice or is there good reason for disliking the nickname *cop?*

Well, good reason there is—in abundance. Though many people think that *cop* is merely a shortened form of "copper" from the buttons once worn by British bobbies, this is untrue. In the first place, "bobbies" did not exist until Sir Robert Peel secured the passage of Britain's first modern Police Act in 1828. But the word *cop* in the sense of "one who captures or snatches" is recorded as early as 1704. Indeed, an ancestor word *cap,* with the same meaning, came into English from French at the time of the Norman Conquest and can be traced all the way back to ancient Rome's *capere* (to capture).

But there seems nothing derogatory about this meaning of *cop*—one who seizes or captures. However, over the centuries, the word *cop* has been used by unsavory underworld characters in many different meanings. To steal, for instance: an auto thief *cops a heap.* To assault from the rear by stealth: a crook *cops a sneak.* And, of course, there's the well-known *cop a plea*—to plead guilty to a lesser crime in order to get a lesser penalty.

In these and many more ways the word *cop* has acquired distasteful connotations for anyone concerned with law enforcement. A policeman's life, noted W. S. Gilbert, is not a happy one—but how much pleasanter life would be for our lawmen if only we, like the French, called policemen *gendarmes.* A *gendarme,* you see, was originally *gens d'arme* and, in medieval French armies, ranked just below a knight in the line of chivalric honor.

copasetic

Copasetic—also spelled *copacetic* or *copesettic*—means "excellent, top-notch." It is a slang word, chiefly heard in Negro dialect until recently. Merriam-Webster recorded it in their unabridged dictionary in 1934, but it is not to be found in most of the general-purpose dictionaries.

This is rather surprising, since it was long the favorite word of perhaps the greatest Negro entertainer of our time, Bojangles Bill Robinson, the tap dancer, who may, indeed, have coined it. Bill used the word in virtually every routine he did during his later years and certainly deserves whatever credit may be due for making it a part of the general language. It's still slang, though, and should be avoided in all save the most informal talk and writing.

corduroy

Of all fabrics used for youngsters' clothing none—save, perhaps, denim —is so sturdy, so well able to withstand the abusive rough-and-tumble wear that young boys give it, as *corduroy.* It is truly the plebeian workhorse of today's fabrics—and yet its name means "cord fit for the king"! Originally *corduroy* (from the French *corde du roi*) was woven from silk and was used exclusively by the Kings of France as part of their hunting costumes.

corned beef

The *corn* in *corned beef* goes back to a time when the vegetable we know as *corn* was called "maize"—as it still is in England today. Originally a *corn* was any small substance or particle—especially a seed or kernel. When beef was laid down in a brine to cure, it was sprinkled with *corns* of coarse salt. So the process came to be known as *corning* the beef and the end product was *corned beef*.

The same use of *corn* to mean a grain or particle remains in words like *peppercorn*—whole black peppers—and *barleycorn*.

corny

Corny—originally a contraction of "corn-fed"—was first used by actors and vaudevillians to describe audiences in "the sticks." To a show business professional of the early days of this century "every town outside New York was Bridgeport"—by which he simply meant that away from the main stem, audience reactions were unsophisticated, in a word *corn-fed*. So that great entertainer George M. Cohan once pointed out in a well-remembered song, "only forty-five minutes from Broadway" you would find "hicks" and "jays" galore.

Since these *corn-fed* audiences relished a broad and unsubtle brand of humor, it became known as "*corn-fed* humor"—a phrase which now is simply "*corny* joke."

It's interesting to note that no one in the theater today would draw the distinctions that were commonplace a generation ago. Television and the motion pictures have brought polished, sophisticated entertainment to every part of the country. You would be hard pressed today to find an audience that would merit the contemptuous *corn-fed* label that a vaudevillian of the 1920's might have used.

cosmonaut. *See* astronaut.

cotton to

When we say we *cotton to* a person or idea, meaning that we have taken a fancy to it, we are referring directly to the way cotton can cling to our clothing. If you have ever tried picking cotton lint from a man's suit, you'll understand the origin of the phrase.

countdown

Intriguingly enough, the creator of the *countdown* technique is motion-picture director Fritz Lang, whose chief claim hitherto to fame was his direction of the silent-film classic, *M*. In the late 1920's Lang directed one of the very earliest science-fiction films, *The Lady in the Moon*. A highlight was the launching of a mammoth rocket which looked uncannily like the ones we launch from Cape Canaveral. It occurred to Lang that greater suspense could be obtained by switching from the conventional "one-two-three" to exactly the reverse. Thus the first *countdown* occurred in a science-fiction film of more than thirty-five years ago.

Science imitated art not only by taking over the *countdown* technique but actually by using some of Lang's other props in early rocket experiments in Hitler's Germany—after Lang himself had been forced to flee.

counter jumper

To a lumberman, a clerk is not a clerk. He is a *counter jumper*. See also LUMBERMEN'S JARGON.

counterwords

"Isn't he *darling?*" "Isn't that puppy too *cute* for words!" "I just think that's the most *precious* purse I've ever seen!"

Remarks such as these look silly in print, don't they? Yet each of us hears such statements many times a day and, though men would surely claim that women are the worst offenders, the fact is that men all too often repeat such outworn and inaccurately used adjectives. We all know, for instance, men to whom everything is either *grand* or *lousy*.

The explanation for the use of such expressions is simple, and the matter of whether they are applied to animate or inanimate objects is irrelevant. Such adjectives are used, you see, with no special regard to their true meanings or application. They are the cheapest currency of contemporary slang and signify nothing more than broad approval or disapproval.

No woman using the word *cute* when describing a hat or purse realizes that the real meaning of *cute* is "sharp, clever or shrewd." Nor does a man who says that he had a *lousy* day at the office mean that his day was infested with lice.

Both are using these words merely as generalized expressions of approval or disapproval. By falling into the habit of using what grammarians call "counterwords"—such as *nice, terrible, grand* and *awful*—they weaken their speech in two ways. They have used adjectives which have no real impact on the hearer, since the very commonness of their use has eliminated all element of surprise or shock from the words. And they have helped further to debase the original meaning of each of the words.

Such "counterwords" cannot be entirely avoided in ordinary conversation but they should be rigorously eliminated from all forms of writing and formal speaking.

course of sprouts

This expression has been traced by the *Dictionary of American English* to 1851 and means, of course, stern discipline or training.

It probably was originally a *course for sprouts*—*sprouts* being any offshoot, including offspring of a family. The transition from *for* to *of* in such a phrase is commonplace enough and the meaning of a disciplinary course for youngsters is obvious.

court shoes

It is not difficult to imagine why the term *court shoes* means to the British what "dress shoes" means to Americans. See also ENGLISH ENGLISH.

cousin. *See* baseball jargon.

Cousin Jack

Cousin Jack comes from the slang of British coal miners. It means a Cornish mine worker or, by extension, any native of Cornwall. *Cousin,* in this phrase, is probably a corruption of "Cornish."

covert of coots. *See* clowder, kindle and cowardice.

covey of quail. *See* clowder, kindle and cowardice.

cowardice of curs. *See* clowder, kindle and cowardice.

cowboy

Cowboy is an American term, which, incredibly enough, was being used during Revolutionary times. The cowboys of those years, however, were a very different lot—guerrilla bands of Tories operating in what is now Westchester County, New York. According to one authority: "The *cowboys* were the worst kind of Tories; they went around in the bushes armed with guns and tinkling a cow-bell so as to beguile the patriots into the brush hunting for cows."

cowboy jargon

One of the most colorful jargons is that of the American cowboy. In the early days of the opening of the West, the trail rider had to be a pretty tough customer and most of them simply didn't have much time for "book learning."

As a result, they talked a salty and colorful lingo—a language all its own. Over the years it has contributed *hoosegow, maverick, hoodlum* and many other fresh and lively words to the working vocabulary of all Americans. But there's a lot more to cowboy jargon than this. For example, do you know what a cowboy means when he says he's *on the prod?* If you don't, partner, watch out because it means he's fighting mad and it's just not healthy to stay in the vicinity. If he says he's *on the peck* he means the same thing. But if he tells you he's *on the drift,* there's nothing to worry about because he just means he's out of work and riding the grub line (i.e., picking up free meals at ranch after ranch) until he can find another job.

Incidentally, that phrase *on the prod* probably came from the *prod pole,* a metal-tipped pole which cowboys used to goad cattle into stock cars. In the old days, cowhands used to ride cattle trains, and every time the train stopped they would poke the prod through the slats on the open cars and make sure all cattle were erect and alive. From this practice came the terms *cowpuncher* and *cowpoke.*

A *cow waddy* nowadays means nothing more than a cowboy, although the term originally was used chiefly for rustlers and for third-rate cowhands who could get jobs only when ranches were shorthanded, usually at the time of spring and fall roundups. *Rustlers,* of course, are cattle thieves—the villains in countless thousands of Western movies. Curiously enough, though the term *waddy* was originally applied to thieves and has come to mean an honest cowhand, *rustler* originally meant only a very hard-working *hustling* cowhand. When he began *hustling* (or *rustling*) mavericks and cattle that didn't belong to him his name fell into disrepute.

A *lariat* (from Spanish *la reata*) is not quite the same as a *lasso.* Originally, at least, the *lariat* was a rope used for hobbling and tethering cattle. The *lasso* (correctly pronounced LASS-oh, not lass-OH), of course, has a running noose on one end and is used for roping cattle and horses.

Nowadays the closest contact most of us have with cowboys reared and accoutered in the great tradition of the early West is when we go to see the rodeo. Here, too, the working cowpoke has developed a special lingo for the rodeo, which, like every other sport, has a language all its own and its technical terms may well prove puzzling to the "dudes" among us. So here are a few of the more common items in the jargon of the rodeo contestant:

Association saddle—Saddle adopted by the rodeo association and required in all official contests. It is designed so that, as the riders say, "it gives the horse all the best of it."

Blow a stirrup—To let the foot come out of the stirrup. In rodeo contests this disqualifies the rider.

Dally—In roping, to take a half-hitch around the saddle horn, using the leverage thus obtained to loosen or take up on the rope as the situation demands.

Git-up end—A horse's hind end.

Notch in his tail—Used of a man-killing bronc who has, like gun fighters notching the handles of their six-shooters, put a *notch in his tail* for each man he has killed.

Op'ry house—The top rail of the breaking corral where ranch hands sit and watch the *buster* at work.

Pile driver—A horse which, in bucking, comes down with all four legs stiff.

Scratching—With boots and spurs raking the forequarters of the horse. In bronc-riding contests, under rodeo rules, each entrant must *come out scratching*.

And when a cowboy talks about his *John B.* and *hair pants* he means his sombrero and chaps. When you stop to think about it, *hair pants* is a perfectly simple and straightforward description of the ornamental angora-hide chaps worn by cowboys as sort of dress uniform. The *John B.* comes from the first part of the name of the John B. Stetson Company of Philadelphia, who made the best broad-brimmed hats known in the early West. Even to this day, this hat is the acknowledged preference of most working cowboys.

cracked up

A well-established colloquial usage is *crack up,* meaning to extoll or praise highly. Also we often use the adjective *crack*—as in *crack shot*—to mean some person or thing that is absolutely at the top of its class. So when you say that something isn't what it is *cracked up* to be, you merely mean that it doesn't merit the high reputation it has obtained.

The first recorded use of the phrase in this country appears in Davy Crockett's direct and candid comment on a fellow politician who at the time was far better known than Crockett but who has since become one of the forgotten men of American politics. "Martin Van Buren," wrote Davy in 1835, "is not the man he's *cracked up* to be." History has certainly supported his verdict.

cracklin'

For all his occasional boastfulness, Davy Crockett had moments of earnest and becoming modesty. Once, drawing on the vocabulary of his native Tennessee, he remarked, "I looked like a pretty *cracklin'* ever to get to Congress!"

Cracklin' in this sense has nothing to do with the *crack up* discussed above. *Cracklings* are the bits of crisp rind left after lard has been rendered, usually by frying. Esteemed by Southern epicures—especially when used in *cracklin' bread*—they remain a relatively unimportant by-product and Davy's estimate of himself as a pretty *cracklin'* is one that few American youngsters would accept.

crambo

Crambo, a word familiar to few others than Scrabble players, is the name of a word-rhyming game. Its origin is found in the Latin word *crambe* (cabbage) and more particularly in the Latin phrase *crambe repetita* (cabbage served repeatedly).

cranberry sauce. *See* turkey talk.

crawfish. *See* political language.

credence

Credence (pronounced KREE-d'ns) from the Latin *credere* (to trust or believe) is applied usually to the claims or statements of another person. You can *give credence to* or *have credence in* or *place credence in* his statements. Any such expression shows that you believe him. At the same time, it is possible for circumstances or proven facts to *lend credence to* what he says.

creek, up the

This and its fuller form *up the creek without a paddle* are somewhat laundered versions of a very commonly heard expression. The meaning— to become trapped in an awkward or embarrassing situation—is obvious. Just who was the first person trapped *up the creek* is not a matter of record.

creepie-peepie

The *creepie-peepie* is a portable TV camera, used to get informal close-ups, often of moving subjects. Its name comes from an analogy to the wartime *walkie-talkie,* a combination radio receiver and transmitter that could, like the *creepie-peepie,* be carried by a single person.

Crichton. *See* Admirable Crichton, The.

cricket

At a meeting of a celebrated New York club, the Right Honorable Lord Bancroft, a member of the British Cabinet, demonstrated that, though the British may have lost their empire, they still retain their wit. *"Cricket,"* according to Lord Bancroft's definition, "is a game which the British—not being a spiritual people—had to invent in order to have some conception of eternity." Later, referring to some of his own experiences in international diplomacy, Lord Bancroft described himself as an expert in "dentopedology—the art of opening your mouth and putting your foot in it."

cripple. *See* baseball jargon.

crocodile tears

The *crocodile* was a favorite figure in ancient Greek and Egyptian folklore. Indeed its name comes directly from the Greek *krokodeilos*. The legend was that this giant lizard attracted its victims by loud moaning and then shed tears while it devoured them.

In America the *crocodile* is more commonly called *alligator*—a word that also has an interesting history. Early Spanish settlers called it *el legarto* (the lizard). Later this was corrupted to *alligarta* and finally to the word as we spell it today, *alligator*.

cropper, come a. *See* come a cropper.

crummie

To the lumberman, the chap who manages the bunkhouse is a *crummie* and the bunkhouse itself is a *bullpen*. See also LUMBERMEN'S JARGON.

cubbyhole, cuddy

A small closet beneath the stairs—too small for a grown person to stand in—is called a *cubbyhole*. A sloop's small cabin—not high enough to stand in—is called a *cuddy*.

There is a close relationship between *cuddy* and *cubby*, both of which come from the same Anglo-Saxon word *cofa*, meaning "cave" or "cell." As a matter of fact, the word *cuddy* in British dialect means not only a small cabin aboard ship but any kind of small closet. In other words, *cuddy* and *cubbyhole* not only have the same root but are virtually synonymous. Since *cubbyhole* was originally a word used by British children, it's possible that the two were originally the same and the variant developed, as so often happens, from a child's mispronunciation.

cubby locker. *See* automobile slang, British.

cuddy. *See* cubbyhole.

cue in, clue in

I have heard the expression *Cue me in* for many years and suspect that it probably originated in theatrical jargon. In my time in the theater, actors in rehearsal were forever looking for an unoccupied prop man or fellow actor to *cue* them in their lines.

The expression *Clue me in,* however, first came to my attention in the early 1950's. It probably started as a variant form of *Cue me in,* with the *clue* gaining quick currency with teen-agers because of the popularity of crime and detection shows like *Dragnet.*

Perhaps the simplest explanation of the difference between the two phrases today may be given in the slang of teensters themselves. Most of them would regard *clue you in* as *hip,* while *cue you in* is *square,* the kind of talk used by *prehistorics* (anyone over twenty).

culpable

From the Latin root *culpa* (blame), *culpable* gets its meaning of deserving of censure, blameworthy.

cummerbund

Cummerbunds were first adapted by British colonial officials from an item of native Indian dress. Originally the Hindustani word for loincloth was *kamarband.* Later the word was applied to a sash worn around the waist and eventually it came to mean the sort of demiwaistcoat worn as a part of formal dress today.

cupboard love

Cupboard love is love that has more than a bit of self-interest involved. It can best be described as the love of a child for an older person who may be in a position to gratify its whims with presents of delicacies from her cupboard.

Cupid. *See* Dan Cupid.

curfew

No one knows when the first *curfew* took place, for the custom was common throughout Europe during the Middle Ages. At that time the danger of fire spreading through a village or town was obviously very great, so at a given hour of night a signal—usually a loud bell—was sounded, warning all citizens to put out their fires. The word *curfew* comes direct from the French *couvre feu* (cover the fire).

Legend has it that the practice was introduced into England by William the Conqueror, as a method of political repression, but there seems little evidence to support this theory.

curry favor

The phrase *curry favor* is a variation (or "corruption," to use the technical term) of the Middle English expression *to curry Favel*. Favel was a chestnut horse in a medieval satire called *Roman de Favel,* which was a sort of parallel of the better-known fable of "Reynard the Fox." Favel, sometimes spelled Fauvel, was a symbol of cunning duplicity. Therefore, anyone *currying Favel* would be trying to gain favor by resorting to duplicity, especially insincere flattery.

curvaceous

Curvaceous is a fairly recent coinage, a blend of "curve" and "aceous," and means "characterized by curves." It is entered in all save the most conservative dictionaries, though labeled "colloquial"—by which the dictionary editors mean that *curvaceous* is perfectly acceptable in conversation or in such informal writing as newspaper and advertising copy. It should, however, be avoided in reports, speeches and the like.

cut a dido

No one knows for sure where the expression *cut a dido* originated. The first recorded appearance of this phrase was in the early nineteenth century and it may well be the forerunner of such common phrases as today's *cutting up* or *He's a great cut-up*. All these expressions, of course, have to do with pranks and pranksters.

One theory—and it's as good as any—is that the *dido* of this phrase was the legendary queen of Carthage, the same who committed suicide when Aeneas broke off their love affair and sailed for home in one of the more touching episodes of Vergil's *Aeneid*.

When Dido was a young princess, newly come to Africa, she made a deal with the natives whereby she bought a piece of land that could be enclosed by a bull's hide. After the deal had been agreed on, she cut the hide into one continuous hair-thin thread—long enough to encompass a huge tract of land. According to legend, this land later became the walled city of Carthage. So Dido was the first—but assuredly not the last—real estate operator to *cut a dido* on some unwary landowners.

cutlass

Cutlass came into English from the French *coutelas* which in turn came from the Latin *cultellus,* meaning "knife." This source also gave us the common word *cutlery* and the currently less common *cutler,* which survives today chiefly as a proper name but once was widely used to designate a person who made or sharpened knives and scissors for a living.

cutie pie. *See* bev, ev, mev and cutie pie.

cut to the quick. *See* quick, cut to the.

cutty, cutty sark, cutty stool

This is simply a Scottish dialect version of *cut* and means short or abbreviated. The Scots call their short shirts *cutty sarks.* Another common use of the word is in the phrase *cutty stool,* which was a short-legged bench in Scottish churches where sinners were required to sit while being publicly rebuked by the minister.

cynosure

Cynosure (pronounced sy-nuh-shoor) is a remarkable word. Literally it means "a dog's tail"—hardly an object that a beautiful woman would like to be likened to. Here's how it comes about. The Greek word *kynosoura* (dog's tail) was used for the constellation of Ursa Minor, which includes the North Star. Navigators since the dawn of recorded history—and probably beyond—have used the North Star in plotting their courses. So *cynosure* became the point toward which all eyes are inevitably drawn and that, by extension, is why any person or thing that attracts widespread interest is called the "*cynosure* of all eyes."

czar, kaiser

Julius Caesar is responsible for several words in our language. Both *czar* and *kaiser* were derived from his name and the surgical operation known as the *Caesarian section* was named after him because, according to popular belief, he was brought into the world through such an operation.

D

Dad

Dad is now used in teen talk to mean any member of the male sex whom you're addressing directly. Family relationship has nothing whatever to do with this use of *Dad*. Indeed, a teen-ager's father would almost invariably be referred to as "Pop," not "Dad."

dahlia. *See* flower names.

damn, not worth a

Not worth a damn originally came from the common phrase "not worth a tinker's dam," this *dam* being a pellet of bread used by old-time tinkers to block small holes in pots and pans while they poured in solder to fix the leak. When the patch was secure, the *dam* was discarded. So anything "not worth a tinker's dam" was something utterly worthless.

The popularity of this phrase and others derived from it is, of course, based on the fact that they are euphemisms for the profane expressions they duplicate in sound if not in spelling. See also *Tinker's dam*.

dampers. *See* automobile slang, British.

Dan Cupid

The *Dan* in *Dan Cupid* is not so much a name as a title. Comparable to the Spanish *Don*, it was used as an honorific in the early days of English writing and meant "Sir" or "Master." Among the memorable lines of our early literature are these of Spenser saluting his most eminent predecessor:

> Dan Chaucer, well of English undefiled,
> On Fame's eternal beadroll worthy to be filed.

Cupid, of course, was the Roman god of love.

dark-complected. *See* complected.

datum, data

"In an issue of *Fortune*," wrote a Washington correspondent, "I came on the following sentence: 'I have been developing facts and figures about that very subject for a study I am doing. . . . On the whole my data confirm the picture Burck has drawn.'

"Now this sentence brought me up sharp," continued my reader. "It so happens that I work with statistical data much of the time but my associates and I always use data as a singular word. Have we been wrong all this time? If so, there ought to be a lot of red faces among the Harvard Business School faculty because that's where several of us studied, and we all recollect our instructors using *data* with singular verbs, as 'The *data* is correct.' What do you say?"

First, may I observe that crimson is the color for Harvard, not red. Second, there's no need for embarrassment on anyone's part, although it's true that *data* is technically a plural form of the little used noun *datum*. This has been the fact for more than two thousand years, for these words are directly inherited from Latin, where *datum* was the gerund form of *dare* (to give) and meant literally "that which is given." Over the centuries it came to mean "things known or assumed to be true"—hence, facts from which conclusions can be drawn, the meaning common today.

Data, nowadays, is considered a "collective" noun. When its user refers to a group of facts as a single unit, it should be followed by a singular verb. When you mean the individual facts that make up the total data, the plural form is preferred. In the instance cited by my reader, it seems clear that the writer is thinking of the individual "facts and theories" he has been developing, and thus the plural form is correct. However, most authorities agree that—except in very formal writing—this fine distinction can be ignored.

Davy Jones's locker

Though there have been many wild and wondrous theories of the origin of this phrase, nobody knows for sure where it came from. Perhaps the most common idea is that *Jones* is a corruption of "Jonah," the name of the Biblical character who spent so much time underseas inside the whale. The trouble with this theory is that the common meaning of "He's gone to *Davy Jones's locker*" is "He's dead—drowned." But the Jonah of the Old Testament story did not drown. He was restored to dry land, unharmed, three days after his watery adventure began.

Another theory is that Davy Jones was the owner of a dockside public house—or barroom—in England. He was supposed to have stored the ale he sold in a locker and somehow this locker was supposed to be greatly feared by seamen. But this also sounds pretty farfetched, for, if you remember the swashbuckling seamen of *Treasure Island,* I think you'll agree they wouldn't be much in awe of a locker full of ale.

But one thing we can report on with accuracy is that the phrase *Davy Jones's locker* has been part of the popular slang of sailors for more than two centuries. In 1751, in a book called *The Adventures of Peregrine Pickle,* Tobias Smollett wrote: "Davy Jones is the fiend that presides over all the evil spirits of the deep, and is often seen in various shapes, perching among the rigging on the eve of hurricanes, shipwrecks, and other disasters to which seafaring life is exposed."

D-day

The *D* in *D-day* has so simple an explanation that it's perhaps not surprising that so few people know it. It simply stands for "day," so *D-Day* literally means "Day-day."

The term was first used in World War I, as the code designation for the Allied offensive at Saint-Mihiel. The most important D-day was, of course, June 6, 1944, the day Allied forces began their invasion of Western Europe.

dead as a doornail

The *doornail* in ancient times was the heavy knob against which a heavy metal knocker struck. Since the doornail was regularly and sharply rapped, it could be assumed that there was no life in it.

The expression was often used by Dickens. In *A Christmas Carol* Old Marley "was as dead as a *doornail.*" Shakespeare used it more than once. Falstaff in *Henry IV, Part II* asks: "What! is the old king dead?" and Pistol replies: "As nail in door." In fact, the expression goes back to the earliest beginnings of English literature, Langland's *Vision of Piers the Plowman* (fourteenth century), in which the expression was used just as we use it today.

debacle

The word *debacle* came to us direct from the French. Originally it was a geologist's term meaning the sudden breaking up of ice in a river. At the time of an early spring thaw, a sudden breaking of the ice may cause a violent rush of water, bearing with it stones and other debris, making a *debacle.* This technical term was later applied, about 1850, in a figurative sense to any catastrophic rout or stampede. Recently its meaning has been extended still further to cover any great catastrophe.

Because the word has figured in our language for only a century or so and because it is still a rather uncommon word, it retains much of its original French accent. The preferred pronunciation is deh-BAH-k'l; indeed, this is the only pronunciation accepted by the *Oxford Dictionary*. However, most American dictionaries list deh-BACK-ul as a second but acceptable pronunciation. You will also hear day-BAH-k'l from those who are trying to approximate as closely as possible the original French version.

debilitate

Debilitate (pronounced dih-BIL-ih-tayt) is easily traced to the Latin. Coming from the word *debilitare* (to weaken, make feeble), it carries the same meaning into English usage. "The prisoner was *debilitated* by his long hunger strike."

debriefing

Debriefing is Pentagonese for what in World War II was known simply as postflight interrogation. All pilots flying missions—including, of course, those of our astronauts—are subjected to intensive "briefings" beforehand. In the course of the briefings they are instructed in procedures to be followed, route, weather conditions, target, destination, probable enemy activity or any other subject pertinent to the mission—including the best way to get back.

Debriefing—a word obviously coined as the opposite of "briefing" —involves, in normal wartime cases, the interrogation of pilot and other personnel in order to obtain information valuable to the intelligence arm of the service. In the case of the astronauts' flights, of course, the *debriefing* procedure was designed to elicit specific data about the out-of-this-world phenomena observed during their orbital missions, to guide our scientists in planning further space forays.

debunk

William E. Woodward is generally credited with creating the word *debunk* in a novel titled *Bunk* which exposed the pretentiousness in the family and social life of a wealthy automobile maker. Woodward later *debunked* George Washington (here Parson Weems' cherry-tree legend went into the discard), General Grant, Lafayette and other historical figures.

Quite a band of imitators, noting the popularity of these "unvarnished" biographies which reflected the twenties' mood of cynicism, delightedly took up the task of exposing all the petty aspects in the careers of our great men. On the whole, the movement was probably a healthy one: the truly great figures of our past suffered no permanent damage and a few who had been extolled beyond their true importance were reduced to proper stature. Biography today is generally candid, less given to glossing over minor defects of a subject's character, than was the case before the debunkers enjoyed their brief turn in the spotlight. See also BUNK.

decapitate

Decapitate is a less dramatic version of the Queen of Hearts' dictum "Off with their heads!" in *Alice in Wonderland.* It comes from the Latin *caput* (head) and *de* (off).

deck. *See* painter.

decoke. *See* automobile slang, British.

defenestration

Defenestration comes from the Latin *fenestra* (window) and *de* (out of). It means the act of throwing or jumping out of windows. As one social commentator, writing about the stock market crash of 1929, remarked wryly: "In Wall Street *defenestration* reached a new high."

defugalty

What we have here is a dialect variation of the simple word "difficulty." Pronounced dif-FYOO-gul-tee, it started out, no doubt, as a deliberate mispronunciation for comic effect. Gradually it became so common that many people came to think of it as a word in itself. The meaning of the phrase "What's the *defugalty?*" is simply "What's the trouble?" or "What's going on here anyway?"

Incidentally, Wentworth's *American Dialect Dictionary* records an odd "switch" on this term. Down east in Maine, he tells us, the natives sometimes say "What's the *cafugelty?*"

deign, disdain

Deign (pronounced DAYN), like the word *dignity,* stems from the Latin *dignus* (worthy) and originally meant "to think something worthy of doing" in the sense of being consistent with one's dignity. In general usage it has the meaning of condescending to do something, of lowering oneself to act. The word *disdain* (originally spelled *disdeign*) is no longer the direct opposite of *deign,* but now has the meaning of to scorn or to look upon with contempt. *Deign* can be used as either a transitive or intransitive verb, as "He did not *deign to* come" or "He would not *deign* an answer." *Disdain,* always transitive as a verb, is also a noun.

deleterious, delete

Deleterious (pronounced del-uh-TEER-ee-us) means injurious in the sense of being pernicious, detrimental to health or life. Some authorities believe it to be derived from the Greek word of almost the same spelling, *deleterios,* which means "to injure." Others give it the same origin as *delete,* which is the Latin *deletus,* past participle of *delere,* "to blot out or destroy." Regardless of origin, the words *deleterious* and *delete* as used today are not synonymous, since *deleterious* carries a special connotation of destruction.

denim. *See* blue jeans, and dungaree.

dentopedology. *See* cricket.

dentophobia

From the Latin *dentis* (tooth) and the Greek *phobos* (fear), *dentophobia* acquires its meaning of fear of dentistry.

depressed beetle. *See* confused beetles.

derby, bowler

The *derby* hat, which the British call the *bowler,* was named after the twelfth Earl of Derby, who also instituted the famed *Derby Day* at Epsom Downs—after which our own *Kentucky Derby* was named.

derrick

The *derrick* that we see used daily to lift and move heavy objects has a very sinister origin, indeed. The first *derrick* was a gallows invented in the early seventeenth century by the most notorious London hangman of the time, whose name was Derrick. See also GUILLOTINE.

derringer. *See* dillinger.

deucer

Dictionary editors carefully enter *deuce* (from the French, *deux* and Latin *duo,* both meaning "two") and give its meanings in card and dice playing, as well as in tennis. But they neglect *deucer* which, in the popular tongue, has half a dozen meanings—a two-dollar bill being the most common. In underworld slang, it is a person serving a two-year term. Baseball players use *deucer* as meaning either a two-base hit or the second game of a double-header. In vaudeville and circus slang it's the second spot on the bill, and to racing enthusiasts it's the horse that finishes second. So, dictionaries to the contrary, there most assuredly is such a word as *deucer*.

device vs. bomb, nuclear

According to the experts there is a difference between a *device* and a *bomb*. A *device* technically is any kind of weapon under development. Only when it has proven itself after extensive testing and is ready for combat use does it become a *bomb*.

devil's dozen. *See* baker's dozen.

dexterous

Dexterous is one of several words in the language that indicate a prejudice for right-handed persons and against left-handed ones. Derived from the Latin *dexter,* which simply means "right," *dexterous* now has the meaning of skillful, while *sinister* (from the identical Latin word for "left") means today ominous or evil. See also GAUCHE.

dhoti. *See* jodhpurs.

diagnosis, prognosis

Two terms from the language of medicine that occasionally trip up the layman are *diagnosis* and *prognosis*. The first, *diagnosis,* means the act of deciding, on the basis of analyzing symptoms, what disease is affecting the patient. It comes, like most medical language, from Greek, specifically from *dia* (between) and *gignoskein* (to know).

The *prognosis* follows the *diagnosis*. It is the prediction made by a physician of the course and probable termination of the disease. It has the same root as *diagnosis,* of course, and the prefix *pro* means "before." Thus a *prognosis* is a "knowing before"—or prediction.

dichotomize

Bernard Schwartz, a counsel for the House subcommittee investigating federal regulatory agencies, didn't last long in Washington but he made at least one fresh—and, let's hope, ephemeral—contribution to the mystifying language known as "governmentese." In commenting on the tendency of committee members to draw too fine distinctions between the legislative and judicial aspects of the inquiry, he accused them of *overdichotomizing*.

Dichotomize (pronounced dy-KOT-uh-mize) is a term borrowed from the language of botany and means "to divide into two." He could have made his point with greater clarity by accusing the committeemen of *hair-splitting*—but that kind of talk is too simple and direct for bureaucrats.

dickel

A *dickel* is an unofficial unit of currency worth seven and one-half cents. *Dickel* is a name made up of the first two letters of "dime" and the last four of "nickel." For students of language, this word qualifies as both a "blend word" (one made up of parts of two or more other words) and a "nonce word" (one of fleeting popularity, especially one coined for a particular occasion or situation).

Dickels were invented in 1953 for use in connection with a celebration in Lincoln, Illinois, of the hundredth anniversary of the town's founding. Made of wood and bearing a picture of Honest Abe, they were redeemable at cash value during the period of the celebration. Reportedly coin collectors from all parts of the nation added them to their collections.

dictionary, unabridged. *See* unabridged dictionary.

dido, cut a. *See* cut a dido.

Dieu et mon droit

The British royal family's motto literally means "God and my right." It was reportedly first uttered by Richard the Lion-Hearted at the Battle of Gisors in 1198—though it did not become the royal motto until much later, during the reign of Henry VI. Richard's meaning was that he—as King of England—ruled by the mandate of God and owed no fealty to the French against whom he was warring. Incidentally, the British won the battle.

Common and amusing mistranslations of this phrase are "My God, I'm right!" and "With the help of God and a good right arm!"

diffident

Diffident (pronounced DIF-uh-d'nt) is the adjective form of the word *diffidence,* which is a combination of two Latin words *dis-* (not) and *fidere* (to trust). We can literally and accurately translate *diffidence* as lacking in trust in oneself. Substitute the prefix *con-* (with) for the prefix *dis-,* and you have *confidence* or, again, literally, "faith in oneself."

dillinger

This is a name youngsters use for short-barreled cap and water pistols. Out of ten children questioned, all called the pistols *dillingers* but none had ever even heard of John Dillinger, the gunman who died so ingloriously during the thirties.

My surmise is that this name came to be applied to the toy pistols by a process known to linguists as "folk etymology." In truth, *dillinger* is merely a variant form of *derringer*—long used as the name of pistols with a short barrel and large bore. *Derringers* were, if memory serves, chorus girls' favorite weapons of self-defense back in Diamond Jim Brady's day.

The original name, by the way, came from its inventor, an American gunsmith named Henry Deringer (one "r") who made the first of his name-sake guns around 1850.

diplomate

A *diplomate*—and I am astonished to note that this word is not included in the major desk dictionaries—is simply a person who has received a diploma certifying to his completion of a course of study in an accredited institution. More common in England and in Europe than here, it is frequently used to indicate that a person has been accredited as an expert in one of the specialized areas of knowledge.

disc jockey. *See* jockeys, bench, disc, et al.

discography

Discography is a word coined by analogy to "bibliography." It means a listing of records devoted to a single composer or performer. Occasionally you will encounter a *critical discography,* containing, in addition to the date and label for each performance, some commentary on the interpretation, quality of recording and other related data.

My first acquaintance with *discography* came in 1931 when I discovered that the French music critic Hughes Panassie was reviewing American jazz records in *La Revue Musicale* with a seriousness then quite inconceivable on this side of the Atlantic.

Already a devoted admirer of Armstrong and Ellington, I was delighted to find that Panassie and a few other French critics were commenting on Louis and the Duke in language usually reserved for performances by Elman and Kreisler. In many instances, their reviews of the recorded performances of these then little-known American performers was supplemented by a *discographie*.

discombobulate

Discombobulate, meaning "to discomfit or embarrass or confuse," is a dialect term, first reported about 1890 but only recently coming into anything like general use. It still rates as "dialectal."

disdain. *See* deign, disdain.

disingenuous

Disingenuous (pronounced dis-in-JEN-yoo-us) is made up of *dis-* (not) and the Latin *ingenuus*. Because of the Latin meaning of the second part of the word, which was "freeborn, frank or noble," *ingenuous* was originally used to describe one of honorable birth or character but came to mean "candid, straightforward, sincere." A *disingenuous* person is one who is not sincere but rather crafty and cunning.

disparage

Disparage (pronounced dis-PAIR-ij) comes to us from the Old French *desparagier* (to marry one of lower rank) which in turn came from *des-* and *parage* (rank). The present-day meaning of *disparage* is to belittle or to lower in esteem. One speaks of another *disparagingly* when being critical of his worth or ability. While there is still such a word as *parage,* it is a noun, not a verb and is not in common use. *Parage* is a legal term for equality in rank or in distribution of property.

dissuasion. *See* suasion.

diva

Diva is the Italian word meaning "leading woman singer or prima donna." The correct pronunciation is DEE-vuh. Diva comes from the Latin, where it means "goddess"—which gives you an idea of how highly Italians regard opera singers.

Dixie. *See* Mason-Dixon Line.

Dixieland

There are many stories about this word. Perhaps the most credible is that the phrase originally was *the land of dixies*—dixie being the popular name for ten-dollar notes issued in Louisiana and bearing the French-Creole word *dix* (ten) on one side.

Another fanciful story is that the original *Dixieland* was a slave plantation in New York City. According to a Southern newspaper of the immediate post-Civil War period: "When slavery existed in New York, one Dixie owned a large tract of land in Manhattan and a large number of slaves. The increase of slaves and of the abolition movement caused an emigration of the slaves to more secure slave sections. The Negroes looked back to their old homes where they had lived in clover with feelings of regret, as they could not imagine any place like Dixie's."

That sounds pretty farfetched to me. But one thing all can agree on is that the song "Dixie" was written in 1859 by the greatest minstrel man of his time, Dan Emmett. First performed in New York, it rapidly swept the country and was enthusiastically adopted as the favorite marching song of the Confederacy.

docile, docility

Docile (pronounced DOSS-'l) means "easily taught," as does the word from which it is derived, the Latin *docilis*. (*Docilis* in turn had its origin in the Latin verb *docere*, "to teach.") It also means "easily managed" and in the noun form, *docility* means "gentleness or easy manageability."

Dodgers, the

Just how did the baseball team get the name *Dodgers* anyway? For the answer we have to turn back to the start of this century when the chief means of transportation in the bustling borough of Brooklyn was the trolley car. So numerous were the trolleys, especially in the central area around Borough Hall, that all Brooklynites were labeled *trolley dodgers*. Later the label was shortened to *Dodgers* and applied to the ball team. In the mid-twenties and early thirties the team was often called the Brooklyn Robins, after their famed manager Wilbert Robinson.

dog, hair of the. *See* hair of the dog.

dog days

This is the season of the year Charles Dudley Warner probably had in mind when he remarked that, "Everybody talks about the weather but nobody does anything about it." Despite the efforts of artificial rainmakers with cloud-seeding experiments, it still appears that nobody can do very much about what Webster defines as the "close, sultry part of summer." At least, though, we can tell you how this period of the year got its name.

First, there's nothing new about the phrase. In the days of the Romans, the six or eight hottest weeks of summer were known colloquially as *caniculares dies* or "days of the dog." The Roman theory was that the dog star Sirius, rising with the sun, added its heat to the sun's and thus the period—roughly from July 3 to August 11—when Sirius' rise coincides with that of the sun was the hottest season of the year.

Humanity has suffered through *dog days* for quite a few centuries now.

So we may as well console ourselves with Don Marquis' advice: "Don't cuss the climate. It probably doesn't like you any better than you like it."

dogie

Probably the best book ever written on the language of the range is *Western Words* by Ramon F. Adams. His comments on the origin of *dogie* are characteristically colorful. Here's what Mr. Adams has to say: "A dogie, in the language of the cowboy is 'a calf that has lost its mammy and whose daddy has run off with another cow.'

"One version of the origin of the word 'dogie' is that it started in the eighties after a very severe winter had killed off a great many mother cows and left a number of orphan calves. Grass and water were too heavy a ration for these little orphans, and their bellies very much resembled a batch of sourdough carried in a sack. Having no mother whose brand could establish ownership, and carrying no brand themselves by which they could be identified, these orphans were put into the maverick class. The first to claim them was recognized as the owner, no matter where they were found.

"One day on a roundup a certain cowman who was trying to build up a herd, drove a bunch in from along the river. 'Boys, there's five of them dough-guts in that drive and I claim every dang one of them,' he yelled excitedly.

"During that roundup all orphans became known as 'dough-guts' and later the term was shortened to 'dogie' and has been used ever since throughout cattleland to refer to a pot-gutted orphan calf."

dog in the manger

This expression, meaning a person who selfishly refuses to give to others things he himself has no use for, comes from one of Aesop's fables. You probably remember hearing, as a child, the fable of the dog lying in a manger full of hay. He snarled at and bit the ox who tried to eat the hay —despite the fact that he couldn't possibly eat it himself. Thus, down the centuries, *dog in the manger* has designated a person who neither enjoys a thing nor allows others to enjoy it.

donnybrook

A true *donnybrook* consists of a knockdown-drag-out brawl with any-where from a handful to a mob of participants. It takes its name from the town of Donnybrook, a suburb southeast of Dublin. There, from medieval times up to the middle of the nineteenth century, were held annual fairs which for riotous debauchery rivaled the Saturnalian revels of Caesar's time. They always wound up in fisticuffs and worse—much worse.

Over the centuries the Irish have displayed a notable disinclination to avoid a good fight. Indeed, their hankering for a brawl is as legendary as their ability at handling their traditional weapon, the shillelagh. So it's hardly to be wondered at that the annual spectacle of thousands of sons of the Old Sod flailing lightheartedly about with splendid disregard for the Marquis of Queensberry rules should have made the name *donnybrook* synonymous with riotous brawling.

doodad, doohickey

Either of these terms can be used colloquially for a small object or device, the proper name of which is not known or is forgotten. See also GADGET.

doornail, dead as a. *See* dead as a doornail.

Doppelgängers, theory of

An alleged psychic phenomenon that your editor finds fascinating is the theory of *Doppelgängers.* And that's not double-talk! Briefly the theory is that each of us has, somewhere in the world, an exact double—a person entirely unrelated by blood but absolutely identical in physical appearance and voice. It's a notion that has long intrigued novelists. Only a few years ago one of the better mysteries, *The Man With My Face,* used the *Doppelgänger* theme.

Like poltergeist, *Doppelgänger* is of German origin, from *doppel* (double) and *gänger* (goer or walker). Being something of a cynic in such matters, I should be interested in hearing if any reader of this dictionary has ever met his or her *Doppelgänger.*

dotage

Dotage is derived from *dote* which has the twin meanings of "to lavish affection on" and "to be of feeble mind." A person in his *dotage* (pronounced DOH-tij) is in his foolish, feeble old age.

double entendre

A *double entendre* is a phrase with two meanings, one of which is usually risqué or improper. The phrase comes from the French, where it was originally *double entente,* meaning "double understanding"—a phrase that can be understood in either of two meanings.

doubting Thomas

The first *doubting Thomas* was St. Thomas, one of the twelve apostles.

According to Scripture, he expressed skepticism about Christ's crucifixion and demanded to see the marks on Christ's body (John, 20:25–29). After Christ had appeared before him and convinced him, he said: "Thomas, because thou hast seen me, thou hast believed; blessed are they that have not seen, and yet have believed."

down East

It happens that I am what folks from other parts of the country call a *down-Easter*—a native of New England. (In New England itself a *down-Easter* is a native of Maine.) Yet I am unable to supply a firm and final answer to the origin of the expression *down East*.

Why can't this transplanted *down-Easter* supply the answer? Simply because nobody really knows, though there are several theories as to how this phrase, which dates at least as far back as the Revolution, got its start.

One theory is that a sailing ship bound from New York or Boston to Maine would be sailing "down wind"—but a mariner friend assures me that there are no "prevailing" winds on the coast and that, if the direction indicated on the ship's charts were considered, the ship would more logically be said to be going "up" east.

A sounder theory, it seems to me, is that our New England forebears simply borrowed the expression from England. In England to this day, a native goes "up" to London—no matter whether he is coming from the north, south or west. Similarly, when he returns to his own less important town, he goes "down."

Boston of the nineteenth century—the "Athens of America" it was often called—was certainly as important in relationship to surrounding states and communities as London to its neighboring towns. So my theory is that the British manner of speech was adopted, with the result that Bostonians went *down East* or *down to Maine* for vacations and Maine businessmen went *up to Boston* to trade.

down of hares. *See* clowder, kindle and cowardice.

draconian

Draconian comes from Draco, an ancient Athenian lawgiver, one of the first to draft a written code. His penalties in most cases called for death —so a common observation of the period (seventh century B.C.) was that "The Draconian Code is written in blood."

dragged. *See* jazzmen's jargon.

drawing room

In books about life among the lords and ladies of Old England and, indeed, in novels about our own landed gentry of fifty years or so ago, one frequently runs across references to *drawing rooms*. Even today on Pullman cars, one can reserve a *drawing room* and travel in comparative elegance.

How did these rooms, which in today's houses we'd call "living rooms," ever get to be called *drawing rooms*? Can it be that the amateur artists we now call "Sunday painters" were so plentiful in the past that each manorhouse had a room reserved for them?

Such guesses are far wide of the mark. Although a little tasteful daubing at innocuous still-life compositions was as much a part of a young lady's social training in those days as piano playing and petit point, I'm sure it would seldom occur even to the most indulgent of Victorian papas that they should devote a whole room to this pastime.

Rather, the name *drawing room* comes from the phrase "withdrawing room" and refers to the now nearly forgotten custom of the ladies "withdrawing" from the dining room at the close of dinner. This was so that the gentlemen could enjoy their cigars, brandy and an exchange of masculine banter with no fear of offending any lady's delicate sensibilities. *O tempora, O mores! Sic transit* . . . and similar expressions indicating that times —perhaps regrettably—surely do change!

drift, on the

A cowboy *on the drift* is out of a job, riding from ranch to ranch until he can find work.

drop head. *See* automobile slang, British.

drove of kine. *See* clowder, kindle and cowardice.

drunk as a lord

Anyone who is *drunk as a lord* is very drunk indeed. The expression comes to us from the reign of George III of England, the same who reigned during the American Revolution. In those days drunkenness was the mark of a gentleman. "Two- and three-bottle men" were commonplace among leaders in society and quite a few formal state dinners ended with many of the guests collapsed in drunken stupor—literally "under the table."

druthers, if I had my

The phrase *if I had my druthers* has been common throughout Southern and Western America at least since 1875, when Bret Harte used it in his book *The Argonauts*. *Druthers* is a corruption of "rathers" and the phrase simply means "if I had my choice or preference."

Harold Wentworth's *American Dialect Dictionary* records other variations in common dialect—*ruther, ruthers, rathers* and *druther*—and notes that the term is used interchangeably in the singular and plural. It remains, however, a folk phrase—not one to be used in formal writing or speaking.

dry behind the ears, not

The expression *not dry behind the ears yet* literally means "as innocent as a newborn babe." According to tradition, at least, the last place where a newly born animal becomes dry is the slight indentation behind each ear.

dry cleaning

Dry in this phrase has a meaning very different from the customary definition: "without moisture of any kind." Actually, *dry cleaning* is more accurately called, in some sections of our country, "French cleaning," for the phrase is a literal translation of the French phrase *nettoyage à sec,* which means cleaning by the dry method, or cleaning without water.

In other words, the true meaning of *dry* in *dry cleaning* is "without water," which means that any of a large variety of liquid solvents—benzine, carbon tetrachloride and naphtha, for example—may be used in the process.

The method was first developed in France midway through the nineteenth century and its great merits are that it causes no shrinking of the materials cleaned nor does it cause a garment to lose its shape. Any man who has been trapped in a mid-July downpour wearing a pre-Dacron suit knows how utterly shapeless his clothes become when well wetted with water. And any wife who has tried to press out the wrinkles after such a mishap knows what a thankless task it is—all because water "wets" a fabric in a way that solvents like benzine cannot.

So the *dry* in *dry cleaning* means only "without water" and you'll no longer be puzzled about why your suit or dress is immersed in an obviously liquid-filled vat.

dry fluids

French vintners for many a long year have been using the word *sec* (dry) to designate wines that are not sweet. The contrast between a *sweet* and a *dry wine* is perhaps most obvious in the distinction between sweet and dry vermouth. So, in our American speech, a beer, gin, rum or even a ginger ale with little or no sweetness came to be labeled *dry*.

ducks and drakes, playing

Playing ducks and drakes is simply the literary expression for what I, as a youngster, called "skimming" flat stones across water. Samuel Butler centuries ago wrote—and this is just as true today as every child knows:

> Flat figured slates are best to make
> On watery surface duck and drake.

dudgeon

What is a high *dudgeon*—and how does it differ from a low *dudgeon?* We have a neat problem here since *dudgeon,* according to most authorities, has two distinct meanings. The less common is "a kind of wood used for dagger hilts and, hence, the handle of a dagger." The second and only frequently heard use of the word today is in the phrase "in high *dudgeon,*" meaning in a state of irate indignation. "High" is here used in the sense of great or intense. And, since there is little likelihood that anyone ever was just a little bit irate or a tiny bit indignant, there simply is no such phrase as "in a low *dudgeon.*"

Though most linguists contend that there is no direct connection between the *dudgeon* of the dagger hilt and the *dudgeon* of deep resentment, it seems to me that they are blinding themselves to a simple fact of medieval life—the period when this phrase first gained wide currency. What would be more likely than that a man of noble birth, feeling indignant over an insult to his name or reputation, would reach for his dagger as the first gesture of revenging the damage? How probable, indeed, that the dagger—instrument of vengeance—became by extension the term used to describe the high degree of wrath which would lead to its use!

So *dudgeon,* in today's meaning of wrath or resentment, almost surely came from the medieval name of the instrument commonly used to avenge the cause of wrath.

Duggan's dew

Duggan's dew is the name given the liquid lightning (illegally distilled spirits) which triggered many a Glencannon adventure in the famous stories by Guy Gilpatric. The name is as fanciful as the stories themselves.

dumps, down in the

Dump is thought to be derived from a Dutch word *domp* (meaning haze or dullness). During the Elizabethan period a *dump* was also any kind of a slow, mournful song or dance.

In *The Taming of the Shrew,* Katherina after her first lively quarrel with Petruchio is asked by her father "Why, how now, daughter Katherina! In your dumps?" So even in Shakespeare's time, *in the dumps* meant out of spirits. But—as everyone who recalls the recent and lively adaptation of this play, *Kiss Me, Kate,* will remember—Katherina was by no means ready for discard to the town dump.

dunce

This word comes from the middle name of one of the most learned and brilliant scholars of the Middle Ages, John Duns Scotus. He was of a strongly conservative bent and soon gathered around him many followers who shared his opposition to many of the changes brought about by the Reformation. After his death, these "Dunsmen" or "Duncemen," as they were called, persisted so long in their blind opposition to change of any kind that they came in time to be considered a pretty stupid lot. So with the passage of centuries *dunce* came to mean a person precisely the opposite of the man who first bore the name.

dungaree

More than 250 years ago, traders began to bring back from India to England a coarsely woven cotton cloth which was known in Hindustani—the trade language of India—as *dungri.* At first it was used chiefly for sails and tents but seamen, noting its long-wearing qualities, began fashioning it into work clothing. As time passed, *dungri* picked up another syllable, becoming *dungaree.* What's more, *dungarees* became the standard work uniform of the Navy and the Merchant Marine and it's a fair guess that the present popularity of *dungarees* can be traced, at least in part, to the fact that millions of young Americans wore them for the first time during World War II.

The textile industry prefers to label the fabric "denim" but it's a safe bet that most of its wearers will continue to call their apparel *dungarees.*

dust and duster. *See* baseball jargon.

Dutch auction

A *Dutch auction* is one that proceeds directly in reverse of an ordinary auction. Instead of starting with a low bid and attracting progressively higher bids, the auctioneer in a Dutch auction starts with a high figure, reduces the price by regular stages and finally sells to the first person who accepts his price quotation.

The term—like such others as "Dutch treat" (when each pays for himself) and "Dutch courage" (courage obtained from the bottle)—reflects what the Oxford dictionary calls the "contempt and derision" in which many Britons held the Dutch people in the seventeenth and eighteenth centuries.

Dutch courage, Dutch treat, in Dutch, etc.

Probably no nationality has come in for so consistent a torrent of verbal abuse from the English as their neighbors across the channel, the Dutch. *Dutch courage*—the kind of courage that comes out of a bottle— is surely an unflattering phrase. When you're invited to a *Dutch treat* or a *Dutch luncheon,* the host expects each guest to pay his own way. *Double Dutch* is a kind of talk deliberately intended to deceive the listener. And *to do the Dutch* is to commit suicide.

In these few phrases—and there are dozens more—the English have implied that the Dutch are cowardly, niggardly and deceitful. Yet the rest of the world sees Holland and its people as a land of tulips, windmills, sunny-faced skaters and brave fellows tending the dikes. Why should the British take such a contrary view?

It was not always thus. Until well after Shakespeare's time, the Dutch were usually well regarded in all literary references by British authors. But during the seventeenth century the two nations became rivals in international commerce. For a while, at least, the Dutch colonial empire loomed as a real challenge to Britain's. So the disrespectful references began. One of the earliest—a reference to *Dutch courage*—was penned by the poet Edmund Waller in 1665:

> The Dutch their wine and all their brandy lose,
> Disarmed of that from which their courage grows.

Today, of course, Great Britain and the Netherlands have lived in peace and fellowship for many years. But the damage done by the derogatory phrases created in a time of wars and rivalry remains. To this day one hears of *Dutch reckoning* (guesswork), *Dutch defense* (retreat or surrender), and a pigheaded or stubborn man is one whose *Dutch is up*. It surely does beat the Dutch!

dynaschmo

Variety, the show business newspaper, coined a word for the big-time operator who "makes like a whirling dervish, acts as though he knows everything, but in the final showdown always comes up blank." *Variety's* name for him? *Dynaschmo.*

E

ears, not dry behind the. *See* **dry behind the ears, not.**

eat crow. *See* **political language.**

eavesdrop

This word comes to us virtually unchanged from Anglo-Saxon days. In those times a house had very wide overhanging eaves, not unlike those which may still be seen on thatched cottages in Devon. Since rain gutters and spouts were unknown then, the purpose of the wide overhang was to allow rain to drip safely away from the house's foundation. So the *eaves-drip*, which later became *eavesdrop*, provided a sheltered place where one could hide to listen clandestinely to conversations within the house.

EDVAC. *See* ENIAC, EDVAC and ORACLE

effete

Effete is a word which has strayed far in popular use from its correct meaning of "worn-out, barren, exhausted." Perhaps because it is a favorite adjective of society columnists, it is now often and not very accurately used as a synonym for "sophisticated" in phrases like "the *effete* social whirl of Monte Carlo."

Pronounced eh-FEET, it literally means "exhausted from bearing young," and thus should properly be used to describe people or a society which once was productive but now is barren and uncreative.

efficacy, efficacious

Efficacy (pronounced EF-ih-kuh-see) is a noun meaning ability to produce the effects desired. It comes from the Latin verb *efficere,* "to bring to pass" or "to accomplish." A doctor might well comment on the *efficacy* of a certain drug. Its adjective form is *efficacious* (pronounced ef-ih-KAY-shus).

effigy, hang in

The practice of venting one's wrath on a facsimile of the person hated is probably as old as the human race. In every society from primitive Samoans to certain of the Pennsylvania "Dutch" sects of the present day, people have believed that they can do harm to their enemies by sticking pins into images or effigies of them.

Our word *effigy* comes from the French word *effigie,* meaning "likeness or copy." The practice of hanging a person in effigy dates back to a French tradition in the years before the Revolution. Then, if a wanted criminal could not be found, it was the duty of the public executioner to hang an *effigie* of him.

Nowadays, of course, the custom does not necessarily imply that the object of a group's wrath would literally be hanged if he could be found. Rather it is an indication that the person is held in complete contempt by the people presiding at the mock hanging.

eighty-eight. *See* jazzmen's jargon.

eight ball, behind the

This phrase comes from the game of Kelly pool. In one version of this game the player is required to pocket the balls in numerical rotation, except for the black ball, which is numbered eight. If another ball hits the eight ball, its player is penalized. So a position directly behind the eight ball is a position of great hazard.

egghead

Egghead was first used by Owen Johnson in one of the Lawrenceville novels beloved by boy readers of the early days of the century. Even then, the connotation was of a person who was quite bright even though he might not, on all occasions, use his brains to their highest potential.

The word was revived during the 1952 Eisenhower-Stevenson campaign. There's no doubt that it was often used invidiously and disparagingly by commentators of an anti-intellectual stripe. But, though Stevenson and his associates were lampooned as *eggheads,* I don't believe anyone using the term questioned that so far as formal education was concerned, the *eggheads* rated very high.

During more recent campaigns the word was not so often heard, perhaps because the country was ready to concede that there might be some place for intellect in our government after all.

86, and bartenders' number code

Practicing barkeeps of the nation aren't going to like this explanation, but indications are that *86* may well have come from a number code created by the comparatively effete soda fountain clerks of the nation. (As a one-time member of the honorable fraternity of soda-poppers, I hasten to add that nothing derogatory should be read into that phrase "comparatively effete." It's just that some bartenders, from the nature of their clientele, have to be of a hardier breed than most counter jumpers.)

But back to *86*. Originally, according to the *American Thesaurus of Slang,* it was a password used between clerks to indicate: "We're all out of the item ordered." The transition from this meaning—common enough in soda fountains of the 1920's—to the bartender's sense of "Serve no more because of the shape he's in" is fairly obvious.

The number code developed by soda clerks was very extensive, incidentally. The head fountain manager was *99,* the assistant manager was *98*—which also meant "pest." A hissed "*98*" from one soda-popper to another indicated, "The assistant manager is prowling around. Watch out."

And, for some reason, *33* meant a cherry-flavored Coca-Cola, *55* meant root beer and *19* was a banana split. And—most cheerful warning of all—*87½* meaning, "There's a good-looking girl out front!"

elephant, white. *See* white elephant.

elhi

For the past decade or more *elhi* has been publishing trade jargon for the divisions of textbook publishers that prepare texts for elementary and high schools. As a cant word, it will probably never find its way into the general lexicons but will remain restricted in use to publishers and their educator customers.

emote

There may be many who wish there were not such a word as *emote,* many who view it with the same disdain they reserve for "enthuse," and similar verbs newly formed from nouns by the process known to students of words as "back formation."

But the fact of the matter is that *emote*—formed from "emotion" by analogy with "devote"—is now acceptable on an informal or colloquial basis. Thus you may find it appearing in newspaper and magazine features about movie personalities—but it would be highly inappropriate in a formal report from the chairman of the board of a motion picture corporation to his stockholders.

Actually *emote* was originally used humorously. Only recently has it been adopted as a relatively serious verb meaning to conduct oneself in an emotional manner, as if giving a theatrical performance.

empathy

Empathy (pronounced EM-puh-thee) is a psychological term meaning the projection of one's own personality into the mind or personality of another in order to understand him better. This special meaning is, of course, not at all the same thing as "sympathy," which merely means a sharing of similar emotions. *Empathy* comes from the Greek *empatheia,* meaning "affection or passion."

Empire State. *See* excelsior.

emulate

To *emulate* (pronounced EM-yoo-layt) is to try to equal or surpass. It comes directly from the Latin *aemulatus,* the past participle of the verb *aemulari,* which has the identical meaning as the English word. Its noun and adjective forms are *emulation* (emyoo-LAY-shun) and *emulative* (EM-yoo-luh-tiv). It is commonly used in the sense of imitating, as in "He will have to *emulate* the advertising practices of his competitors if he wishes to match their sales."

encomium

Encomium (pronounced en-KOH-mee-um) means high praise, especially praise of a formal nature. A music critic might write, "The orchestra's performance was of such excellence as to merit the highest *encomium.*" The word is derived from the Greek *komos,* meaning "revel," and originally referred to songs sung in village revels in praise of Comus, the god of joy. It is amusing that this word which had its origin in the lusty atmosphere of Bacchanalian revelry is now reserved for relatively staid and formal expressions of praise.

enemies. *See* friends, enemies.

English English

Ladies, do you know what your British cousins mean when they speak of *Kirby grips, fringe, Wellingtons* or *suspenders?* Well, *Kirby grips* are bobby pins, *fringe* means bangs (haircut), *Wellingtons* are overshoes—also called *gum boots*—and *suspenders* means a garter belt. For British men, incidentally, *suspenders* are garters and what we call suspenders are *braces.*

Any man should know that a derby hat is a *bowler* but not many will guess that a fedora is called a *trilby.* Our vest is, in England, a *waistcoat,* pronounced "weskit." Dress shoes are *court shoes* and *rubbers* are not worn on the feet, for a *rubber* in England is an eraser.

Radio is, of course, the *wireless* but the English don't have static. They have *atmospherics*. Girls who chatter aimlessly are said to be *blowing out their tongues,* while a courageous chap is called *spartan.* At the seaside whitecaps are known as *white horses* and a swimming pool is known as a *swimming bath.*

If you're having fun, everything is *frightfully jolly* and the answer to the perennial question of "Tennis, anyone?" is "Yes, *let's knock it up a bit"*—which is the equivalent of our "Let's rally!"

ENIAC, EDVAC and ORACLE

Those first two words are not the names of creatures from other planets, nor does this *ORACLE* mean the wise soothsayer of antiquity. In truth, these words are the acronymic designations for three of the early stages in the development of the electronic brain—and there's a story behind each of them. In the early 1940's, a group of scientists, working at the School of Electrical Engineering of the University of Pennsylvania, announced that they had developed a "brain" with the ability to solve mathematical problems 100,000 times faster than the best human mind. They named the device ENIAC from the first letters of the phrase "electronic numerical integrator and computer." Rather sagely they pointed out that the miracle machine could handle only mathematical problems and was unable to cope with more complex human problems like, "How are chances for maintaining world peace?" Shortly after World War II, the same scientists were back in the news again with EDVAC, which, they said, made their previous Frankenstein monster a puling babe by contrast. EDVAC worked a million times faster than the human mind and had extraordinary powers of memory, being able to memorize a thousand ten-digit figures at a time. And its name, like that of its predecessor, was an acronym (a word made up of the first letter or letters of a phrase or title) of the phrase "electronic discrete variable computer."

ORACLE from "Oak Ridge automatic computer, logical engine" does everything its predecessors could accomplish, only more so. It multiplies twelve-digit numbers two thousand times a second. It can accomplish in twenty minutes what two humans, using desk-size calculators, would need six years to figure out.

There are still faster computers now, of course, but the vogue for acronymic names for them has, perhaps happily, waned.

entendre. *See* **double entendre.**

entomologist. *See* etymologist, entomologist.

eon

Eon simply means any extremely long period of time—thousands and thousands of years. It comes from the Greek word *aion,* which meant an age or all eternity.

epidemic—pandemic

An *epidemic* describes the spread of a disease which affects many people in a community at the same time. An *epidemic* may cover a wide area— even, on occasion, an entire country. A disease which is *pandemic* is one which affects many if not most people over a very large area, usually including many countries. *Pandemic* may be understood to mean "internationally *epidemic.*"

epitome

You will occasionally find *epitome* used as a synonym for "ideal" or "acme" but there is a distinction to be made and careful users of the language make it.

Epitome came to English from Greek and literally means a sampling representative of the whole. It may either be a summary or a sample section characteristic of the whole. In correct usage *epitome* has no qualitative implications. For instance, a piece of text can be "the *epitome* of graceless prose" just as another may be "the *epitome* of brilliant writing."

equanimity

Equanimity (pronounced eek-wuh-NIM-ih-tee) denotes calmnness or serenity of temper and is a combination of the Latin *aequus* (even) and *animus* (mind). *Equanimity* really means a calmness or serenity that is not easily disturbed, as in "Nothing she could say affected his *equanimity.*" Incidentally, one of its root words, *animus,* has—when used as an English word—acquired a meaning of enmity or ill-will. In *equanimity* it retains its original meaning of "mind."

equivocate

Coming from the Latin, *equivocate* literally means to speak with two voices: *aequi* (equal) and *vocare* (to call). From this has evolved the present-day meaning of hedging or using double-talk in an effort to mislead or deceive.

esoteric

Anything *esoteric* is intended for a chosen few, the insiders. The word comes from the Greek *esoteros* (inner).

esq. or esquire

In the Middle Ages the first *esquires* were candidates for knighthood, attendants and shield-bearers for the knights. The word came into English at the time of the Norman Conquest, via the Old French *esquier* from the Latin *scutarius* (shield-bearer).

The term *esq.* was later quite commonly used to indicate that the person addressed was of social rank slightly higher than that of tradespeople, who were called simply *Mr.*

Now, in America at least, *Esq.* is used chiefly as a courtesy title when addressing letters to lawyers. One never, incidentally, uses *Mr.* and *Esq.* in the same salutation.

etymologist, entomologist

Everyone has trouble with words. Even the experts find occasional pairs of words—similar in sound or meaning—which they never can quite seem to keep straight. One of America's most eminent dictionary editors once confessed to me that his tongue sometimes slipped when he tried to say the word *etymologist*—meaning a student of word origins. Occasionally it would come out *entomologist*—one who studies insects and their habits.

This editor friend told me how he finally licked his problem. He trained himself to remember this simple sentence: "An *etymologist* is a man who knows the difference between an *etymologist* and an *entomologist*." End of egghead humor.

euphemism

The word *euphemism* is derived from the Greek *euphemismos* (to use a good word for an evil or unfavorable word). A *euphemism* itself is a word substituted for another which is actually more precise or accurate. See also SPADE A SPADE, TO CALL A.

ev. *See* bev, ev, mev and cutie pie.

evanesce, evanescent

Evanescent (pronounced eh-vuh-NESS-ent) stems from the Latin *ex* (out) and *vanescere* (to vanish), and from these roots it has come to mean fleeting, fading or on the point of vanishing, as a vapor would *evanesce.* The noun form is *evanescence.*

everyone to his own liking

The expression "Everyone to his own liking, as the farmer said when he kissed the cow" is a variation on an English folk saying that goes back at least to the mid-1500's. The version then current went like this: "Every man as he loveth, quoth the good man, whan he kyst his coowe." A similar notion is contained in the well-known French proverb, "*Chacun à son gout*"—"Everyone to his own taste."

evince

Evince (pronounced eh-VINSS) is a verb meaning "to make manifest or to show plainly." Derived from a combination of the Latin *ex* (out, from) and *vincere* (to conquer), it is commonly used in relation to emotions, thoughts or qualities of a person as in "He *evinced* a knowledge of science which amazed me." Though it has lost its original English meaning of conquering, it now means "to show beyond a doubt" and, in that sense, some trace of "conquering" remains.

exaltation of larks. *See* clowder, kindle and cowardice.

excelsior

When used to mean shredded wood this word has a curious history. Apparently *Excelsior*—with the *e* capitalized—was first used as a trademark to denote a certain brand of this commonly used packing material. But behind this fact lies an interesting tale involving the now long-forgotten nickname of New York—"The *Excelsior* State."

Although New York's present nickname, "The Empire State," was occasionally heard in the nineteenth century, the more popular designation was *Excelsior* State, from the fact that the state seal bears the word *Excelsior.* This Latin word is the comparative of *excelsus* and simply means "higher." It was apparently chosen as the state motto on the erroneous assumption that it was an adverb meaning "upward."

However that may have been, the word enjoyed great popularity, especially after Longfellow used it as the title of one of his most popular poems. During the Civil War the New York troops, of course, carried the state motto on their campaign flags and "*Excelsior!*" became a popular rallying cry.

Astute merchants began labeling their products *excelsior* under the common delusion that the word was a fine-sounding synonym for "excellent." Some of these old trade-marks exist to the present day, of course—if memory serves, a favorite brand of Fourth of July sparklers bears this label—but most have been long forgotten. The state nickname, which caused all the excitement in the first place, has likewise long been superseded by the "Empire State" label.

But the businessman who, about 1860, first labeled his new brand of thin wood shavings *Excelsior* wrought better than he could ever have dreamed, for his brand name has now become the popular designation for this packing material.

exculpate

Exculpate (pronounced EX-kul-payt) has literally retained the meanings of its Latin roots, *ex* (out) and *culpatus,* past participle of *culpare* (to blame). For example: "The story told by the eyewitness *exculpated* (freed from blame) the suspected man." The accent shifts to the third syllable in the noun *exculpation* and to the second syllable in the adjectives *exculpable* (able to be freed from blame) and *exculpatory* (tending to *exculpate*).

exosphere

A creation of the space age, the word *exosphere* denotes the outer fringe of the atmosphere—out past the stratosphere and the ionosphere.

exotic

According to one authority, *exotic* means "different" or "strange" only in the sense of "from a foreign land." This, of course, is the original sense of the word. It comes from the Greek *exotikos,* meaning "foreign" or "alien." But, over the past few decades, it has also come to mean, in the words of the *World Webster Dictionary,* "having the charm or fascination of the unfamiliar; strangely beautiful and enticing." The *American College Dictionary* puts it this way: "Strikingly unusual or colorful in appearance or effect."

expeditious, expedient

Expeditious (pronounced ex-peh-DISH-us) has its origin in the Latin *expedire* which literally means "to free one caught by the foot" (*ex,* "out," and *pedis,* "foot"). From the same Latin word come the more commonly known *expedite* (to facilitate or speed up) and *expedition. Expeditious* is an adjective and means in a speedy or prompt manner; efficient. (Adverb: *expeditiously.*)

This word should not be confused with another word of the same origin, *expedient,* a noun which means an immediate purpose or a convenient or makeshift device. Used as an adjective, an *expedient* measure may contribute to an *expeditious* completion of a project—or it may have to do only with an isolated incident.

expertise

The word *expertise* (pronounced ek-sper-TEES) is a recent and, in Washington circles, very fashionable borrowing from the French. It means an evaluation or assessment by an expert.

expostulate

Expostulate (pronounced eks-POSS-chuh-layt) is usually followed by *with* and means to reason (with another) and argue against the advisability of an act, intended or in the process of being committed. It has practically the same meaning as *remonstrate.* "He *expostulated* with his friend about his reckless driving." As you see, its meaning today is slightly different from that of the word from which it stems, the Latin *expostulare,* which means to demand vehemently, to require. In its noun form *expostulation,* the accent shifts to the fourth syllable.

extirpate

Meaning to root out or destroy completely, *extirpate* comes from the Latin *ex* (out) and *stirps* (root).

eye service

A person who does *eye service* is working against his will and only when the eye of his employer is on him. The phrase appears in the Bible (Ephesians 6: 5): "Servants, be obedient to them that are your masters . . . not with eye service as men pleasers; but as the servants of Christ."

F

falderal, falderol, folderol

Falderal, falderol, folderol are variant spellings of the same word. Actually *falderal* is the oldest, though *folderol* is now more common, at least in this country.

The whole nonsense—for that's exactly what it is—started in British music halls early in the nineteenth century. Popular comic songs often had nonsense verses like our own "Hot Sut Ralston on the Rillerah" of World War II vintage. These nonsense verses were called *falderal* and the term eventually came to mean any form of nonsense.

fall dough

One of the many terms for undercover bribes to secure success of a project, *fall dough* is an older one for the more recently publicized payola. See also PAYOLA.

fall of woodchucks. *See* clowder, kindle and cowardice.

fallout, fallup

One of the most sinister of the words invented by our generation is *fallout*—to describe the minute particles of radioactive material dropping to earth after the explosion of an atomic or thermonuclear device. Now that we have all become accustomed to the ominous sound of *fallout,* the scientists have come up with a new one for us to ponder. It's *fallup*—contamination of ocean areas by the dumping of radioactive wastes.

false colors, to sail under. *See* sail under false colors.

familiarity breeds contempt

Many writers, including Shakespeare (*Merry Wives of Windsor,* Act I, Scene 1), have used this expression but the earliest recorded appearance is in the *Maxims* of Publius Syrus. Perhaps the most trenchant comment about this saying was made by Winston Churchill when he remarked: "Without a certain amount of familiarity, you will never breed anything."

fan

The word experts have been at work recently retracing the origin of *fan* in such phrases as *sports fan.* Most scholarly opinion for years regarded this as a shortened form of "fanatic." Now the theory is set forth that it may have come instead from "fancy," a now outmoded term for gentlemen who frequent prize fights. I am inclined to think that this comes closer to the true spirit of the *fan* as we know him today. While he is enthusiastic, he is not likely to be actually fanatical.

fantastic. *See* spectacular.

far from the madding crowd. *See* madding crowd, far from

fascism

Despite the fact that we fought our last full-scale war against foes labeled *Fascists,* it's unlikely that many of the Allies were aware of the fact that the enemy's name had its origin in one of Aesop's fables. It's true, though—for it all goes back to the fable in which Aesop showed that, while sticks could easily be broken one by one, they could not be broken if several were tied together in a bundle. The moral was, of course, "In union there is strength."

The Latin word for a bundle of sticks was *fasces* and such bundles were borne as symbols of authority by the lictors of ancient Rome. When Benito Mussolini marched on Rome in 1922, he appropriated the symbol so proudly borne two thousand years previously and named his followers *Fascists* and his form of dictatorship *Fascism.*

fashion talk

The operative word in the world of fashion (according to Eve Merriam, author of *Figleaf: The Business of Being in Fashion*) is "obsolescence." How fads are launched, the carefully plotted strategy behind seemingly spontaneous vogues, the deadly earnestness of manufacturers, wholesalers and retail merchants add up to what Miss Merriam calls "a seemingly illogical business—but only seemingly."

Here are a few choice items from her glossary of common terms as they are used in the world of fashion:

Adult—A grown-up customer (not to be confused with *adulterated,* a used-up consumer).

Basic—Noun, a simple black dress that costs more than $50.

Conversation—Compound word with *piece,* generally descriptive of a charm bracelet, mink-tailed can opener, or rhinestone-studded piggy bank.

Exclusive—A product offered to the broadest possible mass market.

Fun—A total state of being, as "the fun of being in fashion." Also an adjective: "A *fun* blouse, a *fun* hat, a *fun* fur."

Functional—A simple black dress that costs more than $100.

Mature—In whiskey a good thing; in humans, a taboo word.

Nothing—A black dress costing more than $200, as in "a little Nettie Rosenstein *nothing.*"

Permanent—A hair-curling device that may last several months.

Timeless—A style that remains fashionable more than one season.

Understated—A simple black dress that costs more than $300.

Wonderful—The most common adjective, denoting anything run-of-the-mill. Synonyms are: *terrific, amazing, sensational, fabulous, astounding, adorable, cunning, charming, lovable, slimming, slenderizing, thrilling.*

fatuous

Fatuous (pronounced FAT-choo-us) is useful in describing persons or actions which are asinine, silly or complacently stupid. (A person so described is guilty of *fatuity*). It can also mean empty or unreal. Its origin is the Latin *fatuus* (foolish). In its present form it carries a stronger meaning than simply foolish. "His *fatuous* behavior made me dislike him intensely."

fell. *See* swoop, one fell.

fenberry sauce

The cranberry sauce of the first Thanksgiving dinner in this country was undoubtedly called *fenberry sauce* at the time, since the cranberry was known in England as the fenberry and it was not until years later that the Dutch gave it the name of cranberry from their *kranbeere.*

ferninst

Coming from the relatively unexplored lexicon of Irish contributions to American folk speech, this word means "opposite, near or against." It is heard in such expressions as, "Put the table over *ferninst* the wall." In various other spellings—*fernent, forninst, fanent* and *fornent*—it was brought to America by the colonists from other parts of the British Isles, but *ferninst* seems to be the Irish form, brought over midway through the last century when Irish immigration was at its peak.

Sometimes *ferninst* is made into a noun as *ferninster,* meaning one who is chronically "agin" everything. Back in the early forties, William Allen White, the late, great Kansas editor, noted: "The trouble with the Republican leaders in Congress . . . is that they are just *ferninsters*."

fetid

Fetid (pronounced FET-id) means simply having a repulsive smell and comes from the Latin *fetidus* of the same meaning. It is used to describe the offensive odor of rotten matter.

fetish

A *fetish* originally was a sort of charm, often in the form of an inanimate object like a doll or statue, which primitive tribes believed possessed magical powers. *Fetish* is used, in a somewhat different context, by writers in the field of psychoanalysis and has gradually moved into the popular tongue in a broader meaning. However, *fetish* should still not be used except in the sense of something that is held in altogether unreasoning devotion or veneration. If a person is passionately devoted to an idea or an object, you may correctly say that he "makes a *fetish*" of it.

fey

What does the word *fey* mean to you? Slightly daft in a bright rather amusing way? Would you or wouldn't you speak of the *fey* wit of the lamented Kukla, Fran and Ollie? Or Pogo, for that matter?

All right now, look at your lexicons and see if you find this—as I see it, the most common—meaning of *fey* listed anywhere. What's wrong with the dictionaries anyway? The dictionaries that come first to hand enter two main meanings for *fey:* "doomed to death" and "under a spell"— neither of which is very close to the current meaning.

The *World Webster* comes fairly close with this: "in an unusually excited or gay state, formerly believed to portend sudden death." Drop off that last phrase and we would be getting a little closer to the popular meaning of *fey*.

So "who goofed?" Everybody and nobody. The dictionary editors, usually a conservative lot, are probably just getting around to *fey*. Look for it again in five years. You'll probably find the current meaning listed then.

Fido

Fido is indeed a noble name befitting man's most loyal friend, the dog. It comes from the Latin word *fidus,* meaning "faithful."

Fido is also the acronymic designation for a method of fog dispersal along airport runways (Fog Investigation Dispersal Operations).

fiesty, ficety, et al.

A correspondent asks: "I wonder if you can tell me the spelling, origin and meaning of a word that I have been using for almost fifty years. The word is *fiesty* or *fighsty* or some other spelling.

"To me its meaning is somewhat similar to that of the new word *spunky*—but not quite and so not at all the same. I think of a *fiesty* little man, a *fiesty* little boy, a *fiesty* little dog (rat terrier, for example), as one who is rather small in a wiry sort of way and exhibiting a good-natured, 'snappy' antagonism with a lot of nervous energy. The word brings a strong picture to my mind, but I've never heard anyone else use it, nor have I ever seen it in print. I spent a few years in Tennessee in my early childhood."

Were my correspondent to return to the hill country of Tennessee, I'm sure that even today she would hear her favorite word. She might also encounter it—as I first did—in Missouri or in many other parts of the Midwest and South. Her definition is quite a good one and her spelling is one of many variations recorded by students of American dialect terms.

My good friend, Harold Wentworth, whose *American Dialect Dictionary* is one of the landmarks of this country's language research, lists seven possible spellings: *ficety, feisty, fisty, fysty, fiesty, feesty* and *fausty*. Originally the word came from "fice," a small, snappy dog or, as one Eastern Tennessean wrote in 1902: "A *feist* is one o' them little bitty dogs that ginerally runs on three legs and pretends a whole lot."

The same Tennessean also defined the adjective *feisty* this way: "*Feisty* means when a feller's allers wigglin' about, wantin' ever-body to see him, like a kid when the preacher comes." A less colorful but more comprehensive definition comes from H. B. Allen, who reported that of sixty-four natives of southern Illinois interviewed, fifty-one knew the word and gave the following synonyms for it: angry, pestiferous, teasing, spunky, peevish, snippy, lively, peppy, catty, quarrelsome, cantankerous, touchy, restless, fidgety, playful and stubborn. So you see, *feisty*—no matter how you spell it—is one of the most colorful and versatile of our native dialect words.

FIFO. *See* LIFO, FIFO.

fifth column

Ernest Hemingway deserves credit for having established *fifth column* as a term for secret subversives working within a country. The phrase was first uttered by General Mola, who said, during the Spanish Civil War, that he was commanding five columns in the assault on Madrid, four converging on the city from various directions "and the fifth column within the city." But it was Hemingway's use of the phrase in a play called *The Fifth Column* that established it permanently in our language.

filibuster

Surprisingly enough, *filibuster* was originally a Dutch term and had nothing whatever to do with organized government. Indeed, it originally meant "freebooting"—the practice of private citizens engaging in warfare against a state with whom their country is at peace, usually for personal gain.

The Dutch word *vrijbuiter* literally meant freebooter or pirate, and its derivative *filibuster* was first used in this country during the 1850's to describe adventurers who were running guns to revolutionists in Cuba and other Central and South American countries. This kind of *filibustering* still continues. However, the term *filibustering* has become so completely identified with delaying tactics in the Senate that the word is not used for gun-running or piracy any more.

The first use of *filibuster* to describe obstruction of legislation by invoking parliamentary delays and resorting to prolonged speechmaking appeared in 1853, when one member of Congress sharply criticized the tactics of his rivals as *"filibustering* against the United States."

The word grew in popularity and, by 1890, was so well established that the *Congressional Record* used it, noting that "a *filibuster* was indulged in which lasted nine calendar days." That record has since been broken, of course.

filthy lucre

The common expression *filthy lucre* usually brings forth two theories as to its origin: one that it obviously means "dirty bills"; another that it's just a figurative expression, indicating that money is the root of all evil.

Theory Number 2 is closer to the truth—and not just because the expression originated before paper money was known, either. It comes from the New Testament (I Timothy 3:2–3), in which the qualifications of a bishop are set forth: "A bishop then must be blameless . . . of good behavior, given to hospitality, apt to teach; not given to wine, no striker, not greedy of *filthy lucre*." The word "filthy" in the Biblical sense means "dishonorable," rather than dirty or unclean. So *filthy lucre* really means "dishonorable gain."

However, the expression is seldom used seriously today. Instead it is —as the dictionaries say—a "humorously derogatory" phrase.

finalize

President Kennedy's use of *finalize* prompted some casual comments to the effect that this unnecessary coinage must now be deemed a proper part of our language. Such suggestions betray a basic ignorance of our language and the way it grows.

No one person—not even the President—can establish a word as an item of correct usage by favoring it with his mark of approval. The first of the Presidential Roosevelts—Theodore—learned this to his sorrow when he undertook to simplify American spelling. With his enthusiastic approval, all sorts of bizarre spellings—*fonograf, filosofer* and other examples of *fonetic* spelling—were approved for use in official government publications. But the public blithely ignored T.R.'s preachments and he learned a fundamental truth: you can't legislate changes in language.

The basic reason why *finalize* is not likely to find a lasting niche in our language is that it is wholly unnecessary. It says nothing that "end," "complete," "terminate," "finish," "stop" or "close" doesn't say equally well.

Finalize actually started as advertising agency slang just after World War II. In the parlance of Madison Avenue, an account executive could *finalize* an advertising campaign but it remained for the client's approval to concretize it.

Now it has been taken up by the bureaucrats, who will do it to death, and in a few years *finalize* will be a nostalgic memory like the *boondoggle* of Franklin Roosevelt's day or the *normalcy* of Harding's.

Already the evidence is at hand that Washington's men of destiny are moving on to wider linguistic horizons. The head of the now happily renamed "Dynasoar" missile program spoke of improved *capabilities* as projects now in work become more *definitized!*

Still another theory as to the meaning of *finalize* was advanced by a reader of my newspaper column.

"It's very seldom that I find the opportunity to disagree with you," wrote Air Force Captain Richard C. Hicks from Omaha. "Your comments on the word *finalize* give me that opportunity. The synonyms you list (complete, terminate, finish, stop and close) simply do not fit the meaning conveyed by *finalize*.

"The word, at least as it's used in the U. S. Air Force, means 'to perform those actions necessary to assure completion.' When a superior officer directs a junior officer to finalize, the junior performs the tasks so that the senior may end, complete, terminate, finish, stop or close. The staff officer *finalizes* so that the commander may complete."

Weeeell, that's a new slant on this much discussed verb. It's apparently fairly new to the Air Force too, because the really excellent *Air Force Dictionary,* published in 1956, seems unaware that *finalize* means taking steps necessary to but just short of completion of an action. This dictionary defines *finalize* as "to bring an action to a close; to finish a report, plan or the like." It also lists the word as "cant," which is not a pejorative word as used here; it merely means that this word is part of the special jargon of the service.

If *finalize* is to acquire the meaning that Captain Hicks says it already has, at least in his area of the Air Force, I can have no objections. As I have often said, no one can legislative language and many words have changed their meanings with the passage of time. It seems unfortunate, though, that a word whose every connotation is one of finality, of "ending" something, now seems to be used to designate all steps short of ending.

fine Italian hand

This term is used to indicate the accomplishment of one's ambitions by devious, subtle and slightly disreputable techniques. But it is by no means always used in this derogatory sense. Many times the person using it is confessing a certain grudging admiration for the results obtained.

In truth, the origin of the phrase seems to have been of the highest and holiest. During the Middle Ages, papal secretaries used a type of handwriting—technically known as *cancelleresca*—that was easily distinguishable by its delicacy and grace from the cruder Gothic styles of Northern Europe. Hence the *Italian hand* was one noted for its finesse.

fink. *See* labor's lost lexicon.

fireman. *See* baseball jargon.

first-day cover. *See* philatelic jargon.

fishybacking

The practice of transporting loaded truck trailers by boat is called *fishybacking*. See also BIRDIEBACKING.

flabbergast

Flabbergast (pronounced FLAB-er-gast) means, of course, to astonish or make speechless, especially by an unusual remark. The origin of this splendid and expressive word seems to have escaped the language experts, though the Funk & Wagnalls *Unabridged* speculates that it may be a combination of *flabby* or *flap* and *aghast*.

flack

Flack is a slang term common in the theatrical and popular music fields, meaning "press agent." I have been familiar with it in this sense for about fifteen years and suspect it antedates the World War II meaning of *flak,* that of antiaircraft fire (*q.v.*). However, it has never enjoyed the wide popular acceptance given, for example, to the term *disc jockey,* which became current in entertainment circles at about the same time. Perhaps the word is just too blunt and unlovely to find favor among practitioners of the fine art of "space grabbing." The best of them even frown on the term "press agent." Nowadays they are "public relations consultants."

flag down, to

You often hear the expression *"flag down* a cab"—even though it simply means waving one's hand to attract the driver's attention so he'll stop. Originally this expression came from the vocabulary of automobile racing, where the officials signal to the winner that the race is over by waving a flag up and down. This signal is also sometimes used to signal other drivers that they should stop or proceed with caution.

flagstone

There's no connection between *flagstones* and patriotic flags. Actually the *flag* in *flagstone* comes directly from the Norse word *flaga,* meaning "flake." A true *flagstone* is a hard stone split ("flaked") into flat pieces for use as paving.

flak

In World War II *flak* was the generally used British term for antiaircraft fire. It was borrowed from the German *flak,* an abbreviation of *fliegerab-wehrkanone,* "antiaircraft cannon." The word was used earlier by combat fliers in World War I as a part of the jargon or private language of the air arm of the services. If memory serves, there was little need for ordinary civilians to use a word descriptive of antiaircraft fire for, with the exception of a few zeppelin raids on London, the man in the street saw nothing of air attack in that war. By the start of World War II, though, the situation was radically different and the sudden appearance of *flak* in 1940 was merely the emergence into the popular tongue of a word first used a quarter-century earlier in service slang.

flap

In Washington, *flap* has pretty well replaced *hassle* as the slang term used to describe a lively argument, especially one about an important matter. A bureau chief can—and often does—*stir up a flap* by calling a few subordinates on the carpet for an inquiry into methods and procedures of operation. But a truly monumental *flap* can develop when two departments become involved in a struggle to take over some newly defined area of government authority. For fairly obvious reasons, the Pentagon is sometimes nicknamed *The Five-Sided Flaphouse.*

flapper

According to H. L. Mencken, *flapper* was in use in England during the 1890's to describe a young woman who, in the euphemism of the period, "was no better than she should be." By 1910 the word was common in this country, but without any derogatory implications. In America a *flapper* has always been a giddy, attractive and slightly unconventional young thing who, in Mencken's words, "was a somewhat foolish girl, full of wild surmises and inclined to revolt against the precepts and admonitions of her elders."

The *flapper* was also noted for her revolt against conventions of dress. *Flappers* of the twenties used to delight in wearing their overshoes ("galoshes" they were sometimes called) with the hooks unfastened, so that each boot would "flap" against the other as the pretty thing made her way down the street. The practice sounds clumsy and noisy—and it was. But it was also attention-getting and no pretty young lass, in the *flapper* period or since, ever objected to attention.

flash in the pan

The phrase *flash in the pan* is generally thought to have originated in the days of flintlock muskets. Just as an ineffective flash of the primer in the pan of the musket would result in no explosion of the charge, so a person who failed to live up to his early promise came to be known as a *flash in the pan.*

There are those who subscribe to the following theory: The early miners in California and the Yukon originated *flash in the pan* to describe their experiences in "panning" gold in the streams. The *flash* meant that some was there. The later expression, "It didn't pan out," meant it wasn't worth the work. The expression "It didn't pan out" is still heard describing a venture that didn't pay. *Flash in the pan* means "showed promise—doesn't work out well."

At first glance, that seems plausible enough—especially since it's perfectly true that the phrase "didn't pan out" originated with miners panning for gold. However, though they undoubtedly used the expression *flash in the pan,* it was not original with them. The flintlock rifle, you see, had been in common use since the seventeenth century—many, many years before gold miners reached California or the Yukon—and the phrase *flash in the pan* was firmly established in our language long before the first sourdough shook a pan of gravel searching for the elusive flash that would signify gold.

flat

Flat comes from the Anglo-Saxon "flat," meaning ground or floor. In England it designates any suite of rooms on a single floor. In America the word is now little used but formerly it meant a single-floor lodging in an unpretentious or "tenement" building. See also PIED-À-TERRE.

flautist, flutist

In years past among symphony musicians the term *flautist* (pronounced FLAWT-ist) has been more commonly heard, though today the simpler *flutist* would surely be the layman's preference and probably the musician's as well. *Flautist,* like so many terms in the musical vocabulary, comes from an Italian word *flautista,* meaning one who plays a *flauto* or "flute."

During the years when European conductors and artists dominated our musical life—with Caruso, Schumann-Heink, Melba and Martinelli heading the top rank of singers, and Koussevitsky, Toscanini and Stokowski among the foremost symphony conductors—European influences were understandably strong on our musical vocabulary. Thus the form *flautist,* being more nearly akin to the Italian form, was more widely used. One hazards the guess that your local paper would have preferred *flautist* a quarter of a century ago.

Today, though a few of the old figures remain, there is a much more American cast to the musical scene. The literature of our symphonic heritage is increasingly enriched by the contributions of Copland, Ives, Thomson and others of our native-born composers, while American instrumentalists have won world renown.

So it is really not surprising that, as Americans come more and more to dominate the musical life of their own country, their genius for simplification becomes noticeable in the terms they use—*flutist* for *flautist,* and *double bass* for *contrabass,* to note only two examples.

flip. *See* jazzmen's jargon.

flock of sheep. *See* clowder, kindle and cowardice.

flotsam and jetsam

The word *flotsam* is used in maritime law to describe goods swept from a vessel and found floating in the sea. *Jetsam* refers to cargo deliberately thrown overboard (or *jettisoned*) from a ship when it is in imminent danger of wreck, especially goods which sink and remain under water. *Flotsam and jetsam* is often loosely used to refer to wreckage either floating or washed up on shore.

flower names

Many flowers, not surprisingly, have taken their names from the men who first developed the species. *Begonias* are named after an eighteenth-century French botanist, Michel Begon; *magnolias* from Pierre Magnol, a near-contemporary of Begon; *gardenias* from the appropriately named Alexander Garden, an American; and *dahlias* are named after A. Dahl, a Swedish botanist. See also CAMELLIA, FUCHSIA, WISTERIA.

fly

A *fly* in the days of Sherlock Holmes was the British equivalent of the Oriental jinricksha, designed for quick passage from place to place in the British seaside resort of Brighton. Later, according to the *Oxford Dictionary*, the name "was extended to any one-horse covered carriage, as a cab or hansom, let out on hire."

fly off the handle

Flying off the handle implies a sudden wild outburst of wrath—much more than simply getting angry. It suggests the kind of trouble that would result if an ax-head flew off its handle.

folderol. *See* falderal.

food from the opera

Perhaps the most famous dish to bear the name of an operatic diva is *Chicken Tetrazzini,* named after Luisa Tetrazzini, whose Lucia di Lammermoor thrilled opera lovers throughout Europe and North and South America during the early decades of this century. As might be expected of an Italian-born singer, her favorite dish contains *pasta*—specifically, thin spaghetti—chicken and a rich cheese-and-mushroom sauce. Delicious—but not for anyone counting calories!

Madame Tetrazzini, of course, was not one to worry about the caloric content of her food. When I saw her on her last tour of America—she was well into her sixties—the magnificent voice was the palest echo of its one-time brilliance but the figure was, simply, enormous. Many hours of devotion to the dish named in her honor were evident in her tremendous girth —and she acted as though she had enjoyed every minute of the time spent at the table.

The greatest tenor of our era, Enrico Caruso, was also one of the notable gourmands of his time. He has left us *Sauce Caruso,* which is marinara sauce, with sautéed mushrooms and chicken livers added. Characteristically again, this is designed for service with spaghetti.

And, topping off the menu, we have *Peach Melba,* named after the great Australian soprano, Dame Nellie Melba. This concoction involves peach halves, vanilla ice cream and a sauce of currants and raspberries.

foof

Do you number any *foofs* among your circle of acquaintances? Before you jump to a hasty conclusion and aver that you wouldn't be caught dead talking to a *foof,* perhaps you'd better find out what they are.

A *foof* is a member of an informal fraternity of Friends Of Old Films. They scorn Rock Hudson, Diana Dors and Anita Ekberg. For a faithful *foof* there have been no great movies since the days of Richard Barthelmess, Norma Talmadge and—of course—Garbo.

In all seriousness, there is such a group in New York City and they have a special schedule of Saturday morning screenings of cinema classics at the Museum of Modern Art. Similar groups are reported forming in other parts of the country.

foolscap

Foolscap is a term used to designate stationery measuring from 12 by 15 inches up to 13½ by 17 inches. The most common size is 13 by 16 inches, which is often folded to make pages of 8 by 13 inches. Originally it was a printing paper used in England and got its name from the ancient watermark of a fool's head and cap used to identify the paper. The earliest specimens of paper using the *foolscap* watermark date back to before the time of Shakespeare.

foopah, faux pas, foxpaw

Foopah is a dialect version of *faux pas* (false step), a term we have borrowed from French to indicate a blunder or error, particularly in etiquette. In some parts of the country another dialect variation, *foxpaw,* is heard.

forcemeat

A term at least as interesting to a word expert as to a master cook, *forcemeat,* believe it or not, comes from the same root as the dramatic term *farce* and both originally meant the same thing—"stuffing."

During the Middle Ages it was the custom of acting companies to insert a brief, rowdy and highly comic interlude between the acts of the main drama. These short pieces were figuratively "stuffed" between sections of the performance and so were called *farces* from the French word for stuffing.

Farcemeat—finely chopped and seasoned meat or fish used as stuffing —in the course of time came to be *forcemeat,* possibly through confusion with the totally unrelated word *force*—since, as anyone who has stuffed a twenty-pound turkey knows, a certain amount of *force* is involved in the operation.

Nowadays a *forcemeat* stuffing is occasionally encountered, especially among items from the *haute cuisine* like *"chaud-froid* of boned chicken" —a dish which the average housewife would have neither the energy nor the patience to prepare. But *forcemeat* balls as garnish for soups rank among the true culinary delights. So you see, there's really nothing *farcical* about *forcemeat*.

forecastle

Forecastle comes from medieval naval warfare. It was customary then to build up the fore part of a fighting ship with a battlement similar to those found in castles. The idea was to dominate the enemy's deck, so that your bows, guns and what not could shoot down on him.

Speaking from personal experience of not too many years ago, I can assure you that, though the crew's living quarters have improved greatly in the past thirty years or so, they are still far from "castles."

forgotten man, the

While Franklin D. Roosevelt was surely the person who made this phrase popular, he was not the first to use it. Back in 1883 Professor William Graham Sumner, of Yale University, used it in a speech. What he said—and the words still ring true today—was: "Such is *the forgotten man*. He works, he votes, generally he prays—but he always pays."

fortnight

The *fort* in *fortnight* is simply a contraction of "fourteen"—and who first abbreviated "fourteen nights" that way is not known to history. Anyhow it must have been many centuries ago, for the terms *fortnight* (two weeks) and *sennight* ("seven nights" or one week) are at least as old as written English. Indeed, they are thought to have been borrowed from the ancient German method of measuring time by counting nights rather than days.

Sennight is now obsolete throughout the English-speaking world, but *fortnight,* while something of an affectation, continues to be heard in America and is very common in England. There, indeed, a two weeks' vacation is commonly referred to as a *"fortnight's* holiday."

fourth estate, the

The term *the fourth estate* is commonly used to refer to newspapermen. Indeed, it is the subtitle of the trade journal of the newspaper business, *Editor & Publisher. The fourth estate* gets its name from a famous remark of Sir Edmund Burke in the British Parliament. He noted the various estates of the realm: the Lords Spiritual, the Lords Temporal and the Commons—the powers that hold in their hands the control of British governments. Then Burke added, pointing to the press gallery, "And yonder sits the *Fourth Estate,* more important than them all."

frantically, franticly

A correspondent writes: "If I read you correctly, you concede that, on dictionary evidence, *franticly* may be correct as the adverbial form of *frantic,* but *frantically* is preferred. Mind answering a rebel's 'Why?' I don't like *frantically* and would never have thought of using it nor, to be truthful, would I have ever thought it correct before seeing it in your article. I've known people who were *frantic* but would never have called them *frantical.* As a friend of mine says about the income tax: 'It may be correct—but it ain't right!' "

My answer is that, though the case for *franticly* may be logical, it isn't correct. The dictionaries, it's true, admit *franticly* as an acceptable spelling, but always as the second choice, with *frantically* preferred. Several of the word books label *franticly* as "rare."

Frantic, as it happens, comes from the Greek *phrenitikos,* meaning a suffering caused by inflammation of the brain. Let's not add further to the brain fag of writer and reader alike, to say nothing of the typesetters and proofreaders who surely must be *frantically* seeking the end of this entry. And here it is.

frappé, frosted

This American language of ours is really many languages—and this fact is nowhere more evident than in the area of slang and the colloquial idiom. Scholars have devoted years of research to the attempt to track down and codify in book form the various slang languages of America and occasionally, especially in *The American Thesaurus of Slang* by Van den Bark and Berry, have done a very creditable job of it. But such research is never complete or completely satisfactory because it is part of the American genius to be everlastingly creating new words—even when perfectly good words for the same thing already exist in other parts of our nation.

So it is with *frappé* (Boston) and *frosted* (New York), the self-same drink with different names—merely a milk shake with ice cream added before the mixture is blended. But a *frappé* in some places (a scoop of ice cream with chocolate syrup over it) is called in other places a "sundae" or maybe a "college ice." So even the lexicon of soda jerkers has its infinite variety.

free lance

Free lance is a term that goes back to medieval times. Originally it referred to the so-called free companies, both Italian and French, of mercenary soldiers who were willing to serve under any banner—for a price. The word *free* has no reference to the rates they charged; it merely means that they were free of loyalty to any one standard and were free to fight for whoever paid the best fee. (Change "fight" to "write" in that sentence and you have a pretty fair definition of today's *free-lancer.*) Since this newer meaning of a writer or artist who places his talents at the service of many employers has completely replaced the older military meaning of the word, this could be evidence that the pen really is mightier than the sword.

friends—enemies

A current witticism runs: "With a friend like you, who needs enemies?" This notion has been commonplace for centuries. When leaving Louis XIV, Maréchal Villars is supposed to have said: "Defend me from my friends; I can defend myself from my enemies." And George Canning wrote:

> Give me the avowed, the erect, the manly foe,
> Bold I can meet—perhaps may turn his blow!
> But of all plagues, Good Heaven, thy wrath can send,
> Save, save, Oh, save me from the candid friend!

frieze, frise

Here are two kinds of fabrics very similarly named. *Frieze* (pronounced FREEZ) is correctly used to designate a heavy wool cloth with an uncut, shaggy nap on one side. It is generally used as an overcoat material. The cloth is believed to have originated in Friesland, Holland, where it got its name.

The upholstery fabric, however, is correctly spelled *frise* and, in its original French form, had an acute accent on the final *e*—thereby calling for the pronunciation free-ZAY. *Frise,* which comes from the French word *friser* (to curl), is a fabric with a thick pile made of uncut loops or a combination of cut and uncut loops.

fringe

While the American miss may have her hair cut with bangs across the forehead, the same haircut is, to the British, one with fringe. See also ENGLISH ENGLISH.

fruit salad

As a slang term, *fruit salad* is used to describe the collection of service and combat ribbons worn on the chest of military personnel.

fuchsia

Fuchsia takes its name from Leonhard Fuchs, a sixteenth-century German botanist.

funny bone

Actually what causes that painful, tingling sensation when you bump your *funny bone* is the impact not on any bone but on the ulnar nerve. However, the term *funny bone* has been part of the language for many a long year and is apparently here to stay. It results from a rather learned pun on the name for the bone running from the shoulder to the elbow, the humerus. Humerus—humorous. Get it?

I agree the joke is rather less than howlingly funny. But standards of humor in the early nineteenth century were very different from those of today and the bearded pre-Victorian medical student who coined *funny bone* was doubtless considered a truly topping wit—a veritable Bob Hope of the stethoscope set.

furtive

Furtive (pronounced FUR-tiv), with its meaning of "stealthy" or "sly," is another of the many words derived from Latin. From *furtum* (theft), the Romans made *furtivus* (stolen or hidden) and it was the latter meaning that carried over to English. Thus a *furtive* movement is one which the maker tries to conceal; a *furtive* glance is one stolen with the hope of not being seen. As an adverb it becomes *furtively* and as a noun, *furtiveness*.

fuzz

Fuzz is underworld slang for "policeman" or "the law" in any of its guises. It is a comparatively recent addition to the argot of crime and probably originated in the secret language of narcotics addicts and pushers. *Fuzz*, most likely, is a corruption of "Feds," referring to agents of the Federal Narcotics Bureau.

G

gabardine, gaberdine

The spelling *gabardine* is preferred to *gaberdine* for the twilled fabric widely used in the making of suits and topcoats. Indeed, it is the only spelling accepted by George Linton's authoritative *Modern Textile Dictionary*.

During the Middle Ages, Jewish merchants wore a loose-fitting coat or cloak called a "gaberdine." Shylock refers to his costume by this name in *The Merchant of Venice*. The same sort of garment was worn by wanderers and pilgrims. Indeed, the word originally came from the Old High German word *walvart* (pilgrimage) via the Old French *gauvardine*.

Although the *er* spelling for the second syllable is still acceptable in England for both the historical meaning of "loose cloak" and the present-day meaning of "twilled fabric," American authorities generally agree that the *er* spelling, if used at all, should be restricted to the historical sense of the word.

gadget

No one knows for certain where *gadget* began, but it has been in the language for nearly eighty years and was popularized by sailors. It means, of course, any small mechanical device, particularly one whose precise name escapes the speaker. Originally it was a sort of seagoing equivalent of the landlubber's *thingamajig* or *doodad*. It has long since been an accepted part of the landman's vocabulary, though, sharing honors with *doohickey* and World War II's *gismo*.

One theory of the origin of *gadget* is that it is an engineer's corruption of the now obsolete Scottish word *gadge*, a variant of "gauge," the measuring device. Still another possible origin is in the French word *gachette*, meaning a catch or staple. Take your choice.

gaggle of geese. *See* clowder, kindle and cowardice.

gallery gods. *See* peanut gallery.

galore

In English we are accustomed to thinking of adjectives as preceding the nouns they modify, though there are many instances (notably predicate adjectives) where they follow. Some adjectives are regularly placed "post-positively," as grammarians say. For example, "court-martial." These usually follow the French pattern. But *galore* (as in "He makes mistakes *galore*") comes from Gaelic. Perhaps the word order follows that of the original Gaelic but, as a non-Gaelic speaking descendant of the Old Sod, I can only hazard a guess.

galoshes

Galoshes—which sound like an item from hillbilly dialect—actually come direct from the royal courts of the French monarchs. In the days when shoes were made of silk and other kinds of cloth, *galoches,* which were a sort of wooden sandal, were worn to protect the shoes on wet days. Over the centuries these wooden clogs were transmuted into the rubber overshoes we know as *galoshes* today.

gang of elk. *See* clowder, kindle and cowardice.

gardenia. *See* flower names.

Garrison finish

The Garrison of *Garrison finish* was jockey Edward H. Garrison, usually called "Snapper" Garrison. He left the turf before the start of the twentieth century but, in the days when Diamond Jim Brady was living high on the hog, the Snapper was one of America's folk heroes. It was his almost invariable practice to hold his horse far back in the pack, moving up with a rush only when entering the home stretch. Since most of his races were won in the last furlong, the *Garrison finish* became part of the American sporting language.

gas. *See* jazzmen's jargon.

gastrosoph

Many times items from newspapers seem to require explanation or correction. For example, this bit comes from the writings of one of our most heralded cooking authorities: "One could buy a whole meal from this appetizer corner [she's talking about a supermarket], a Gargantuan meal. Being a *gastrosoph,* we didn't eat again until several days later."

A *gastrosoph* (from the Greek *gaster,* meaning "stomach," and *sophos,* "wise") has precisely the same meaning as *gastronome*—one who is fond of good eating. *Gastrosoph* is, however, much less frequently seen in print and it is my guess that the cooking expert used it deliberately to pique the curiosity of her readers. If you want similarly to intrigue your friends, the word is pronounced GAS-truh-sof.

gauche

Gauche (pronounced GOHSH) means "graceless, tactless or socially awkward." In French, from which the word comes directly, *gauche* means simply "left."

Here we have an example of the way our language seems always to discriminate against left-handed people. Have you ever noticed that *dextrous* (from the Latin *dexter,* meaning "right") and *adroit* (from the French *droit,* also meaning "right") both have the connotation of skillfulness and cleverness, while the "left-handed" words like *sinister* (from the identical Latin word for "left") and *gauche,* which we discussed above, have derogatory implications? Even the word *gawky* originally came from a dialect phrase *gawk-handed* meaning left-handed.

gazebo

"He's a big *gazebo*," back in New England of the 1920's, was as common as "He's a wheel" or "He's a real operator" on college campuses of a later day. However, the dictionaries give only this definition: "a summerhouse . . . a projecting window or balcony."

Just how a rather high-flown word like *gazebo,* which is believed to have been formed from the word *gaze* in pretentious imitation of a Latin form, could have come to mean "guy" or "chap" is a minor linguistic mystery. In the process, of course, the pronunciation was altered from guh-ZEE-boh to guh-ZAY-boh and the word dropped from proper usage to colloquial or slang use.

Gemini. *See* Project Gemini.

gendarme

In France, a *gendarme* is a policeman. Originally a *gendarme* was *gens d'arme* and, in medieval French armies, ranked just below a knight in the line of chivalric honor.

geomorphologist

Your editor is fortunate in numbering among his friends a number of specialists in different areas of knowledge—men and women to whom he can refer questions requiring special technical knowledge. Recently the word *geomorphologist* cropped up, so I asked Harold Fahy, map editor for the *Grolier Encyclopedia* people, how he would define it. His reply seemed to me a masterpiece of careless erudition: *"Geomorphologist,"* said Harold, "is just a fancy way of saying 'physiographer.' " A physiographer is defined as "a person who studies the features and nature of the earth's surface, atmosphere and climate with special reference to the distribution of plant and animal life."

Geronimo

From the earliest wars in recorded history, men have plunged into battle shouting battle cries. Indeed, our common word "slogan" was origi-nally the Gaelic *sluggh-ghairm,* meaning the call to battle used by Scottish Highlanders and Irish clans. The newest, and one of the most interesting, of these cries is the one used by the U.S. airborne paratroopers: *"Geronimo!"*

Recently we speculated in print on why our soldiers should use the name of a dead Apache chieftain for their slogan and several alumni of the airborne regiments reported various stories of its origin. A plausible one came from Arthur A. Manion of Mount Lebanon, Pennsylvania. "At Fort Sill, Oklahoma," he wrote, "a series of rather steep hills called, I believe, Medicine Bluffs, was pointed out to all new arrivals. It was said that one day Geronimo, with the army in hot pursuit, made a leap on horseback down an almost vertical cliff—a feat that the posse could not duplicate. The legend continues that in the midst of this jump to freedom he gave out the blood-curdling cry of 'Geronimo-o-o!' Hence the practice adopted by our paratroopers. I hope this helps. It's at least colorful, if not authentic."

Another correspondent, Mrs. Elizabeth Windsor, who once lived at Fort Sill while her husband was stationed there, added the useful infor-mation that the bluff from which Geronimo made his daring leap "is a cliff overlooking a small river (at least, it was small when we were there)." So we know that Geronimo and his steed had water, rather than desert floor, to break their fall.

Now this is indeed an interesting tale and one that may very well be the real inspiration for the paratroopers' shout. But one niggling uncertainty remains. Fort Sill was at the time the Army's Field Artillery and Guided Missile School. Paratroopers were trained at Forts Bragg and Campbell. Why, then, did they reach to Fort Sill for inspiration for their battle cry?

R. Collier of Milwaukee offered a less glamorous but probably more accurate account of the origin of the call. "In the early days of the 82nd Airborne," he wrote, "the men used to go to the nearby movie in Lafayette-ville. During the week scheduled for the division's initial jumps, they saw a movie named *Geronimo.* (If that wasn't the title, at least the Indian chief played a leading part.) Anyway, one guy hollered the name and one of those things no one can explain happened. The whole division took it up and from them it spread to the later-activated airborne forces."

And why do they shout anything? Well, Mrs. B. Berns, also of Milwaukee, had a theory about that—and, again, it ties in nicely with our Indian brave. "According to my encyclopedia," she wrote, "Geronimo's Indian name was Goyathlay—One Who Yawns. I am under the impression that yawning is nature's way of assisting the shallow breather. Deep breathing is requisite to the paratrooper and drawing in breath for the shout automatically eliminates any possibility that he may forget to breathe deeply."

Well, those are the theories. Take your choice but, whatever you do when you jump—*Geronimo-o-o-o.*

gerrymander. *See* candidate.

gesundheit

The common cold takes much of our time, energy and patience. Excepting only the vendors of nose drops and tissues, it seems that nobody can be found who will say a good word for colds.

And yet that is not entirely true, for one has only to sneeze in a public place and, almost invariably, someone will murmur "God bless you" or *"Gesundheit."* The speaker may be a friend or a complete stranger but you would be an ingrate indeed if you didn't feel a momentary twinge of gratitude for these kind words.

Have you ever wondered about where and when this custom began? Well, nobody knows for sure. Certainly the ancient Greeks and Romans uttered very similar expressions. It is recorded that whenever he heard one of his followers sneeze, the Roman Emperor Tiberius would say, *"Absit omen"* ("Let any omen or mischance be absent"), which is a rather backhanded way of saying "Good luck!"

The almost universal use of such phrases probably stems from the plague years of the Middle Ages. A sneeze was regarded as a probable indication that the sneezer had contracted the plague and thus was certainly in need of divine help.

Gesundheit (pronounced geh-ZOONDT-hite) is the German word for "health" and, as a matter of fact, is often used as a toast (like *prosit, skoal* and "your good health") as well as in benediction to one who has just sneezed.

Incidentally, the gravity with which sneezing was regarded by our forebears is indicated by the colloquial phrase, "Not to be sneezed at"—meaning something to be taken seriously.

ghost, to give up the

This expression—meaning "to die" or, in colloquial use, "to surrender" —derives simply from the belief that life exists independent of our mortal bodies and that, when death comes, the *ghost* or soul leaves the body and lives on. The phrase is at least as old as the King James version of the Bible where (Job 14:10) we find: "Man dieth, and wasteth away; yea, man giveth up the *ghost,* and where is he?"

Gidget

A fictional heroine known as *Gidget* seems likely to figure in as many cinematic adventures as did the Andy Hardy of old. Her name, according to the novelist who created her, is what linguists call a "blend" or "portmanteau" word. It's made up of "girl" and "midget"—or so, at least, the author thought.

But a note from "Old Salt," San Diego, California, protested: "Your arm of philology doesn't reach back far enough. Although today *gidget* apparently has the new meaning of which you spoke, any WW II sailor can tell you that back then a *gidget* was whatever wasn't a *gismo*. And if you were to ask a sailor the definition of a *gismo,* he'd reply, 'It's a *gidget* for a *gadget.*' I myself used the word many times."

It happens that I spent a couple of years at sea in World War II myself, without ever running on the word *gidget*. Of course, radio and communications officers were scarcely regarded as human beings, let alone "sailors," so that may be part of the reason why I didn't hear the word at that time. Perhaps, too, the fact that my service was all in the Atlantic and Mediterranean areas, while Old Salt's seems to have been in the Pacific, might have something to do with it.

Anyway, it was a great war for amateurs. They really won it, you know, and if they weren't always sure of the precise name for a dingus—well, *gidget, gadget, gismo* or *doohickey* usually filled the bill. The *dingbat* was attached to the what-you-may-call-it. It usually worked—and another blow was struck for freedom. See also GISMO.

gig. *See* jazzmen's jargon.

gimmick

This word comes to us from the slang of carnival midways. The first *gimmicks* were hidden devices by which a carny confidence man or *grifter* could control the stopping point of the wheel of chance. Magicians were next to take up the word. For them a *gimmick* was any small device used secretly in the course of an illusion. Then, about 1930, the word passed into our general language and came to mean any clever device or gadget.

There are two theories of its origin. One is that it comes from the German word *gemach,* literally meaning a "convenience." The other, and the one I'm inclined to favor, is that it's simply an altered form of *gimcrack* —a term long associated with carnivals and circuses to mean any showy but useless object.

gin

Gin originally was *Geneva.* However, this *Geneva* or *genever* as it was often spelled, had nothing to do with the Swiss city. It was the British translation of the French *genièvre,* meaning "juniper." As all veterans of the Prohibition era will recall, essence of juniper—"juniper juice," it was commonly called—was widely regarded as an essential ingredient of bathtub gin. Probably few concocters of that foul potion realized, as they added juniper juice drop by drop, that they were putting in the ingredient from which the drink itself got its name.

Mr. T. F. Warffemius from the admirably appropriate town of Brandywine, Maryland, added this to my information on the subject: "Probably you would like to know that the Dutch name for the gin flavored with the juniper berry is *Genever* pronounced jeh-NAY-ver." Thus he supplied the link between the original French word for juniper and the name which the British, by folk etymology, converted first to *Geneva* and then to *gin.*

One may also notice in liquor ads a remarkable bottle-shaped earthenware jug bearing the legend "Bols Holland Genever Gin" and the further information that "Our firm was founded in 1575 and has been advantageously known all over the world since." The *Oxford Dictionary* notes that the word "Geneva" or "Hollands Geneva" was first recorded in England in 1706, indicating that it took somewhat longer than a century for the product to become "advantageously known" across the channel in England. However, the first use of *gin* is listed for 1714, indicating that once the British discovered the liquor, they lost no time in making it their own by giving it the distinctive name it has borne to this day.

Incidentally, the cotton-cleaning machine which Eli Whitney invented takes its name, *gin,* from a Middle English contraction of the Old French *engin,* meaning a mechanical contrivance.

gismo

There are many theories of the origin of this handy word which the GI used to designate any kind of gadget or "what-you-may-call-it." Perhaps the likeliest explanation was given by George Yost, Jr., writing in *American Speech* magazine. Yost thinks it comes from a common Arabic phrase

shu ismo which has the same meaning. And where did our GI's pick it up?
In Moroccan bazaars during the North African campaign. See also GIDGET.

give the hook. *See* hook, give the.

give up the ghost. *See* ghost, to give up the.

Glaswegian. *See* Liverpudlian.

glove money

Glove money, simply put, means a bribe. In ancient days it was the
custom in British law for the client to present a pair of gloves to the attorney who agreed to handle his case. On one celebrated occasion, a Mrs.
Croaker gave Sir Thomas More, then the Lord Chancellor, a pair of gloves
which contained the sum of forty pounds. The Lord Chancellor retained
the gloves, in accordance with prevailing custom, but returned the money.

glutinous, gluttonous

Glutinous (pronounced GLOO-tin-us) should not be confused with *gluttonous.* Derived from the Latin *gluten* (glue), *glutinous* means sticky, tena-
cious or resembling glue.

Gluttonous (pronounced GLUT-'n-us) stems from the Latin verb *glutire*
(to devour) and is used to describe one who eats too much or too greedily.
Glutton, one who eats voraciously, may also be used figuratively to mean
a person with a great capacity or appetite for anything, as "He's a *glutton*
for work."

go by the board

Board in this phrase refers to the side of a ship. It's a term that originated in sailing-ship days. When, at the height of a storm, a mast broke, it
was up to the skipper to decide whether to attempt to salvage it or to let it
go by the board—fall over the side to complete and utter destruction.

Today when we decide to let a matter *go by the board,* we mean that
we are washing our hands of it—are finished with it for good and all.

gob

Gob has rather an uncertain ancestry but neither of the two possible
origins of the word confers dignity on the word. As H. L. Mencken reports
in *The American Language:* "Gob has been traced variously to 'gobble,'
an allusion to the somewhat earnest methods of feeding prevailing among

sailors, and to *gob,* an archaic English dialect word signifying expectoration. The English coast-guardsmen, who are said to be free-spitters, are often called *gobbies.*"

In fact, *gob* grated so on the ears of Navy brass that in 1928 the commander-in-chief of the U.S. fleet ordered it banned from ships' newspapers as "undignified and unworthy." The ban—like most efforts to legislate language—failed and the word *gob* is still commonly heard.

gobbledygook

Gobbledygook is, according to Webster, "inflated, involved and obscure verbiage characteristic of the pronouncements of officialdom." Indeed, the word was first credited to one-time Texas Congressman Maury Maverick, who, as wartime chairman of the Smaller War Plants Corporation, became infuriated at the tortured language used in official reports that came to his desk.

In a memorable message to the memo manufacturers under his direction, he ordered them to: "Be short and say what you're talking about. Stop 'pointing up' programs. No more 'finalizing,' 'effectuating' or 'dynamics.' Anyone using the words 'activation' or 'implementation' will be shot."

But it looks as though we'll have to start rewriting the dictionaries, if evidence presented by Clarence Denslinger of Sequim, Washington, stands up under close scrutiny. At least we'll have to rewrite one important entry in such word books as the Merriam-Webster *Collegiate,* Berry and Van Den Bark's *American Thesaurus of Slang* and H. L. Mencken's *The American Language.* For all of these illustrious authorities agree that the word *gobbledygook,* meaning "pretentious, meaningless prose," was coined in 1944 by the late Congressman from Texas.

"But," exclaimed Mr. Denslinger, "I disagree! I first heard this word when I was a schoolboy in northwestern Pennsylvania and it had the same meaning—confused, meaningless words—that it has today. Could it be that the Congressman had heard it in the same way I did and carried it in an unused cell in his brain until exasperation caused him to remember it and use it?"

Another note of dissent came from D. D. Robins of Sharon, Pennsylvania, setting forth an interesting and plausible account of *gobbledygook*'s origin: "Mr. Maverick may have been the first to use the word in a sufficiently high area to attract public attention, but he was not the originator. From my personal knowledge I can report that the word was coined by Mess Sergeant Bacher, Co. F, 112th U.S. Engineers, at Camp Sheridan, Montgomery, Alabama, in August, 1917.

"Sergeant Bacher was so exasperated at the Quartermaster Corps' inefficiency in filling his ration orders that he stormed into the First Sergeant's tent and said, 'This profanity profanity Quartermaster Corps don't know beans from potatoes. When I order beef, I get corned Willie! When I order spuds, I get beans! And when I holler at them, all I get is a bunch of *gobbledygook!*'

"The word caught on and spread through the whole division and later through Pershing's army. Sergeant Bacher was widely known for his ad lib origination of picturesque phrases punctuated by educated profanity!"

Well, this is the earliest report we have yet had of the origin of *gobbledygook*. It's intriguing to think that this colorful contribution to our language may well have fallen first on the famed "hairy ears" of our U.S. Engineers.

go condition

Go condition, as used by America's astronauts, is simply a shortened form of "ready-to-go condition"—and that is self-explanatory.

Goldberg, Rube. *See* Rube Goldberg, a.

golf

Amazing as it seems, golf was introduced in America as recently as 1888. The first players were an immigrant Scotsman named John Reid and several friends who set up the first golf course in Yonkers, New York. They came to be called the Apple Tree Gang because their third course, laid out in 1892, was on a thirty-four-acre apple orchard. Incidentally, it was only a six-hole course.

The game itself dates back at least to the fourteenth century, however, and no one is quite certain where it started. As the *American People's Encyclopedia* discreetly puts it, the game is "possibly of Dutch origin, but generally identified with Scotland." The idea that it started in Holland derives from the theory that the word *golf* came from the Dutch word *kolf,* meaning a club for hitting balls. A more recent theory, however, traces *golf* to the Scottish word *gowf,* meaning "to strike." I incline to accept this latter theory—especially since there is no history of any game even remotely like golf being played in Holland down through the centuries. See also CADDY.

gonfalon

CHISOX SNATCH GONFALON read a headline sent in by a Midwest reader who asked: "Just what is the word *gonfalon* doing in a headline on the sports page? I gather it means 'flag' but why can't they say so? I can't even find it in my dictionary."

Well, the reader was right: *gonfalon* does mean flag, specifically a flag once used in medieval Italy and designed to hang from a crosspiece instead of from an upright staff. For some reason *gonfalon* has long been a favorite of sportswriters, many of whom go to great lengths to use elaborate words where simple ones will do. The best sportswriters never fall into this trap. But others—too many others—use "spheroid" when they mean "ball," "three-play swat" for "triple" and so on. They belong to what humorist Charles Morton calls the "elongated yellow fruit" (for "banana") school of writing. No *gonfalons* in the writing sweepstakes for them!

goo-goo and gook. *See* Old Army slang.

goober

The peanut was native to South America originally and came to America by way of Africa, during the era of slave trading. There it got the *goober* name, a variation of the Congolese word *nguba*.

goof

In the case of *I goofed,* it seems clear that the comedian Jerry Lewis can be credited with popularizing it through repetition of the phrase in motion pictures and on television.

But Lewis didn't create the phrase. Far from it. *Goof* as a noun meaning simpleton has been common in the United States for at least forty years. Some scholars believe it originated as a colloquial form of *goff,* an obsolete word meaning dolt or stupid fellow.

Very likely the presently popular phrase *I goofed,* meaning "I made a foolish mistake," had its origin in this earlier noun meaning. During World War II, the phrase *goof off* was widely popular in two senses: to shirk onerous assignments and to make a mistake. *I goofed* has been recorded as long ago as 1946 and probably was current during the war as a streamlined variant for *I goofed off*.

It appears, then, that we can credit the ever-fertile imagination of the American serviceman for first evolving the terse and expressive *I goofed*.

googol

The word *googol* was originally a facetious coinage by the nephew of Edward Kasner, distinguished American mathematician. Asked to suggest a name for the number 1 followed by 100 zeroes, the youngster said: "*Googol.*"

Today the word is accepted and used by mathematicians throughout the world. Incidentally, a *googolplex* is the figure 1, followed by a *googol* of zeroes—and, if you can follow that, you have left me a *googol* of miles behind.

goop

Goop started its career in our language as the coinage of Gelett Burgess, one of America's favorite humorists in the early years of this century. Burgess is the same chap, by the way, who invented *blurb* to describe the descriptive material appearing on a book's cover to praise the book's contents. He also invented *bromide,* meaning a trite remark or cliché, whence we have the adjective *bromidic* to describe trite, unimaginative speech. Quite an inventor, this Burgess!

Originally a *goop* was a silly, boorish, ill-mannered fellow and the first *goops* appeared in Burgess' book *Goops and How to Be Them,* published in 1900.

Sometime later *goop* began to develop other meanings, but always with the connotation of something distasteful and frequently of something messy or unpleasant to handle. Auto mechanics took to calling lubricating grease *goop.* Beauty shop operators used the same label for the thick fluid used for making finger waves. And, most recently, in World War II, soldiers labeled the mixtures used in incendiary bombs *goop.*

Goop in any of these uses should be classified as slang. In the jargon of carnival workers, frozen custard or so-called "soft" ice cream has long been termed *goop,* so it would appear that *goop* is an appropriate term for all the weird and wonderful assortment of sweets that a child will consume at a circus or carnival.

goose, cook their. *See* cook their goose.

gopher ball. *See* baseball jargon.

gorilla

The word *gorilla* is an African word and describes the largest anthropoid ape of West Africa. It has also been used in underworld slang to denote a mobster, usually one who acts as bodyguard for a big-shot gangster.

gossip

A *gossip* in the time of Chaucer was a godparent, usually the godmother. The word then was spelled *godsibbe*—god, of course, having the same meaning it has today and *sibbe* meaning kin or relative.

How did the meaning of *gossip* as we know it today develop? Well, over the years the original meaning was extended to include not only god-parents but any very close or intimate friends. Since it's the nature of friendship to entrust one's closest secrets to one's friends, and since it seems to be human nature to pass on such secrets, the evolution of *gossip* should be fairly obvious.

Gotham

The name *Gotham* was originally applied to New York City by Washington Irving in *Salmagundi,* a series of satirical pieces, published in 1807. But that's only a small part of the story.

Gotham (pronounced GOT-um in England but GOTH-um here) was originally a village near Nottingham known as "the town of wise fools." The story goes that King John once made a trip to Gotham for the express purpose of acquiring land and building a castle. The shrewd burghers realized that, with the royal presence at hand, they would be subjected to frequent tax levies. Not to put too fine a point on it, the king could make life unbearable if he were a resident of their town. So they decided to play the fool and, when the king's outriders neared Gotham they found most of the townspeople running wildly in circles, obviously daft.

Equally obviously this was no place for his royal highness to take up residence, so he abandoned his original plan and betook himself elsewhere. The townsfolk then remarked: "More fools pass through Gotham than remain in it"—and Gotham's reputation for "wise fools" was established.

Washington Irving, in choosing this epithet for New York, intended to satirize the wiseacre, know-it-all attitude of its inhabitants. Though much about New York has changed in the century and a half since he first applied the label, obviously the "wise guy" attitude has not.

goulash

The highly spiced stew, *goulash,* owes its name to the shepherds of Hungary. Indeed, *goulash*—or *gulyas,* as the Hungarians spell it—originally meant simply "shepherd." Then it came to mean the food the shepherds ate, specifically the stew made with beef or veal and vegetables—and lots of paprika.

gourmand, gourmet

The distinction between *gourmet* and *gourmand* is a nice one, but one worth observing. A *gourmet* is a person who is an authority on the selection and preparation of fine foods; almost invariably he or she is also a qualified judge of vintage wines. But a *gourmet* is not necessarily a heavy eater.

Indeed, he is likely, by reason of the discrimination that he brings to his choice of viands, to eat sparingly.

A *gourmand,* on the other hand, while he often shares the gourmet's liking for rare and unusual delicacies, is primarily a trencherman, one who loves good eating—and, usually, plenty of it. The word *gourmand* (pronounced GOOR-mund) was originally a French adjective meaning "gluttonous" and some slight vestige of this earlier meaning carries over into our language.

Both words, by the way, come from the same French word, *groumet,* which originally meant groom or stableboy. Gradually *gourmet* came to mean any manservant and eventually the term was reserved for the wine-taster or steward. Since the prime requisite of a wine steward is the ability to discriminate among the choicest vintages, the word *gourmet* came to have the meaning of "epicure," a person with a refined and cultivated taste in both eating and drinking—and that is the sense in which it is used most accurately today.

go west

"Go west, young man, *go west"* is generally credited to the New York *Tribune* editor Horace Greeley, though he often said that John Soule, in an article in the Terre Haute *Express,* had created the expression. In any event, it was first written in 1851 when the Gold Rush had focused public attention on the vast potential of this part of the continent. As Greeley later amended his advice, the idea was *"Go west,* young man, and grow with the country." Now that our West has developed so tremendously in the past century, today's Greeley would probably advise a young pioneer to "go northwest"—to Alaska.

The other meaning of *go west*—to die—was common in World War I. Actually, though, it is many years, perhaps many centuries, older. It derives from the legend believed by many American Indian tribes and by primitive civilizations the world over that each day is newly born in the east and dies in the west. Thus the "land of the setting sun"—the west—is where a person goes when he dies.

gowk, hunt the. *See* April Fool's Day.

graduation and commencement

Every year hundreds of thousands of American families share pride-fully in the excitement that attends school *graduation* or college *commencement.* Nowadays, it is not just a ceremony for high school and college seniors. I am reliably informed that some of our more progressive school systems even have *graduation* festivities—complete with caps and gowns —for youngsters winding up their year in kindergarten!

Be that as it may—and you'll admit it conjures up a rather grim picture —let's look at two of the words most closely associated with this occasion.

Commencement, from the Latin words *cum* and *initio,* "to go into together," quite literally means a beginning. The reason why it is used to designate the day on which college education ends is because the ending is also a beginning—the start of the new career or vocation for which college has trained the student.

Grade and high schools, by contrast, usually and properly designate their ceremonies *graduation.* From the Latin *gradus* (step or grade) this indicates that a pupil has completed an important step toward his educational goal but that more remains to be done.

grand slam. *See* baseball jargon.

grass roots. *See* political slang, nineteenth century.

gratuitous

This word is most often encountered in phrases like *"gratuitous* insult." While the meaning "uncalled-for" and the opprobrious connotation of "without cause or justification" do attach to this meaning of *gratuitous,* it has still another meaning of "given or received without charge or obligation." This, indeed, is the meaning closer to its Latin root *gratuitus,* meaning "free or spontaneous." In law *gratuitous* has the special meaning of "given without receiving any return value."

grease. *See* payola.

green cheese. *See* moon is made of green cheese, the.

green room

The *green room* is the off-stage retiring room used by the acting company in a theater. Most Broadway theaters are so cramped for space backstage that *green rooms* are nonexistent. However, the old phrase remains in such terms as *"green room* gossip" as loosely synonymous with "back stage."

The *green room* took its name from the fact that its walls were often painted green to rest the eyes of actors after exposure to bright stage lights.

Grey, Major. *See* Major Grey of chutney fame.

grog blossom

A beer garden is the only garden where you would be likely to find a *grog blossom*. *Grog,* you see, is the British sailor's term for spirits— usually rum—diluted with water. And a *grog blossom* is a facial blotch or blemish resulting from overindulgence in grog.

grog shop

Grog shop as a name for a bar and grill is a British term, as British as the Royal Navy. Originally, grog was a ration of spirits, usually rum and water, issued to British sailors. This issue was first authorized by an eighteenth-century officer, Admiral Vernon, who was nicknamed "Old Grog" from his habit of wearing a grogram coat. You'll find no grogram in a *grog shop* today, though.

groundnuts

The *groundnut* is nothing more than the common peanut or, in Southern dialect, the *goober*. *Groundnuts* figured large in the news from England a decade or so ago when the Tory party made political capital of an abortive attempt by Attlee's Socialist Government to develop a successful groundnut "industry" in Africa.

grout

In an article about methods being employed in the construction of a new building on New York's Park Avenue the word *grout* appeared. Referring to the need for having a completely solid base for the structure, which must withstand the vibration of hundreds of passenger trains passing through the tunnel under the avenue each day, the piece said, "In the case of a faulted rock, the fault might be cleaned out and grouted." Such an unfamiliar word ought to be more clearly explained in anything short of a technical article designed for professionals. However, though the term is unfamiliar, the procedure is not really too involved. After the fault in the rock has been cleaned out, a mixture of concrete and, perhaps, stones and other reinforcing materials is poured into the fault and left to harden. The substance poured in is called *grout* and the procedure *grouting*.

growler, rushing the. *See* rushing the growler.

grubstreet hacks

The phrase *grubstreet hacks* means underpaid free-lance writers. ("Underpaid free-lance writer" must seem to many in the craft a redundancy—but let it pass.)

The original Grub Street was a lane in the London ward of Cripplegate Without. Dr. Samuel Johnson, first of the great English dictionary makers, once described the street as "much inhabited by writers of small histories, dictionaries and temporary poems; whence any mean production is called *grubstreet.*"

If you go to London today, by the way, don't waste time trying to find Grub Street. Its name was changed more than a century ago to Milton Street—not out of deference to John Milton, the poet, but after the landlord who owned most of the houses on the street.

grues

It was the famed novelist and poet, Robert Louis Stevenson, who coined the name for those macabre little verses which so delighted our parents and grandparents. *Grues* was the collective label he chose—obviously taking his inspiration from "gruesome"—for the rhymes about Little Willie and his grimly comic mishaps. Here we quote the best-known *grue:*

> Little Willie in the best of sashes
> Fell in the fire and was burned to ashes.
> By and by the room grew chilly,
> But no one liked to poke up Willie.

And that reminds us of an eight-line *grue* from our boyhood:

> Little Willie from his mirror
> Licked all the mercury off,
> Thinking, in his error,
> That it would cure the whooping cough.
>
> But next week when Little Willie's funeral came around,
> Little Willie's mother said to Mrs. Brown,
> " 'Twas a cold day for Little Willie
> When the mercury went down!"

Although many wits of the Victorian era turned their hands to the creation of *grues,* the master seems to have been a chap named Harry Graham, who sometimes wrote under the pseudonym of "Colonel D. Streamer" and whose masterpiece was aptly entitled *Ruthless Rhymes for Heartless Homes.* William W. Vosburgh, Jr., editorial director of the Waterbury *Republican,* submitted this sample of a Graham *grue* at its most gruesome:

> When with my little daughter, Blanche,
> I climbed the Alps last summer

I saw a dreadful avalanche
About to overcome her.
And as the stones came hurtling down
I vaguely wondered whether
It would be wise to cut the rope
Which bound us twain together.
I must confess I'm glad I did—
And yet I miss the child, poor kid.

guaranty. *See* warranty, guaranty.

guerrilla

Guerrilla was originally a Spanish word, the diminutive form of *guerra*, meaning "war." *Guerrilla* originally meant a fast-moving, skirmishing type of warfare. Gradually it came to mean a soldier engaged in that kind of warfare. Today *guerrillas* are members of small groups—usually volunteers —whose specialty is quick, hit-and-run attacks on supply lines and installations of the enemy. Often their activity is carried on behind the enemy lines.

guillotine

Here is one of the wry footnotes to history: the inventor of the *guillotine* was a French physician (named, of course, Dr. J. I. Guillotin) who thought that his invention was a great humanitarian contribution. In a sense perhaps he was correct, for the guillotine was at least a speedier and more efficient method of administering the death penalty than the drawn-out tortures which had been used before his time. But—thanks to the bloody abuse of the instrument during the French Revolution—the very word *guillotine* is now synonymous with needless and brutal slaughter. See also DERRICK.

gum boots

Gum boots is British slang for overshoes, which are also called Wellingtons by some over there. See also ENGLISH ENGLISH.

gung-ho

Gung-ho is a Chinese phrase, meaning "work together." During the early phase of World War II, it was the slogan of the 2nd Marine Raider Division, which served with distinction in raids on Guadalcanal and the assault on Little Makin Island. The division, also known as Carlson's

Raiders, was led by Lieutenant Colonel Evans F. Carlson, who had served as an observer with the Chinese 8th Route Army during 1937–39. Some of his guerrilla tactics, as well as the *gung-ho* slogan of the division, seem to have been derived from his experiences there.

Today *gung-ho* seems to be enjoying a revival in the slang of teen-agers. They use it not as a rally cry, of course, but rather as an adjective descriptive of a person ambitious or zealous beyond the norm.

gyrene

Gyrene is a World War II slang term—a slightly derogatory name for a U.S. Marine. Curiously, this word has been overlooked in most of the postwar dictionaries—perhaps because of the mystery surrounding its origin. Now, though, the new *World Webster* comes forth with a fairly plausible theory—that *gyrene* comes from the initials GI plus the last syllable of Marine. Just why the new word would contort two *i*'s into *y* and *e* respectively is, as the saying goes, a puzzlement.

H

Haganah. *See* Irgun, Haganah.

hair of the dog

The theory—and a most unsound one it is—that the best remedy for a hangover is another drink (*the hair of the dog that bit you*) goes back to ancient times. The Romans believed that the best antidote for a dog bite was the burned hair of the dog that had attacked you. They even had a proverb *Similia similibus curantur* ("Like things cure like") to express this belief.

hair pants. *See* cowboy jargon.

hairsbreadth

The expression *hairsbreadth* means a measure as narrow as a human hair. It's very old. The *Oxford Dictionary* traces it to 1561 and that sprightly young dramatist, Will Shakespeare, was using it only a few years later. In *Othello,* he had the leading character reminisce about the story of his life and "most disastrous chances, of moving accidents by flood and field, of hair-breadth 'scapes i' the imminent deadly breach, of being taken by the insolent foe, and sold to slavery."

In England, at one time, the *hairsbreadth* was recognized as a formal unit of measure—one forty-eighth part of an inch. And many newspaper readers of an older vintage will remember that wonderfully satiric comic strip character, *Hairbreadth Harry,* who brightened many a Sunday with his miraculous rescues of beautiful blond heroines from certain death.

halcyon

Halcyon (pronounced HAL-see-un) is an adjective meaning "calm and peaceful." Most often used by Fourth of July orators in the phrase "the *halcyon* days of yore," it comes from the Greek word for kingfisher. Legend was that the kingfisher's brooding period was the seven days before and the seven days after the shortest day of the year. Since the kingfisher's nest was believed to be borne on the waves of the ocean, it followed that during this period the weather would surely be calm and peaceful—or *halcyon.*

halloo. *See* hello and hi!, hello.

ham actor

Ham in this phrase has two rather distinct meanings. First, probably by analogy to "amateur," there is the use of *ham* to mean an actor who is incompetent or unskilled. That's the meaning intended in such phrases as "Hollywood *hams.*"

Then there is *ham* in the sense of one who overacts or outrageously overplays a scene—especially when his intention is to center all attention on himself to the exclusion of other players. Such devices as upstaging other actors, grimacing at the audience and pointedly fiddling with one's pocket handkerchief during another player's speech are common practices of actors bent on *"hamming* it up."

Whichever the meaning, though, there seem to be several theories as to the origin of the term. In the days of blackface minstrel shows before the turn of the century, one popular song was "The Hamfat Man" and it clearly referred to second-rate actors of the type that appeared in such shows. But nobody knows for sure whether the song inspired the name *hamfatter* for these actors or whether the name preceded the song.

I am inclined to think that the name came before the song, probably from the minstrel's practice of using ham fat to remove the heavy black makeup used during performances.

It has even been suggested that the name came to be applied to actors because they all want some day to play the title role in Shakespeare's *Hamlet*. Were this true, actors would have been labeled *hams* for centuries. Actually, though, there is no record of the word's appearance much before 1880—and it's very definitely an American slang term, not British.

hamburger

Hamburger was originally "Hamburg steak" and took its name from the city of Hamburg, Germany. The dish was brought to this country at the time of the first great wave of German immigration, midway through the nineteenth century. With the passage of time, "Hamburg steak" dropped its capital *H*, acquired an extra *er*, lost the "steak" and moved from the platter to a place between the slices of bread or roll to become the *"hamburger* sandwich" we know today.

hame. *See* jazzmen's jargon.

Hancock, John. *See* John Henry.

handwriting on the wall. *See* mene, mene, tekel, upharsin.

hangar

At a luncheon meeting of a famous New York club, Harry Ashmore, editor of the Encyclopaedia Britannica, found himself seated between the skipper of the British aircraft carrier *Ark Royal* and John Chapman, the club president. When he rose to speak, Ashmore remarked that since he had become an encyclopedia editor, even his old friends tended to assume that he knew everything in his encyclopedia from "aardvark" to "zygote." The truth was, he wryly noted, that he shared with other encyclopedia editors a certain knowledge that he would never be able to read every word in the set he edited—much less know all of them.

To illustrate his point, he quoted a bit of conversation between Chapman and the *Ark Royal*'s commander. "On your ship," remarked Chapman, "airplanes not alerted for flight are stored on the hangar deck. Now that's a word that has long puzzled me—*hangar*. Where did it come from?" Without a moment's hesitation, the British skipper replied, "In the early days of aviation, when lighter-than-air craft were quite common, airships were stored in big sheds 'hanging' from the roof. Hence, *hangar*."

"I was so grateful that our British friend knew the answer," continued Ashmore, "because otherwise Chapman would have asked me—and I didn't have the faintest notion where *hangar* came from, though, as an encyclopedia editor, I might have been expected to know."

"But Mr. Ashmore," interrupted the British officer, "I shouldn't want anyone to think that that's the true origin of *hangar*. Assuming that nobody else knew either, I improvised it on the spur of the moment. Truth to tell, I haven't the foggiest notion where it came from either!"

It's rather a pity that this charming "origin" of *hangar* was so speedily disclaimed by its creator, for the fiction is far more interesting than the prosaic truth. Actually, we took the word over direct from the French where it means simply "farm shed." Apparently Bleriot and the other French aviation pioneers simply put their craft in vacant sheds and—*Voila!* —*hangar* acquired a new meaning.

Harvard beets

A half-century or so ago, when Harvard had some of the finest football teams in the country (don't laugh, boys, they really did!), Harvard crimson was a color known throughout the land. About that time, a chef, whose name unfortunately has been lost to history, confected a dish of cooked beets warmed in a sauce of vinegar, sugar and cornstarch whose resulting deep red color was very close to the crimson in Harvard's then proud banners. Eureka—an inspiration—and the name of *Harvard beets* was coined!

hassel, hassle

Though the origin of *hassel* in the sense of a heated discussion is uncertain, some language experts believe it is derived from a Southern dialect word variously spelled *hassle, hassel* and *hessel*. This term means "to pant or to breathe noisily"—as "The dog is *hassling*." Since the participants in a lively *hassel* (argument) might well lose their breath as well as their tempers, perhaps this is as good an explanation of the origin of *hassel* as we are likely to find.

Hassel is listed in the *World Webster Dictionary,* College Edition, with the label "slang." The Merriam-Webster Third Edition, in another indication of its casualness about labeling levels of usage, enters *hassel* with no indication that it is anything short of completely acceptable on every level of speech and writing.

If its popularity continues to spread and if it comes to be used by literate speakers and writers, it may eventually be classed as "colloquial" —meaning that it will then be standard usage in informal speech and writing. At this time, however, it is still considered "slang" and should be avoided.

hatch, down the

The phrase *down the hatch,* which is common among patrons of small bars, is from the jargon of sailing men, the mouth being regarded as analogous to the hatches down which cargo is lowered.

hatter, mad as a

The explanation of this phrase that I find most believable holds that *hatter* is really a variant form of the Anglo-Saxon word *atter,* meaning "poison." *Atter,* of course, is closely related to "adder," the venomous viper whose sting was thought to cause insanity. This explanation has much to recommend it. For one thing, it explains why the phrase, in one form or another, was current before hatmaking became a recognized trade. Secondly, it removes the stigma from an otherwise honorable means of employment.

Incidentally, the wide popularity of the phrase can, of course, be credited to Lewis Carroll, whose Mad Hatter in *Alice in Wonderland* is one of our most delightful comic creations. The phrase itself, however, was used often before Carroll's time, notably by Thackeray in *Pendennis.*

havoc

Havoc (pronounced HAV-uk) has an interesting history. Its meaning today is destruction or devastation, especially that resulting from a great catastrophe. But back in the Middle Ages when we took the word into English from the Norman French word *havok,* it was a war cry—a signal for invading warriors to attack, sack and plunder a village.

Perhaps the word is best known nowadays to readers and playgoers in the memorable sentence from Mark Anthony's soliloquy over the body of the newly fallen Caesar: "And Caesar's spirit ranging for revenge . . . shall in these confines with a monarch's voice cry 'Havoc!' and let slip the dogs of war." Here, as in so many other instances, Shakespeare's use of a word in memorable context has been incomparably the best insurance that the word would remain a part of the living language.

heinous

Heinous is a word often misused and even oftener mispronounced. Meaning "hateful" or "atrocious," it is a word of Teutonic origin which came into English through the Old French word *Hainos.* Pronounced HAY-nus, it was used with notable effectiveness by Cole Porter in his delightful "Brush up Your Shakespeare" number in *Kiss Me, Kate,* wherein he managed to rhyme *heinous* with Coriolanus.

heirloom

An *heirloom* today is, of course, any valued possession which has been passed on within a family for several generations. Originally, however, it was much more closely related to the family's traditional trade or occupation.

For the *loom* in *heirloom* was not necessarily the loom used in weaving. In Anglo-Saxon times (when the word was spelled *geloma*) the loom was any kind of tool or implement. Not until after the Norman Conquest did *loom* come to mean specifically the weaving apparatus that we call by that name today.

hello

At a guess, there's probably no other word (excepting "I") so much used as *hello*. Practically every phone conversation opens with it, and that alone must account for millions of uses every day. But where did it come from in the first place? The earliest English ancestor seems to be *hallow*, a word of greeting common in the time of Chaucer. It was pronounced with the accent on the second syllable.

By Shakespeare's day, it had become *halloo*—a form still used by foxhunters and perhaps by more plebeian hunters as well. Then we come closer to the present form because by the nineteenth century our fellow countrymen were greeting each other with *hullo*.

Legend has it that Thomas Alva Edison himself was the first to say *hello* over the telephone—and this is one instance where legend may well be accurate. It is indeed true that *hello* came into widespread popularity within a very few years of the introduction of the telephone. Amusingly enough, the very first telephone exchange, set up at New Haven, Connecticut, in 1878, did not use *hello, hullo* or even the "View, Halloo" one might have expected from Yale's sporting bloods. Instead the phones were answered "Ahoy, ahoy!" We may all be grateful that that custom didn't persist.

Hell's Corner

Hell's Corner was a section of the British coastline along the English Channel near Dover. It got its name from the fact that during the trying months of the Battle of Britain (1940) it was under shell fire from German cross-Channel guns and also under constant air threat because much of the fighting between Goering's *Luftwaffe* and Britain's gallant Spitfires was going on right overhead.

Henry, John. *See* John Henry.

herd of cattle. *See* clowder, kindle and cowardice.

heroes, thin red line of. *See* thin red line of heroes.

herring, neither fish nor fowl nor good red

This expression (which sometimes also appears as "neither fish nor flesh nor good red herring") goes back at least as far as the Middle Ages. At that time the three chief classes of society (aside from nobility, a class by itself) were the clergy, lay people generally and paupers. Fish was food suitable to the clergy. Fowl (or flesh) was food appropriate for the mass of the common people. Red herring was food fit only for paupers. So something that was *neither fish nor fowl nor good red herring* would be suitable for no one. Nowadays, the phrase is often used to characterize a plan or idea that is so vague that nobody can make anything of it.

hex signs, hexagon

The colorful *hex signs* painted on barns in the Pennsylvania Dutch country to ward off evil spirits are sometimes six-sided (hence, *hexagons*) but this is mere coincidence. There is no direct connection between *hex* and *hexagon*. The former comes from an old German word *hagazussa,* from which the Anglo-Saxon word *hag* also comes. *Hexagon,* on the other hand, comes straight from the Greek *hexagonon,* a six-sided figure.

hi!, hello

Hi! is an abbreviation of *hiya,* which in turn is a corruption of *How are you?* While common enough as a casual, informal greeting, especially among young people, *Hi!* can certainly not be considered correct for use in a formal situation. Better say *Hello.*

Incidentally, the word *hello* itself is comparatively recent in general use, as we have noted before in the entry "hello." For centuries the calls *hulloa, halloo* and *hollo* were commonly used by sailors and huntsmen to attract attention. It's likely that the term first came into English—as did so many other terms associated with hunting—at the time of the Norman Conquest. Originally *hola* from the French *ho* and *là*—"Ho, there"—the salutation gradually took other forms and, by the middle of the last century, was generally pronounced and written *hullo.*

Then came the invention of the telephone and for the first few years people began each conversation with *Are you there?*—as many still do in England today. But Edison, impatient as always with waste of time or energy, decided this was too wordy and settled on *Hello* for his own telephone salutation. His example was widely imitated and has since been standard American practice.

hide your light under a bushel, to

The *bushel* in this phrase is the container, usually made of earthenware or wood, used to measure a quantity (four pecks, as a matter of fact) of grain, vegetables or fruit. The phrase *hiding your light under a bushel* now means displaying excessive modesty about one's abilities.

The phrase first appeared in the Bible (Matthew 5:14–15) when Jesus, after urging his disciples to be "the light of the world" added that "A city that is set on a hill cannot be hid. Neither do men light a candle, and put it under a bushel, but on a candlestick."

hi-fi

The designation *hi-fi* is popular among devotees of the hobby of high-fidelity reproduction of broadcast or recorded music. In the minds of many, the terms *high fidelity* and *high frequency* are confused, since the first thing you notice about music played through a *hi-fi* "outfit" is the clarity with which you can hear high notes of instruments like the flute and celeste— notes which can only be heard poorly, if at all, when records are played through conventional phonographs. Recent developments in electronics have made the reproduction of sounds up to the limit of human hearing —approximately 15,000 cycles per second—commercially feasible. Non-*hi-fi* reproducers seldom range above 8,000 cycles.

It is important to remember, though, that true high-fidelity reproduction encompasses faithful and realistic reproduction of sounds in the low-frequency range as well. If you keep this in mind, the difference between *hi-fi* and high frequency will be clear.

highball

Highball comes from bartenders' slang of the 1890's when they called all glasses *balls*. Naturally, the tall glass used for whiskey and soda became the *highball*. Its popularity is doubtless partly due to the meaning *highball* has for railroaders: the signal to speed up on a clear track.

high dudgeon. *See* dudgeon.

highfalutin, highfaluting

Highfalutin or *highfaluting* was originally an American slang word, first recorded in print about 1850. It was part of our frontier language and originally was used to disparage high-flown, bombastic orators. As a matter of fact, some language students think the *highfalutin* is simply another form of "high-flown" or "high-floating"—to refer to the puffed-up phrases used by old-time Fourth of July orators.

Nowadays the word is listed in most dictionaries as "colloquial" rather than "slang." That means that you will hear it used in informal conversation among well-educated people. Truth to tell, it's one of my favorite words—very useful in telling off pompous pedants who keep putting on *highfalutin* airs!

high man

To circus and carnival folk, the *high man* is not the boss of the circus but the man who winds up on the top of a human pyramid. See also CIRCUS JARGON.

hip, hep

Hip is a latter-day variant of hep. During the early big-band swing days of the 1930's, bands like Benny Goodman's and Count Basie's were labeled *hep*—meaning that the musicians, arrangers, *et al.*, were "in the know." For a brief period about that time, devotees of jazz were popularly known as *hep cats,* a term that was never very popular with musicians themselves.

Hep first appeared in soldier slang around 1900 as a borrowing from the drillmaster's cadence count: *"Hep,* two, three, four. *Hep,* two, three, four." The troop that always hit the beat properly was in step, hence *hep*.

About the end of World War II, new voices were heard in the jazz world. *Bop* flourished for a while, later giving way to *cool* jazz. With these transitions, a new jazz argot came in, a new form of verbal communications between musicians themselves. *Hep,* in the words of one musician friend, "wasn't *hip* any more." The variant form *hip,* in other words, had completely displaced *hep*.

hit the panic button. *See* panic button, hit the.

hitting on all six

This particular phrase comes straight from the slang of auto fans of about 1915. In an age when most cars had only four cylinders, a six-cylinder car was something pretty special. So if all six cylinders of a car were functioning properly (*hitting on all six*), the car and its driver were cutting a very fancy figure indeed. The phrase came to be used to apply to any person whose performance was better than usual.

H.M.S. *See* U.S.S.

hobby

So popular have hobbies become in these years of comparative leisure that many magazines, hundreds of guidance books and reams of newspaper copy are devoted to the activities of hobbyists. But where did the word *hobby* come from?

Actually *hobby* is a contraction of "hobbyhorse" and originally meant a small or medium-sized horse. Then it came to mean a light wicker framework, draped with colored cloth to simulate a horse, which was used by dancers in the medieval English country dances called Morris dances. In the course of these revels, various characters from the Robin Hood legend were depicted, so the function of the hobbyhorse as an instrument of make-believe is pretty obvious.

Later the hobbyhorse came to be a child's plaything—what Yorkshiremen call "a stick with an 'orse's 'ead 'andle"—and the phrase "to ride a hobbyhorse" came to indicate the pursuit of a childish game with a zeal worthy of more adult interests. Readers of Laurence Sterne's *Tristram Shandy* will recall with delight the relentless hobbyhorse riding of My Uncle Toby. Quite possibly his endearing addiction to his hobby may have contributed greatly to the establishment of *hobby* in its present meaning of an occupation or pursuit bordering on the frivolous to which a person is devoted.

The word *hobby* has by now come a long way from the time when it meant merely a small pacing horse. But through all its changes of meaning, the element of fun has been implicit in it. Perhaps it might be argued that the *hobbyists* who most truly represent the historical meaning of the term are those improvers of the breed who devote time, energy and plenty of money to watching the bangtails pound down the stretch and the totalizator lights flash the final odds on win, place and show.

hobnob

Hobnob is a word of impeccable ancestry. In its present form it has been in our language since Shakespeare's day. In fact, it is found in at least one of his plays. Originally, it appeared in Chaucer's time as *habnab*, meaning literally "to have and have not" or "hit-or-miss."

In those days, and through the centuries since, the term was used to describe the social practice of alternating in the buying of drinks: one chap buys a round, then his friend buys the next. First he has, then he has not, the honor of treating.

Gradually the term *hobnobbing* came to mean any form of social intercourse on easy, familiar terms—the sense in which the word is most often used today.

Hobson's choice

Back toward the end of the sixteenth century, one Thomas Hobson operated the leading livery stable in the university town of Cambridge, England. Devoted to the welfare of his horses, he established a firm rule that each customer in turn must take the horse nearest the door when he arrived. He tolerated no picking and choosing, insisting that this strict order of rotation be followed. Thus, when someone offered you *Hobson's choice,* you were actually being offered no choice at all.

Popular, early in this century, was a sort of "folk etymology" for this phrase, some people asserting that the term had its origin in the heroic action of Richmond Pearson Hobson, who sank the collier *Merrimac* in an attempt to bottle up the Spanish fleet in Santiago Harbor in 1898. The theory was that, seeing his duty, he made his choice—*Hobson's choice* —and scuttled the ship. Pleasant though this account is, Thomas Hobson's stable pre-existed our national hero by some three centuries and thus must receive credit for the origin of the phrase.

hodgepodge

The original English spelling for this word was "hotchpotch," meaning a kind of stew. Logically enough, the word in time came to mean any kind of jumble or mess. In America today the spelling *hodgepodge* is far more common. Most people would regard "hotchpotch" as an affectation.

hogging moment

This is the moment of stress to which a ship is subjected when she is water-borne amidships but out of the water at both ends. The opposite situation is the *sagging moment*. And, either way, it bodes ill for the ship.

hog on ice, independent as a

Of all the many thousands of colorful folk expressions used from border to border in this great land of ours, few have proven as fascinating to word sleuths as the phrase *independent as a hog on ice*. One scholar even used *A Hog on Ice* as the title for a book on word origins. When my newspaper column mentioned some theories of its origin, the mail was flooded with comments from readers who had heard the expression from parents and grandparents, each of whom had a different explanation of the story behind this seemingly contradictory phrase. When you stop to think of it, just how "independent" can a hog on ice be?

The question arose when Minnesota's Governor Orville Freeman used it in a speech in its present meaning of a person who takes an exasperatingly stubborn and self-assured position. It's a phrase to challenge anyone's curiosity since, at first thought, there's hardly anything less independent than a squealing porker sliding around on a frozen pond.

The late Charles Funk attempted to trace the origin of the phrase and came up with a theory that the *hog* referred to is not the ordinary farm animal at all but a marker used in the Scottish game of curling, in which flat stones are slid along ice. That seemed to me and to many readers a singularly unconvincing explanation. Here are some of the interesting theories sent in from readers in all parts of the country.

First, an explanation that goes back nearly 140 years to the childhood of the grandmother of my correspondent, Olive L. Cluver of Etiwanda, California. "When I was a little girl," she wrote, "I asked my grandmother (who was born in 1812) how a hog could show his independence. She told me that when she was a child, her grandfather raised hogs. When he wanted to move these hogs from one side of a stream to the other, he waited for the stream to freeze over to a thickness that would hold the weight of the hogs. Then he sanded a strip across the stream. A helper would go to the opposite side with feed and call the hogs. If one or more of them got off the sanded strip, they would begin to slip around. Then they would lie down and not move until the men got them back on the sanded ice."

Well, that's a plausible theory—and certainly not quite so grim as one from Rev. R. O. Gates of Akron, Ohio. "This is how I 'heered' it," he wrote. "A hog does not go on ice until after it's butchered. Then it goes into the freezer. Since it is dead, it needs nothing, wants nothing, and cares about nothing. Therefore it is quite independent of people and things."

This explanation surely sounds conclusive, but I somehow doubt if the expression would have earned such widespread popularity if its origin had been in the slaughterhouse.

Here's a suggestion from Miss Freda F. Graves of Ashtabula, Ohio, in reaction to Governor Freeman's use of the expression to describe the voters of his state:

"I believe it was the custom of many farmers to turn their hogs out to fend for themselves part of the year (as in the phrase 'root, hog or die'). When the time came to round up these animals for butchering or to be penned up, some of them had different ideas. Perhaps they were cunning enough to try to cross frozen streams or get out on thin ice which would make their capture a difficult, exasperating and sometimes dangerous business.

"So you have the picture of an animal just out of reach, where he's a hazard to go after, but too valuable to be left to drown or freeze. Our ancestors valued self-reliance and independence very highly, but they realized that it can sometimes be carried too far or used unwisely. Therefore, anyone who steadfastly refused badly needed help or advice—perhaps to his own detriment—was said to be as *independent as a hog on ice*.

"It seems to me that the governor of Minnesota must have had a meaning similar to this in mind, though, of course, he was using the expression in a joking way. Just think how annoying voter independence can be to the plans of a political candidate!"

Well, that's an intriguing idea and one which gives the hog credit for some slight degree of intelligence. Unless and until some reader of this book comes up with an even more persuasive theory of the origin of this phrase, we shall—if you'll forgive the expression—put the whole discussion on ice.

hoicks

Hoicks is a variant of the better-known "yoicks"—a call to the hounds in fox hunting.

hoi polloi

Hoi polloi (pronounced hoi puh-LOI) comes from the Greek. It means "the many" and is generally used to refer to the great mass of humanity, the common people. Purists shudder at the sight of *the hoi polloi* in print, pointing out that it is equivalent to "the the many." However, theirs is probably a futile struggle. Even such conscientious writers as John Dryden refer to *the hoi polloi,* and in British university slang that is the common designation for students who graduate without honors.

hoist by his own petard

This is a figurative expression meaning "destroyed by his own trickery or inventiveness." A *petard,* in medieval warfare, was an explosive charge which daring warriors would affix to the walls or gates of a castle under siege. This action in itself was a most hazardous one but the greatest danger came after the *petard* was in place. The explosive was detonated by a slow-match or slowly burning fuse. Occasionally, of course, the explosive went off prematurely, in which case the warrior was *hoist* (lifted or heaved) *by his own petard.*

It is unlikely that this archaic phrase would have persisted in our language, even in a figurative sense, had not Shakespeare conferred immortality upon it with this line from *Hamlet:* " 'Tis the sport to have the engineer *hoist with his own petard."*

Today it is chiefly used to describe a person ruined by plans or devices with which he had plotted to ensnare others.

hoity-toity

Meaning "haughty or snobbish," this term has been in common use for nearly three centuries. Some scholars say it comes from an obsolete verb *hoit,* meaning "to romp around noisily," but that seems to me very far-fetched. More possibly, it is a corruption of *haughty.* This latter theory, at any rate, comes much closer to the present meaning of the word.

Incidentally, it is one of a group of words the scholars call "reduplicated words"; others of its ilk are harum-scarum, hugger-mugger and the like.

hole, in the. *See* baseball jargon.

holocaust

Holocaust (pronounced HOL-oh-kost) is a word we sometimes see in the headlines, yet it is not one that many of us find in our speaking vocabularies. Originally a holocaust was a sacrificial burnt offering to pagan gods in pre-Christian times. It is derived from the Greek words *holos* (whole) and *kaustos* (burnt). Nowadays it is generally used to mean slaughter and destruction on a very wide scale, especially by fire, as in the sentence: "All London was a *holocaust* after the bombers left."

homonyms

Remember the old nursery rhyme about Fuzzy Wuzzy, the bear? It went like this:

> Fuzzy Wuzzy was a bear.
> Fuzzy Wuzzy had no hair.
> Fuzzy Wuzzy wasn't fuzzy, was he?
> No, he was a bare bear!

Perhaps because it's a rhyme that has been repeated times without number in the Morris nursery over the years, I found it running through my head when I received this inquiry from a column reader. "Isn't there a word," she asked, "to designate words which sound alike but have different meanings, like *alter* and *altar,* or *road, rowed* and *rode?*"

There is indeed a word for such pairs of sound-alike words. In fact, there are two words for them—*homophone* and *homonym.* Technically speaking, a *homophone* (from the Greek *homos,* "the same," and *phone,* "sound") means a word which sounds like another word of different meaning, while a *homonym* (from *homo* plus *onyma,* "name") is one which has the same sound and spelling as another word of different meaning. However, this distinction is seldom observed and, to all intents and purposes, *homonyms* and *homophones* are considered the same.

Homonyms, of course, are the source, not only of confusion, but of many of our puns. Note the "bare bear" of our nursery rhyme or the remark of a television entertainer that President Eisenhower had invited him to "tee."

While *homophones* are not strictly a phenomenon of the English language, it's true that we have many more of them than are to be found in other tongues. The reason? Simply because English has borrowed so widely from a great variety of languages that it was inevitable that words of different meanings but of similar spelling and sound would come from different source languages.

"Bear," the animal, comes from the German *bar* by way of the Old English *bera,* while "bear," to carry, comes from the Anglo-Saxon *beran* and has, indeed, been traced by some scholars back to the Sanskrit *bharati.* "Tea" and "tee," as you might expect, come from countries half a world apart, the former from a Chinese word *t'e* and the latter from the Scottish dialect word *teaz.*

homophones. *See* homonyms.

honeymoon

The explanation of the origin of *honeymoon* is, I fear, a bittersweet one. First as to the *honey:* It was a custom in ancient times for a newly married couple to drink a potion containing honey on each of the first thirty days —a *moon*—of their marriage. Attila, King of the Huns, was reputed to have drunk so heavily of this potion that he died of suffocation.

The thirty days, of course, roughly correspond to the lunar month, but there is still another explanation of the use of *moon* in this phrase. According to the *World Webster Dictionary,* this referred "not to the period of a month, but to the mutual affection of newlyweds, regarded as waning like the moon."

There, my friends, speaks a disillusioned etymologist. Let's cast off his cynical interpretation and revert to the happier thought of the young couple, steeped in bliss and honey, at least for the first thirty days of their married life.

hood

Hood is a contraction of *hoodlum,* an underworld slang term first reported in San Francisco where it was used to describe gangs of rowdies who specialized in maltreating Chinese laborers in the latter part of the nineteenth century.

There are a few fanciful theories of its origin, the most unlikely being that it was first a backward spelling of Muldoon ("noodlum") and gradually became *hoodlum*. Incidentally, sources with closer connections with the underworld than I report that hoods themselves pronounce the word to rhyme with "brood." The real hoods, apparently, never use the pronunciation given to "hood," the head covering.

hook, on his own

This is a phrase from the lore of fishermen. Whatever the angler takes *on his own hook* is done on his own responsibility and redounds to his credit.

hook, to give the

The *hook* here is straight out of vaudeville. In Grandfather's time a weekly event at the local vaudeville house was Amateur Night, when local talent competed for modest prizes and an opportunity to get a start in show business.

Very bad acts were hooted vehemently and, when the boos reached a peak, the manager would reach out from the wings with a long pole bearing a hook at the end and unceremoniously jerk the ham out of the limelight. Nowadays anyone who gets or is given *the hook* is a person discharged for incompetence.

hoolihan

Hoolihan has two closely related meanings in the colorful jargon of the cowpoke. An untamed or unbroken horse may buck in any one of a number of different ways. If he *swallers his head,* he drops his head between his forelegs. If he *crowhops,* he pitches with short, stiff-legged jumps. If he *jackknifes,* he clips his front and hind legs together. But if he *hoolihans* or *wildcats,* he actually somersaults. So a rider able to *throw the hoolihan* would have to be as skillful as they come.

The word *hoolihan*—sometimes written *hooley-ann*—has a second meaning in ranching. Cowpokes use various techniques to rope and throw cattle at roundup time. *Bulldogging* a steer means to get a grip on its horns and twist its neck until it hits the ground. *Hoolihanning* a steer is a very similar operation—knocking it down by leaping on its horns.

hoosegow

A jail or prison, *hoosegow* is derived from the Spanish word *jusgado*. The earliest recorded use of the word in American English is given as 1920, but, almost without question, the word was picked up by American cowpokes from their Mexican saddlemates back in the mid-1800's.

Hoosier

Referring to a native of Indiana, this designation derives from the Cumberland dialect word *hoozer,* meaning anything unusually large. It has been found in its present-day meaning of Indianan as far back as 1829. All sorts of variations have been created, including *Hoosierdom, Hoosierism* and even *Hoosierina,* meaning a woman who lives in Indiana.

hootch

One minor contribution of the Alaskan Indians to our cultural history might be noted. The slang term *hootch* so popular in the 1920's as a nickname for any of the then forbidden alcoholic beverages comes from *hoochino,* crude firewater which made those long Alaskan nights bearable for Alaskan natives many decades before they enjoyed the privileges of American citizenship—and the luxury of central heating.

Hore-Belisha

Lord Leslie Hore-Belisha, onetime head of the British War Office, among other notable accomplishments succeeded in making his name a part of the language during his tenure as Minister for Transport in the early thirties.

Always a controversial figure, blessed with a flair for publicity that rivaled that of New York's Mayor LaGuardia, Hore-Belisha burst into print soon after his appointment to office with the brash announcement that he was going to bring a halt to the "mass murder" of pedestrians on British roads and highways. Among his contributions to this end was a special pedestrian warning signal, an amber light mounted on a black-and-white striped post, which was supposed to warn drivers that they were nearing an intersection where pedestrians had the right-of-way. With characteristic modesty, the Minister of Transport named them *Belisha Beacons.* The man in the street, more often than not, called them *Hore-Belishas.*

And thus Lord Leslie has attained a sort of immortality, for that peerless chronicler of the English tongue, the *Shorter Oxford Dictionary,* now devotes six lines to Belisha and his beacon—as much space as is given to Queen Victoria's consort, Prince Albert, and the frock coat named after him.

hornswoggle

Unfortunately there's not much light to be shed on the origin of *hornswoggle.* Experts agree that it's an American coinage that can be traced to the early days of the nineteenth century. One Australian word authority recently commented: "The only American coinage which has left us breathless with admiration is *hornswoggle*"—and this from a nation that coined *bonzer, bushwhacker* and *billabong!*

Some theorists hold that the *horns* in *hornswoggle* may refer to the traditional symbol of the husband victimized by infidelity and that this would account for the element of deceit and trickery implicit in the word.

hors d'oeuvres

The literal meaning of the original French phrase *hors d'oeuvres* is "outside the work" and it was originally an architectural term referring to an outbuilding not incorporated into the architect's main design. The phrase was borrowed by France's culinary experts to indicate appetizers customarily served apart from the main course of a dinner. Thus *hors d'oeuvres* are, quite literally, outside the main design of the meal. *Vraiment, c'est simple, n'est-ce-pas?* See also CANAPÉ.

horse latitudes

The *horse latitudes* are regions characterized by calms, fickle breezes and high barometric pressure. They are found at 30 degrees North and South latitude. There are two theories as to how they got their name. The first is that sailing ships carrying horses to the New World might, when becalmed, have been forced to cast some of the horses overboard to lighten the vessel and take advantage of whatever breeze might be stirring.

The second theory is that *horse latitudes* is a translation of the Spanish phrase *golfo de las yeguas,* "gulf of the mares." The poetic Spaniards thus compared the fickleness of the breezes with the well-known capriciousness of mares.

horse Marines. *See* Marines, tell it to the

horseshoes as good-luck symbols

The story behind this good-luck symbol goes back at least to the tenth century. St. Dunstan, later to become the Archbishop of Canterbury, was known for his remarkable horseshoeing ability. One day the devil asked him to shoe his cloven hoof. St. Dunstan, recognizing his customer despite the disguise, performed the task after tying the devil to the wall. He made the treatment so painful that he soon had the devil begging for mercy. Dunstan finally let him go in return for the promise that he would never again enter a place which had a horseshoe nailed to the wall.

Among the notables who have shown their faith in this symbol we can count Lord Nelson, Britain's hero at Trafalgar. Nelson had a horseshoe nailed to the mast of his flagship, *Victory,* but its magical powers seem to have been somewhat circumscribed. Britain won the battle, but Nelson lost his life.

hotchpotch. *See* hodgepodge.

hot corner. *See* baseball jargon.

hot dog

The first recorded appearance in print of the term *hot dog* is in 1903. The late Henry L. Mencken, as would be expected by anyone familiar with his massive and enormously entertaining tome, *The American Language,* did some very thorough research on the origins of *hot dog.* His findings: although sausages in rolls have been sold in this country for many years, the first person to heat the roll and add mustard and relish was Harry Stevens, concessionaire at the Polo Grounds, home of the New York Giants. And the coiner of the name *hot dog?* None other than the late T. A. Dorgan, who, signing his work "Tad," was undoubtedly the best-known sports cartoonist of the era.

hot rod language

Here are a few items from the jargon of the denizens of the drag strip, those special runways where drag races are held. A *drag race,* incidentally, is really an acceleration-time trial, the object being to see whose car can make the fastest time over a quarter-mile course from a standing start.

To *chop and channel* a car is to cut out part of the body of a sedan or coupé in order to reduce wind resistance, and then lower the entire body by dropping it down over the frame rails. This results in a machine with an oddly truncated appearance much admired by devotees of the sport.

This is only the beginning. Until the car's *mill* or engine has had a *build-up*—which may involve the addition of *twin pots,* dual carburetors —it cannot qualify as a *rod,* much less as a *full house,* a car whose engine has been completely modified for high-speed performance.

The accessories added to improve an engine's speed and power are known as *goodies.* But a car decked out with flashy ornamentation and without a properly *modified* engine is scorned by all true rodders as a *gooker* or *gook-wagon.*

For some years now, Western rodders have been using airplane belly tanks as bodies for cars designed for racing on the dry lake beds of Southern California. These rods are known variously as *tankers* or *lakesters.*

Some racing rods have to be pushed, or *nerfed,* when warming up for a speed run. The bumper used on the pushing car is called a *nerfing bar.*

An *A-bone* and an *A-bomb* are both Model A Fords, but the second is a souped-up version, modified for greater power. A *T-bone* is a Model T Ford—remember them, Pop?—but these are really more of interest to fanciers of antique or "classic" cars than to rodders.

If you had a choice in the matter, you'd do well to choose a *beast,* rather than a *goat* or a *gook*. A *beast,* you see, is a really powerful hot rod, while a *goat* is a poor performing rod and a *gook* is despised by all true hot-rodders who judge their cars more by performance than appearance. While they like to keep their rods well tended and polished, they know that, in Fred Horsley's words, "Beauty starts on the inside and a good rod combines performance and safety with good looks."

A *chopped fly* is a flywheel lightened by cutting off metal. This is done to give the rod faster acceleration. Obviously, then, a rod with a chopped fly will get a better *bite*—hold traction better for a quick getaway—*if the rubber doesn't break loose.*

You don't know what that last phrase means? Get with it, Dad. That merely means if the tires don't spin or skid when you're trying for a fast getaway in a rod race.

house, on the

The chances are that the original *house* was a British inn or tavern. In the years before Prohibition, it was the custom of most saloons or, as they are known in England, *public houses,* to give a free drink with every third or fourth one bought. This drink was *on the house*—meaning at the expense of the establishment.

Nowadays, of course, such as practice is unknown. Indeed, it is prohibited by law in many states. So the expression *on the house* has come out from behind the bar, so to speak, and is now a common and respectable part of the language.

Hoyle, according to

Edmond Hoyle was a sixteenth-century British clubman and games expert. One of the most popular games of the time was whist, which continued in popularity until the advent of auction and contract bridge. Hoyle was the first person to prepare a really authoritative handbook on it: *A Short Treatise on the Game of Whist*. Later he added rules for other card games and he became accepted as the final authority on the playing of card games. To this day the phrase *played according to Hoyle* means "played in accordance with the rules of the game."

hugger-mugger

Hugger-mugger is a word seldom come upon these days. Elliot Paul wrote a better-than-average mystery *Hugger-mugger in the Louvre* some years ago but if the word has been much in evidence elsewhere, it has escaped this writer's attention. It originally meant secrecy or stealth, and Mr. Paul pretty obviously extended this meaning to something bordering on skulduggery. It has also the meaning of an untidy, disorderly mess.

Hugger-mugger is one of a large class of words known to scholars as "reduplicated" words or "ricochet" words. Chitchat, ding-dong, harum-scarum, hoity-toity and hodgepodge are a few more. Sometimes these words have been coined for humorous effect; more often the repetition tends to intensify the meaning of the root word. So it is with *hugger-mugger,* which is thought to be a variant of *hoker-moker,* from the Middle English *mokeren,* "to conceal or hoard." Thus the meaning of secrecy is inherent in the root of the word—and strengthened by the repetition.

humble pie

Here we have a play upon words which dates back to the time of William the Conqueror.

First, the *pie* referred to in "eating *humble pie"* was really *umble pie,* made from the umbles—heart, liver and gizzard—of a deer. It was made to be eaten by servants and huntsmen, while the lord of the manor and his guests dined on venison. Thus a person who had to eat *umble pie* was one who was in a position of inferiority—one who had to humble himself before his better.

The pun resulting from *umble* and *humble* is even more precise when you recall that in several British dialects—notably Cockney—the *h* on *humble* would be silent.

Actually the two words come from quite different roots, *humble* from the Latin *humilis* (low or slight), and *umble* from the Latin *lumulus,* meaning "loin."

humbug

This amusing word for "hoax" or "fraud" first appeared during the eighteenth century as a bit of popular slang and quite possibly came out of the jargon of the underworld. At any rate, it is first recorded by the Earl of Orrery who termed it a "new-coined expression which is only to be found in the nonsensical vocabulary and sounds disagreeable and absurd."

Its great popularity during the nineteenth century can be credited to P. T. Barnum who probably never said, "There is a sucker born every minute," but most assuredly did say, "The American people like to be *humbugged."* Indeed, Barnum once lectured in England on the subject: "The Science of Money Making and the Philosophy of *Humbug"*—which sounds remarkably like a more forceful and candid exposition of the same sort of pragmatic approach to business success that is peddled today under labels such as "Influencing People," "Positive Thinking" and the like.

hunting the gowk

An April Fool's Day trick practiced by the Scots, *hunting the gowk* translates to "hunting the cuckoo bird." See also APRIL FOOL'S DAY.

hush puppies

Department stores the country over are selling a brand of rubber-soled shoes called *hush puppies*. The adman who thought up the name is doubtless proud of his cleverness, but I can't help wondering what he'd think if he knew the history of the term.

Throughout the South, of course, *hush puppies* are known as tasty bits of deep-fried corn-meal batter often served as accompaniment to fried fish. The most common theory of the origin of the term traces it back to the years immediately following the War Between the States. During those days of Reconstruction, food was shockingly scarce and a staple on all diets was corn meal in various guises. According to legend, many a mother fried up bits of corn batter to quiet the plaintive cries of hungry children —and dogs—with the words "Hush, child. Hush, puppy!"

Another and perhaps more authentic explanation was offered to me by Troy West of Encinitas, California, who explained that he was born and raised in the South, and that the original *hush puppy* was the salamander, an aquatic reptile almost always called a "water dog" or "water puppy."

"Over fifty years ago," Mr. West wrote, "my mother told me that no one wanted anyone to know they were reduced to eating water dogs. So 'hush, don't say anything about it and just eat it.' The water dogs were generally fried with the fish and the corn dough, which was formed into small sticks—so they could easily be called *hush puppies* too."

The salamanders Mr. West mentions were also called "hell benders" and "land pike." As long ago as 1687 an early visitor to America described the land pike as "another strange reptile so called from its likeness to that fish; but instead of fins it hath four feet." So it's easy to understand how it could have been used as a substitute for the genuine article—and why people would want to keep that fact hush-hush.

I

ice. *See* payola.

iconoclast

Iconoclast (pronounced eye-KON-uh-klast) is a word which has come almost unchanged from the Greek *eikon* (image) and *klastes* (a breaker). Literally one who shatters sacred images, it has come to mean anyone who scoffs at our treasured beliefs. During the 1920's it was the fashion to "debunk" history and, as a result, a whole rash of *iconoclastic* books about America's heroes was published.

ill wind that blows nobody good, It's an

Today the most common meaning of *ill* is "not healthy," but for many centuries after it came into English from Old Norse, it meant "evil." So the real meaning of this expression is "It's an evil wind that blows nobody good." Among musicians the piccolo is sometimes facetiously called "the woodwind nobody blows good."

implosion

The new vocabulary of science is full of words that are, often quite literally, beyond the comprehension of older generations. *Implosion* is such a word. It has long been used in the technical vocabulary of speech experts to describe the sudden cutting off of breath in the pronunciation of such consonants as *p, t* and *k.* With the development of the atomic bomb, *implosion* moved into the field of nuclear terminology, for the effect produced by the detonation of one of these weapons is the opposite of that produced by the ordinary explosion of bombs. The atomic bomb actually does "explode inwardly."

In dictionary language, then, "*Implosion* is a bursting inward, especially a guided explosion focused inward, as in the atomic bomb."

impugn—impute

It's not surprising that many people confuse these two "look-alikes." Even our learned brethren of the legal profession who nowadays can lay almost sole claim to *impugn,* since it rarely is heard outside courtrooms and legislative chambers, have been known to mistake one for the other. *Impute* means to ascribe to another the credit or blame for an action or event. Usually it is used in a derogatory sense, as, "Kennedy *imputed* to Khrushchev the responsibility for the breakdown of negotiations."

Impugn likewise is often used in a deprecatory sense and means to assail with insinuations or accusations. Thus one occasionally will hear an attorney protesting to the judge that his "worthy opponent" is attempting to "*impugn* his veracity." For a means of keeping the two words straight in your mind, I suggest you remember that *impute* (literally "think against" from the Latin *in* and *puto*) obviously implies greater subtlety in discrediting an opponent than *impugn* (from the Latin *impugno,* "to fight against").

inchoate

Inchoate (pronounced in-KOH-it), derived from the Latin verb *incohare* (to begin), is an adjective meaning "just commenced" or "incipient." It has no relation to *chaotic,* which describes a state of confusion or disorder.

incipient

Meaning "just beginning to exist," *incipient* comes to us from the Latin *in* (in or on) and *capere* (take).

indemnify

Indemnify (pronounced in-DEM-nih-fy) means either to secure against loss or damage or to compensate for such. Its roots are Latin: *in* (not) and *demnum* (hurt). Other forms of the word are *indemnification* or *indemnity* and *indemnifier* or *indemnitor* (the person or company that provides compensation or insurance).

independent as a hog on ice. *See* hog on ice, independent as

Indian corn. *See* Indian giver.

Indian giver

Thanks to the trend in recent years to motion pictures showing the American Indian in a sympathetic light, the old concept of the Indian as a ruthless, bloodthirsty warrior is not shared by today's youngsters. Some credit for the new and more accurate evaluation of the Indian and his role in our history doubtless should also go to the teachers who have worked hard to erase the stereotype which colored the thinking of earlier generations.

But the changeover from a harsh to a sympathetic delineation of the Noble Redskin has not been without its complications. Terms such as *Indian giver* remain in our language and the stories of their origin and meaning are no longer entirely consistent with the picture of the Indian.

Originally an *Indian giver* was one who made a gift only in expectation of getting an even better one in return. It is only comparatively recently that an *Indian gift* became one which was itself to be returned.

Actually the term was one of several—*Indian summer, Indian corn* and *Indian tea,* for example—invented by the earliest colonists to describe something which resembled the genuine article as they had known it in England but actually was not the same. Thus, *Indian summer* is the brief period in the fall when we have a temporary return of summer's warm climate. *Indian corn* is not what the British called "corn"—which we know as wheat—and so on.

If you are willing to concede that the Indians occasionally employed trickery in their dealings with the whites, you will understand why the white man came to use the word *Indian* as a synonym for "bogus" or, to use a favorite adjective of children, "pretend." So an *Indian giver* is, in a youngster's own language, only a "pretend giver."

Indian summer. *See* Indian giver.

Indian tea. *See* Indian giver.

inexorable

Inexorable (pronounced in-EX-er-uh-b'l)—this negative form is much more common than the positive *exorable*. Meaning inflexible, relentless, merciless and unmoved by any plea, the word *inexorable* is a combination of the Latin *in* (not) plus *ex* (out) and *orare* (to pray).

infracaninophile

Many years ago the late Christopher Morley coined the word *infracaninophile* to describe a person who favors the underdog. Pronounced in-fruh-kuh-NIN-oh-file, it is based on the following word elements: *infra* (under), *canino* (dog) and *phile* (one who loves).

This odd word—actually what linguists call a "nonce word," one coined for a single occasion—moved Joseph A. Davis, Jr., of Woodcliff Lake, New Jersey, to observe: "I am a zoologist (more specifically, a mammalogist) with a background of Greek and Latin in school. Christopher Morley to the contrary, shouldn't the word be *infracaniphile* or *infracanophile?*

"The root is *canis* (dog). *Caninus* would be 'doglike.' An *infracanino-phile* would root for the 'underdog-like'—which is an awkward expression for one who is a nonbeatnik.

"Or is *canino* justified because the underdog is not *really* a dog? And what when he *is* a dog?"

Then, to cast further confusion, came a letter from Sidney P. Goodrich of the Classics Department, Ripon (Wisconsin) College: "As a professional palaeoglottist (student of ancient languages)," he wrote, "I am spurred to a state resembling animation by your report on *infracaninophile*. If the word is to be Greek, it should be *hypocynophile* (*hypo*, "under" and *cyno*, "dog," plus *philos*, "friend"). If it is Latin, I suppose it should be *infracaniary* (*infra*, "below"; *canis* "dog"; and *arious*, "one associated with.") With best wishes and the hope that this will add to the confusion, I remain, Waxlessly yours, S. P. Goodrich."

In a footnote, Dr. Goodrich noted that *waxlessly* is his way of writing "sincerely"—from the Latin *sine* (without) and *cera* (wax).

Well, he has certainly compounded the confusion—to the extent that I'm beginning to hate underdogs and wish that Mr. Morley had never brought the subject up. Unfortunately it's no longer possible to summon Christopher Morley—that delightful sage and wit—to defend his word creation. My guess is that he too would concede the puristic propriety of the suggested variations but argue that, since the word was created wholly in the spirit of fun, the spoofing *infracaninophile* trips off the tongue with a brighter lilt.

ingénue. *See* ingenuous.

ingenuous—ingenious

Ingenuous (pronounced in-JEN-yoo-us) is not to be confused with *ingenious*, the more common word meaning "inventive" or "resourceful." Though both come from the same Latin verb, *ingignere* (to produce), *ingenuous* comes directly from the Latin *ingenuus*, which meant "freeborn, noble or frank." In English it has come to mean candid, frank, straightforward or naïve.

The French took the same root and developed the word *ingénue* as a name for a naïve young woman or an actress playing that part.

The noun form of *ingenuous* is *ingenuousness*, while *ingenuity* is the noun for the quality of being *ingenious*.

innocuous desuetude

Innocuous desuetude means, in plain English, "harmless disuse." It was coined by President Grover Cleveland and used in a message to Congress, March 1, 1886. The complete quote from President Cleveland runs: "After an existence of nearly twenty years of almost *innocuous desuetude,* these laws are brought forth."

inscrutable

Inscrutable (pronounced in-SCROO-tuh-b'l) describes that which is beyond comprehension, mysterious, incapable of being understood. Stemming from the Latin *in* (not) and *scrutari* (to search), it is related to the English word *scrutiny* which means a careful or close examination. As an adverb it becomes *inscrutably,* and, as a noun, *inscrutability.*

intelligentsia

The pronunciation of *intelligentsia* with a hard *g* is a snobbish affectation—not wrong, mind you, but not normal either.

Here's how it comes about. *Intelligentsia* followed a very curious path in coming to English. It is derived originally from the Latin *intelligentia,* meaning "perceptiveness and discernment." From the beginning it appeared in Italian, logically enough, as *intelligenza* (intelligence), but then it detoured to Russia where it became *intelligentsiya* with the meaning it has today—people who are or regard themselves as being the intellectual elite.

When it arrived in the Russian language the soft Italian *g* became the hard Russian *g*. However, the soft *g* is much more commonly heard and, by analogy with other related words (*intelligence* itself, for instance) which did not take the Russian detour, it is a more logical pronunciation.

intransigent

Intransigent (pronounced in-TRAN-suh-junt) is both a noun and an adjective. It is used to describe or identify a person who is uncompromising or who refuses to be reconciled, particularly politically. From the Latin *in* (not) and *transigere* (to come to an understanding), it gained its political significance in Spanish when the name *los intransigentes* was the term applied to the extreme Left (Republican) party.

intrinsic

Intrinsic (pronounced in-TRIN-sik), also, *intrinsical,* describes that which is both inherent and essential. Derived from the Latin *intra* (within) and *secus* (beside) it is used in anatomy to describe that which is located within a part of the body.

inveigle

Inveigle (pronounced in-VEE-g'l) means to entice or persuade by flattery or other deception. It is the English version of the French word *aveugler* (to blind) and goes back in Latin to *ab* (from) plus *oculus* (eye). The word *inveiglement* applies to either the act of *inveigling* or that of being *inveigled*. He who commits the act is an *inveigler*.

Inverness cape

There are several garments and fabrics which bear place names, rather than names of individuals like cardigan and raglan. The *Inverness cape,* beloved of Sherlock Holmes enthusiasts, is one of these. This combination overcoat and outer cape is named after Inverness, a county seat in Scotland where the winters are surely such as to make a man appreciate the added warmth of his *Inverness*.

inveterate

Meaning "firmly established or habitual," *inveterate* stems from the Latin *in* (in) and *vetus* (old).

Irgun, Haganah

Irgun (full name: *Irgun Zvai Leumi*) was the name of an underground organization in Palestine especially active during the trying period immediately following World War II. According to the *Columbia Encyclopedia,* when the British in 1946 set quotas for the immigration of stateless Jews, "secret organizations attacked British military installations. . . . The most violent were the Irgun Zvai Leumi. . . . Haganah, the large and well-trained secret defense army of the Jews, abstained from violence."

As to pronunciation, the *Irgun Zvai Leumi* may be pronounced EAR-goon TSWAH-ee leh-OO-me, while *Haganah* (also sometimes spelled *Hagana*) is simply HAH-gah-nah.

irony

Irony comes to us from the Greek *eiron,* meaning a person who dissembles (pretends) in his speech. Thus *irony* is the speech of one who says the opposite of his true meaning. Grammarians classify this figure of speech in two ways: *light irony,* which is humorous banter, and *severe irony,* which is usually sarcasm or cutting satire.

itching palm

The exact origin of this phrase is unknown but it derives from a superstition that if your palm itches, you're about to receive money, usually from some unexpected source.

The expression goes back at least to the time of Shakespeare, for in *Julius Caesar* he writes:

> Let me tell you, Cassius, you yourself
> Are much condemned to have an itching palm.

itmo

Itmo is an odd word and worth at least a casual glance. It is a Tagalog name for the betel vine and nut. In case you're still mystified, Tagalog is the native language of the Philippines and betel nuts are the mildly narcotic nuts chewed throughout Southeast Asia. Bloody Mary in *South Pacific,* you recall, was "always chewing betel nuts."

ivory tower

A phrase of comparatively recent origin, *ivory tower* means a place where intellectuals go to think and to be away from the world. It is credited to the nineteenth-century French literary critic Charles Augustin Sainte-Beuve. As he used it, of course, the phrase read *un tour d'ivoire.*

I.W.W. *See* labor's lost lexicon.

J

Jabberwocky

Lewis Carroll, creator of the ever-young *Alice in Wonderland,* invented the language he called *Jabberwocky* by blending two words into one and coming up with such words as *slithy,* made up of "lithe" and "slimy," and *mimsy,* made up of "miserable" and "flimsy." Carroll termed the words *portmanteau words* because they were "packed together" as in a portmanteau (suitcase). See also BLEND WORDS.

Jack Armstrong, all-American boy

During the 1930's a very popular afternoon serial show on radio was called *Jack Armstrong, All-American Boy.* The announcement fanfare with a glee club hymning the virtues of a popular breakfast cereal soon became the butt of juvenile humor and *Jack Armstrong* took his place in folklore and in the language, just as Frank Merriwell had a generation or two earlier.

Abe Lincoln had a celebrated rough-and-tumble fight with a Jack

Armstrong who later became his friend, but this does not appear to be the origin of this fairly common American expression.

jack, balling the. *See* balling the jack.

Jack Robinson

Quick as you can say Jack Robinson is older than baseball's Jackie Robinson—about two centuries older, in fact. While no one knows for sure where the expression started, it was listed as early as 1785 by Francis Grose in his *Classical Dictionary of the Vulgar Tongue*. Grose gave the following unlikely explanation of its origin: "Before one could say Jack Robinson is a saying to express a very short time, originating from a very volatile gentleman who would call on his neighbors and be gone before his name could be announced."

Jacob's ladder

A *Jacob's ladder* is a ladder made of rope or cable, usually with wooden rungs. It is dropped over the side of a ship to enable people to ascend from or descend to small boats alongside. Harbor pilots usually come aboard via a *Jacob's ladder*.

The *Jacob's ladder* gets its name from an incident in the Book of Genesis (28:12). The patriarch Jacob falls asleep and has a vision: "And he dreamed, and behold a ladder set up on the earth, and the top of it reached to heaven; and behold the angels of God ascending and descending on it."

Jacob's ladder has been used in at least two other quite earthly meanings. A small plant with a flower-and-leaf formation resembling a ladder bears this name. In England, also what we Americans call "runs" in hosiery were formerly called *Jacob's ladders*. Nowadays they are simply *ladders*.

jaded

Jaded (pronounced JAY-d'd) is an adjective, the past participle of the verb *jade*. In the Old Norse language *jalda* meant "mare" and in English *jade* means "horse," particularly one which is old and tired. Thus the verb *jade* came to mean to make or to become old and tired. The adjective *jaded* can be applied to many things, most commonly to the appetite. "As a result of overindulgence, the gourmand's appetite became *jaded*."

jargon

There are two schools of thought about why practically every profession or academic discipline invents and maintains its own peculiar type of vocabulary. After considerable search a novice can usually convert these arcane words into common, everyday English. Specialists in these areas claim that the origination of their "own" terms is occasioned by the need to express certain nuances of meaning not readily found in day-to-day speech. On the other hand, outsiders often feel that the primary motivation is a desire for exclusivity and a wish to impress outsiders with an artificial profundity.

The jargon or argot of learned professions—and even the shop talk of less pretentious trades—often leaves the layman puzzled. When a schoolteacher, for instance, showers a questioning parent with remarks about *core curriculum, structured compositions, root subjects, semantic concepts* and *structural linguistics,* the parent is justified in wondering whether the instructor's intent is to clarify or confuse.

But when a chef speaks of *persillade,* a seamstress refers to *bar fagoting* or a lawyer mentions *torts* we realize that each is using a term of his trade because it is a more precise indicator of true meaning than any word in the general vocabulary.

So the suggestion that the chief reason why people use special jargon is to "impress outsiders" merits the traditional Scotch verdict: "Not proven." Surely the desire to impress—and confuse—those outside a trade or profession is often the reason for the use of a private language. But, equally often, such terms are resorted to because they supply a precision lacking in the common language.

For anyone curious about the examples of trade talk given above, *persillade* is a mixture of finely chopped parsley and garlic used to garnish meat dishes; *bar fagoting* is a decorative ladderlike seam stitch, and a *tort* is a wrongful act (not involving breach of contract) for which one can bring a civil action.

jarhead. *See* Old Army slang.

jawbone. *See* Old Army slang.

jaywalker

The word *jaywalker* dates back to the early part of the century when *jay* was a popular slang term meaning "countrified" or "rustic." A *jay* was pretty much the same as a *rube* and, if memory serves, was so used by George M. Cohan in the lyrics of one of his most famous songs, *Forty-five Minutes from Broadway.*

A farmer, strange to the ways of the city and perhaps frightened by the newfangled automobiles churning down the streets at fantastic speeds up to fifteen or twenty miles an hour, might have been expected to cross the street in an erratic fashion, without paying too much attention to signals. Hence, *jaywalking.*

You'll find that some dictionaries say that *jay* in this word means "stupid" or "dull-witted," but anyone who has *jaywalked* in New York City traffic knows that he must have his wits about him at all times, if he wants to live dangerously—successfully.

jazzmen's jargon

Some of us in the thinning hair and thickening paunch set can remember away back to the early thirties when jazz was a furtive thing heard only in a handful of night clubs and speakeasies. Never were the raucous, wailing notes of jazz and the blues allowed to sully the nation's airwaves and seldom did a recording company stoop to record what was then known as "race" music. Indeed, almost the only time the dedicated jazz fan could hear his favorite music was when he was fortunate enough to be allowed to sit in on an after-hours jam session where the musicians made their kind of music for their own mutual enjoyment.

My, how things have changed! But for all the lavish trimmings given jazz on TV—which must amuse Duke Ellington when he thinks back to the Cotton Club of three or four decades ago—one thing has changed little, the argot spoken by the musicians themselves. Like all secret languages, the jive talk of the working musician exists chiefly because he wants a way to communicate with his fellow musicians without the general public (*squares,* to musicians) knowing what is going on. But, as always, some insider is willing to unravel the mysteries of the jargon for the enlightenment of the baffled *squares.*

This time it's Mitch Miller who reports some of the latest language findings. According to Miller, any instrument may be labeled the *ax*—though the term is usually reserved for one or another of the horns. A *bash, gig, hame* or *bake* is an engagement where the musician works. But a *ball* to a jazz musician is never a formal dance; it's an occasion for exuberant enjoyment, a real good time. *Ball* is also used as a verb: "I'm going to *ball* tonight."

A *benny* is a pawnbroker and a *bill* is a hundred dollars. Money, generally speaking, is *bread* and, for the most part, bread comes from the *bossman,* who may be booking agent, bandleader or music contractor.

A *cat* is *dragged* by a dull, boring experience, but a stimulating, enjoyable occurrence will *gas* him—sometimes to the extent that he will *flip.* When low in funds, the musician may speak up for a *taste*—meaning an advance upon the *bread* to come. If the *taste* is big enough, he might treat himself to a new *set of threads*—a suit.

Now that jazz is being recognized by television as an exciting entertainment form, TV has begun to rate high in the jazz musician's professional interest. Indeed, a pair of new phrases have been coined to fit the new situation. When a musician is appearing on local TV, he is *on the tube*. If it's a network show, he's *on the Big Tube*.

One last word for the guidance of future chroniclers of *Le Jazz Hot*—and there's a dated phrase, by the way—comes from Phil Sterling, Mitch Miller's amanuensis. "Musicians do not use the term *the eighty-eight* for the piano, except as a sort of bad joke," writes Sterling. "They do call it *the keys,* though." So don't goof, Jack. When you're digging Shearing from a seat in Frontsville, it's the keys that gas you, not the eighty-eight! See also MUSICIAN'S SLANG.

jazz slang. *See* musician's slang.

jeans. *See* blue jeans.

jeep

This designation is generally believed to have developed from the letters GP (for "general purpose"), used by the Army as the code designation for this vehicle. Undoubtedly its immediate widespread acceptance can be credited in large part to the popularity of a comic strip character, Eugene the Jeep, a tiny creature with supernatural powers, created by the late E. C. Segar, a widely syndicated cartoonist in the years just preceding World War II.

jemmy twitcher. *See* sandwich.

jerkwater

Small towns are often referred to as "*jerkwater* towns." The general meaning of the term is obvious, its origin not quite so much so.

In the days when most trains were powered by steam, it was necessary for them to stop at regular intervals to refill the water tender, the first car behind the engine. Since the water requirements of the trains did not always coincide with the regularly scheduled passenger stops, they often paused briefly in small way stations where the fireman would jerk a cord attached to an enormous spigot hanging from the water tower and fill the tender with water. Hence, *jerkwater* to describe a hamlet with no other reason, from the railroaders' viewpoint, for existence.

jerry-built

Jerry in this case has nothing to do with Germans, although confusion has arisen because *Jerries* was a common British nickname for German soldiers in World Wars I and II.

Actually *jerry-built,* meaning poorly built or constructed of inferior materials, was originally a shipbuilding term and was first used in the shipyards of Liverpool midway through the last century. It is probably a corruption of "jury" as in "jury rig" or "jury mast," meaning something contrived for emergency or temporary use.

jersey

Jersey, a knitted fabric, is so called because it was originally produced on the island of Jersey, one of the Channel Islands.

jetsam. *See* flotsam and jetsam.

jew's-harp

The *jew's-harp* is a small metal instrument held between the teeth and plucked with a finger. It produces a twanging noise which bears about the same relationship to music as the sound of bagpipes does.

The origins of the *jew's-harp* are indeed ancient, however. It was known in France as the *jeu tromp,* literally the "play trumpet." Then Beaumont and Fletcher, the Elizabethan dramatists, converted the *jeu* to *jew* to make the phrase *jew tromp.* Still later the "trumpet" idea gave way to the "harp"—which the instrument in a very remote way does resemble—and the word *jew's-harp* came into being.

jig is up, the

The jig is up, meaning "Your game has been exposed," was first heard during Shakespeare's time. *Jig* was then a slang word for "trick," so the phrase simply meant your trick or deceit has been found out.

Jimmy Higgins. *See* labor's lost lexicon.

jockeys, bench, disc, et al.

The *disc jockey* (or *D.J.*) is a familiar figure on the radio scene, the chap who plays records interspersed with comment and commercials. Writing in *American Speech* magazine—Dr. Ruth Aldrich of the University of Wisconsin reported that the term *disc jockey* goes back "at least until 1946." I can attest that it appeared in a dictionary I edited (*Words: The New Dictionary*) in early 1947. Taking into account the time involved in getting a dictionary ready for publication, this means that it must have been current in the early 1940's.

The date of its first appearance is not nearly so interesting, though, as the remarkable collection of variations Dr. Aldrich has collected. Most of them are self-explanatory, and all reveal that genius for improvisation that makes the American brand of English the lively and often bewildering language it is. Here are a few: *bus jockey* (bus driver); *typewriter jockey* (typist); *plow jockey* (farmer); *car jockey* (parking lot attendant); *jet jockey* (jet pilot); *chopper jockey* (helicopter operator); *slide-rule jockey* (airplane's navigator or research engineer); *motorboat jockey* and *switchboard jockey.*

Baseball, of course, has used the phrase *bench jockey*—a player who heckles the opposing team from the safety of his own dugout. And, amusingly enough, elevator operators—a vanishing breed, judging from the popularity of automated elevators—are honored in Dr. Aldrich's collection with two separate listings: *elevator jockey* and *vertical jockey.*

Some authentication of the origin of *jockey* in such connotations came from a Washington, D.C., correspondent, who wrote that in the early 1920's ball players were already being called *bench jockeys.* One of the sportswriters of that era referred thus to Fritz Maisel, Baltimore Orioles third baseman. The logic behind the term was that a *jockey* does the riding and directing, with the help of his reins and whip, and Maisel was —metaphorically, at least—applying the same tactics to the opposition. To *jockey a fall guy* into an undesirable position seems to be an outgrowth of this same sense, somewhat different from *jockeying* a bobsled or motorcycle. It would be this latter sense, I guess, though the distinction is not great, which led to *disc jockey,* but trying to catch the exact connotations of such a phrase is like trying to put a rubber stamp on a slippery ghost.

jocose

Derived from the Latin *jocus* (joke), *jocose* is another word for humorous or facetious.

jodhpurs and dhoti

A few years ago one of our favorite night club comedians used to brighten the midnight hours with a mournful plaint called "Sam, You Made the Pants Too Long." Whether the song is still being sung, your editor cannot say. With the passage of years, his visits to the bistro beat have become fewer. But the old refrain came mockingly to mind as we read of the involvement of Prime Minister Nehru of India in a saga which might well have been titled, "Jawaharlal, you wore the pants too long!"

It seems that Nehru favors *jodhpurs* (pronounced JOD-perz or JOHD-perz, never JOD-ferz) rather than the traditional Hindu loincloth, the *dhoti* (pronounced, again with the "h" silent, DOH-tih). *Jodhpurs* take their name from Jodhpur, a state in northwestern India. As adapted in the form of riding breeches, they are associated in the minds of some Hindus with their one-time overlords, the polo-playing British colonials.

By contrast, the *dhoti*—a nearly knee-length garment somewhat re-sembling a wraparound bed sheet—has become practically a symbol of patriotism, since it was the garment invariably worn by the late Mahatma Gandhi. Not long ago a native of Bengal tried to insist upon his right to wear the *dhoti* into the main dining room of a leading New Delhi hotel. The management, invoking a rule requiring "lounge suits or evening dress," de-nied him admission.

The result was a furor which landed on the front page of every Indian newspaper. Editorialists rushed to the defense of the *dhoti,* which was called "as graceful for men as the sari is graceful for women." And Nehru, though not even in town at the time of the incident, was sharply criticized for favoring *jodhpurs* instead of the *dhoti.* Some newspapers even insisted the *dhoti* should be prescribed as the national dress.

Well, if that New Delhi hotel has a night club, its comedian has some seasoned material ready at hand. You guessed it: "Sam, you made the Pandit's pants too long!"

Joeys

Joey is the backstage name for a circus clown, chosen in honor of the first great modern clown, Joseph Grimaldi, who charmed children and grownups alike in England more than a century and a half ago. See also CIRCUS JARGON.

John B. *See* cowboy jargon.

John Henry, John Hancock

As every schoolboy knows, the biggest, boldest and most defiant sig-nature on the Declaration of Independence was scrawled by John Hancock of Massachusetts. So completely did it overshadow the autographs of the other founding fathers that the term *John Hancock* has become synony-mous with "signature" and each of us at one time or another has spoken of "putting his *John Hancock"* at the bottom of a document.

In the West, a half-century and more later, the phrase became altered to "John Henry," and nobody knows quite why. Suffice it that, in the words of Ramon Adams' excellent collection of cowboy jargon, *Western Words:* "John Henry is what the cowboy calls his signature. He never signs a document, he puts his *John Henry* to it!"

Incidentally, there seems to be no connection between the John Henry of cowboy slang and the fabulous John Henry of railroad lore who was so powerful that he could outdrive a steam drill with his hammer and steel. This legend has been traced to the drilling of the Chesapeake and Ohio Big Bend Tunnel through West Virginia in the 1870's—substantially later than the first use of *John Henry* by cowpokes of the Old West.

johnnycake

Where *johnnycake,* the name for flat corn bread cooked on a board or griddle over an open fire, came from nobody seems to know, for sure. There's one widely held theory that it is a corruption of "journey cake," since corn bread lasted longer in the saddle bags of early travelers than bread made of wheat flour.

More likely, however, is the theory that it was originally "Shawnee-cake"—from the Shawnee Indians, who certainly knew and used corn in cooking and baking long before any white men came to America.

Joneses, keeping up with the

Keeping up with the Joneses was originally the title of a comic strip by A. R. Momand, first released in 1913 and—perhaps ironically—a casualty of the depression year of 1931. The author says that he originally planned to call the strip "Keeping up with the Smiths" but changed the name to Joneses as being more euphonious. Apparently the Smiths, then as now, were quite as well-to-do as the Joneses.

juberous

The word *juberous* is rather more than just a synonym for "dubious." It *is* "dubious."

Actually *juberous* started as a joking mispronunciation of "dubious" and figured prominently in humorous writing of the early and mid-nineteenth century. In that period, the days when Bill Nye was the ranking American humorist, mispronunciations and misspellings were the chief characteristics of our humor.

Juberous, according to Harold Wentworth's *American Dialect Dictionary,* is still very widely heard in many parts of the country, chiefly in rural regions. He reports that it is also sometimes spelled *jubous, duberous* and *jubious.* Sometimes, instead of being used subjectively to describe a state of mind ("I'm *juberous* about our chances"), it is applied to the object of the anxiety ("That car looks mighty *juberous"*—meaning in poor shape for the trip ahead).

Please note, however, that all these uses are labeled "dialectal." That means that they figure perfectly properly in the easy, informal speech between you and your friends. Such expressions, indeed, add color to our daily speech. However, such words as *juberous* should surely be avoided in written communication of a formal nature, as well as in sermons or talks intended for a general audience.

juke box

Pinball machines and "one-arm bandits" are not *juke boxes.* A *juke box* is a coin-operated phonograph and only a coin-operated phonograph.

The earliest *juke boxes,* actually, were known as "jook organs" and were coin-operated devices which produced sounds like those heard from hurdy-gurdies or barrel organs. They took their name from the "jooks" or "jook joints," which the dictionaries politely label "unsavory resorts." The word "jook" is Gullah Negro dialect, perhaps originally related to the West African word *dsug.*

K

kaiser. *See* czar.

kangaroo court

A *kangaroo court* is an illegal mock or sham court, usually one set up by inmates of a prison to levy fines and punishment on other inmates who violate the "code." Such organizations, usually very informal in nature, exist in most large prisons and are even encouraged by some wardens as a useful device for maintaining order.

The name probably originated at the time when Australia, land of the kangaroo, was the penal colony for the British Empire.

The term has occasionally—and inaccurately—been applied to the kind of roadside justice of the peace court which exists only to collect fines from motorists caught in speed traps.

kaput

Kaput comes straight from German. It means "spoiled, done for, broken down." Apparently Yankee soldiers in World War II picked it up from their German counterparts for whom the war did indeed "go *kaput.*" *Kaput* is pronounced "kuh-POOT."

keeping up with the Joneses. *See* Joneses, keeping up with.

kegler

Kegler comes from the old German word *Kegel,* meaning a ninepin or tenpin. The game, and, with it the origin of *Kegel,* goes back to the Middle

Ages. Bowling began—believe it or not—in cathedral cloisters as a diversion for monks.

These medieval German monks devised a game in which a single pin (the *Kegel*), similar in appearance to the present-day bowling pin, was set up at one end of the cloister. Then the monks would take turns hurling something—usually a stone—from the other end. The objective, of course, was to knock down the *Kegel,* and if you succeeded it was considered proof that you were leading a pure life.

keister. *See* pratfall.

Kentucky fire. *See* mountain dew.

kettle of fish, pretty

Here is an odd phrase. Except to the devoted fisherman, there's no such thing as a *pretty kettle of fish*—and most truly sporting fishermen prefer to broil or fry their catch anyway.

The phrase came from a custom common along the Scottish border. At the start of the salmon run each year, groups would gather for outdoor picnics along the banks of the streams. The main course at these affairs was salmon boiled in a huge pot of well-salted water and eaten in catch-as-catch-can fashion, rather in the style of our "chicken in the rough."

Give thought for a moment to the shambles likely to result from dozens of people trying to eat hot, boiled salmon with their fingers while sitting along the banks of a woodland stream—and you'll understand why the phrase a *pretty kettle of fish* has long been synonymous with confusion, muddle and mess.

keys, the. *See* jazzmen's jargon.

keystone sack. *See* baseball jargon.

kibosh

There are two theories put forward by the experts about the origin of *kibosh* and they couldn't be more dissimilar. A leading dictionary avers that it is "probably Yiddish in origin" and indicates that it comes from a Middle High German word *keibe,* meaning "carrion." On the other hand, the famous Irish poet, Padraic Colum, believes it comes from the Gaelic *cie bais,* meaning "cap of death." Well, as the saying goes, "you pays your nickel and you takes your choice." At any rate, today's meaning of "put the *kibosh* on"—to put an end to something—is well known and has, according to H. L. Mencken, been widely used in America for more than a century.

kick the bucket

There are two theories on the origin of *kick the bucket*. The first, and less likely, traces it to England where, centuries ago, the frame from which a newly killed pig was hung was called a bucket. Presumably the pig would thrash about a bit and *kick the bucket*.

The second, more likely, origin is simply that the bucket referred to is the pail traditionally used by the suicide to stand on while tying a noose around his neck. Then, with a kick of the bucket, the fatal deed is done.

kidult, video

Maybe you have noticed that many television programs seem aimed at young and old alike. In place of straight children's fare through the twilight hours and, later in the evening, relatively mature adult programming, there is a distinct tendency to slant the subject matter in such a way as to retain youthful interest while picking up adult listeners. Well, those grownups who have been enjoying these programs may be interested to know that the television industry has a name for you. You're a *kidult!*

At any rate that's better than the name sportswriter Red Smith coined some years ago when television was given over chiefly to Gorgeous George and Milton Berle. At that time he labeled televiewers *videots*.

killer. *See* philatelic jargon.

kindle of kittens. *See* clowder, kindle and cowardice.

Kinescope

Kinescope, a trade-marked name for a filmed recording of a television show, has been shortened by the trade to *kine* (pronounced KINNY) and, despite legal restrictions on its public use, is in general use in the studios as such.

king's disease

The *king's disease* or *king's evil* is *scrofula,* a tubercular infection of the lymphatic glands, usually causing swelling of the neck. It was very common, especially in young people, during the Middle Ages and later. First known in Middle Latin as *regius morbus,* it derived the name *king's evil* from the widespread belief that a touch from the royal hand would cure it.

From the time of Henry the Confessor to the reign of Queen Anne, reigning monarchs touched great numbers of persons afflicted with the disease. One king (Charles II) reportedly touched nearly 100,000 sufferers during his reign. The number of cures, if any, is unreported.

kirby grips. *See* English English.

kit and caboodle

Kit, meaning a collection of anything, comes from the kit bag of a soldier in which he had to carry all his belongings. The earliest record of its use is in England in 1785. Combined with *boodle,* it came to mean a collection of people.

There's a difference of opinion as to where *boodle* originated, some authorities attributing it to *buddle* (which in turn was probably Old English *bottel*), meaning "bunch" or "bundle." Others think it came from the Dutch *boedel,* meaning "property." In this sense it has long been used by New England longshoremen.

How did it become *caboodle? Caboodle* is said to be a corruption of *kit and boodle.* All of which certainly makes *the whole kit and caboodle* an all-inclusive phrase.

kith and kin

Kith in Anglo-Saxon was *cyth* and earlier *cuth*—the same root that we see in the word "uncouth." It simply meant "known," so a *cyth* or *cuth* person was an acquaintance or friend. Thus *kith and kin* equals "friends and relatives."

kitty-cornered

Kitty-cornered is a colloquial variation of *cater-cornered,* meaning "diagonal." *Cater-cornered* comes from the French word *quatre* (four) and "cornered." It has a long history, appearing in print as early as 1519, so it probably was well established in the popular tongue not long after the Norman conquest.

A couple of similar, though not directly related, expressions popular in folk language to express the same idea of "diagonal" or "diagonally," are *slaunchways* and *skewgee.* See also CATER-CORNER.

kiwi

The *kiwi* (pronounced KEE-wee) is a nearly extinct New Zealand bird whose most remarkable characteristic is a complete inability to fly. A very odd-looking creature with large four-clawed feet and a disproportionately long beak, it lives—when in captivity—on a diet of earthworms and drinks fluids only when it is sick. It is almost unknown outside New Zealand, where it is considered the national bird.

Whether the use of the nickname *kiwi* to designate flightless aviation cadets originated with the Australian and New Zealand armed forces is not certain, but the phrase has been in general use with our forces at least since World War I.

A Chicago contributor has documented this point:

"During World War I there were thousands of administrative officers' (nonflying officers) commissioned directly from civilian life without any military training whatever, and in grades ranging from lieutenants to colonels. These very unpopular 'officers,' who were appointed in many cases through pull and politics rather than merit, were dubbed *kiwis* by flying cadets and flying officers alike. In those days *kiwi* was a term of derision, and was never applied to flying cadets who had not yet soloed.

"While there were many qualified nonflying officers at that time, *kiwis* did most of the administration and nontechnical training of the flying cadets. Their tendency to 'pull their rank' and generally to try to impress both cadets and also experienced and well-trained ground officers, at a time in flying history when flying was at least rarer, if not more hazardous, than it later became, caused the *kiwis* to be thoroughly disliked by the flying cadets.

"Many times I stood in military formations which were in charge of a *kiwi* and heard the subdued cry of '*Kiwi, kiwi!*' from portions of the rear ranks where the callers could not be definitely located. As a result of one of these incidents a whole squadron of cadets was confined to the post for a week.

"During World War II I never once heard the word *kiwi* applied to anyone but I was not on duty at any primary flying school. One reason was that in World War II direct commissions went only to qualified men, and the great bulk of administrative officers were both well trained and respected."

kowtow

Kowtow comes from the Chinese *k'o-t'ou* and koh-TOU nearly approximates the original Chinese pronunciation. However, the word has long been completely Americanized and, while that pronunciation cannot be called wrong, it is surely far less often heard, even in the speech of literate people, than KOU-TOU.

To *kowtow* to a person, of course, means to show great respect to him. Originally, in the China of the mandarins, this respect was shown formally by kneeling before a superior and touching the ground with the forehead.

kudos

A fairly common error, especially in headlines, is the use of this word as if it were plural: MAGNATE WINS MANY KUDOS. But *kudos* (from the Greek *kydos*) is singular. If you want to say that a man received many honors, you must say that he has many *kudoses*—a repulsive word if I ever saw one.

There are many ways out of the dilemma posed by *kudoses,* of course. The simplest is merely to avoid the word completely and use "fame," "honor" or "glory"—all perfectly good English words well established in our tongue long before *kudos* became used as British university slang in the early 1800's.

Kudos would probably never have enjoyed any vogue in America, had not *Time* magazine used it frequently during the 1920's and 1930's. Indeed *kudos* and *tycoon* are about the last vestigial remnants of the *Time*-style vocabulary evolved by Henry Luce and his cohorts when that magazine was a brash upstart just beginning to challenge such well-established organs as the *Literary Digest.*

Besides odd words dredged from the small print of unabridged dictionaries, *Time*-style also favored an inverted sentence structure, now happily abandoned. Its death knell was sounded by the late Wolcott Gibbs who, in a classic *New Yorker* parody of *Time,* observed that after several paragraphs of *Time* prose "backward reels the mind" and "where it all will end, knows God."

L

labanotation

Labanotation is the name of the first satisfactory method for noting down by diagram the various movements and positions of a ballet. In the past choreographers (the persons who design or direct ballets) have had to base their revivals of classic ballets on old pictures or the memories of dancers who had appeared in previous performances of the ballets.

Now, thanks to *labanotation*—which is named after its creator, Rudolf Laban—every dance director can have at his fingertips the dance equivalent of the score an orchestral conductor follows. Perhaps of equal importance to the creators of ballets is that, by transcribing their works by *labanotation,* they will be able to have them copyrighted and thus enjoy the same sort of protection from plagiarism which writers and composers have had for many years.

labor of moles. *See* **clowder, kindle and cowardice.**

labor's lost lexicon

The scene of labor's struggles today has moved from the picket line to the hearing chamber and courtroom. It's a fair bet, indeed, that more labor unions are now undergoing some form of legislative or judicial inquiry than are actively on strike.

It wasn't always this way, of course, as anyone with a memory for events of twenty years ago can attest. Nor does the polite, lawyer-guided testimony of today's labor leaders bear even a remote resemblance to the lusty, salty language used by the hard-fisted founders of America's labor movement. Before they're all forgotten, let's look at a few of the expressions used by workingmen when the century and the labor movement were young.

Ever hear of a *scissorbill?* Well, a *scissorbill* was a laboring man who was militantly antiunion. *Finks* and *scabs* were men who would take the jobs of striking workers, but *scissorbills* went one step further. They took the strikers' jobs and then campaigned actively against the union. Sometimes they were also called—facetiously, of course—*missionary workers.*

Jimmy Higgins? He was any conscientious, hard-working member of the rank and file, especially the sort of chap who could be counted upon to work selflessly at the drudgery of union work. The *Jimmy Higgenses* never made headlines and seldom got thanked for their labors, but they did the jobs nobody else wanted.

The term *yellow dog* was once firmly implanted in the lexicon of popular American slang to designate any kind of worthless or mongrel thing. It survives today chiefly in the phrase *yellow-dog contract,* the union's term for a contract which stipulated that an employee would not join a labor union.

Early in the century *wobblies* were active on the union scene, though they and the organization they represented have vanished. *"Wobblies"* were members of the I.W.W., initials which stood for "International Workers of the World" to its sympathizers but signified "I Won't Work" to its opponents.

This is, of course, only a smattering of the jargon which grew out of the early struggles of America's laboring men to form their unions. Sounds long ago and far away, doesn't it?

laches

This is a legal term meaning "failure to carry through an action at the proper time"—especially if such failure to act results in loss to a party in an action. An attorney who is engaged to bring an action but, through inexcusable delay, fails to do so until such time as the action is disqualified by the statute of limitations would be guilty of *laches*. Pronounced simply LACH-iz, it has been a common term in law for centuries. It is derived from the Latin adjective *laxus,* meaning "lax" or "negligent," and it came into Middle English shortly after the Norman Conquest in the form *lachesse* along with many hundreds of other terms for the languages of the various professions—church, law and medicine.

lachrymatory

Lachrymatory comes from the Latin *lachrima,* meaning "tear." It has two meanings. First, a vase designed to contain tears, found in the sepulchers of the ancient Romans and so called from a notion that tears of the deceased person's friends were collected in them. Second, *lachrymatory* is used humorously to mean a handkerchief.

lackadaisical

Lackadaisical, meaning "indolent, languid or slow-moving," comes from the early English *alackaday,* an exclamation implying lighthearted dismissal of cares and worries.

lagniappe

Pronounced lan-YAP, this is a Creole term derived from the Spanish *la napa* (the gift), and means a trifling present—a "bonus gift"—formerly given by New Orleans tradespeople to their favored customers.

lame duck. *See* political language.

lampoon

Lampoon, nowadays most often encountered as part of the name of the Harvard College undergraduate humor magazine, is not a new word. Indeed, it's almost as old as Harvard itself. The *Oxford Dictionary* traces it to 1645, nine short years after John Harvard guaranteed his fame by donating a few books to a fledgling school in England's youngest colony.

The practice of writing bitingly satirical pieces (*lampoons*) flourished during the seventeenth and eighteenth centuries. And who were the first *lampoonists?* Appropriately enough, students—and drunken students at that. The word *lampoon,* you see, comes from the refrain of a drinking song popular in the early part of the seventeenth century: "*Lampone, lampone, camerada lampone,*" which, translated, means "Guzzler, guzzler, my fellow guzzler."

landlubber

Most people think that *landlubber* is a corruption of "land-lover" and means a person unhappy to be aboard ship and yearning to be back home on shore.

But no. A *landlubber* quite conceivably could love the sea and still merit that label, for a *landlubber* is an awkward novice aboard ship—a stumbling, bumbling greenhorn, whose lack of experience is apparent in everything he does.

Nor does *lubber* come from "lover." It's a word derived from the Anglo-Saxon *lobbe* and means a slow, clumsy, inexperienced person. Apparently the original intent of the sailors' derisive label *landlubber* was a "person so awkward that he'd be clumsy even back on land."

land-office business, to do

The original "land offices" were those set up by the government after the Civil War to allot lands to citizens who qualified for migration to the Western territories. So tremendous were the lines of citizens waiting when the offices opened that the phrase *land-office business* has been part of our language ever since.

larboard. *See* starboard.

lariat. *See* cowboy jargon.

Latin Quarter

In New York City there is a night club called the Latin Quarter which gets its name from Paris' Quartier Latin. This area, famous as the locale of student life and Bohemian ways, got its name during the Middle Ages because tutors and students of the University of Paris (located there) conversed in Latin.

lay an egg

Believe it or not, this expression originated in the very British game of cricket. When a player failed to score, he was said to have "achieved a *duck's egg*"—an allusion to the resemblance between a duck's egg and the figure zero.

As baseball became popular in this country, the term was domesticated as *goose egg* and, in the days when sports-page prose was more luxuriant than it is today, you might read of Walter Johnson setting down the opposing team for "nine consecutive *goose eggs*."

Gradually the "goose" dropped out of the expression and it became a favorite of vaudevillians in such expressions as "The new comic opened in one and really *laid an egg*." From vaudeville to radio and TV was the shortest of jumps and *to lay an egg* is now a common slang expression for "to fail utterly."

layover to catch meddlers

This phrase is a dialect variant of a very common answer used by adults to evade a direct answer to children's questions. Instead of saying to the child, "It's none of your business," he would be told "It's *layover to catch meddlers.*"

So what's a *layover,* you ask. A *layover* is a trap for bears or other unwary animals, made of a pit covered with boughs. And a *meddler,* of course, is a person who interferes in other people's business.

The phrase has been recorded in Eastern and Southern states as long ago as 1890. It also appears as *larovers for meddlers, layos to catch meddlers* and even as a single word *larofamedlers.*

lb.

If you want to find this abbreviation in the dictionary, look under *lb.* rather than *pound,* for most modern dictionaries enter abbreviations along with words in alphabetical order. *Lb.* is the abbreviation for the Latin *libra,* meaning "pound." The original phrase was *libra pondo* (a pound in weight). Over the centuries *pondo* (in weight) acquired the meaning of "pound" and *libra* was lost, except in *lb.*

leatherhead

The term *leatherhead* once played an important role in our American slang. During the nineteenth century watchmen and policemen were often called *leatherheads,* apparently from the fact that the "men of the watch" —the earliest policemen in many towns and cities—often wore leather hats. The term *leatherhead* was once also used as a nickname for natives of Pennsylvania, though no one now seems able to recall the reason.

leatherneck

The term *leatherneck* originated as an epithet in the lively intraservice rivalry between sailors and Marines. During the middle years of the nineteenth century the Marine uniform jacket had a leather-lined collar or stock. In hot weather it became very uncomfortable and was finally eliminated in 1875—but not before it had given the sailors a handy weapon in the not-so-lighthearted badinage which took place whenever Marine and sailor met off duty.

The sailors contended that *leatherneck* really meant a neck long unwashed. Indeed, they coined *leatherneck wash* and *Marine wash* to describe a method of washing one's face without taking one's shirt off.

By now the phrase *leatherneck* has become a prideful label among our U.S. Marines, with all thought of the derogatory implications of its original use long forgotten.

lees

One of my acquaintances once sent me a copy of the *Bulletin* of the Harvard Club of New York, marking for my attention this sentences: "The Club's chess team can neither drink the wine of victory nor the *lees of defeat*." In the margin is the scribbled notation, "What it mean?" This ungrammatical formulation must, I am sure, be attributed to haste in writing, not—obviously—to any fault of my friend's education.

Well, what the sentence means is that the chess team hasn't done either well or badly. The drinking of wine in celebration of victory is a custom which goes far back into classical antiquity. The *lees* of wine are the dregs, the bitter sediment which settles to the bottom of the wine vat in the aging process. Obviously, to the victors go the choicest portions of wine while the vanquished must be content with the dregs or *lees*.

left-winger

Left, leftist and *left-wing* came to their present meaning of "radical" from the practice of most European legislatures of seating the conservative members to the right of the chair and the liberal and radical members on the left. Very likely this resulted from the ritual of always seating honored guests on the host's right at formal gatherings. Since the most distinguished and noble members of a parliament would almost invariably be politically conservative in their views, their parties became known as the parties "of the right" and the less well-endowed and more radical groups were the parties "of the left."

legislator. *See* candidate.

lemon sole

This phrase does not mean that lemon is squeezed on the fish before it is cooked. The word *lemon* in *lemon sole,* in fact, has nothing to do with the fruit. It is a translation of the French word *limande,* meaning any kind of flat fish. Incidentally, it adds up to a redundancy for who ever heard of a sole that was anything but flat?

leonine contract

This phrase, more common in British usage than American, harks back to the ancient fable of the lion and his fellow beasts. As Aesop told the story, several animals went along with the lion on a hunt. When it came time to divide the spoils, the lion announced that he would demand one-quarter share as his due as king of beasts; another quarter because of his superior bravery; the third quarter to feed his dam and cubs; and "as for the fourth, let he who will dispute it with me."

So here we have the origin of the common expression "the lion's share," meaning the greater part or all of a reward. Here too is the origin of *leonine contract,* any agreement which is entirely one-sided.

leotard

The *leotard* is often used by ballet dancers, chiefly as a rehearsal costume, not for actual performance. It is a close-fitting garment, usually of knit fabric, covering the entire body from wrist to ankle and having a fairly high neckline.

The costume originated under the big top. One of France's most famous aerialists in the nineteenth century was M. Leotard, who designed and introduced the garment—still worn by trapeze artists—which was tight-fitting, low at the neck and sleeveless, but otherwise very similar to the ballet dancer's *leotard.*

let the cat out of the bag. *See* pig in a poke.

Levant

The *Levant,* a term used as far back as the time of Shakespeare, meant the eastern part of the Mediterranean Sea and the islands and countries of that area. It was so called because the sun rose there, *levant* being the present participle of the Latin verb *levare* (to rise). Thus *Levant* (pronounced leh-VANT) literally meant "a rising."

Naturally the makeup of the *Levant* varied over the centuries as the political fortunes of its countries changed. Generally, though, the *Levant* was considered to consist of the regions from Greece to Egypt, including Syria, Lebanon and Palestine.

Levis. *See* blue jeans.

lewd

Lewd—or, in its Anglo-saxon spelling *laewede*—originally simply meant "ignorant" or "uncultured." With the passage of centuries, it came to be used to describe the lower orders of society, the "vulgar" herd. (*Vulgar,* incidentally, originally meant "belonging to the common people.") Then *lewd* came to mean base, unprincipled and vicious.

The meaning of obscene or lascivious for *lewd* is not recorded until about 1712. Today, however, this meaning with its connotation of moral impropriety is practically the only one heard.

life. *See* baseball jargon.

life of Reilly

There are several theories of the origin of this popular catch phrase which means, of course, to live luxuriously without working. One authority says it comes from a song of the 1880's "Is That Mr. Reilly?" popularized by Pat Rooney, founder of that great American song-and-dance dynasty, "The Dancing Rooneys."

No less an authority than H. L. Mencken, however, is quoted as dating it near the turn of the century and attributing it to a song called "The Best in the House is None Too Good for Reilly," written by the Tin Pan Alley team of Lawlor and Blake, who also created the immortal "Sidewalks of New York."

Be that as it may, the phrase came into wide favor in the early 1900's and later—with "Reilly" simplified to "Riley"—became the title of a popular television program.

LIFO—FIFO

Among the gentler side effects of our increasing preoccupation with taxes, we note that new words and expressions are coming into the language to cope with changing situations "taxwise," as the Wall Streeters would say.

One of the most significant recent developments was the court decision permitting a major New York department store to reckon its taxes on the LIFO inventory system, a decision which may mean rebates retroactive to the early 1940's, totaling several millions of dollars.

"What," asked an incurable punster among my correspondents, "does *LIFO* mean? For the life o' me I can't figure the whole thing out."

Well, it's really not that complicated. LIFO is an acronym—a word made up of the initial letters or syllables in a phrase—and stands for "Last In, First Out." It is a technique of inventory maintenance which assumes that the most efficient handling of merchandise results from selling off first that stock which has most recently arrived.

Thus the stock on hand at inventory taking time is assumed to be "first in," and is valued at the earliest cost obtaining during the period covered. Since our prices have been steadily mounting over recent years, this results in a stock evaluation at the lowest possible cost, thereby reducing the amount of taxes to be paid. Naturally, the system works in reverse in a shrinking economy, and one rather doubts if the proponents of *LIFO* would have fought quite so hard for this new interpretation of the tax law if our economy had been on the decline these past two decades.

Incidentally the more conventional method of handling inventories is called FIFO—First In, First Out.

Light Brigade, The Charge of the

The legendary charge of the gallant and doomed "Six Hundred" took place at Balaclava (now Balaklava, U.S.S.R.) on October 25, 1854. An account of the incredibly bumbleheaded leadership that committed these gallant men to their fate is given in *The Reason Why* by Cecil Woodham-Smith, one of the finest historical works of our time.

I am reminded, for no very good reason, of something I read in an English magazine. At a large gathering celebrating many prosperous years of the London Gas Light and Coke Company an official, in lavish praise of the achievements of the company, said: "If I may be permitted a pun, I would say 'Honor the Light Brigade.'" A consumer in the audience shouted: "Oh, what a charge they made!"

limelight

The *lime* in *limelight* has nothing to do with the fruit from which the color lime is derived. *Limelight* gets its name from calcium oxide, popularly known (in various compounds) as lime, quick lime, slaked lime and so on.

Calcium oxide was first isolated in 1808 by Sir Humphry Davy, famed British chemist, who soon demonstrated that it would give off a brilliant white light when heated. The phenomenon inspired Thomas Drummond to devise methods of concentrating and projecting the light for theatrical use. The light, first called the "Drummond light" and later used in lighthouses, gradually became known as *limelight*.

It has long since been supplanted by arc and Klieg lights but a man *in the limelight* still is a person center stage, so to speak, receiving the full intensity of the public spotlight.

Limerick

Despite the fact that the *Limerick* undoubtedly derives its name from Limerick County, Ireland, the Old Sod cannot claim credit for the origin of the *Limerick*. The verse form was first used by Edward Lear, an English writer, whose *Book of Nonsense* remains popular today, more than a hundred years after its publication. One of his earliest *Limericks,* appearing in 1846, was:

> A flea and a fly in a flue
> Were imprisoned, so what could they do?
> Said the flea, "Let us fly!"
> Said the fly, "Let us flee!"
> So they flew through a flaw in the flue.

Interestingly enough, Lear did not call these verses *Limericks.* That name was first attached to the verse form more than fifty years later when,

about 1898, it became a popular taproom fad to bawl out the line "We'll
all come up, come up to Limerick" between verses of *Limericks* rather
more robust and indelicate than the one quoted above.

limey

Limey originated as a derogatory nickname for a British sailor. He was
so called because of the long-standing custom in His Majesty's Navy of
serving lime juice to the crew to prevent scurvy. The term has, with the
impetus of two world wars to give it wider currency, come to serve as a
somewhat contemptuous term for anyone of English birth.

line. *See* painter.

lingerie

The pronunciation of *lingerie* as lahn-jer-RAY is a good sample of what
the late Frank Colby used to call "bargain-basement French." In truth, it's
not French, English or American. It's as utterly senseless a pronunciation
as any I know.

The correct French pronunciation closely approximates lan-zh'-REE.
Note that there's no *ay* sound in that last syllable. Best American pronunciation is—or should be—lahn-zhuh-REE.

Incidentally, the word *lingerie* itself is an oddity. Its American meaning
has nothing whatever to do with its French origin. In France *linge* means
"linen" and *lingerie* means "linen clothing" or "linen closet." Little wonder
that a native of France is bewildered when she first hears Americans talk
of "nylon *lingerie*."

lingua franca. *See* pidgin English and bêche-de-mer.

lion's share. *See* leonine contract.

Listerine

One of the most widely sold mouth washes, *Listerine,* takes its name
from Lord Lister, the English surgeon who is generally considered the
father of aseptic surgery. H. L. Mencken reports in *The American Language* that Lister was unhappy about this use of his name and objected to
it, but to no avail.

lived, short- and long-

There is only one correct pronunciation of *lived* in such compounds—
with a long *i* to rhyme with "shrived" or "wived." Yet all of us have heard
otherwise well-spoken people pronounce it with a short *i*, as in the past

tense of the word "live"—"He lived there once." Why is this error so common?

Simply because *lived* is not the word many people think it is. It has no connection with the verb "to live" when used in such combinations as *short-lived* and *long-lived*. Here it is actually a blend of "life" and "ed" and means "having a certain kind of duration of lives." So if you'll bear in mind that this *lived* is derived from "life," rather than "live," you'll have no trouble pronouncing it correctly.

Liverpudlian

This is the name for a native of Liverpool. With the subtlety characteristic of British humor, some wit centuries ago substituted "puddle" for "pool" in Liverpool, came up with *Liverpudlian,* and the name stuck.

Other odd names for natives of British cities are *Glaswegian* (pronounced glas-WEE-jun) for inhabitants of Glasgow and *Cantabrigian* for residents of Cambridge. The latter comes from the Latin name of the town, applied during the Roman occupation of England. See CANTAB.

lock, stock and barrel

The meaning of this phrase—the whole of anything—should be instantly apparent to any huntsman, for the lock, stock and barrel are the three parts of a firearm and together they make up the whole gun.

log book

This started about the time of Columbus when sailing ships kept track of their speed by means of a *log*—a thin quadrant of wood, loaded so as to float upright and connected to a line wound around a reel. The record of distance traveled was kept in a *log book* and that term, by extension is applied to any record of travel. So the first *log* was actually made of wood.

loggerheads, at

The *loggerhead* expression (two people *at loggerheads* are involved in a quarrel) goes back to Shakespeare's time, long before the term was applied to sea turtles. Here's how it came about. The first *loggerheads* were long-handled instruments with large metal cups on the end, used to melt tar over open fire. In naval warfare during the Middle Ages, sailors would heat pitch and tar in *loggerheads* held over open fires, and then hurl or dump the contents on attacking craft. Thus the two crews would be *at loggerheads* with each other.

The turtle gets his *loggerhead* name from the fact that his chief characteristic, besides great size, is a remarkably big, knobby head.

The epithet *loggerhead* was formerly used the way we now use "blockhead" and "knucklehead," as a label for a singularly dull and stupid fellow.

logophile

Logophile comes from two Greek words, *logos* (word) and *philos* (lover). Hence its meaning is obvious. It's a word which you won't find in many, if any, dictionaries, perhaps because dictionary editors tend to be a somewhat churlish lot to whom words are a business—with amateurs or *logophiles* not especially to be encouraged.

logothete, Byzantine. *See* Byzantine logothete.

logrolling

Logrolling goes back to the earliest days of Western migration. When a settler was clearing his land before building a home, he would often call on his neighbor for help in rolling heavy logs with the tacit understanding that he would help the neighbor when he was in need.

In politics it refers to the practice common among legislators of helping one another with favorite pieces of legislation. If a Congressman from one state wants a bill passed which will benefit the voters of his community, he may engage in a little *logrolling* with representatives from other states whereby each agrees to support the pet projects of the others. In the common phrase, "I'll scratch your back if you will scratch mine."

longest word in the language

One question people never tire of asking is "What is the longest word in the English language?" Youngsters run across this query in their earliest books of riddles, complete with the answer: "Smiles, because there's a mile between the first letter and the last."

But the matter is one that grownups frequently debate and the belief is widespread that *antidisestablishmentarianism* is the longest meaningful word in the language. This word was coined by onetime British Prime Minister Gladstone to describe the beliefs of those who opposed his bill to disestablish the Church of Ireland.

Actually, there are other longer words, notably a term found in the *Oxford English Dictionary—floccinaucinihilipilification*. It's a noun defined as "estimating as worthless" and is rather forthrightly labeled a "nonsense" word. However, it is in the dictionary and, with its twenty-nine letters, is one letter longer than *antidisestablishmentarianism*.

As you may have guessed by now, dictionary editors are not above a little prankishness in the compilation of their solemn tomes. Speaking as one of the clan, I feel certain that the *Oxford* editors entered "floccinauc— you finish it" more to be able to point to it as the longest word than through any feeling that the sweet uses of scholarship were aided by its inclusion.

The same prankish spirit, I suspect, motivated the editors of the Merriam-Webster *New International Dictionary* when they solemnly included in the "New Words" supplement the word *pneumonoultramicroscopicsilicovolcanokoniosis*. It's a disease of the lungs to which miners are particularly susceptible. But I'd be willing to give rather high odds that no doctor has ever used the term in telling a coal miner what's wrong with him.

How many letters are there in this jawbreaker? Well, you can count them for yourself, dear reader, and if the typesetter happens to lose a letter or two, I'm sure it will still add up to more letters than the word from the *Oxford Dictionary*. I guess that's a victory for our side—though the typesetters won't thank us for it!

long-lived. *See* lived.

longshoreman

Longshoreman, meaning a dockside worker who helps in the loading and unloading of ships, is simply a contraction of "along-shore-man." These workers are often also called "stevedores," a word taken from the Spanish *estivador,* one who rams or packs things. In Britain, they are called "dockers."

loony bin

This slang term for insane asylum is a fairly obvious coinage from "loony," a dialect form of "lunatic," and "bin," a place where objects are stowed away. See also BOOBY HATCH.

loran

Loran is an adaption of radar, used as a long-range aid to surface navigation, and the name comes from the first letters "long" and "range." Comparatively simple to operate, it was found indispensable by our naval forces navigating in the Aleutians in World War II. The fact that we had *loran* and the Japanese didn't is probably one reason why the enemy found himself so completely outmaneuvered that he abandoned the Aleutian theater for the duration of the war.

Month-long fogs which, over the centuries, had caused thousands of wrecks in these perilous waters were reduced to hazards of secondary importance by the miracle of *loran*. This enabled our naval navigators to "fix" their position through impenetrable fog with just as high a degree of accuracy as the most expert navigator using the conventional sextant and compass at high noon on a perfectly clear day. Some authorities, indeed, predict that the installation of *loran* on all merchant ships will eventually make the old methods of celestial navigation as obsolete as the square-rigger and whale-oil lamps.

lot lice

Only in towns where it is still possible to see a circus under a canvas big-top does the term *lot lice* apply. Nostalgic Americans who can remember gathering early in the morning to watch the big top go up would not have relished it so much if they had known the circus jargon name for them. They were *lot lice*.

love (in tennis). *See* amateur.

love apples

Tomatoes were once known as *love apples*. Apparently some of our forefathers thought tomatoes were aphrodisiac but that represents a distinct triumph of mind over matter for science tells us that as a love potion tomato juice simply doesn't have what it takes.

The whole idea comes from a mistake in etymology. Tomatoes originally grew in South America and were imported to Spain not long after Columbus discovered America. From there, they were taken to Morocco and eventually were introduced to Italy, where they were known as *pomo dei Moro* (apple of the Moors). A romantic Frenchman mistakenly translated this as *pomme d'amour* (love apple) and a legend was born.

lox. *See* bagel and lox.

lucre, filthy. *See* filthy lucre.

lucubration

Lucubration (pronounced loo-kyoo-BRAY-shun) comes from the Latin *lucubrare* (to work by candlelight) and has acquired the meaning not only of work done late at night but of any study or literary work of a laborious nature. It also applies to the product of scholarly work, particularly an elaborate one. The verb form is *lucubrate*.

Lucy Stoner

Lucy Stone was one of the most ardent women's suffrage leaders in the nineteenth century. She was so intent upon making the point of woman's equality with man that she refused to change her name when she married. Although legally Mrs. Henry Brown Blackwell, she would not answer to any name but Lucy Stone all the years of her married life.

Her example was much emulated by "emancipated" women of the early years of this century. Heywood Broun's first wife, Ruth Hale, was a *Lucy Stoner,* as were many other literary and artistic women of the period. Perhaps the furthest point to which the crusade for women's equality in

names was carried, though, was in the case of the political commentator
Raymond Swing. During more than a score of years of marriage to Betty
Gram, he dutifully signed himself Raymond Gram Swing. When he
married another lady in 1945, he reverted to Raymond Swing.

lukewarm

Luke is simply the modern spelling of the Middle English *louke,* meaning "tepid," which in turn came from the Dutch *leuk.* Since tepid itself
means barely warm, *lukewarm* certainly seems redundant—but that won't
diminish its popularity after all these centuries.

lumbermen's jargon

Ever hear of *flatheads, shavin' crews* or *swampers?* Would you recognize a *crummie, sky pilot* or *counter jumper* if you saw one? Well, these
are all expressions from the jargon of lumbermen of the Northwest.

Lumbermen can be roughly grouped into three groups, the woods crew,
the mill crew and the bunkhouse gang. There often is, as one veteran
noted, "quite a bit of brick-throwing between the woods crew and the
mill crew." But both are usually tolerant toward the bunkhouse gang
because food and shelter are involved. When cookie brings in a really
poor meal, though, the lumberjacks react by *walking the table*—which
means that two lumberjacks mount the table, one at each end, and walk
down it kicking everything off. Cookie usually leaves by the next train.

But back to those words in the first paragraph. A *flathead* is a sawyer.
The *shavin' crew* are mill hands who plane the lumber. *Swampers* are the
lowest caste among lumbermen. They lob the limbs from the felled timber
and cut the roadways.

A *crummie?* Well, he's the chap who manages the bunkhouse, often
called the *bull pen.* A *counter jumper* is merely a clerk and a *sky pilot* is a
preacher. Incidentally, should you hear a burly lumberjack suggest that he
and his pal *go to Sunday school,* don't be misled. That's lumberman's
slang for "Let's get up a poker game!"

lush

Lush as a generic term for beer and other intoxicating drinks has been
British slang for more than a century. It is supposed to have originated as
a contraction of the name of a London actors' club, the City of Lushington.
The use of *lush* to describe a drunken person and *lushed* or *lushed up* to
describe the state of intoxication has been common in America for at
least forty years.

M

macadam

A surprising number of our common words were proper names before they became part of the common currency of our tongue. When we speak of a *macadam* road, for example, we are unwittingly paying tribute to John L. MacAdam, the Scottish engineer who invented this method of paving highways. MacAdam, a Scot who came to America in the late eighteenth century, earned a fortune and returned to his native land. When he got back there he was appalled at the poor condition of the roads and put his time, thought and money into the development of new and better methods of paving them—with today's *macadam* roads the long-range result.

mace

Mace is political slang for extorting contributions for political purposes from public employees, usually engaged in by political bosses. Most dictionaries list it as "origin unknown" but it may well be related to the earlier mace, a club or staff used as a symbol of authority by officials.

mach-breaker

Mach is the term used to denote the ratio of air speed to the speed of sound. An airplane traveling at a speed of *Mach 1* is traveling at the speed of sound. A *mach-breaker,* then, is a person who has traveled faster than the speed of sound.

Mach, by the way, comes from the name of a noted Austrian physicist, Ernst Mach, who died in 1916—more than thirty years before the first *mach-breaker.*

machine. *See* political language.

mackintosh

The well-known *mackintosh* raincoat bears the name of its inventor, Charles Mackintosh, who was the first man to make truly waterproof fabrics.

[223]

mad as a hatter. *See* hatter, mad as a.

madding crowd, far from the

Most of us remember Thomas Hardy's novel *Far From the Madding Crowd*. However, the phrase was not original with Hardy. He quoted it from Thomas Gray's famous "Elegy Written in a Country Churchyard" in which the following lines appear:

> Far from the madding crowd's ignoble strife
> Their sober wishes never learned to stray;
> Along the cool sequestered vale of life
> They kept the noiseless tenour of their way.

The distinction between *madding* and *maddening* is well worth observing, by the way. *To mad* is a verb, now almost wholly archaic, meaning "to act madly or insanely." A *madding* crowd, then, is one that is acting like a group of lunatics. However, a *maddening* crowd would merely be one that causes vexation or annoyance, like the crowd that fills all the elevators in an office building, forcing you to wait.

Madison Avenue

Madison Avenue, as a generic term to describe advertising agencies and their employees, first came into use in 1944 when an article on advertising's contribution to the war effort appeared in the *New Republic* magazine signed "Madison Avenue." Articles in the New York *Herald Tribune* by Joseph Kaselow, a most perceptive chronicler of the folkways of the advertising gentry, have often referred simply to *the Avenue*. None of his readers needs to be told what *Avenue* meant, any more than sons of Harvard or Yale need to be told what "The Game" is.

In recent years some of the larger agencies have moved to Fifth and Park avenues, perhaps in a conscious effort to evade the opprobrium which now attaches to the *Mad Ave* label in the public's mind. Thus the label is rapidly becoming a misnomer as agencies show a marked inclination to locate their offices anywhere *but* on Madison Avenue.

New York has many such misnomers, as any student of the metropolis can attest. The Madison Square Garden of today is more than thirty blocks removed from Madison Square. Times Square no longer is the location of the *New York Times,* whose editorial offices are a block away and whose new printing plant is many blocks distant. Park Avenue, once synonymous with swanky society living, is now the location of many stunning new office buildings. And Broadway, legendary home of the theater, no longer can boast a single legitimate playhouse.

Madison Avenuese. *See* adman's jargon.

madras

This word, when it is used as the name of the Indian city, is pronounced muh-DRAS or muh-DRAHS. The fabric *madras,* a kind of cotton cloth, usually striped, obviously derives its name from the name of the city where it is believed to have originated. Indeed, the fabric *madras* is still commonly used in India.

However, in American usage at least, the common pronunciation of the fabric is MAD-ras and I can marshal a rather formidable array of authorities to support my point. For instance, two recent and competently edited desk dictionaries, the *American College Dictionary* and the *World Webster,* College Edition, both indicate MAD-ras as the preferred pronunciation.

This isn't to say that anyone pronouncing it muh-DRAS would be in error. That pronunciation is also entered as "acceptable" for the fabric and "preferred" for the Indian city.

maelstrom

The original maelstrom was much more exciting than just a simple whirlpool. The Maelstrom (note the capital M) is located off the northwest coast of Norway and is caused by strong tidal currents capable of swamping and sinking many small ships.

In ancient days, so legend has it, two magic millstones ground out so much salt that the boat carrying them sank. The millstones continued to grind, even to this day, which is why the seas in that area are so turbulent— and why the oceans themselves are salty.

Maggie's drawers. *See* Old Army slang.

magnolia. *See* flower names.

main guy

The *main guy* is not the circus owner but the guy rope which holds up the center pole in the big top. See also CIRCUS JARGON.

Major Grey of chutney fame

"I have been trying without success to find out who was the *Major Grey* of *Major Grey's Chutney* fame," asked a reader. "Can you tell me what, if any, other contributions he may have made to the military or social history of Great Britain?"

With remarkable uniformity the basic books of biographical reference have ignored *Major Grey.* Indeed, after considerable fruitless search, your editor was almost ready to consign him to the limbo of corporate but incorporeal figureheads like Betty Crocker. However, we have the word of T. J. Finucan of the Crosse & Blackwell Company that there once was a living, breathing and, of course, eating Major Grey.

He was a military officer who became acquainted with chutney—a relish made of fruits, spices and herbs—during his service in India. When he ended his tour of duty in the Punjab, he arranged to have supplies of the raw materials shipped home and set up the manufacture of Major Grey's Chutney in his home.

After a while, the task became too great for him since, with his limited facilities, he couldn't keep abreast of the orders, so he made arrangements for Crosse & Blackwell to take over the manufacture and distribution of his product. So successful was it, according to Mr. Finucan, that "at one time there were several brands in competition, such as Colonel Skinner's Chutney and Sergeant Murphy's Chutney. Apparently the belief was that all you needed was a military title as a guarantee of good sales." But Major Grey's has outlived them all—and has made his name a household word in many parts of the world.

major maladjustment. *See* M.M.A.

malaprop

As you all should remember from your high school English courses, Malaprop is the name of a character in Richard Brinsley Sheridan's comedy *The Rivals*. Mrs. Malaprop's utterances were highlighted by the affected misuse of elegant words with hilarious results. As another character remarked, "She decks her dull chat with hard words which she don't understand."

Incidentally, Sheridan did not have to look far for a name for his character. *Malaprop* is simply an abbreviated form of *malapropos,* a word we took directly from the French phrase *mal à propos.* It means "unsuitable, inappropriate, out of place."

We all, I am sure, know at least one person who—especially when writing letters—will try to make an otherwise simple and direct statement sound important by interspersing "high-sounding" words, often with disastrous *malapropian* results. Such a fellow might write: "The speaker tried to arouse his hearers with a truly inflammable speech," when what he means is "inflammatory." Or he might describe an enemy as a "contemptuous fellow"—meaning "contemptible."

man and wife

During a wedding ceremony the pastor says, "I now pronounce you *man and wife.*" Why doesn't he say "husband and wife" or "man and woman?" Why does he split the "go-togethers," contrary to our customary way of speaking?

That's an intriguing question and one which has really only one answer: tradition. Since the earliest days of spoken English, certainly since the Norman Conquest, the phrase used in the marriage ceremony has been *man and wife.* The word *man* then meant, among other things, "husband" —a meaning which the *Oxford Dictionary* says it still has in Scotland, although it is obsolete elsewhere. The word *husband,* in turn, was used to mean a man who tilled the soil or one who managed matters well, a sense we still have in "He *husbanded* his resources."

So here is a case of two words whose meanings have changed and broadened over a span of nine centuries. But, just as the institution of marriage is the unshakable foundation of civilized society, so the forms and traditions surrounding it are virtually unchangeable—and the language used in plighting the troth remains the same as that used when William the Conqueror fought Harold at Hastings.

man, the forgotten. *See* forgotten man, the.

manner born, to the

At first glance, it does seem that there might be more logic in the phrase "to the manor born," if you merely mean "born to high estate or riches"—these being symbolized, of course, by the manor house.

However, *to the manner born* is the correct phrasing, since the meaning of the expression is actually "fitted by birth or endowment for a certain position in life." So you can say: "He's an executive *to the manner born,*" "She's a saleslady *to the manner born,*" or even, "He's a ball player *to the manner born.*"

Bearing in mind this broader application will underscore the appropriateness of *manner* rather than "manor" in the phrase.

Mardi gras. *See* Pancake Tuesday.

margarine

Margarine—properly "oleomargarine"—got its name from a misapplication of the term "margaric acid," a fatty substance in certain animal and vegetable oils. "Margaric" and its first derivative "margarine" were pronounced "MAR-guh-rin." But there's precious little logic to the development of our English language so, by the time *margarine*'s use became widespread, the popular pronunciation of the word had become MAR-juh-rin. In the same fashion the pronunciation of "penicillin" started out as peh-NISS-ih-lin, but soon became pen-ih-SIL-in.

A few dictionaries tried to stand fast against the popular pronunciation and, as recently as 1935, some dictionaries were listing MAR-guh-rin. By now, however, this pronunciation is either omitted entirely or relegated to last place among the possibilities listed.

Marines, tell it to the

One theory is that the Marines referred to in this remark were the "horse marines"—a nonexistent outfit. While it's true that the expression is sometimes heard as "Tell it to the horse marines," the simpler horseless version came first.

As a matter of fact, it originated in the British Royal Navy where Marines were traditionally held in some slight contempt by sailors who considered all Marines green, lubberly and stupid. According to sailors, Marines would believe any story told them, no matter how fanciful.

There's no reason to believe that there was any particular truth in this idea, all services having a fair sprinkling of boobs. But it's indicative of the service rivalries which still exist, despite all talk of "unification," that seasoned sailors still sometimes call Marines "seagoing bellhops."

When, in my syndicated column, I mentioned the "horse marines" as a facetious nickname for a platoon of Marines that never existed, my ears were pinned back by a fusillade of pan letters from ex-Marines, all convinced that I was slandering the Corps and presenting various bits of evidence to prove that there had indeed been units of U.S. "horse marines." The only trouble was that none of my irate correspondents was able to cite any specific official unit, though all agreed (as I would, too) that Marines have served on land, sea, in the air and even on horseback.

Then came an intriguing letter from John A. Childress of Washington, D.C., setting forth another story of the origin of "horse marines." He said: "As is well known, the War of 1812 resulted in the complete blockade of our Atlantic coast by some 300-odd warships of the British—to the extent that no ship could venture out of port. In the emergency, all trade along the eastern shore was conducted by wagons and they soon developed into a fleet. For example, a wagon of shoes and hats would move from Massachusetts and Connecticut south possibly as far as Carolina and return with, say, cotton and rice.

"Facetiously, those wagons became known as 'ships,' their drivers or owners became 'captains' and soon were known as the 'horse marines.' For example, ads would appear in a Baltimore newspaper announcing that a shipload of articles from New England would 'dock' at Lexington and Fayette Streets and 'Captain Jones' would be glad to meet those interested, etc. Of course, those wagons would take on local freight from, say, Baltimore to Washington or Richmond and most of the wagons went along with the pretext to the extent of painting their names on the sides, like ships.

"All of the above I read in a U.S. history some sixty years ago, with actual excerpts of local ads. It's strange but, in the intervening years,

I have never run across another reference to that rather amusing episode in our history. Could it be because we rather like to forget the true facts of that unfavorable war and so even dismiss them from our records? I think that this handling of our disrupted trade was most ingenious—and certainly nothing to be ashamed of."

Agreed, Mr. Childress! And so, surprisingly enough, the first "horse marines" may actually have been "merchant marines" after all.

Mark I, II, etc.

The first use of the term *Mark* as applied to cars of American manufacture was on the Ford Company's first postwar Lincoln Continental, which they labeled *Mark II*. The original, or prewar Continental, was presumably the *Mark I,* although the term was not in use at that time.

Ford did not, of course, invent the *Mark* designation to designate a new model of a car. British auto makers, notably the creators of the Jaguar, had been using it for some time. But the origin of the term seems to be in the military jargon of Hitler's *Wehrmacht,* which designated successive refinements of tank models as *Mark II, Mark III,* etc.

maser

You will find *maser,* a word new to our language, used in connection with reports of findings in outer space. This term from the rapidly expanding field of electronic research is simply too new to be listed in most dictionaries, though all of them will include it eventually. However, the recently published Funk & Wagnalls *Standard Dictionary,* International Edition, enters *maser* with this definition: "a sound-amplifying device which uses a crystal of potassium-cobalt-cyanide to pick up radio waves emitted by remote celestial objects."

The word *maser,* incidentally, is one of that increasingly popular group of words known as "acronyms," words made up of the initial letters or syllables of several other words. *Maser,* for example, stands for "Microwave Amplification through Stimulated Emission of Radiation."

Mason-Dixon line

The Mason-Dixon line was named after its surveyors, Charles Mason and Jeremiah Dixon. It marked the boundary between Pennsylvania and Maryland and was regarded as the demarcation line between North and South in the years leading up to the Civil War.

There's no connection between Mr. Dixon and *Dixie,* though. This name for the Southland gained its popularity from the song "Dixie," composed by minstrel man Dan Emmett in 1859 and adopted as the semiofficial marching song of the Confederacy.

But Emmett did not coin the name *Dixie*. That had been a popular designation for the South for many years. According to the best authorities a *Dixie* was originally a *dixie* note"—a ten-dollar banknote issued by a Louisiana bank and bearing the French word *dix* (ten) in large letters. Traders from the North used to say that they were going south to get some *dixies,* so the section gradually became known as *Dixieland.*

mavericks

Referring to unbranded calves on the open range, *mavericks* got their name from an early Texas rancher named Sam Maverick who either (a) rounded up all strays and gave them his own brand or (b) let his own calves run unbranded so that many neighboring ranchers branded his cattle with their brands. The story is told both ways, so you can take your choice.

Maximum Permissible Concentration, Maximum Permissible Level or Limit. *See* MPC, MPL.

May Day

May Day, as used in radio communications, is merely the Anglicized spelling of the French phrase *M'aidez,* meaning "Help me." It is the distress call authorized by international radio regulations for radio telephone use by ships and aircraft. Not so well known as the radio-telegraph "SOS," it is just as imperative a call. Since it is only used in times of direst peril, it directs every ship and shore station within range to bend every effort to help the craft in distress.

McCoy, the real

The popularizer, if not the originator, of the phrase was "Kid" McCoy, famed prize ring and barroom battler of the 1890's. The story goes that he was being taunted by a saloon heckler with the challenge that if he were *the real McCoy,* he'd put up his dukes and prove it. At length, his patience exhausted, McCoy did exactly that. When the heckler regained consciousness his first remark was "That's *the real McCoy,* all right."

Recently I received a note from a minion of the J. Walter Thompson Company, who must be presumed to have more than a passing interest in the TV show. Conceding that my account is probably the right one, he proceeded to cite a really staggering number of authorities, from H. L. Mencken to the renowned British word expert, Eric Partridge, on various other theories of the origin of the phrase.

Sample a few with me. Item: An Irish ballad of seventy years ago, in which an irate wife proclaims herself head of the household, saying: "I'm *the real McCoy.*" Item: The expression is really "The Real Mackay" and refers to a brand of Scotch whisky popular at the turn of the century. Item: *The real McCoy* was Bill McCoy, a rum runner of the 1920's whose product was always right off the boat. Item: Liquor has nothing whatever to do with the matter. "The Real Mackay" is the phrase and it refers to the quality of a kind of Scottish wool.

Interesting theories all—but I still favor Kid McCoy and the colorful sage of the saloon. That, for me, is *the Real McCoy*.

MCU

In the television world of today, *MCU* is code for a "medium close-up" as opposed to *BCU* or "big close-up." A *BCU* will show only the face of the actor, under stress of some emotion, while a *MCU* will give the audience not only the actor but also some of the background.

meat hand. *See* baseball jargon.

megaton

Mega in classical Greek meant simply "big, great" and it is so used in such words as *megalomania*. A *megaton* bomb thus could mean simply "a big bomb"—but two thousand years and more have passed and, in the long centuries between, that little word has acquired a new and important function.

Besides its original meaning in such medical terms as *megadont* (having large teeth) and *megaprosopous* (having a large face), it has also proven very useful in other areas of science. In physics, for example, *megacycle* is one million cycles. In electricity a resistance of one million ohms is known as a *megohm*.

So it's only natural that nuclear physicists, seeking a simple term to measure the most awesome force that man has ever conceived, would reckon the strength of blast of nuclear weapons first in tons, then kilotons (one thousand tons) and finally in *megatons*.

As a further extension of the use of *mega* in the lingo of today's scientists, we have the deplorable *megabuck* ($1,000,000) to represent the cost of these fearsome bombs and the unspeakable *megadeath* to record the havoc they may wreak.

melton cloth

Melton cloth, from which many men's overcoats are made, gets its name from Melton Mowbray in Leicestershire, England.

mene, mene, tekel, upharsin

Mene, mene, tekel, upharsin (pronounced MEE-nih, MEE-nih, TEK-'l, yoo-FAR-sin) were the words Daniel found written on the wall (Daniel 5:25). Translated from the Aramaic, they mean "numbered, numbered, weighed (and) divided," which Daniel took to mean that God had weighed Belshazzar and his kingdom, found them wanting, and planned their destruction.

mercenary—mercy

It would not be accurate to call *mercenary* a derivative of *mercy*, though both words can be traced back to the same Latin root, *merces*, meaning "payment" or "reward." *Mercenary* has come to us almost unchanged from the Latin *mercenarius*, "one who worked for wages," especially a soldier who served a foreign power for pay, as did the Hessians who served under the British flag in the Revolutionary War. *Mercy* came into English by way of French *merci* and has several closely related meanings, of which the most common is the power or disposition to forgive —especially forgiveness in excess of what might be expected.

meretricious

Meretricious (pronounced mer-uh-TRISH-us) is an adjective meaning gaudy or deceptively attractive. It has its origin in the Latin *mereri* (to serve for hire) and *meretrix* (a prostitute). Its broader meaning is "tawdry or having false charms." Its noun form is *meretriciousness;* its adverb form, *meretriciously.*

Merrie England

According to history, England of the Anglo-Saxon period and the Middle Ages was not a very happy place to be, let alone *merrie*. So why this phrase indicating revelry and joyous spirits, as if England were one perpetual Christmastime?

The answer is that the word *merrie* originally meant merely "pleasing and delightful," not bubbling over with festive spirits, as it does today. The same earlier meaning is found in the famous expression "the *merry* month of May."

mess

War veterans who now have sons in the Air Force may be startled to read letters from them which refer to their eating places as *dining halls* rather than as *mess halls,* the term used by the fathers.

Shortly after World War II, the Department of Defense recommended a number of changes in the terminology used by the various branches of the Armed Forces. Among these changes was the substitution of *dining hall* for *mess.* But only the Air Force acted favorably on the suggestion, the Navy, Army and Marines preferring to retain the old label.

Mess, which today has the rather repulsive meaning of "a sloppy, confused mixture; a muddle," came to us from the Latin *missus* (a portion of food or a course at a meal). This was also its earliest meaning in English as we know from the Biblical quotation, "Esau sold his birthright for a *mess* of pottage."

Gradually *mess* came to mean any group of persons who regularly eat together—especially such groups as officers or enlisted men who by regulation are required to dine as a unit.

The idea of *mess* as a muddle or hodgepodge came much later than these two earlier meanings, perhaps from the popular usage to mix up a *mess* of food, especially for an animal.

But it seems to me most likely that the Air Force's discontinuance of the use of *mess* stems directly from the unpleasant associations of this newer meaning. And it seems logical that the newest of our service arms, lacking the centuries-old tradition of the Officers' Mess, would be the first to scuttle the phrase in favor of the seemingly more genteel *dining hall.*

metaphors, mixed, muddled and mauled

"There are many parts of the earth where the hand of man never set foot." Such expressions are generally classed as *mixed* or *muddled metaphors,* though I would be inclined to label this example *mauled* rather than *mixed.* Technically, however, what we have here is a case of mixed metonymy—"metonymy" being the name of the figure of speech in which an attributive or suggestive word is used for the name of the thing meant. The phrases "hand of man" and "set foot" are intended to suggest "the human race" and "inhabit," just as "White House" is often used in news dispatches when "The President" is meant. All are examples of metonymy. The incongruity arises, of course, when the figurative phrase "hand of man" clashes with "set foot."

Examples of such mixed figures are fairly common both in speeches and writing. There was, for instance, the Congressman who defended our World War II alliance with Russia in these words: "When you're locked in life and death struggle, you can't be too choosy about who you get in bed with." And Hollywood producer Sam Goldwyn, whose muddlings of metaphors resulted in the creation of the word "Goldwynisms" to describe them, once remarked of actors and their agents: "They are always biting the hand that lays the golden egg."

mev. *See* **bev, ev, mev and cutie pie.**

Mexican cinco. *See* **Old Army slang.**

Mho. *See* **volt.**

microphone

Not long ago I received this interesting query. "I am something of an amateur student of words and I especially like to break a word down into its component parts to see how it came to have its present-day meaning, but I'm stumped on *microphone.* The first half is from the Greek *micros,* meaning 'small.' The second part is from *phonos,* 'sound.' Seems to me the word should mean a device for making sounds smaller, not louder. But, obviously it doesn't, so what's wrong with my deduction?"

First, the Greek prefix *mega* (meaning "great" or "large"), which might more logically have been used, had been pre-empted by the word *megaphone,* a device nobody who lived through the Rudy "Vagabond Lover" Vallee hysteria of the late twenties will soon forget.

Equally to the point, the prefix *micro* has several meanings. The first, "little or exceptionally small," is the most common and is the one to which my correspondent referred. However, *micro* may also mean "enlarging what is small." Its most common appearance in this sense is probably in the word *microscope,* and it is in this sense that we find it in *microphone.* Thus we have here a perfectly accurate name for the device whose chief use is to intensify weak sounds.

Mien

Mien (pronounced MEEN) denotes external appearance or bearing. Synonymous with *demeanor,* it probably has common origin in the Latin verb *minari* which originally meant "to threaten" but later became *minare* (to lead). It is closer in meaning today to the French *mine* (look or air) and the German *Miene.* "She bore herself with truly aristocratic *mien.*"

military tattoo. *See* tattoo, military.

militate

Militate (pronounced MIL-ih-tayt). Derived from the Latin *militare* (to serve as a soldier), this word originally meant to fight against in military fashion. Its meaning has changed over the centuries and *militate* now means "to operate or work," and is almost invariably followed by *against.* Its subject should be circumstances, situation or facts. "The heavy rain *militated* against a speedy trip," or "His youth *militated* against his getting the dangerous assignment."

mimeograph

Mimeograph, now a very widely used word, was coined as the trademark of a particular process for duplicating written or typewritten matter. There seems now to be some question as to whether the word has come into sufficiently common use that it should now be regarded as the generic word (with a small first letter) for any of several similar processes or should still be regarded as the trade-mark (with a capital *M*) for the original method. Various dictionaries differ on this point.

mint. *See* pristine.

mint condition. *See* philatelic jargon.

missionary worker. *See* labor's lost lexicon.

mistletoe. *See* Christmas words.

mitigate

Mitigate comes from the two Latin words *mitis* (mild) and *agere* (do), and in today's usage means to make less severe or to give some excuse for, as in "*mitigating* circumstances."

M.M.A.

According to our college-age daughter, fresh from a course in psychology, none of us is normal without at least one *M.M.A.,* the campus abbreviation for "Major Maladjustment." In most of us, this *M.M.A.* takes the form of a *phobia,* with fear of heights (*acrophobia*) and fear of closed places (*claustrophobia*) being the most common.

But there's really no need to settle for one of the run-of-the-mill *M.M.A.*'s. There are more than enough phobias to give us all the variety we want to choose from. Let's take a look at a few of the fancier ones.

Hate animals? You have *zoophobia.* Cats? Your trouble is *ailurophobia.* Dogs? You're a *cynophobe.* Children and dolls? *Pediophobe* is the word for you—and your only consolation is to be found in the words of the immortal W. C. Fields: "A man who hates dogs and children can't be all bad!"

Practically everyone has days when he succumbs to *ombrophobia* (dislike of rain) and February, in the Northern states anyway, is no month for victims of *psychrophobia* (hatred of cold).

That most of us are sociable beings is evidenced by the fact that medical science has no fewer than three words to describe fear of being alone—*autophobia, eremophobia* and *monophobia.*

If you hate flowers, you're an *anthophobe,* but if your employer classes you with the *ponophobes,* watch out. That means you're a hater of work.

Do you hide under blankets during a thunder-and-lightning storm? If so, you can take your choice of four fancy names for what ails you.

Keraunophobia, ceraunophobia and *tonitrophobia* all mean fear of thunder, while *astropophobia* is dread of lightning.

As we see, then, some phobias are so commonplace as scarcely to rate as Major Maladjustments at all. The time to start worrying in earnest, though, is when the doctor hints that you're falling prey to *anthropophobia,* fear of other human beings.

But an end to all this, lest you readers come down with a severe case of *phobophobia*—fear of developing phobias! See also PHOBIAS.

mob

Mob is such a marvelously compact, expressive word that it sees daily service in the headlines of almost every paper, especially in times such as these when *mobs* gather daily in all parts of the world.

In view of its great popularity, it's almost amusing to note the long struggle *mob* had to gain acceptance by the self-anointed arbiters of language. Originally it was part of a Latin phrase *mobile vulgus* (excited or fickle crowd). Gradually it became shortened, during the sixteenth century, to *mobile* and eventually, in the late seventeenth century, to *mob.*

But how the purists did howl at this "vulgarization" of the mother tongue. Richard Steele wrote in his magazine the *Tatler:* "I have done my utmost for some years past to stop the progress of 'mob' and 'banter,' but have been plainly borne down by numbers, and betrayed by those who promised to assist me."

That, sadly perhaps, is the story of many a language arbiter's life, for language remains a fluid, growing thing. It never can be completely fixed. Always there will be new, more vivid words, and, if they are conveniently short and expressive, there will always be a headline writer to give them wide circulation.

modus vivendi, modus operandi

The first phrase (pronounced MOH-dus vih-VEN-dy) comes unchanged (except for the pronunciation of the last syllable) from Latin and means "manner of living"—especially a temporary arrangement pending final settlement of a dispute.

The second phrase *modus operandi* is pronounced MOH-dus op-uh-RAN-dy and means "manner or mode of working." It is often used in the sense of "procedure" in such a sentence as, "The director set up a *modus operandi* to be followed by all employees in fulfilling the contract."

Mohammed. *See* mountain will not come to Mohammed, if the.

monaural, binaural

With the mass production of "hi-fi" radios and phonographs, the attempts of specialists and hobbyists to obtain a new dimension in sound have resulted in the addition of many new words to our language. Among them are *monaural* and *binaural*.

Monaural, obviously, is a coinage from the common prefix *mono-* or *mon-,* meaning "one" and *aural* from the Latin *auris* (ear). Thus one might think *"monaural* sound" means sound heard through one ear, while *"binaural* sound" would be sound heard through both ears. Only in a limited sense is this correct, since the "ears" referred to are not the human ears but actually recording devices or broadcast wavebands.

"Binaural sound" employs two separate but complementary sound signals picked up by different microphones, recorded or broadcast separately and played back through separate speakers. To listen to *binaurally* reproduced music, one places loudspeakers in positions simulating the placement of microphones in the studio. Then, by sitting between the speakers at an angle, you hear music with a depth and breadth of lifelike realism unobtainable by ordinary methods. It sounds, quite literally, as though the orchestra were in your living room and you were on the conductor's podium.

Monaural? Well, that's plain old-fashioned sound recorded or broadcast through only one channel and reproduced through only one loudspeaker. It's what you have been hearing, lo these many years, without ever dreaming it was to be called *monaural.*

money player. *See* baseball jargon.

monicker

This word, meaning "name," is not, as you might surmise, a Damon Runyon coinage. In fact, it's not American slang at all. The word, which is also sometimes spelled *monaker* and *moniker,* comes from the jargon of the British underworld and has been used for at least a hundred years.

Originally it meant a mark left by a tramp on a building or fence to indicate to fellow vagrants that he had been there. Each "knight of the road" developed his own distinctive mark. Thus, a tramp's *monicker* identified him as readily as his signature would and gradually the meaning developed of *monicker* as one's real name—contrasted with one's alias. The word probably was originally a corruption of *monogram.*

monkey drill. *See* Old Army slang.

moon is made of green cheese, the

This is a very old proverb going back almost as far as the beginnings of our English language as we know it today. Its first appearance in English is in the works of Sir Thomas More (1478–1535). Shortly afterward it appeared in this form in a collection of proverbs collected by Thomas Heywood: "The moone is made of a greene cheese"—and Heywood makes it pretty clear that anyone who believes this is a fool.

Heywood didn't claim to have created all his proverbs. He merely collected popular sayings and polished them up a bit, much as Benjamin Franklin did centuries later in *Poor Richard's Almanac*. Some people think that the French humorist François Rabelais, who was a contemporary of Heywood's, said this one first—but chances are they both merely wrote down an expression that had long been spoken by ordinary people.

By the way, *green* in this proverb does not refer to the color of the moon. A "green" cheese is one that is new, and has not had time to age properly. In the earliest days of cheesemaking, such a new cheese often resembled the moon in shape and coloring.

moonlighting

Remember when the word *moonlight* symbolized romance, when "Moonlight and Roses" was a favorite theme song of young lovers the country over? Well, in the world of business *moonlight* now has a much more humdrum and unromantic meaning.

Specifically, *moonlighting* is the term now applied to the increasingly common practice of one person's holding down two jobs. More and more heads of families—notably members of the teaching profession—are finding it hard to make ends meet on the salary earned on one job. So they take on another part-time or full-time job to pad out the family income.

Years ago when your author—and millions like him—were working a basic 56-hour week, such doubling up on jobs was impossible. Indeed, most of us were grateful to have any job at all. But, with the 35-to-40-hour week standard in most industries and employment at an all-time high, the National Industrial Conference Board reports millions of *moonlighters* in the United States today.

It's indeed a far cry from moonlight and romance to *moonlighting* in a factory, but it's a fair bet, as the song goes, that "you can't have one without the other." Or, as Frank Loesser's lyrics ran in *Guys and Dolls:* "You can bet that he's doing it for some doll!"

moot, much mooted

The verb *to moot* is not so familiar as the phrase *moot point,* but in essence the phrase *much mooted* simply means "much discussed." The expression comes from the Anglo-Saxon words *mot* (to meet) and *gemot* (a meeting). The earliest Anglo-Saxon parliament was known as the *Witengemot,* the meeting of wise men. Since debates on current issues were commonplace in such assemblies, the word *moot* gradually came to mean "open for discussion or debate."

Even today in many law schools the pupils and professors try theoretical cases in *moot courts* where, so far as is possible, the circumstances of an actual trial are duplicated. There's one big difference between *moot courts* and real courts, though: in the *moot court* the defendant, no matter what his alleged degree of guilt, always goes free.

morganatic marriage

A widespread belief is that *morganatic* in the term *morganatic marriage,* used to refer to a marriage of wealthy people, refers to people descended from, or as rich as, J. P. Morgan.

Not at all. Indeed, the term was widely in vogue long before J. P. Morgan made his first million. The phrase comes from a Latin phrase *matrimonium ad morganaticam* and refers to the ancient custom by which a husband gives his bride a "morning gift" on the day after the ceremony.

In a *morganatic marriage* the bride forswears all interest in her husband's worldly possessions and agrees that the children of the marriage will also not share in his estate. So the "morning gift" represents just about all she can ever expect to get of her husband's wealth.

moron

Moron was coined as a precise scientific term. Dr. Henry H. Goddard proposed it in 1910 to the American Association for the Study of the Feeble-minded and it was promptly adopted as the official designation for a mentally deficient person whose mental age is between eight and twelve years and whose Intelligence Quotient is below 75. *Moron* is the highest rating in mental deficiency, above "imbecile" and "idiot."

But the word has long since been accepted in the popular tongue as simply synonymous with "fool." Since it was coined from the neuter form of the Greek word *moros,* meaning "foolish," this popular or colloquial meaning is really very close to the original Greek.

Morris dances

Morris dances were originally "Moorish" dances, brought to England from Spain about 1350. Adapted from Moorish military dances, they became very, very British, with the dancers miming various roles from the Robin Hood legends.

Mother's Day

Mother's Day is the occasion when we all join in tribute to the leading ladies in our lives. It may be interesting to see where this celebration had its origin. According to Iona and Peter Opie's delightful *Lore and Language of Schoolchildren,* "A Miss Anna Jarvis of Philadelphia, who lost her mother on May 9, 1906, determined that a day should be set aside to honor motherhood. By forming a league of supporters, by persistent lobby-ing, and by what amounted to emotional blackmail (anyone who opposed her did not love his mother), Miss Jarvis quickly had her way. After one year's campaign Philadelphia observed her day; and on May 10, 1913, the House of Representatives solemnly passed a resolution making the second Sunday in May a national holiday, dedicated to the memory of 'the best mother in the world, your mother!' "

Actually a somewhat similar tradition had existed in England for more than three centuries. The fourth Sunday in Lent was known as "Mothering Sunday" and apprentices and daughters "in service" were permitted by their masters to return home for the day. It was their custom to bring a gift, often a bunch of posies or a small cake. Sometimes, also, they showed their affection for their mother by doing the housework on this day.

As a result of what some Britons call the "American Occupation" of Britain during World War II, the ancient tradition of Mothering Sunday became confused with *Mother's Day*. Today the Yankee version, complete with *Mother's Day* cards and specially inscribed cakes and boxes of candy, is observed throughout Great Britain.

mound, rubber or hill. *See* baseball jargon.

mountain dew

The tradition of illicit distilling of spirits was once as strong in the Scottish Highlands as it is in the mountain regions of Kentucky and Ten-nessee even today. The product of our moonshiners is variously known as *white mule, stump liquor, squirrel whiskey,* or *Kentucky fire.* But gleanings from Highland stills were always known simply as *mountain dew.* The classic version was *Duggan's dew* of Kirkintilloch, the liquid lightning which triggered many a Glencannon gala in the famous stories by Guy Gilpatric.

But there's no point in trying to find *Duggan's dew* at bar or pub. Like Glencannon himself, it can be found only between the covers of the wonderful Glencannon books.

mountain will not come to Mohammed, if the

The common version of this saying goes like this: "If the mountain will not come to Mohammed, Mohammed must go to the mountain." It seems that when Mohammed was bringing his message to the Arabs, they demanded some miracle to prove his power. He then ordered Mount Safa to come to him. When it failed to move, he said that God was indeed mer-ciful for, had it obeyed, it would have fallen upon them, destroying them utterly. He then proposed to go to the mountain to offer thanks to God for his mercy.

Generally speaking, this proverb is used to mean that when a person tries and fails at an impossible task, he is wise to bow to the inevitable.

mouth, down in the

The origin of *down in the mouth* is quite obvious. Take a look at the mirror next time you're feeling out of sorts. Notice how the corners of your mouth seem to turn down? Just the opposite of the smile you wear when you're happy!

moxie

If you have ever lived for long in the New England States, you will surely be familiar with the *Moxie* soft drink which has been popular in this area since 1884. Somewhat similar to root beer and cola drinks, it has a characteristic tartness which accounts for its popularity.

In sports parlance, *moxie* has come to mean courage of a rather high order. It has also the secondary slang meaning of "nerve" or "gall." Just how a respected trade-marked name came to acquire these slang connotations is a puzzle.

By the way, if you should decide to try the original soft drink *Moxie* on a trip to New England, do not make the mistake of calling it "pop" or "soda." Natives of Massachusetts and northern New England, at least, always refer to soft drinks as "tonics." Thus a grocery chain which in New York and other outlets will advertise: "Your favorite soft drinks, 3 for 25¢" will change the copy in the Boston area to read: "Your favorite tonics . . ."

MPC, MPL

Two sets of initials with which we may all become unhappily too familiar in years to come are *MPC* and *MPL*. The former stands for "Maximum Permissible Concentration" and designates that amount of radioactive material in body tissue which specialists feel will not produce significant injury. *MPC* ratings are established to indicate limits of radiation permissible for safe operations in industry and laboratories.

MPL stands for "Maximum Permissible Level (or Limit)." That's the "tolerable" dose rate of radiation to which humans can be exposed. At the present time, scientists throughout the world agree that the *MPL* is 0.3 roentgen per week—a "roentgen" being the unit of absorbed radiation used by radiologists.

When you consider that some scientists estimate that the radioactive contamination from a perfectly feasible attack on an American city would total at least 1,200 roentgens in the first twelve hours, you get some faint notion of how awful is the prospect of radiological warfare.

M.S. (motor ship). *See* U.S.S.

mugg

New York City must take the responsibility for the term, *to mugg,* which is the base of the forms *mugged* and *muggers.*

The *Dictionary of American Underworld Slang,* whose compilation was directed by two long-term convicts and a prison chaplain, gives a graphic definition of the verb *mugg.* First meaning, according to these indisputable authorities, is "to assault by crunching the victim's head or throat in an arm-lock." (It also has the underworld meaning of "to rob with any degree of force, with or without weapons.") The second meaning is an earlier one, supported by Mencken's *American Language:* "to photograph, especially for the Criminal Bureau of Investigation."

Mencken also places the term as originating in New York, describing the process of *mugging* as one in which one stick-up man grabs "the victim around the neck from behind and chokes him while the other goes through his pockets. . . . This is called *mugging* in New York but *yoking* in most other places," he says.

The urge for a lowly pun about no yoking is almost too great. We will quell it by pointing out that *mug* (with one *g*) has long been slang in America and England for the human face or, as a verb, "to grimace." It comes from Gypsy language, perhaps having its origin in *mukha,* Sanskrit for "face."

mugwump. *See* political slang, nineteenth century.

mukluk. *See* sourdough.

mundane

Mundane (pronounced mun-DAYN) denotes that which is of the world, worldly as opposed to spiritual or fanciful. It comes from the Latin *mundus* (world). "Now that the ballet has finished, let's turn our thoughts to more *mundane* matters—such as how we can find a taxi at this hour."

mush. *See* sourdough.

mustache

Mustache (the preferred spelling nowadays) comes from the Italian *mustacchio* by way of French *moustache.* Further back, in Greek, the word was *mystax* and referred to either the upper lip or adornments growing there.

musicians' slang

"Hep ain't hip, Man. Hep is square—really the squarest. Hep's been out for the longest time!" The speaker was Norman Paris, radio and television bandleader and one of the hippest cats in the cool, cool business of jazz.

The occasion for this observation was a discussion of slang with Mr. Paris and his bandsmen during an appearance on a CBS program. And, though he probably didn't realize it at the moment, Paris was making an observation of interest to America's philologists and even to our etymologists.

"Man, I don't dig those labels," one of Paris' sidemen (musicians) might comment. "They sound strictly from Weirdsville. What's with this 'etymologist' jazz?" Well, an etymologist is a student of word origins and development, and an etymologist would be interested in the fact that within the past decade the word *hep* has become entirely obsolete in popular jargon and been replaced by *hip*. The philologist, a specialist in the study of words, would find Mr. Paris' observation interesting because part of the philologist's job is to determine whether either *hep* or *hip* is likely to last long enough to deserve being put in the dictionary.

Since there may well be a few among the readers who don't know either *hep* or *hip* in their slang connotations, it might be well here to explain that both are used to describe a person who is knowledgeable, "in the know."

Musicians for many years have been in the vanguard of developers of the nation's slang. See JAZZMEN'S JARGON.

muster of apes. *See* clowder, kindle and cowardice.

N

naked truth

This phrase—meaning, of course, truth plain and unadorned—goes back to an old fable. Truth and Falsehood went swimming together in a stream. Falsehood came out of the water first and dressed in Truth's clothing. Truth, not wanting to don the garments of Falsehood, remained naked.

nation of shopkeepers. *See* shopkeepers, nation of.

NATO. *See* acronyms.

navel orange

The *navel orange* got its name from the fact that this kind of orange has at one end a depression somewhat resembling the human navel.

Navy, black shoe

Black shoe Navy refers to the traditional seaborne Navy, as differentiated from its newer airborne arm. More specifically, it is a term often used by officers of the fleet air arm—most of whom are alumni of naval training stations, rather than of Annapolis—in deprecatory reference to Naval Academy alumni, who, they feel, exercise too much control over promotions to flag rank.

The origin of the term, of course, goes back to the time when all naval uniforms were either blue or white, and black shoes were part of the prescribed attire. The uniform of naval aviators, which permitted use of brown shoes, was the first deviation from the traditional modes of naval dress.

nebulous

Nebulous (pronounced NEB-yoo-luss) gets its meaning from the noun *nebula* which is a mass of luminous gases in the sky, or a group of stars so far away that they cannot be distinguished and appear as a cloud. *Nebulous* thus has the meaning of "not clear, figuratively speaking; uncertain, indefinite, vague or obscure," as "His proposals are too *nebulous* to be given serious consideration at this time."

neologism

A *neologism* is simply a "new word," a fresh coinage. It comes, as does most of the terminology of linguistics, from the Greek—in this case, from *neos* (new), and *logos* (word).

newly rich

Two terms—both borrowed from French but both perfectly at home in English—*parvenu* and *nouveau riche,* mean a person who has suddenly risen to wealth but does not conform to the customs of the class he now belongs to.

news

One of the most prevalent and erroneous stories of the origin of a word

—what linguists call a "folk etymology"—is that the word *news* is coined from the first letters of the points of the compass.

Apparently the story got its start from the practice of some newspapers, especially those named the *Globe,* of putting a replica of the globe—complete with major compass points N, E, W and S—on the masthead of the paper.

Actually *news*—originally spelled *newes,* by the way—has been part of our language since the Norman Conquest and appears to be a translation of the French *nouvelles* of the same meaning. As a matter of fact, the Latin *nova*—"those things that are new"—had exactly the same meaning. So, for that matter, did the Greek *neos.*

But this pat little story dies hard and I'm certain that—though it couldn't be further from the truth—it will continue to be passed by word of mouth from generation to generation. Many years ago British children had an amusing bit of doggerel which doubtless helped popularize the legend:

> News is conveyed by letter, word or mouth
> And comes to us from North, East, West and South.

So there's nothing new about this bit of misinformation.

nicety

Nicety (NICE-uh-tee), like the word *nice,* has traveled far from the meaning of their common root, the Latin *nescire* (to be ignorant). Also like *nice,* it has many present-day meanings. Most of the meanings of *nicety* have an element of delicacy and minuteness. A *nicety* can be a minute distinction; exactness in treatment or management; delicacy or accuracy of perception; fastidiousness or acts in good taste, as in the common phrase "the *niceties* of life."

Nick, Old. *See* Old Nick.

nicotine

The name of the drug found in tobacco comes from Jean Nicot, a French ambassador to Portugal. An unlikely source, you say? Well, M. Nicot was presented with some seeds of tobacco brought from newly discovered America by Portuguese sailors. In 1560 he planted them in France, introduced tobacco to his native land and thus achieved a fame to which his ambassadorial achievements would never have entitled him.

nightmare

As it happens, the *mare* in *nightmare* has nothing at all to do with a female horse. It comes from the Anglo-Saxon word *mare,* which meant "incubus," and an incubus was an evil spirit or monster which sat or lay on one's breast during sleep. Often in the Middle Ages, this demon was called the "night-hag." Nowadays, of course, a *nightmare* has come to mean any kind of a frightening dream.

nixie

In any discussion of Christmas mail problems, post office officials often use the word *nixie*. The dictionary will tell you that a *nixie* is a "female nix"—which isn't much help, since a "nix" is defined as a goblin. Can it be that the Post Office Department is blaming delays on leprechauns and mischievous little people?

Without much doubt gremlins do affect mail deliveries during holiday periods, else we'd never have those recurring stories about Christmas cards being delivered a year late. But the *nixies* referred to by the postal officials are not the little people of folk legend. These *nixies* are simply pieces of mail which are undeliverable, usually because of faulty addresses. *Nixie* is a term from the private language of postal workers, who, like members of other trades and professions, have a jargon all their own.

Nob Hill

San Francisco's *Nob Hill* traces its name to the fabled courts of Kubla Khan. It is derived, in fact from the language of the ancient Mogul Empire of India.

Before the tragic fire of 1906, the wealthiest of San Francisco's aristocrats—many of whom had made their fortunes in trade with the Far East —built magnificent homes on the steep hill overlooking the bay. So posh was the area that it soon became known as *Nabob Hill*. And a *nabob* (from the Hindustani *navah*) was originally a district ruler under the old Mogul regime. Later the word was applied to non-natives (English and Americans, chiefly) who went to India and became fabulously rich.

So *Nabob Hill* it became, in the lingo of San Franciscans, only to be shortened to *Nob Hill* even before the terrible fire which wiped out the sumptuous homes that gave it its name.

noctiphobia

A child afraid of night and darkness is a victim of *noctiphobia*. Roots of the word are found in the Latin *noctis* (night) and the Greek *phobos* (fear).

no-hitter. *See* baseball jargon.

noisome

Noisome (pronounced NOY-sum), though similar in appearance to *noise* and *noisy,* has nothing in common with them in terms of meaning or of origin. *Noisome* appeared in Middle English as *noyesum* and stems from the same root as the word *annoy* which was the Latin *in odio* (in aversion). Its present meaning is that of being unwholesome and harmful to health. It also means offensive to the smell or the other senses. "Unless the appropriation for a new incinerator is passed, our entire town will be the victim of this *noisome* stench."

Nome (Alaska)

According to George Stimpson, whose *Book About a Thousand Things* is one of the most fascinating collections of oddities in print:

"Nome was originally called 'Anvil City.' The present name was suggested by Cape Nome, near which the town is situated. The cape itself was named in this manner: when a chart of the Alaskan Coast was being prepared by the British ship Herald, it was observed that this point had no name. This was indicated by '? Name,' meaning that the name was unknown.

"A draftsman carelessly copied it as 'Cape Name,' but the 'a' in 'Name' was so indistinct that in London the word was interpreted as 'Nome' and the name of the point was written as 'Point Nome.' There appears to be no foundation for the legend that 'Nome' is a corruption of Eskimo *Ka-no-me* ('I do not know'), the reply of natives when asked by Europeans what the name of the place was."

One may be inclined to question whether such an error could creep into the transcribing of anything so carefully compiled as a coastal survey chart. But nobody who has had much experience with verbal renderings of artists and draftsmen will doubt that the incident could very well happen. See also BORN WITH THE GIFT OF LAUGHTER.

nonplus

Nonplus (pronounced non-PLUSS), a combination of the Latin *non* (not) and *plus* (more), is both a verb and a noun. As a noun it means a "quandary" or "state of perplexity." However, it is more commonly used as an intransitive verb to describe being in such a condition that it is impossible to do any more thinking or take any further action. "I was *nonplused* by his sudden departure."

normal schools

Normal schools derive their name from the French phrase *école normale.* These teacher-training institutions, the first of which was established in France by the Brothers of the Christian Schools in 1685, were intended to set a pattern, establish a "norm" after which all other schools would be modeled. The first *normal school* in America was established in Vermont in 1823.

The name fell out of favor toward the end of the 1920's when the influence of Columbia University's Teachers College became paramount in the field of public education. Most such institutions changed their names to "teachers colleges" during the 1930's. Now that the "progressive education" teachings of the Columbia group have been discredited, the Progressive Education Association itself has disbanded and most colleges have dropped "teachers" from their names. Thus we find that the *normal school* of grandfather's day became a "state teachers college" during father's youth, but today's sprouts are attending "state colleges."

nose, on the. *See* on the nose.

no-see-um. *See* sourdough.

nostalgia

For quite a few years, dictionary editors refused to concede that *nostalgia* had any meaning beyond the purely medical sense of "homesickness." The word came originally from the Greek word *nostos* (return) and *algos* (pain). The *Oxford Dictionary* gives the definition as "a form of melancholia caused by prolonged absence from one's country or home; severe homesickness."

One salient fact about our language is that its development is often completely illogical. The technical medical meaning of *nostalgia* may well be the only one used in England today but in this country the popular, if illogical, meaning of "something to do with the past" is so well established that even dictionary editors are beginning to enter it as completely acceptable usage. Note this from the *World Webster,* College Edition: "a longing for something far away or long ago."

Our language is a constantly changing entity, though purists for centuries have tried to fix it permanently by setting rules of right and wrong, "acceptable" and "taboo." The basic rule by which today's recorders of language are guided is simply that when a word acquires a meaning which is widely used by literate people, that meaning must be recorded as "accepted usage." By this standard *nostalgia* in the sense of longing for things "long ago" as well as "far away" has entered the area of good usage.

not worth two bits. *See* bits, not worth two.

notarize

Notarize, meaning to attest to the authenticity of a document by a notary public, is a word that somehow eluded the dictionary makers for many years. Although it had been in general use for decades, it didn't appear in many dictionaries until after World War II. You'll find it listed in all good recent dictionaries now. Its root is the Latin *notare*, "to note or mark."

notch in his tail

Used by cowboys in speaking of a man-killing bronc, *notch in his tail* has the same connotation as the notched gun handles of gun fighters—one for each man killed.

nouveau riche. *See* newly rich.

nut

Nut, as a theatrical term, means the investment required of a play's backers to put it into production and meet the payroll. Sometimes the term, which is used loosely in the jargon of the entertainment world, also means the "break-even point"—that stage in the show's financial operation when the initial investment has been recouped and the backers begin to make a profit.

nye of pheasants. *See* clowder, kindle and cowardice.

obfuscate

Obfuscate (pronounced ob-FUS-kayt or OB-fus-kayt) has its origin in the Latin *ob* (to) plus *fuscus* (dark) and one of its meanings still is "to darken." By extension it has come to mean "to obscure, confuse or stupefy." Variant forms are *obfuscated, obfuscating* and *obfuscation*. "The complexities of the situation serve well to *obfuscate* a newcomer."

oenophile, oenophilist, oenomaniac

Oenophile is made up of the Greek words *oinos* (wine) and *philos* (love). This word has the added connotation of an "expert or connoisseur of wines." An *oenophile,* in other words, is no mere wine-bibber—that would be an *oenophilist,* who is, according to Funk & Wagnalls, "one who is too fond of wine."

Then there's always the *oenomaniac.* The Bowerys and skid rows of the nation have more than their proper quota of *oenomaniacs,* whom the police label "winos."

oese

Oese, a word found chiefly in crossword puzzles, is the name of a looped platinum wire used by bacteriologists in making cultures. The word comes direct from the German. Without the aid of diacritical marks, one can give only an approximation of its pronunciation: U-say, the first syllable being pronounced like the *u* in "burn" and the second vowel like the *e* in "prey."

ohm. *See* volt.

O.K.

Most common among the legends about what H. L. Mencken once called "without question the most successful of all Americanisms" is that Andrew Jackson, when a court clerk in Tennessee, marked *O.K.* on legal papers as an abbreviation for *orl kerrect.* Though this fiction has been widespread for more than a century, the fact is that Jackson was never a court clerk—he was a prosecuting attorney—and no legal documents bearing *O.K.* in his handwriting have ever been produced.

Still another widely held theory—this one convincing enough to beguile the editors of the Merriam-Webster dictionaries for a few years—is that the term comes from the Choctaw Indian word *okeh,* meaning "it is so." In this spelling it was used by Woodrow Wilson for his initialed approval of state papers. It was also in the spelling *okeh* that the term appeared as the name of a long-defunct record company beloved by jazz antiquarians because under its *Okeh* label appeared the first important recorded efforts of such luminaries as Louis Armstrong, the Dorsey Brothers, Benny Goodman and many more.

The only persuasive explanation of the origin of *O.K.* however, is one which Allen Walker Read proposed back in 1941 and which has since been accepted by virtually all word experts. Read showed that the first printed example of the term in this country was as part of the name of "The Democratic *O.K.* Club," an organization of supporters of Martin Van Buren, who was running for a second term as President. Van Buren was a native of Old Kinderhook, a village in New York State, and had been known throughout his political career as the "Sage of Kinderhook" by his partisans and the "Kinderhook Fox" by his enemies.

American participation in two world wars, plus the tremendous influence of American motion pictures, has served to make *O.K.* a truly international phrase. Prisoners of war in Japan during World War II and more recently in Korea have reported that every native guard used and understood the term. It is perhaps appropriate, therefore, that three American Presidents—Jackson, Van Buren and Wilson—should have figured so prominently in the history of this "most successful" Americanism. See also SK TO O.K.

Old Army slang

In today's world most fathers—and some mothers—have served a hitch in the armed forces. All sons—and a few daughters—know that somewhere along the road from eighteen to thirty they will serve in one or another branch of service. So it's something of a shock to realize that, until twenty years ago, this country had never had a peacetime draft and the armed services were, except in time of war, staffed wholly by "career" men.

The careers certainly varied in duration, depending on a man's willingness to re-enlist but, by and large, our Army, Navy and Marine Corps were made up of dedicated, professional fighting men. And the language they spoke, like the trade language of any well-integrated group sharing the same work and interests, contained some elements of jargon much more colorful and picturesque than the language of the laity.

"Inasmuch as the Old Army was a professional army," Colonel Harry R. Brown of Oconomowoc, Wisconsin, wrote to me, "and we served (most of the Infantry, Cavalry and Field Artillery, at least) in the Philippines and in Western posts near the Mexican border, Spanish influence was very strong. Also Tagalog, the native language of the Philippines. Actually, the Old Army—prior to World War I—spoke a jargon of English, Spanish, Hawaiian, Alaskan, Tagalog, American Indian and what not. During the First World War we of 'The 7000' (Siberian A.E.F.) even added a few Ruski words to our vocabulary."

Colonel Brown sent along a glossary of these "Old Army" terms, some of them going back as far as the Civil War, others still current in the language of our present-day Army. *Artillery pie* has probably gone the way of the horse-drawn field gun, but in the old days it meant a stew with biscuit topping. A *belly robber* then as now was a mess sergeant. *Slum* was stew and a *slum burner,* naturally, was a cook.

In the early 1900's, *goo-goo* was the name given to Filipino natives. Later, as our soldiers learned to know and like them, the name was seldom used. It came from the song "Just Because She Made Them Goo-goo

Eyes." The term *gook* used in World War II and Korea came from the older *goo-goo*.

Woods and jungles were called *bundoks* from a Tagalog word. Now it is usually pronounced and spelled *boondocks,* which is close to the Tagalog pronunciation.

To jawbone was to sell or buy on credit. The term dates from 1898 when U.S. troops were camped near Camp San Antonio Cibad, prior to advancing on the walled city of Manila. A small store sold to the soldiers on a "to be paid payday" basis. The store had a large sign JABON (soap). The soldiers pronounced this *jawbone* and thought it meant "credit." The term is still heard among old soldiers.

The red flag waved in front of a target to denote a miss was known variously as *Maggie's drawers* or *Mexican cinco*. A bull's-eye scored five, a miss nothing. *Cinco,* of course, means "five."

The word *brat,* as used to refer to a person born into the Army, was a proud and honorable title. For instance, one would say "General Mac-Arthur is a *brat*"—i.e., his father was in the Army when Douglas was born.

An *Old Phogy* was an old officer. The increase of pay given to an officer for years of service is known as a *phogy*. *Monkey drill* was calisthenics on horseback, while ordinary setting-up exercises were *physical torture*. And finally, three cheers—also known as *three long years* or *three big beers*—were the three notes played by the band before and after trooping the line at parade or formal guard mount.

It was, indeed, a colorful language. Now that the Jeep has replaced the *jarhead* (mule) and civilian soldiers greatly outnumber the professionals, the old order in Army language will change, too.

Old Nick

It may seem inconceivable that there is any connection between the names of *Old Nick,* the devil, and St. Nick, the embodiment of the Christmas Spirit. But, as a matter of fact, some scholars do think that *Old Nick* like St. Nick may be derived from the name of St. Nicholas. He was a fourth century bishop of Asia Minor whose feast day (December 6) was the children's holiday which, over a period of centuries, came to be celebrated on Christmas. *Santa Claus,* incidentally, is derived from the Dutch name for St. Nicholas.

However, a more likely explanation is that *Old Nick* got his name from Niccolò Machiavelli, Italian Renaissance statesman, who wrote *The Prince,* a book which gained its author a lasting reputation for political unscrupulousness. A brilliant and cynical work, it made its author so famous that the adjective *Machiavellian* is still widely used as a synonym for "crafty," "treacherous" and "double-dealing."

Macaulay, in his biographical study of Machiavelli, wrote: "Out of his surname they have coined an epithet for a knave, and out of his Christian name a synonym for the devil."

So you see, the probability is strong that *Old Nick* got his nickname not from the good saint, but from the evil genius of Renaissance statesmanship.

omadhaun

This is another word for "idiot, fool or simpleton." Dictionaries generally give the pronunciation as OM-uh-don, but I have heard the *thon* sound for the last syllable. It's a word which has come direct from Ireland with no change in spelling and is heard in families of Irish ancestry.

one fell swoop. *See* swoop, one fell.

one foot in the grave

The origin of this phrase, meaning "hovering on the brink of death," is generally attributed to the Emperor Julian, who said that he would "learn something even if he had *one foot in the grave.*"

The Greeks, as is so often the case, had a very similar expression—"with one foot in Charon's ferryboat," referring to the means of transportation across the river Styx to the Elysian fields.

In Genoa there is a famous statue of an old man at the foot of a long flight of stairs with one foot in an open grave. It is a superbly executed piece of sculpture and, as might be expected, tourist guides claim that this statue was the source of the colloquial expression. But, since Julian is on record with his remark some fifteen hundred years before the statue was carved, I'm afraid we have to give him the credit for its origin.

onerous, onus

Onerous (pronounced ON-er-us) is an adjective meaning "burdensome, tedious or troublesome." It is derived from the Latin word *onus,* meaning "load or burden"—a word which has, incidentally, come into English without change. Nowadays one might speak of the *onerous* duties of a street cleaner or say that the *onus* (burden of responsibility) for an international crisis is the aggressor nation's.

on the nose

This common expression does not, as some people think, mean the same thing as "nose-and-nose" when used of a horse race to mean that two horses are finishing at practically the same moment.

No, the term originated in radio from a sign made by directors putting a finger alongside the nose to indicate that a program is running precisely on schedule. There are quite a few similar items in the "sign language" of radio and TV—a language of pantomine made necessary because spoken instructions would go out over the air. The signal to stop—or "cut," for example—consists of the director violently pretending to saw his own throat with his right hand.

opera

Opera in one sense is merely the plural of "opus" and means "works" or "artistic creations." It is in this sense that a movie reviewer once showed his displeasure with what he called "one of the picture's less probable additions, an underwater love-dive lifted from one of the Esther Williams opera." He was merely saying that the underwater scene would more appropriately have been found in one of Miss Williams' films.

The more commonly used *opera*—the one often called grand opera— is an abbreviated form of the Italian phrase *opera in musica,* meaning "work set to music."

op'ry house

The top rail of the breaking corral where ranch hands sit and watch the bronc buster at work.

oracle. *See* eniac.

orange, navel. *See* navel orange.

ostracize

Pronounced oss-truh-size, this word comes from the Greek word *ostrakon*—a "tile," the earliest form of ballot. When Athenians decided that a person had become a menace to the state, they would assemble to vote, by casting an *ostrakon,* on whether he should be exiled. If six thousand voted "yea," the victim was banished for at least five years—and thus *ostracized* very harshly indeed by his fellow citizens.

overhead. *See* painter.

overprint. *See* philatelic jargon.

overt

Overt (pronounced oh-VERT) is an adjective derived from the French verb *ouvrir* (to open), of which *overt* is the past participle. In English it has the meaning of "manifest, openly done, unconcealed." For example, it is possible to suspect a person of malice toward another but until he commits an *overt* act of malice, you might not be sure. *Overtly* and *overtness* are the adverb and noun forms.

oxford (cloth)

Colleges seem to play quite a role in the shirt business. At one time, for example, Scottish weavers invented four special fabrics for shirts and named them after the four great universities of the English-speaking world: Harvard, Oxford, Cambridge and Yale. Of the four, only *oxford* remains popular today.

Ozarkian language

This land of ours often seems, to a student of language, a country of many peoples and many tongues. So varied are the dialects of the New England farmer, the Texas cowhand, the Bronx cliff dweller and the Ozark mountaineer that each would have the greatest difficulty understanding the others. Yet in these regional tongues there is a color and vitality that makes them a delight to those of us with ears to hear and the leisure to enjoy.

One such observer is Mrs. Shelby Steger of Bear Camp Hollow, Van Buren, Missouri. Let me share with you some of the delightful expressions she has collected in ten years residence in the Ozarks.

"Many are the words brought from England and Scotland by the Pilgrims which are still in common use here in the hills. Here are a few.

" 'Wash the baby's hands, they're all *gaumy* (or all *gaumed up*) from that candy.' 'The old henhouse is so *shacklety* it's about to fall down.' 'I bought the biggest *budget* of groceries.' (Pronounced BOO-dget—that is, the *u* of 'push,' not 'bud.') 'Wal, I wouldn't exactly say he's lazy but he *is* right smart *workbrickle*.'

"Many, of course, the dictionary has lost track of. The verb *to wool* —'The baby *wooled* that pore little kitten plumb to death.' *Proud of* used as 'pleased or delighted with'—'My, your new freezer is fine; I'll bet you're just so *proud* of it.' *Sull* as a verb, undoubtedly derived from 'sullen'—'Pa whupped Old Ring for stealing eggs, and now the old hound's crawled under the floor and *sulled up* till he won't come even when you whistle to hie him out.'

"Plus so much picturesque speech," concluded Mrs. Steger, "that I regret I don't know shorthand. Rain? Why hit was a 'raining pitchforks and bull yearlings.' 'Another year of this drouth and the river'll be so low we'll have to start haulin' water to it.' 'I ain't ascaired of him. I ain't very big but if he messes with me, he'll think I'm a circle saw.' "

P

pad, the

The pad was originally criminal slang meaning first a bed, later an apartment or, in jail, a cell. Teen-agers have picked it up from the jargon of jazz musicians and to them it now means "home."

paddle your own canoe

The word *canoe* has been traced back to the time of Columbus and is believed to be derived from a Haitian word, *canoa,* meaning a small hand-made craft, originally one made from a hollowed-out tree trunk. Columbus reportedly used the word in the diary of his voyages and it was taken into Spanish without change.

The phrase *"Paddle your own canoe"*—meaning "Mind your own business"—has been traced back to the early nineteenth century, although canoeing as a sport did not become popular until around 1875. It was a favorite expression of President Lincoln and his frequent use of it probably did much to make it popular.

pagan

This word comes to us from the Latin *paganus* meaning "villager" or "rustic." For many centuries it was thought that *pagan* got its meaning of "heathen" or "non-Christian" from the fact that early Christians were city dwellers and anyone not of the city was *paganus.* However, recent research shows that *paganus* was used by Roman soldiers as a slang term for "civilian." Since the early Christians considered themselves "soldiers of Christ," it was logical that they should adopt the soldier's derogatory label *paganus* to describe everyone who was not a member of Christ's army.

pageant

In medieval times religious "mystery" dramas designed to educate the people in the doctrines of the Christian faith were performed on stages called *pagents*. These rough scaffoldings, sometimes mounted on wheels so they could be moved from place to place, later gave their name, now spelled *pageant,* to the plays acted upon them.

painter

Probably because they used to spend many long months at sea, away from contact with civilization, seamen have always had a colorful language, one uniquely their own. Aboard ship, ceilings aren't ceilings, they're *overheads.* Similarly, walls are *bulkheads,* floors are *decks,* ropes are *lines* and drinking fountains are *scuttle butts.* And we could go on through hundreds of other terms from the salty lexicon of the sea.

One of these words is *painter*—the line by which a small boat is tied to a ship or mooring. What earthly connection can a rope have with paint? The answer is none.

Originally the *painter*—called in French *peyntour*—was the rope holding the anchor to the side of the ship. In this sense the word was used in the Middle Ages and can be traced back to the Latin word *pendere,* "to hang." Today, though the word's meaning has been changed somewhat, it remains a common item in sailor talk.

Pakistan

Although only an autonomous nation since World War II, its name was created back in 1933, in anticipation of the eventual creation of the state. Like so many recently coined words, *Pakistan* is an acronym—that is, a word made up of the first or last letters of a group of other words. Thus *Pakistan* contains these elements: *P* for Punjab; *A* for the Afghan border states; *K* for Kashmir; *S* for Sind; and *TAN* for Baluchistan.

By what is certainly more than just a happy coincidence, *Pakistan* also is composed of the Persian root *pak,* meaning "pure, unadulterated or holy," and *stan,* a common Urdu suffix meaning "land or place." Thus *Pakistan* besides containing elements of the names of each of the states which made it up, also means "Land of the holy."

pale, beyond the

The *pale* in such phrases as *outside the pale, beyond the pale* and even *within the pale* has nothing whatever to do with the adjective "pale," meaning whitish or colorless.

The *pale* we are talking about when we use these phrases actually means stake or fencepost, a meaning which has come to us unchanged from the original Latin word *palus.* Since stakes or "palings" are generally used to mark off restricted areas, the word *pale* came in time to have the figurative meaning of a territory or district.

Back in the fourteenth century the areas of Ireland which had been colonized by the British were collectively known as the British *Pale.* The area, which included Dublin, Cork, Drogheda, Waterford and Wexford, was considered to be under British law, so that anything that took place *outside the pale* would be beyond British jurisdiction. Thus when we say that a person is *"outside the pale* of the law" we mean that by his actions he has forfeited the protection that the laws provide to law-abiding citizens.

No one needs to be told that the Irish regarded British supervision as rather less than a mixed blessing. So it's not surprising that the area known as the British Pale contracted steadily and, by the sixteenth century, it included only an area of about twenty miles around Dublin.

Incidentally, there were two other English *pales* in sixteenth-century Europe—one the city of Calais in France, which had been in English hands for centuries and the other, in Scotland, which, like the Irish domains, had been but recently acquired.

Today, of course, the British *Pale* is merely a phrase to be found in the history books but the common phrases which it made part of our language—*beyond, outside* and *within the pale*—are still in daily use.

pallbearer

The *pall* is the velvet cover sometimes used to cover the coffin. Originally a *pallbearer,* one who attends the coffin at a funeral, held the edges of the *pall.*

pall mall

Originally *pall mall* was the name of a game—a sort of distant cousin of croquet—imported from Italy to London's fashionable West End during the reign of Charles II. A high arch or hoop of iron was mounted at one end of an alley and the sporting blades of the time would engage in contests to see who could bat a boxwood ball through the arch most often. High man, of course, was winner.

So popular was the game with members of the court that the alley where it was played eventually became a center of fashionable club life and *Pall Mall* became a symbol of elegance just as New York's Park Avenue is today.

palm, itching. *See* itching palm.

pan, flash in the. *See* flash in the pan.

Pancake Tuesday

This is an old British name for Shrove Tuesday, the day before Ash Wednesday, which starts the Lenten period of fast and prayer. The serving of pancakes on this day was once as traditional in Britain as eating turkey on Thanksgiving is here in America. Some think the practice started from the understandable desire of British housewives to clear out fats and other foods whose use would be forbidden during Lent.

The same day is, of course, widely celebrated as Mardi gras, a French term meaning "fat Tuesday." This name comes from an ancient French custom of parading a fat cow or ox through the village streets on this day to symbolize the passing of meat during the Lenten season to follow.

This symbolic fasting from the use of meat also gives us the word *carnival* (from the Middle Latin *carne vale*—"Flesh, farewell!"). *Carnivals* are still, of course, highlights of the Mardi gras observation in many countries of Europe, to say nothing of similar revelries in our own New Orleans.

pandemic. *See* epidemic, pandemic.

panhandle, panhandler

There are at least two famous *panhandles* in this country, the one in West Virginia—which is often called the *Panhandle State*—and the *Panhandle* section of Texas. In each case the area gets its name from the fact that a narrow strip of land extends out from the rest of the state appearing, on a map, much like the handle of a pan formed by the rest of the state.

As the natives of either section would be quick to tell you, there is absolutely no connection between this kind of panhandle and the *panhandlers*— beggars and bums—who frequent the slum areas of our big cities. This kind of *panhandler* gets his name from the fact that he originally used tin pans when soliciting alms or handouts, as they'd be known today.

panic button, hit the

Many times one hears the expression *hit the panic button* used when things become—as we used to say in the last war—"snafued,"—all fouled up. As it happens, this phrase—which is rapidly becoming widely used, though not in the meaning originally intended—was researched thoroughly by Lieutenant Colonel James L. Jackson, USAF. Writing in *American Speech* magazine, he reported: "*Hit the panic button,* meaning speaking or acting in unnecessary haste or near panic, is now used in a general way to refer to any kind of precipitate action.

"Discussion with pilots at the Air Force Academy reveals at least four buttons or switches which may be referred to as the *panic button*. The one mentioned most often is the feathering button, which is punched in flight to stop the operation of a malfunctioning engine and turn the prop blades edge-forward. Another candidate is the switch which shoots off the extinguisher materials designed to put out an engine fire in flight.

"A third possibility is the ejection seat trigger. Obviously, when a man must jettison his canopy in flight and eject himself from his plane by use of the explosive charge stored under his seat, he can be excused for calling the trigger *the panic button*. And still a fourth possible source is the button on the panel of the F-84 which salvoes the tip-tanks, either in combat or if the pilot has trouble on take-off.

"But none of these four switches seems to have fathered the expression. Further discussion with Air Force officers and airmen reveals that the phrase *to hit the panic button* was in use during the Second World War, before any of the devices mentioned above were introduced.

"The actual source seems probably to have been the bell system used in bombers (B-17, B-24) for emergency procedures such as bailout and ditching. In case of fighter or flak damage so extensive that the bomber had to be abandoned, the pilot rang a 'prepare-to-abandon' ring and then a ring meaning 'jump.' The bell system was used since the intercom was apt to be out if there was extensive damage. The implications of the phrase seem to have come from those few times when pilots *hit the panic button* too soon and rang for emergency procedures over minor damage, causing their crews to bail out unnecessarily."

panther sweat

Panther sweat is one of the more than a thousand slang words which have been invented over the years as synonyms for the word "liquor." See also SHEETS IN THE WIND.

pantophobia

The most inclusive of all phobias, *pantophobia* makes its victims thoroughly miserable all hours of the day and night. Meaning fear of everything, it is derived from the Greek *pan* (all, every) and *phobos* (fear).

pants

Remember the expression, "You surely can tell who wears the *pants* in that family"? Already it sounds more than a bit dated, almost quaint, in view of the revolution in women's wear which has made trousers—or "slacks"—a commonplace item in the wardrobes of females from eight to eighty.

The wholesale adoption by women of what had been male garb would probably be dated by a social historian to the days of World War II, when the fair sex by the hundreds of thousands took factory jobs previously held by men going into service. So the transition from "outlandish" to routine has taken remarkably few years—far less time than was needed for trousers to become acceptable attire for men in the first place.

About 1790 the first trousers—probably inspired by the *trews*, close-fitting tartan *pants* worn by certain Scottish regiments—were introduced in England. Most males were unenthusiastic, feeling that the breeches and silk stockings then in vogue were more flattering, for those were the days of the male "dandies."

Among military and naval men, though, the newfangled trousers soon won wide popularity since they were far better suited to rough wear. Still for several decades no gentleman would dare be seen at a fashionable gathering dressed in what were mockingly called *pantaloons,* which was later shortened to the word we commonly use today—*pants.* Indeed, no less a hero than the Duke of Wellington was refused admittance to one of his London clubs in 1814 because he was dressed in plebeian *pants,* rather than in breeches and silken hose.

But the revolution in attire which took men of Wellington's stripe nearly forty years to accomplish was duplicated by today's women in less than ten. As the magazine people say, "Never underestimate the power of a woman. . . ."

Come to think of it, isn't that well-known slogan just another way of phrasing the thought behind the now obsolescent, "She wears the *pants* in the family"?

parachute. *See* **bumbershoot, parachute.**

parage. *See* **disparage.**

paranormal

On occasion some radio commentators can be too literate for the average listener. On a program in which the commentator and his guest were discussing psychic research, the statement was made that poltergeists are "*paranormal* but not occult."

Don't be surprised if you are stumped by *paranormal.* It's not even listed in many dictionaries. Here is how we deduce its meaning from a combination of entries that *are* in the dictionaries.

Para- is a common Greek prefix meaning "beside" or "beyond." Thus *paranormal* would mean simply "outside the normal course of human experience," while *occult* implies secret and mysterious machinations of supernatural agencies. Since poltergeists are traditionally impish, prankish creatures, the milder adjective *paranormal* seems better suited to them.

parliament. *See* **candidate.**

parvenu. *See* **newly rich.**

passion for anonymity

This popular phrase was coined by the late Franklin D. Roosevelt. Midway through his Presidency, long after the original Brain Trust had broken up, he announced that he was going to appoint several "Presidential Assistants" who would serve him in an advisory capacity. Perhaps with a rueful recollection of the headline-grabbing antics of Tugwell, Ickes and others of his early associates, he noted that one of the first qualifications he would demand of the new assistants would be *a passion for anonymity.* Apparently he succeeded, for the only one whose name comes to mind at the moment is Lauchlin Currie—and his claim to fame is probably based more on his postwar diplomatic missions than on his work with Mr. Roosevelt.

pastiche

A lighthearted reincarnation of the typical musical comedy of the 1920's, the Broadway show *The Boy Friend* differed from similar period pieces in treating its subject with warmth and affection, rather than ridicule and satire.

To describe his work, its author, Sandy Wilson, chose the wonderfully appropriate though quite uncommon word *pastiche.* Directly derived from the French and pronounced pass-TEESH, it means a composition—literary, artistic or musical or, as in this case, all three—imitating previous works of the same genre or type.

Originally *pastiche* derived from the Italian word *pasticcio* whose root is *pasta* (paste). Thus the earliest meaning of this word was a composition of bits and pieces of other people's work pasted together to make a new whole. In *The Boy Friend,* though, Wilson created a wholly new musical play in the spirit of the twenties but not directly borrowing from any earlier work. So *pastiche* in its present-day meaning was completely appropriate.

patent leather

Patent leather got its name from just about where you would expect— the U.S. Patent Office. The process by which this brilliantly polished black finish is applied to leather used in shoes and handbags was once protected by patent.

patio

The word *patio* comes from Spanish and, when originally popularized in our Southwest, it was given the Spanish pronunciation PAH-tyoh. Gradually this was Americanized and the two syllables of Spanish became three: PAH tee-oh.

With the enormous expansion of suburban living in the years following World War II, the ranch house—usually in hybrid variations no rancher would ever recognize—dominated the home-building scene. Since *patio* sounded more glamorous than "back yard" it became the custom to refer to almost anything in the way of outdoor recreation area as a *patio.* And, since the flat, short *a* of "pat" is far more common, especially in the Midwest, than the broad *a* of the Spanish original, the pronunciation PAT-*ee-oh* became widely heard.

So today all authorities accept both pronunciations, but all still indicate a slight preference for PAH-tee-oh.

payoff pitch. *See* baseball jargon.

payola

Payola is anything but a new word. It has been part of the trade jargon of the music and recording industries for more than a decade. Some years ago, for instance, *Variety,* the show business trade magazine, devoted many pages of several issues to an expose of the *payola* practices which even then constituted a threat to the music industry. It's not an overstatement to say that the revelations of the Congressional hearings were little more than a warmed-over rehash of *Variety's* findings.

Payola appears to be a fanciful variant of "payoff," formed by analogy to at least two words well known in the music trade: "pianola" and "Victrola."

The practice of undercover bribery to assure success of a project is, of course, about as old as humanity. Through the years bribery—for that's what *payola* is, of course—has acquired some interesting and occasionally euphonious labels in the various trades. Politicians are said to be *on the take*. Ticket agents, handling ducats for top-rated Broadway shows, see to it that they get *ice* on *hot* tickets. Other variations are *schmeir, rake-off, grease, fall dough* or simply *the take*.

Perhaps most ominous, for it seems an indication of how deeply the *payola* practice has infected the American business community, is the common phrase *do business,* meaning to obtain special favors through bribery.

peach Melba. *See* food from the opera.

peanut gallery

Back in the nineties—and perhaps earlier—it was the custom of vaudeville audiences to eat peanuts during performances, just as today's moviegoers munch away on popcorn. Theaters in those days consisted of orchestra, balcony and gallery, sometimes called "second balcony."

The "gallery gods"—so-called because their seats were nearest the ceiling, which often was decorated with allegorical paintings of the heavens —were a raffish, undisciplined crew given to direct action when they wanted to express displeasure at the entertainment. The most direct method, of course, was to rain peanut shells and, on occasion, pennies down on the heads of the hapless performers.

Thus developed the practice of *playing to the galleries*—or making an appeal to the least critical element in the audience—since success and, occasionally, physical well-being depended on satisfying these denizens of the *peanut gallery.*

peasant

A *peasant*—a term seldom used in America, by the way—is a man of the soil. His name came into English at the time of the Norman conquest in the form of the French word *paisent,* which is directly derived from *pays,* the French word for "country." Further back, it can be traced to the Latin word *pagus* (district or province). So *peasant* is correctly used only when speaking of farm workers.

peccadillo

Peccadillo (pronounced pek-uh-DIL-oh) is a petty fault or a minor sin. A Spanish word, it is the diminutive of *pecado,* which in turn is derived from the Latin verb *peccare* (to sin). "A child should not be punished for mere *peccadilloes.*"

pedestrian

This term comes from the Latin word *pedester,* "one who moves on foot," and its first meaning is "walking or moving on foot." For centuries, though, it has had the figurative meaning—especially when applied to writing or speech—of "prosaic or dull." Thus one speaks of an author's "*pedestrian* prose."

peeler

Peelers are British policemen, also often called *bobbies.* Both nicknames come from the name of the founder of modern London's police, Sir Robert Peel, who earlier also organized the Irish constabulary. In America, *peeler* is show business slang for strip-tease dancer.

peeping Tom

This expression goes back to one of the most celebrated legends of the Anglo-Saxon period of British history. Leofric, Lord of Coventry, imposed exorbitant taxes upon his subjects. His wife, Lady Godiva, was sympathetic to the complaints of her subjects and repeatedly pleaded with him to reduce their tax burden. He refused but eventually, more to make her be quiet than anything else, said that he would cut taxes if she agreed to ride unclad through the streets of Coventry.

To Leofric's astonishment, she accepted the challenge and, after asking that all townspeople stay indoors and close their shutters while she rode, she made the ride on a white horse. Everyone honored her request except the town tailor, Tom, who peeped through the shutters and, as legend has it, was stricken blind for his impudence.

And, yes, the taxes were lowered.

peeve

Peeve is a "back formation" from the adjective "peevish," just as "enthuse" is a back formation from "enthusiastic." While the verb *peeve* cannot properly be labeled "slang," it surely is too recent a coinage to be admissible in formal writing. Label it colloquial, meaning that it may be used in informal conversation and writing. By the way, the popular expression *pet peeve* would still merit the label "slang."

Pelion on Ossa, piling. *See* piling Pelion on Ossa.

penchant

Penchant (pronounced PEN-chant) is a strong liking or inclination and comes from the French verb *pencher* (to incline). "My wife has a *penchant* for pearls and French perfumes."

penguin

Ever since the earliest of the Byrd expeditions, pictures of the ponderously playful penguins have been a source of delight to young and old. But did you know that these strutting birds in formal dress got their name from Welsh and Breton fishermen who not only never saw a penguin but never got within thousands of miles of the South Pole?

Here's how this paradox developed. The great auk was a flightless diving bird, commonly found during the seventeenth and eighteenth centuries on the islands of the North Atlantic. With its heavy body, webbed feet and short tail and wings, it was as incapable of flight as the penguin of the Polar regions, which, indeed, it much resembled.

Because of the white spots the great auk had near its eyes, it was known to Breton and Welsh sailors as the *penguin* from *pen* (head) and *gwyn* (white). When, many years later, sailors in southern latitudes saw a similar kind of flightless bird, they applied the same name *penguin* to it, though the label by now was inaccurate, since one characteristic of today's penguin is his black head.

Incidentally, the great auk is now entirely extinct. The last one was killed in 1844 and his fate is a prime example of the dire result of man's killing of wildlife, which later generations of nature lovers have fought long and hard to repress.

perforce

Perforce (per-FORSS), an adverb, means "of necessity." The *per-* in the word is Latin for "through," so we have a meaning of "through force," the force being that of circumstances or necessity. The word is found in Old French and Middle English as *par force*. "The circuit court must *perforce* accept the verdict of the court of appeals."

peripatetic

Readers of the "good gray *Times*"—as the *New York Times* is affectionately nicknamed—must have been startled to find a story about one of Mr. Eisenhower's medical check-ups given this alliterative headline: PRESIDENT PROVES A PERIPATETIC PATIENT. Regular readers of the *Times* would not be surprised by the rather obscure and polysyllabic *peripatetic* in the headline. But here was humorous alliteration in a story about the President—and on the front page at that! Well, it was a Saturday morning issue, so the number of *Times* readers unnerved by this unexpectedly light-hearted whimsy was probably relatively small.

It is interesting to note, though, that this *Times* headline writer did not choose the word *peripatetic* merely to achieve the sought-for alliteration. He was trying, of course, to convey the point that the President refused to "stay put" during his hospital visit and insisted on wandering around and chatting with other patients.

You might ask why words like "ambulatory" or even "itinerant" wouldn't serve the purpose as well. For the answer to why *peripatetic* is the one entirely accurate word in this instance, we have to go back to its originator, the Greek philosopher Aristotle. It was his practice to instruct his pupils through discussions held while wandering through the covered walks of the Lyceum at Athens. Since the Greek word for "walk about" was *peripatein,* his system of philosophy became known as the *Peripatetic School*—literally, the "walk-around" school.

And the reason why the President was a *peripatetic* patient rather than merely an ambulatory one is that he did more than walk around the corridors of Walter Reed Hospital. He stopped to chat and exchange views with many other patients, ranging from Philippine Ambassador Carlos P. Romulo to the youngsters in the children's ward.

Thus this *Times* headline writer preserved all the subtleties of meaning inherent in this 2,300-year-old word—and also achieved a headline that, at least by *Times* standards, rates as witty and eye-catching.

pernickety, persnickety

Pernickety or *persnickety*—whichever way you spell it—means "fussy, fastidious or overprecise." The word originally came from Scottish dialect, perhaps from *pertickie,* a Scottish children's form of "particular."

Unquestionably the original form of the word in our American speech was *pernickety,* and most dictionaries still list it that way. But my own researches indicate that *persnickety* is much more widely used today. So one dictionary of which I am advisory editor (Funk & Wagnalls *Standard Dictionary,* International Edition) enters *persnickety* in its proper alphabetical location.

Persnickety remains, however, a colloquial term. That means that you may use it freely in conversation or in informal writing. It should not be used in formal letters or in sermons, full-dress speeches and the like.

persuasion. *See* suasion.

pet peeve. *See* peeve.

phat

Phat is a printing term, sometimes and more logically spelled "fat." It means "profitable" and is used for advertising and other layouts which have an unusually large proportion of open space or illustrations, and hence lower composition costs.

philatelic jargon

Almost since the issuance of the first postal stamp, just a little more than a century ago, the collection of these colored bits of paper has fascinated young and old the world over. The word *philately* itself was coined from the Greek words *philos* (love) and *ateleia* (exemption from tax), alluding to the fact that the first stamps served as evidence that postage charges had been prepaid and thus the receiver was exempted from further charge.

Like all hobbies, *philately* (pronounced phil-AT-uh-lee) has a language all its own—one which its devotees bandy about freely and which contains enough odd and colorful lingo to attract the interest even of noncollectors. Here are just a few of the commoner items from the stamp collector's working vocabulary:

Mint condition describes a stamp or block of stamps in the same condition as when first printed.

A *sleeper* is a stamp more rare—and thus more valuable—than the catalogue listings indicate.

A *first-day cover* means an envelope bearing a stamp used and postmarked on the day of official issue.

A *cachet* (kash-AY) is the inscription, usually printed, on an envelope bearing a special issue commemorating some great event.

Killer means simply the post office cancellation mark.

An *overprint* is a stamp whose face value or designation has been officially altered by printing an inscription or new valuation on it.

philately. *See* timbromania.

Philemon and Baucis

The tale of *Philemon and Baucis* comes from the *Metamorphoses* of Ovid, a Roman poet who lived and wrote at the very dawn of the Christian era and whose works were standard fare, along with Cicero and Vergil, in the classrooms of a half-century ago.

As Ovid told the tale, Philemon and Baucis were poor cottagers in Phrygia, a country in Asia Minor. They were visited by Jupiter, who was so pleased by their hospitality that he promised to grant them any wish they might make.

So devoted were they to each other that they wished only to remain together in death as in life. Their request was granted and Philemon became an oak, Baucis a linden tree, growing so close together that their upper branches were intertwined.

This legend has proven so appealing down through the centuries that many writers, including Goethe, have retold it. Nor did it begin with Ovid, though his version is best known. In the earlier Greek version, the visiting god was, of course, named Zeus, rather than Jupiter, and Philemon and Baucis were made priests in the temple of Zeus before their final incarnation as trees.

phillumenist

A person who collects match-book covers is a *phillumenist,* from the Greek word *philos* (love) and the Latin *lumen* (light). Incidentally, most word coiners prefer to have both elements of a compound word come from the same language rather than one part from Latin, one from Greek. But since there is already a national society of *phillumenists,* I suppose this word is here to stay.

philolexian

Philolexian is the name of a literary society at Columbia University, dating back to 1802, which was recently revived by the undergraduates at the university. The pronunciation is fil-oh-LEX-ee-un. It's from the Greek *philos* (lover) and *lexis* (word).

phobias

Phobias are those fears which, in greater or less degree, haunt all of us.

Are you fearful of high places? Do you flee from subways? Do you tremble at the thought of being alone, or are you, perhaps, terrified of being in a crowd? Whatever your fear, there's a name for it—and by the time we run through a few of the phobias, the chances are that your day will have turned to gloom and you'll be snorting instead of smiling at the passers-by. Don't be too depressed, though. Remember that everyone has his own particular phobia in the weird gamut ranging from *acrophobia,* the fear of high places, to *zoophobia,* fear of animals.

Have you ever had stage fright? Well, that's a special form of *topophobia,* fear of being in a particular place. Don't confuse that with *tropophobia,* by the way; that means fear of moving or making changes.

Most of us are familiar with *claustrophobia,* the fear of being shut up in a closed space, but there is also a more extreme form of this particular dread. It's called *taphephobia* and means fear of being buried alive. One touch of *taphephobia* and you lose all love for cave exploring!

Stenophobia does not, as it happens, mean the awe amounting nearly to fear with which a boss regards an efficient secretary; *stenophobia* is simply the fear of narrow places.

Some years ago H. L. Mencken coined the word *ecdysiast* to describe strip-tease dancers. He might have saved himself the trouble by calling them *vestiophobes,* people with an aversion to wearing clothing.

Unless you are a victim of *sophophobia,* fear of learning, or of *verbophobia,* aversion to words, why not look at a few more common and uncommon phobias?

A child afraid of night and darkness is a victim of *noctiphobia.* By contrast, some people fear bright lights. They are victims of *photophobia.* If you blanch at the thought of going to the top of the Empire State Building, chances are you have a touch of *acrophobia,* fear of high places.

Practically everyone of sense has a touch of *anemophobia,* the dread of hurricanes and cyclones, but *ailurophobes* are relatively scarce. They are people who hate cats. Many soldiers, including some of the bravest, are victims of *ballistophobia,* fear of bullets, but it's a rare person who is prone to *botanophobia,* intense dislike of flowers and plants.

If you're a regular user of that soap that claims to stop "B.O.," chances are you have a touch of *bromidrosiphobia,* fear of body odors. And the makers of color television sets will, I'm sure, have no use for victims of *chromophobia,* dislike of colors.

Practically all of us have suffered at one time or another from a touch of *dentophobia,* fear of dentistry, but no subscriber to the philosophy that "man's best friend is his bed" ever succumbed to *clinophobia,* fear of going to bed.

Well, those are just a few of the commoner phobias. If none of them seem to fit your case, just possibly the reason is that you're a victim of *pantophobia*—fear of everything. See also M.M.A.

phogy, old. *See* Old Army slang.

phonetic spelling. *See* Shaw's linguistic legacy.

pick off, pick up. *See* baseball jargon.

pidgin English

If you have ever tried finding *pidgeon English* in your dictionary, you probably had little success.

The reason why you can't find the phrase is that you should be looking for *pidgin* not *pidgeon* English, although the misspelling is quite common. The word *pidgin* came from Chinese traders' mispronunciation of the word "business." Originally it was a language developed by British traders with China during the seventeenth century—a blend of English words and Chinese syntax. The end result sounds very much like baby talk, in that many short words are used to express the sense of a single word not known to the natives. Thus "bishop" becomes "top-side-piecee-Heaven-pidgin-man," and "Belly-belong-me-walk-about" means "I am hungry."

There are today many varieties of *pidgin English* and, for that matter, *pidgin French, pidgin Spanish* and so on. In Mediterranean seaports, a hybrid language containing elements of Arabic, Turkish, Spanish, Italian, French and Greek is spoken. It is called *lingua franca*—literally, "the Frankish language"—and the Franks, you recall, were a German tribe that, during the Middle Ages, ruled over most of Europe. Thus, the term *lingua franca* originally meant the language through which the Moslem world could conduct business dealings with the Franks.

One of the most interesting kinds of *pidgin* is that known as *bêche-le-mar* or *bêche-de-mer,* a blend of English and Malayan spoken in Samoa, Tahiti and other Polynesian islands. When traders talk together in the islands, you hear such phrases as "Capsize him coffee along cup" for "Pour the coffee," and "Shoot him kaikai" for "Serve dinner." A Frenchman is called "man-a-wee-wee" (the man who says *oui-oui*) and a butcher is called "man-belong-bullanacow."

Partly as a result of American occupation of many Pacific Islands during the last war and partly because of the work of educators and missionaries, everyday English is gradually replacing *pidgin English* in many of these areas. But, so long as trade with untutored natives remains important to our economy, you may be sure that *pidgin* will be used. See also BÊCHE-DE-MER.

pie

The origin of *pie* is complicated and hardly appetizing. First, remember that the original pies—in the British Isles, at least—were very different from what Americans usually refer to as pies today. Instead of dessert dishes like apple pie and lemon pie, British pies were main dishes concocted of meat or fish and a variety of vegetables, under a pastry or potato covering. Indeed, they really were stews in pie form.

Now then, the "magpie," a member of the crow family, has long been famous for his habit of bringing all sorts of useless odds and ends back to his nest. So the theory is that the first pies were so called because they contained a miscellaneous mixture of meats and vegetables, not unlike the oddments collected by the magpie.

Another theory of *pie*'s origin first appeared in the old *Youth's Companion* magazine in 1900.

"In old England and France, shoes were shapeless affairs, making the foot (*pie* or *pied*) an oblong, shapeless object. The toothsome delicacy made of dough flattened out in an irregular shape and filled with meats or fruit, with the edges turned up from the sides to make a cover, resembled the footprints of the shoes (*pies*)—so they too were called 'pies.' "

That's an ingenious explanation—and not one bit more appetizing than the original "magpie" theory.

pied-à-terre

Pied à terre, a French term meaning literally "foot to the ground," is rather a popular expression in England to designate temporary lodgings. Thus an actor in town for the brief run of a show, might rent an unpretentious *pied-à-terre,* rather than take a lavish apartment or, as the British would call it, a "flat" on a long lease.

pigeon English. *See* pidgin English.

pig in a poke

Buying a *pig in a poke,* meaning "buying blind," has an amusing origin. The expression comes from a ruse practiced for centuries at country fairs in England. A trickster would try to palm off on an unwary bumpkin a cat in a burlap bag, claiming it was a suckling pig.

If the "mark"—or victim—was brighter than the sharper expected him to be, he would insist on seeing the pig and thus *let the cat out of the bag.*

Poke, meaning "bag" or "sack," is now chiefly heard in regional dialects in this country and England, though it has a long and honorable history and, indeed, is the word from which *pocket* was derived.

pig Latin

Pig Latin has been a childhood diversion for many decades, though completely ignored by students of language and not even defined in most

dictionaries. It consists, of course, simply of transposing the initial con-
sonant of a word from the front to the end and adding the sound *ay* after
it. Thus "John went home" becomes *"Ohnjay entway omehay."* Iona and
Peter Opie in their excellent book *The Lore and Language of Schoolchildren* report that *pig Latin* was common in England before World War I.
My guess is that *ig-pay atin-lay* is much older than that.

piggybacking

Piggybacking is the method of long-distance hauling of loaded truck
trailers, whereby the trailers are fastened on railroad flatcars and thus
travel to the railroad station nearest their destination. See also BIRDIE-
BACKING.

pile driver

In the colorful language of the West, a *pile driver* is a horse which, in
bucking, comes down to earth with all four legs stiff.

piling Pelion on Ossa

This phrase means "piling embarrassment upon embarrassment." The
reference is to an incident in the *Odyssey* when the Titans, attempting to
attack the gods in heaven, piled Mount Pelion on Mount Ossa, and both
onto Mount Olympus.

pima cotton. *See* broadcloth.

pin money

Originally, this expression may have meant money set aside especially
for the purchase of pins, which, in mid-seventeenth-century England and
America, were very expensive because the manufacture of pins was controlled by a monopoly under grant from the Crown. More likely, however,
the term is merely a figurative one, meaning funds over which the wife
alone has control. Since a husband would be scarcely likely to be buying
pins, the term is not inappropriate. The phrase *pin money* is recorded in
the *New English* [Oxford] *Dictionary* as early as 1697.

pithy

Pithy (pronounced PITH-ee) is the adjective form of *pith,* which was
Anglo-Saxon and has kept its original meaning of the central substance of
certain plant stalks. It has acquired the further meaning of "strength, force,
or essence." *Pithy,* when used figuratively, can be defined as containing
the central substance in terms of meaning. Statements, comments, remarks
can all be *pithy*. Comparative and superlative forms are *pithier, pithiest.*

"George Bernard Shaw's plays are notable for *pithy* succinctness of dialogue."

pitted. *See* battle royal.

platform. *See* political language.

platter. *See* baseball jargon.

play a hunch

We often hear the phrase *play a hunch,* meaning "to act upon intuition or premonition." It goes back to the gamblers' superstition that good luck would follow if one touched a hunchback on his hump.

playoff

That long list of credits at the end of many a television show which gives the names of everyone from the cast to the make-up man is, in television parlance, the *playoff.*

playing to the galleries. *See* peanut gallery.

Plimsoll mark

All cargo- and passenger-carrying vessels bear marks, usually on either side of the bow and stern of the ship, to indicate the depth of the ship's draft under various conditions of loading.

The most important mark carried by ships, however, is the *Plimsoll mark,* sometimes called the *Plimsoll line.* It is distinguished from the ordinary draft markings by being not simply a line but a circle with a horizontal line drawn through it. It is located amidships on both sides of the ship and marks the maximum depth to which that ship may be loaded.

The *Plimsoll mark* gets its name from Samuel Plimsoll, a member of Parliament who waged a long campaign against shippers who, during the early nineteenth century period of migration from the Old World to the New, persisted in sending to sea ships that were overloaded and undermanned. So infamous and so widespread was this practice that such ships came to be known as "coffin ships." In any kind of a heavy gale, the ship's chances of survival were slight but the owners, having heavily insured the ships, stood to make a handsome profit if they were lost at sea. This murderous practice was finally halted in 1876 when Parliament passed Plimsoll's bill and from that day onward all British ships—and virtually all the rest of the world's shipping—have carried this symbol of safe loading.

American flag ships also carry what are known as *A.B.S.* (for "American Bureau of Shipping") marks. These, like the *Plimsoll line,* are carried amidships, but they are four in number and mark the maximum permissible load under four sets of conditions: fresh water—summer; fresh water—winter; salt water—summer; salt water—winter.

pocket. *See* **pig in a poke.**

podiatry. *See* **chiropody.**

poisson d'Avril. *See* **April Fool's Day.**

poke, pig in a. *See* **pig in a poke.**

polecat

A *polecat* takes its first syllable from the French *poule,* meaning "chicken." Thus, chicken thief. As a further oddity, the European *polecat* lacks the characteristic stripe down the back flaunted by the American skunk.

police. *See* **politics**

political language

The language of politics, especially in the United States, is colorful and ever-changing. The contrast with the long-established terminology of Great Britain's political parties is, in a sense, symbolized by the different terms used to describe a candidate for office. In England one *stands* for Commons, while in America a candidate *runs* for Congress.

With the establishment of a new nation and a radically new form of government after the Revolution, it was necessary to coin a great many words and phrases, for the reason that the customs and institutions being described simply hadn't existed before. Thus our early Founding Fathers were responsible for such now commonplace political terms as *machine* (coined by Aaron Burr), *favorite son,* a term first used in reference to George Washington, and *platform,* which was in use as early as 1789.

Later ingenious inventions included the phrase *to send up Salt River* (to defeat a candidate), *to crawfish* (to backtrack from a position previously taken), *to straddle, to split the ticket, to boodle* and *to eat crow.* Many of these terms are so much a part of everyday speech that most of us aren't even aware of the fact that they began life as part of the slang of politics.

Then there are such phrases as *lame duck,* to designate an officeholder who fails to be re-elected but still has a few weeks or months to serve, and *gerrymander,* to rearrange Congressional or other electoral districts in order to benefit the party in power. *Gerrymandering* will probably be a lively topic of political controversy for years to come as a result of an important Supreme Court decision. Thus a word coined in Massachusetts in 1812 still finds useful application clear across the country nearly a century and a half later. See POLITICAL SLANG.

And remember this: our political heritage is at least as lively and colorful as the language we have coined to describe it—and far more important.

political slang

Election time is a biennial phenomenon in our fair country and down the length and breadth of the land candidates take to the stump to explain to their fellow citizens why they—and they alone—are fit to run the people's government. Over the years since our earliest Continental Congress, we have developed a varied, colorful and characteristically American collection of words to make up our vocabulary of politics. Let's look at some of the more interesting of these terms.

That phrase *taking to the stump,* for example, pretty obviously goes back to the early days of our Western migration when the campaigning politician would mount any platform—even a tree stump—where he could find a handful of voters willing to listen to his speech. (See also STUMP, TO.)

No primary campaign would be complete, of course, without the claim of the defeated candidate that his opponent's election was actually dictated by the *bosses in the smoke-filled room.* This phrase is a comparative newcomer to our political scene and is credited to a former Associated Press reporter, Kirke Simpson, who used it to describe back-stage maneuvering for Warren Harding's nomination at the 1920 Republican convention.

The word *boss* itself is no stranger to the American scene. It comes from the Dutch word *baas* meaning "master." Quite possibly, then, the first American political boss was none other than old Peter Stuyvesant.

Among native American political terms few are more colorful than *Tammany* and *gerrymander.* You may be surprised to learn that Tammany Hall was originally an exclusive social club, founded in 1789 by a group of politically minded New Yorkers including Aaron Burr. It was named after a Delaware Indian chieftain who, some historians believe, was the person who negotiated with William Penn the transfer of the territory which eventually became Pennsylvania.

Gerrymander—a word meaning rearrangement of political districts in such a way as to benefit the party in power—owes its origin to an eighteenth-century Massachusetts Governor who was later a U.S. Vice-President, Elbridge Gerry. Interestingly enough, though the Governor pronounced his name GEH-ree, with the *g* as in *get,* the noun which assured him a lasting place in the history books and dictionaries is usually pronounced JEH-ree-man-der.

So, a person who alleges that, "The third *senatorial* district was *gerrymandered* to benefit the *Tammany candidate*," would unwittingly be running the broad gamut of our language, using two words from our great store of Latin borrowings and two of native American origin. See also CANDIDATE.

political slang, nineteenth century

The relatively mild epithets exchanged by candidates for public office in recent campaigns contrast sharply with the brash, colorful and occasionally downright libelous language of campaigns in the nineteenth century. Perhaps we should be thankful that today's talk is of "social security extension" rather than of *boodle* and *boodlers* and that our candidates choose to address themselves to such topics as "better schools and more teachers" rather than to *pork barrels* and *bulldozing.* But if our nation is the gainer for this more serious-minded approach to politics, our language is the poorer. Just as the torchlight parades have been replaced by sober, sedate television appearances, so the lusty language of old has given way to the polished platitudes of eggheads and ghostwriters.

Before they're all forgotten, though, let's look at a few of the terms popular in Granddad's day. A *roorback,* for instance, is a defamatory lie about a candidate given wide circulation on the eve of election. Its success —when it does succeed—depends upon its timing, for if the libeled candidate has sufficient time to present the facts to the electorate, public opinion is likely to swing to his support and away from the candidate who stooped to vicious libel.

The original *roorback* took the form of a printed account, back in 1844, of the alleged trip through Southern states of one Baron Roorback. He reported seeing a number of Negro slaves bearing the brand of James K. Polk, Democratic candidate for the Presidency. Since no Roorback really existed and since Polk was elected anyway, one might say that the first *roorback* backfired. This hasn't kept unscrupulous politicians from attempting the trick many times since, however.

A *mugwump* is a political figure who refuses to follow faithfully the dictates of his party. The term, originally an Algonquian Indian word for "chief," first came into wide use in its political sense when many Republicans refused to support the party's candidate (James G. Blaine) in the election of 1884. Democratic politicians who bolted to President Eisenhower in 1952 and 1956 might well have been labeled *mugwumps,* although the label is usually reserved for nonconformist Republicans. An attempt was made to revive this term in the recent New Deal days to

describe a fence-straddling politician—one who had his *mug* on one side
and his *wump* on the other. The revival effort, not surprisingly, failed.

Carpetbagger, as most of us recall from our school history courses, is
the term used for unscrupulous Northern politicians, adventurers who,
carrying their meager belongings in the then fashionable carpetbags, roamed
through the shattered South in the years immediately following the Civil
War, The shameless way in which they took advantage of the impoverished
Southerners has made *carpetbagger* a lasting symbol of political trickery
and venality.

A *boodle* was a bribe and a *boodler* one who dealt in bribes, especially
in an effort to "fix" an election. The *pork barrel* was—and is—the device
by which government appropriations are used for local political patronage,
disregarding the interests of the nation as a whole. *Bulldozing* was an
attempt to intimidate elected officials by threat of physical violence.

Nowadays, *grass roots* is usually considered to mean the rural sections
of our country and *"grass-roots* sentiment" is thought to be reaction arising
spontaneously from the people, especially the folks on farms. It didn't
always have that meaning, however. As long ago as 1876 *grass roots* was
a mining term meaning the soil just beneath the surface of the ground.
To describe a mining site in North Dakota's Black Hills as one in which
gold could be found even *at the grass* roots was a certain "come-on" for
Eastern speculators.

Later *grass roots* developed a new meaning, in the phrase "get down
to *grass roots"*—getting down to basic facts. This may well have been
because many of the naïve Eastern speculators found nothing but hard
rock instead of dreamed-of gold when they reached the grass roots.

In any event, the term in the political sense of "sons of the soil" seems
to have been introduced about 1920 by the Farmer Labor party and it was
taken over by the Republicans when, in 1935, at the nadir of their fortunes in this century, they held a *"Grass Roots Conference"* at Springfield,
Illinois. The ill-fated Alf Landon Presidential campaign of 1936 also
stressed the *grass-roots* theme and doubtless did much to bring the phrase
to wide popular recognition and use. See also BUNK, BUNKUM and PORK
BARREL.

politics, politician

Politics has its origin in the Greek words *polis* (city) and *polites*
(citizen). From the same source, incidentally, came the word *police.*

Originally, then, *politics* meant whatever had to do with the rights and
status of a citizen. Gradually it has come to have at least two clearly
defined meanings: the art and science of government, sometimes called
"political science," and the day-to-day professional management of political affairs from the city precinct to the White House.

An expert manipulator of political affairs, especially one who regards the great game of politics as his career, is known as a *politician*. This word has always had somewhat unsavory connotations with, as one authority puts it, "implications of seeking personal or partisan gain." For this reason even the most skilled political operators often shun the label *politician,* much preferring to be called "statesmen."

The press has reported one charming exception to this prevailing rule, however. When British Transport Minister Ernest Marples was invited to talk before pupils of his old school, he reminisced about the day on which he received his first report card. Noting that the grades left a great deal to be desired, he first rummaged through the family attic until he found one of his father's old report cards. He then handed both cards to his father. "And that," he told the assembled schoolboys, "began my career as a *politician!*"

poltergeist

The *poltergeist*—from the German *Polter,* meaning "uproar," and *Geist,* "spirit" or "ghost"—is a prankish sort of spirit, the Middle European equivalent of Erin's elves, leprechauns and little men. See also PARANORMAL.

pomp and circumstance. *See* circumstance, pomp and.

popinjay

A young housewife and mother once wrote me that she came across the word *popinjay* in a bedtime story. Her six-year-old loved the word and decided for himself that it meant a funny kind of a bird. She tried to tell him that it meant an empty-headed, boastful person—but he still insisted it was a kind of jaybird.

Actually, there is more than a trace of truth in her young son's interpretation of *popinjay*. The word comes from the Arabic word *babaga* by way of the Greek *papagos,* meaning "parrot." One of the notable characteristics of parrots is their ability to chatter away without having a thought in their heads. Another is the dazzling beauty of their plumage. Put these two characteristics together and you'll see how easily we came to the present-day meaning of *popinjay*—a foppishly dressed chatter-mouth.

pork barrel

Pork barrel originally was the total amount of contributions to the campaign fund of a candidate for public office. Since midway through the last century, however, it has meant the government funds appropriated for projects on the basis of local patronage—specifically, appropriations from which a successful politician can reward his supporters. The most notable example of *"pork-barrel* legislation" is the Rivers and Harbors Bill, which, by tradition, is loaded with special projects of little benefit to the nation as a whole but important to individual legislators as rewards for the faithful among their constituents. See also POLITICAL SLANG, NINETEENTH CENTURY.

portmanteau words. *See* blend words.

posh

A word you'll not find in most dictionaries is *posh*—a borrowing from British slang, meaning "smart, sophisticated or elegant." Thus one might be complimented on a "very *posh* party" or a well-turned-out sportsman could be applauded as "looking very *posh* today."

Perhaps the omission of this particular word from our dictionaries is not especially serious, but there is a charming, if highly improbable, story of the word's origin. It dates back to the era when Great Britain was truly a seat of empire and her colonial emissaries were making regular trips from London by steamer to India, Australia and other far-flung territories. Preferred accommodations aboard ship were "away from the weather" —port side outward-bound and starboard side homeward-bound. And that, so the story goes, is where *posh* came from—Port Outward, Starboard Home.

posting of the banns. *See* banns, posting of the.

pot likker

This does not refer to homemade moonshine, brewed in the hillbilly sections of the country. Such moonshine may be called *silo drippings, mountain dew* or, perhaps, *stump liquor. Pot likker,* on the contrary, is an entirely respectable and assuredly nonalcoholic beverage.

Pot liquor, to give it its formal spelling, is a sort of broth made from greens or field peas boiled with a fat meat, usually that cut of pork known as fat back. Its praises have been sung by no less an authority on Southern cuisine than the late Marjorie Kinnan Rawlings, whose *The Yearling* remains one of the authentically great books of our time. In *Cross Creek* she wrote: "Turnip greens cooked with white bacon, with cornbread on the side, make an occasion. *Pot liquor* and cornbread have even entered into Southern politics, a man addicted to the combination being able to claim himself a man of the people."

potter's field

A *potter's field* is a burying ground for destitute or unknown people.

It has its origin in the Bible (Matthew 27:7) when the chief priests and elders of the people are faced with the problem of what to do with the thirty pieces of silver which Judas cast down in the temple. "And they took counsel, and bought with them the *potter's field,* to bury strangers in."

pox upon you!, A

This expression comes straight out of the eighteenth century! In that era, when smallpox was one of the most widespread and deadly maladies, the expression *A pox upon you!* was a very serious oath. Today, thanks to the success of medical science in virtually eliminating smallpox, it is merely an archaic and amusing euphemism.

practical joke

A *practical joke,* as we all know, is a trick played upon another person. Usually it is intended to be funny but occasionally the trick goes awry and the result is painful to both perpetrator and victim. Such practical jokes as the "hot foot" fall into this category.

But the quality that distinguishes a practical joke from the ordinary jest is that it depends upon some practical action by the person perpetrating the joke. In the case of the "hot foot" it is the action of igniting a match previously inserted between the sole and upper part of the victim's shoe.

pragmatic, pragmatical, pragmatist

Pragmatic (pronounced prag-MAT-ik) is the adjective form of *pragmatism,* a form of philosophy based on the practical utility of any given function or conception. Stemming from the Greek word *prassein* meaning "to do," it has the same origin as *practice* and *practical.*

Pragmatical has the meaning of meddlesome or officious, opinionated or conceited. These same meanings apply to *pragmatic;* however, this shorter form has other broader meanings including: practical, busy, pertaining to the civil affairs of a state, concerned with the historical evolution of causes and effects.

Pragmatist is the usual word for a *pragmatic* person, although *pragmatic* alone is sometimes used as a noun to designate such a person.

The term *pragmatic sanction* is applied to a royal decree which has the same force as fundamental law.

pratt fall

Pratt fall, meaning a fall on the buttocks in an effort to obtain laughs from an audience, is certainly slang, a part of the trade talk of show business for as long as I can remember. Just by the way, a commonly heard synonym for *prat* or *pratt* in show business circles is *keister* (pronounced KEE-ster). You won't find that in most dictionaries, either.

prehistoric. *See* warden.

prejudice

Some authorities on usage maintain that *prejudice* may only be used in an unfavorable sense—that is, one must always be prejudiced *against* something, never *for* something. The assertion was often made in the early days of this century—when language proprieties were perhaps more closely observed than they are today—that one might be *partial* or *predisposed* in favor of a person or thing but never *prejudiced.*

Actually there was never any linguistic basis for this "rule." *Prejudice* comes from the Latin prefix *prae-* (before) and *judicium* (judgment) and merely means a preconceived idea—either favorable or unfavorable. So both etymology and today's usage indicate that if you wish to be prejudiced in favor of something, that is not only your civil right, but perfectly acceptable English.

premiere, premier

Premiere—with the final *e*—is the correct word to designate the first performance of a play or other public event. Pronounced prem-YAIR or prih-MEER, it comes direct from French where it appears as the feminine form of the adjective *premier.*

We have also borrowed the masculine form, *premier,* and use it as an adjective just as the French do—in the sense of first or foremost. When we use it as a noun, however, it means a top-ranking official, usually a prime minister. It is never used in the same sense as *premiere.*

pretty kettle of fish. *See* kettle of fish, pretty.

preventive, preventative

STROKES REDUCED BY ANTICOAGULANTS, read the headline of a recent science story in one of the major New York City newspapers. The subhead continues: MAYO, CORNELL STUDIES INDICATE DRUGS' WORTH AS PREVENTATIVE. Interestingly enough, the reader can search as he will through the story itself and never find the word *preventative* which appears in the headline.

Why? Because the author of the story knew what the headline writer did not know, that there is no such word in the vocabulary of careful speakers and writers as *preventative.* The word to use is *preventive.*

The word *preventative* is what H. W. Fowler calls "a needless lengthening of an established word, due to oversight or caprice." I should say that this is one of the rare occasions when the waspish Mr. Fowler was being kind to offenders against linguistic proprieties.

The truth of the matter is that the use of *preventative* instead of *preventive,* of "filtrate" instead of "filter," of "experimentalize" instead of "experiment," is part and parcel of what seems at times to be a concerted attempt to eliminate simple and exact words from our language and substitute flowery, pretentious gobbledygook.

A great deal of confusion and ambiguity can be avoided by the use of simple, precise words wherever possible. The correct word for the headline quoted is *preventive,* not *preventative*—and I say this in full knowledge of the fact that the latter word has become so common that leading dictionaries have had to enter it, albeit grudgingly.

pride of lions. *See* clowder, kindle and cowardice.

primordial

Primordial (pronounced pry-MOR-dee-al) comes from the Latin *primus* (first) and *ordiri* (to begin) and is an adjective meaning first in order, original, primitive or fundamental. "The first life developed from the *primordial* ooze."

pristine

Pristine (pronounced PRISS-teen) comes to us directly from the Latin word *pristinus,* meaning "primitive." Properly defined as "earliest" or even "primeval," the word has come to mean "unchanged" or "uncorrupted." Thus an antique dealer might refer to a Victorian highboy as being in *"pristine* condition," meaning that it has been preserved by its previous owners so carefully that it is truly "as good as new." The meaning of *pristine* in this use is practically the same as that of a stamp or coin dealer when he refers to his merchandise as in "mint" condition, meaning "as fine as the day it left the mint."

prod, on the

Watch out, pardner. A cowboy *on the prod* is fighting mad and it's just not healthy to be in his vicinity.

prognosis. *See* diagnosis.

Project Gemini

The second phase of America's manned-spacecraft operation is called

Project Gemini. Gemini is the Latin word for "twins" and refers to the fact that the spacecraft is planned to carry two men into orbit.

prolix

Prolix (pronounced PROH-lix or proh-LIX) is an adjective meaning "wordy, profuse, tedious or long-winded" and is derived from the Latin *prolixus* (extended). It becomes *prolixity* or *prolixness* as a noun, *prolixly* as an adverb. "Dr. Samuel Johnson's prose style was notable for its *prolixity.*"

propaganda

In today's battle of ideas and ideologies what our side says is "information," what the opposition says is *propaganda.*

It's curious that this word should have come to the point where its use today is almost wholly in derogatory connotations, for few words ever had more estimable sponsorship and few were ever coined with the idea of describing a more worthy cause. *Propaganda,* you see, was the coinage of Pope Urban VIII, who organized a *congregatio de propaganda fide,* a "congregation for propagating the faith." The original intent of the word *propaganda,* then, was the spreading of Christian faith by missions throughout the world.

Through the centuries *propaganda* came to mean any doctrine circulated on a broad scale and, late in the last century, began to be used in what H. L. Mencken calls "the evil sense." During the two world wars of this century, *propaganda* was used so widely to describe the content of enemy broadcasts that it is now used almost exclusively as a pejorative word.

psychosomatic

During the past few years much has been written about *psychosomatic* medicine and many authorities have labeled it a great step forward in medical history. Put briefly, *psychosomatic* medicine is that branch of medicine which treats physical ailments caused by mental illness.

Not only colds but many more serious physical illnesses—such as asthma—often may be caused by worry. They may, in medical language, be "of *psychosomatic* origin." As one doctor stated: "We have always known that illness can make us unhappy. Now we are beginning to realize that unhappiness can actually make us ill."

Appropriately enough, *psychosomatic* is derived from two Greek words *psyche* (mind) and *soma* (body). Pronounced sy-koh-so-MAT-ik, it will roll easily off your tongue if you practice it a few times.

public be damned, The

William Henry Vanderbilt, son of the famed "Commodore" Vanderbilt, is alleged to have said this in an interview appearing in the Chicago *News* in 1882. At the time he had recently started a high-speed luxury express between New York and Chicago to compete with a similar "flier" on the Pennsylvania Railroad. In response to a reporter's inquiry, he said he was losing money on the train and would cancel it if it weren't for the competition.

"But wouldn't you continue it for the benefit of the public?" the reporter queried. *"The public be damned,"* exploded Vanderbilt. "Railroads are not run on sentiment but on business principles."

Vanderbilt later denied having used these words but, like all denials, it never caught up to the original quotation.

pugilist

Pugilist comes straight from the Latin *pugil*, (boxer), which in turn came from *pugnus* (fist).

pug-nosed

Pug-nosed comes from the name of the *pug* dog, now a relatively rare animal but not so long ago a great favorite. The pug is a small, short-haired dog whose chief facial characteristic is a blunt snub nose. It was a great favorite with ladies of fashion a century or so ago and it's thought that the name is probably a variant form of "puck," a term of endearment.

pulling the wool over his eyes. *See* wool over his eyes, pulling the.

pumpernickel

According to a magazine article, this type of dark rye bread got its name from the fact that, when first made, it was popular with all the inhabitants of the German province of Westphalia except one French cavalry officer. He dubbed the bread *bon pour Nicolas*—Nicolas being the name of his horse. The implication that the bread was fit only for horses was greeted with derision, so the story goes, but his description in the abbreviated form *pumpernickel* has lasted to this day.

"Farfetched" is a mild term for so fanciful a story. On the very face of it, the idea of Westphalian Germans paying much heed to the opinion of a French cavalry officer is ridiculous. Nor is there any reason to seek the origin of *pumpernickel* in French words, since its elements are clearly of Germanic origin. In fact, the German word *Pumpernickel,* with a somewhat different meaning, existed long before the bread was originated.

Three centuries ago, a *Pumpernickel* was a dolt, a fool or a blockhead.

The word was made up of *Pumper,* the sound made by a person falling, and *Nickel,* a dwarf or goblin. Thus the original *Pumpernickel* was an object of derision and the butt of the heavy-handed and occasionally savage humor of the period.

Why the name was later applied to loaves of dark rye bread is a matter for speculation. Possibly the characteristically round shape of the loaves reminded Westphalians of the expressionless moonface of the village half-wit. In any event, we may be sure that no French cavalry officer with a horse named Nicolas had anything to do with the naming of this bread.

push-over wipe. *See* television language.

put the kibosh on

Putting the kibosh on, in the sense of putting an end to something, is a well-known phrase that has been widely used in America for more than a century.

Authorities differ widely, however, as to the origin of *kibosh* itself. One theory is that it is Yiddish in origin, coming from the Middle High German *keibe* (carrion); others believe it comes from the Gaelic *cie bais* (cap of death). In any event, it is slang.

put your best foot forward

Put your best foot forward is an expression dating back at least to the time of Shakespeare. It means, of course, to make your very best effort, especially at the start of a new endeavor. A variation can be found in Shakespeare's *King John:* "Nay, but make haste; the better foot before."

quandary

Quandary (pronounced KWAHN-der-ee) is a state of perplexity or indecision, particularly one where several equally acceptable solutions are possible. In this it differs from a *dilemma,* which presents only unpleasant alternatives. Although its exact origin is obscure, it may have come from the Latin interrogative *quanda* (when) or it may be a corruption of the Middle English *wandreth* (evil, perplexity).

quarter horse

Quarter horses were originally developed by the earliest settlers in Virginia more than two hundred years ago. They got their name from the fact that, since there were no race tracks in those days, they were raced on short paths about a quarter of a mile long. Later they were crossbred with thoroughbreds to improve their quality and performance. Because of their remarkable speed for short dashes, they make ideal cow ponies and are widely used on Western ranches as "cutting ponies."

quick as you can say Jack Robinson. *See* Jack Robinson.

quick, cut to the

Historically, both the noun *quick* and the adjective and adverb forms come from the same root, the Anglo-Saxon *cwicu,* meaning "alive" or "living." Thus the phrase "the *quick* and the dead," from the King James Bible, merely means the living and the dead. During the Middle Ages, farmers customarily referred to their herds of livestock as *quickstock* and a hedge was a *quickfence,* signifying that it was a growing thing as contrasted with a stone fence.

Then, just as we have today such phrases as "look alive" and "step lively," the common folk began to use *quick* in phrases like "move *quickly*" and "she has a *quick* wit." Soon this usage became standard, as it has now been for many centuries.

The phrase "You have cut me to the quick" is, of course, a holdover from the original meaning of the word. Literally, it means to cut through the skin to the living tissue. Figuratively, it merely means "You have hurt my feelings."

quiz

This word has become very popular in educational jargon and, of course, it's almost impossible to turn on TV or radio without getting some sort of a *quiz* show. Where did the word come from?

Nobody really knows. Nearly all dictionaries list it as "origin unknown" or "origin uncertain." However, there is one pleasantly Gaelic story of its origin and, if it smacks a bit more of 100-proof Irish whiskey than of 100 percent accuracy, don't say I didn't warn you.

It seems that late in the eighteenth century one James Daly, the manager of a theater in Dublin, being somewhat in his cups, made a very rash wager. He bet that he could introduce a word into the language overnight

—specifically within twenty-four hours. What's more, he wagered that this would be a word absolutely without meaning.

There were takers for his bet—of that you may be sure. So it was up to Jim Daly to make good his boast and he did. He hired all the urchins in Dublintown, equipped them with pieces of chalk, and sent them out into the night with instructions to chalk a single word on every wall and billboard in the city.

The word? Well, of course you know it. The word was *quiz*. And, as a result of Daly's enterprise, it was on the lips of all of Dublin in the morning.

At first, though, it became synonymous with practical joke—for that was what he had played on the citizenry. Gradually it came to mean making fun of a person by verbal bantering. So, in time, it came to mean what *quiz* means today—to question a person in order to learn the extent of his knowledge.

quonking

Quonking is just what it must sound like to the sound men on television set when a pair of bit players, unaware of an open mike, carry on a private conversation that interferes with the main dialogue of the show. In any event, that is what they call it.

R

℞

℞ has been a symbol used by pharmacists since ancient times. The *R* in the symbol means *recipere* (Take this). The slant bar across the base of the *R* is the sign of the Roman god Jupiter, patron of medicines. According to Brewer's *Dictionary of Phrase and Fable,* the sign can be paraphrased this way: "Under the good auspices of Jove, patron of medicines, take the following drugs in the proportions set down." That little symbol packs in a lot of meaning!

race is not to the swift, the

The original quotation, *"The race is not to the swift,* nor the battle to the strong," is from the Bible (Ecclesiastes 9:11). It was Franklin Pierce

Adams, best-known as a stellar performer on *Information, Please* in the golden days of radio, who, in his "Conning Tower" column which appeared for many years in the old New York *World,* once observed: *"The race is not to the swift,* nor the battle to the strong; but the betting is best that way."

race music. *See* jazzmen's jargon.

raft (of things)

The *raft* that means "a great number," "a lot," has no connection with the raft you dive from or float on. It comes from the Old French word *raffe,* meaning a large number or collection and, theoretically at least, should be spelled *raff.* However, it picked up the terminal *t* along the way, undoubtedly from its resemblance to "raft."

Raff, by the way, persists in the word *riffraff,* meaning people of no consequence, the dregs of society. This word came into English after the Norman Conquest from the French phrase *rif et raf,* meaning a collection of people who steal. The *rif* in this phrase was closely related to the Old French *rifler* from which we got our word "rifle" in the sense of stealing ("The bandits *rifled* the safe of its contents").

raglan. *See* cardigan, raglan.

railroad, railway

Railroad and *railway* are both nouns but also have adjective forms identically spelled. In years past the word *railway* was generally reserved for streetcar systems or other forms of rail transportation lighter than the full-fledged *railroads* with locomotives and rolling stock. This distinction, which was never observed by the British, incidentally, has gone by the boards in America with the gradual disappearance of our urban trolley-car systems and today the two words are generally used, as guide books use them, interchangeably.

railroad, to

Railroad as a verb has acquired two rather interesting colloquial meanings—both, in a sense, reflecting our national admiration for the speed and sureness with which railroads work. Important legislation being put through in a rush is said to have been *railroaded.* And a person sent to prison after a speedy trial on trumped-up charges is said to have been *railroaded.*

raise Cain, to

In the term *raising Cain* the allusion is to Cain, brother of Abel and traditionally the world's first criminal. In earlier times, *Cain* was used by God-fearing folk as a euphemism for "devil" and the expression *to raise Cain,* meaning to create a loud disturbance or to cause a great deal of trouble, was used instead of "to raise the devil."

As long ago as 1840, newspapermen were making puns on the phrase, as witness this howler from the long defunct St. Louis *Pennant:* "Why have we every reason to believe that Adam and Eve were both rowdies? Because they both raised Cain!"

I think we can agree that standards of newspaper wit are a little higher than they were a century ago.

rake-off. *See* payola.

rambunctious

Another of the Irish contributions to American folk language, *rambunctious* (pronounced ram-BUNK-shus), means "wild, disorderly or unruly." The word's popularity is attested by the fact that it turns up in various forms in different parts of the country—*rambustious, rambuctious* and *rambumptious* being three variants often heard.

ramshackle

Ramshackle comes from the Icelandic *ramskakkr,* meaning "badly twisted." Thus it comes to its present meaning of "about to fall to pieces."

rank and file

Originally a military term, this has been applied in recent years to the membership of the labor unions in this country. *Rank and file,* of course, is the enlisted component of an army, as contrasted with the officers. The designation comes from the fact that ordinary soldiers are required to muster in *ranks*—drawn up side by side—and in *files*—one behind the other. Obviously the leaders—officers—are not required to assemble in such group formations.

rasher

Rasher has been a part of our language since the Norman Conquest, when it came into English from the French *raser,* meaning "to shave or slice thin." So not only does a *rasher* mean a single slice, it means a thin slice. It has no connection at all with "rash," meaning "reckless or hasty."

real McCoy. *See* McCoy, the real.

rebus

A *rebus* is the kind of puzzle in which pictures of objects suggest words or phrases by the sound of their names. For example, a picture of a pair of gates and a head would be a rebus for Gateshead. The word is the ablative plural of the Latin word *res* (thing). So *rebus* literally means "by things." Originally the phrase was *rebus non verbis* (by things not words).

recant

Recant (pronounced rih-KANT) is a verb meaning to retract, renounce or withdraw in a formal or public way a previous statement or belief. It is derived from the Latin *re* (again, back) and *cantare* (to sing). The act itself is called *recantation*.

Interestingly enough, when an underworld character confesses to the misdeeds of himself and his accomplices, thus *recanting* his previous statements, he is said to "sing."

recap

This word may mean to put a new rubber tread on a used auto tire, but not when used as follows by a newspaperman: "Tomorrow I'll give you a *recap* of the whole thing."

Recap in this context obviously is an abbreviated form of *recapitulation*, meaning a review or summary of information previously transmitted. In this sense, it is in common use in newspaper offices, and an order familiar to every rewrite man is: "Give me a quick *recap* on this story," meaning, "Give me a shortened summary, omitting none of the essential facts."

receipt, recipe

The similarity between these two words is understandable since they both come from the same Latin word *recipere* (to take back or receive). *Recipe* is the present tense, imperative, meaning literally "Take!" From the earliest days of medicine, *recipe* has been used as the first word in prescriptions, either spelled out or, in recent times, abbreviated by the letter *R* with a slant mark across its base. Though *recipe* is still used primarily in this medical sense, it has also long been used to designate any list of ingredients, as in cooking *recipes*.

Receipt comes from the past participle of *recipere* and originally meant "that which has been received." Since *receipts* are traditionally handed down from experienced to inexperienced cooks, these formulas are "received" by one from the other.

Formerly *receipt* was used to indicate a list of medical ingredients as well as a table of ingredients for cooking, but in modern times it is used solely as a culinary term.

Incidentally, the *Oxford English Dictionary* notes that *receipt* first appeared in print in 1582, while *recipe* didn't appear until about 1652, so the evidence is clear that *receipt* always had that meaning, and didn't acquire it as a mispronunciation of *recipe*.

red dog

Red dog is a term much used and abused by football fans these days. Originally it meant a defensive tactic whereby a line backer shot through the offensive line to hit the quarterback and stall the play before it got started.

The *dog* part is fairly obvious, since the job of the line backer was to "dog" or "hound" the passer. The *red* comes from a color code developed by Clark Shaughnessy, one of the game's greatest coaches. If one backer was sent through, the code would be "red"; if two, "blue"; if three, "green."

No one today speaks of "blue dog" or "green dog." Only *red dog* remains, and it is carelessly used to mean almost any kind of shooting a gap in the offensive line.

red-eye

Another slang word for "liquor," one of the thousand or more synonyms invented over the years. See SHEETS IN THE WIND.

red herring

Former President Harry Truman's use of this term in the midst of the political storm over the Alger Hiss case was probably the most poorly chosen phrase in national politics since the Rev. Samuel Burchard injected the issue of "Rum, Romanism and Rebellion" into James G. Blaine's campaign for the Presidency in 1884.

The expression itself is, of course, as old as the sport of fox hunting and originally had nothing whatever to do with Communism. It seems that a *red herring* dragged across a fox's trail will effectively destroy the scent that has been laid and thus divert the dogs to a false trail or "fault the hounds," to use the hunter's expression. Thus, in popular speech, a *red herring* came to mean any device used to confuse or divert attention.

The actual *red herring,* incidentally, is one which has been dried, salted and smoked—what our British friends call a "bloater" and which, so help me, they sometimes eat for breakfast.

Reds

The use of *Red* as a synonym for "Communist" derives, of course, from the *red* flag which has been the international symbol of Communism for a century or more and is now the official flag of the Soviet Union. Since the time of the French Revolution, however, it has been a symbol of anarchy and rebellion, and the extreme partisans of that period were known —strange though this sounds to American ears—as *red republicans*. Reportedly their hatred of the nobility they had vowed to overthrow was so intense that they dipped their hands in the blood of their victim, then brandished them aloft in triumph—whence the label *red*.

It seems to this observer unfortunate that the word *red* has taken on such unpleasant connotations in the past century or two because throughout history *red* has been a color associated with honor (note its use in royal and ecclesiastical robes) and good fortune and magic (for, as Yeats pointed out, *"Red* is the color of magic in almost every country. . . . The caps of fairies are well-nigh always *red."*). Here's to the day when *red* again will describe only things of grace and beauty!

red tape

The practice of tying official documents with tape of a reddish hue began in seventeenth-century England. By the nineteenth century its use to mean inaction or delay caused by official sluggishness had become well established. In America, early in the 1800's, Washington Irving described a bureaucrat thus: "His brain was little better than *red tape* and parchment."

Reilly, life of. *See* life of Reilly.

relevant, relevancy, irrelevant

Relevant (pronounced REL-eh-vent) means pertinent to or applicable in a given situation or matter, as in "the only discussion permitted was that *relevant* to the major issue before the convention." It is derived from the same Latin words as the word *relieve* (*re,* "again" and *levare,* "to lift") but its meaning is quite different. *Relevancy* is its noun form and *irrelevant* its opposite.

remuda

A *remuda* is the string of horses herded in reserve during a roundup. It's a term borrowed by American cowboys from their Mexican counterparts. Originally, of course, the word was Spanish.

reprehensible

That which is reprehensible is deserving of censure or rebuke. Its sources are logical Latin ones: *re* (back) and *prehendre* (take).

res gestae

Race JEST-eye is a fairly accurate, phonetic rendering of *res gestae,* favored "legal Latin" phrase for "all the essential circumstances attending a given transaction." However, most lawyers would pronounce the phrase race JEST-ee. The long-*I* pronunciation is more characteristic of classical Latin than of lawyer's Latin.

rhubarb

In my newspaper column I once used the term *family rhubarb*. The piece was about a difference of opinion about whether the phrase should be *Welsh rabbit* or *Welsh rarebit*. "Where does *rhubarb* come in?" some readers asked.

Rhubarb is a fairly recent item from the jargon of sports slang. It means a heated argument—and that's what the husband and wife were having about the Welsh rabbit. The husband was right but that, as any husband can attest, doesn't mean he was victor in the *rhubarb*.

Richmond, another in his field

The expression comes from Shakespeare's *Richard III*. The King, speaking of Henry of Richmond, who later became Henry VII, says:

> I think there be six Richmonds in the field;
> Five have I slain today, instead of him—
> A horse! a horse! my kingdom for a horse!

The meaning, of course, is that still another, and unexpected, opponent has turned up to do battle.

riffraff

Riffraff originally came to English from the French—*rif et raf,* meaning "one and all." Later, thanks perhaps to the influence of a Swedish word *raff,* meaning "sweepings," it came to mean the offscourings of society, the dregs of humanity. See also RAFT.

rigadoon

Rigadoon is a dance, lively and spirited, performed by two people. It originated in the eighteenth century. Since the dancers in a *rigadoon* spend most of their time pirouetting at some slight distance from each other, the resemblance to the modern "twist," though rather farfetched, does exist.

Riley. *See* life of Reilly.

rill

"I was amazed," a woman from Wisconsin wrote me, "at hearing a well-educated woman on a quiz show get stuck on the question: 'What is the meaning of *rills* in 'I love thy rocks and *rills,* thy woods and templed hills'? I was even more amazed the next day when I told a couple of recent University of Wisconsin graduates and, instead of laughing, they gave me a blank stare. Neither had any idea of its meaning. I kept trying and found that few, if any graduates knew this word. Finally, after about six tries, I found a man who knew it. He hadn't been to school much but he read because he liked to."

It is indeed astonishing that so many well-educated people should be ignorant of the meaning of such a simple word as *rill*—especially one which is often on the lips of every schoolchild in the verse quoted from *America.* A *rill* is, of course, a small stream or rivulet. It comes, interestingly enough, from the Dutch word *ril* of the same meaning.

ringing the changes

This comes from the almost forgotten art of bell ringing. A set of bells (from three to twelve) tuned to the diatonic scale are rung in a series of variations from the regular striking order. Theoretically every possible variation is rung without any repetition. The phrase *ringing the changes,* figuratively speaking, now means trying every possible way of doing something.

river, up the

The phrase *up the river* was originally an underworld term for a sentence in a reformatory or jail. It probably derives from the fact that New York State's most famous prison, Sing Sing, is *up the river* from New York City.

Robin Hood

Is it true that Robin and his crew are only legendary? Wasn't there once a real Robin Hood? This is a hard question to answer, for leading authorities on the history and legends of pre-Chaucerian England are divided on the answer. Some hold that Robin was an actual outlaw, perhaps the Earl of Huntingdon, who harassed the Norman invaders, stealing from the rich and giving to the poor.

Another theory is that he was a relatively obscure local hero of the thirteenth century around whom stories and legends handed down from Scandinavian mythology gradually gathered. And at least one eminent historian considers him merely the folk representation of traditional Saxon defiance of the Norman oppressors.

While it may be impossible to show with certainty that an actual Robin Hood lived, the ballads, stories and legends associated with his name have entertained and inspired generations of English-speaking youth from his first appearance in the pages of *The Vision of Piers Plowman* before 1400 to the televised performances of today.

Robin Hood's barn, all around

Robin Hood had no barn. His domain was Sherwood Forest and the lands and fields surrounding it. When you say that someone arrived at a conclusion *by way of Robin Hood's barn,* you mean that he wandered in a roundabout fashion.

Robins. *see* Dodgers.

rock hound

Though *rock hound* hasn't reached the pages of many dictionaries, it's well established in the popular tongue as a name for geologists and especially for amateur geologists who collect specimens of rare rocks as a hobby.

rococo

Rococo (pronounced roh-кон-koh) is a word which frequently confuses even those who know its meaning and pronunciation, since the temptation to double the first or second *c* is almost irresistible. *Rococo* designates a style of architecture and decoration, originating in France in the early eighteenth century and characterized by curved designs, over-all delicacy and much ornamentation. The word is believed to have come from the French *rocaille* or "shellwork," used extensively as decoration during the reign of Louis XIV. Thus one might say, "The scrollwork in the formal drawing room is simply too *rococo* for modern tastes."

Roger

The word *Roger*—in the meaning of "Yes, O.K., I understand you"—is voice code for the letter *R.* It is part of the "Able, Baker, Charlie" code known and used by all radiophone operators in the services. From the earliest days of wireless communication, the Morse code letter *R* (dit-dah-dit) has been used to indicate "O.K.—understood." So *Roger* was the logical voice-phone equivalent. With the return of servicemen to civilian life, *Roger* came into the common speech.

roman à clef

The phrase *roman à clef* comes from French and translates as "novel with a key." Generally speaking, it means a novel whose leading figure or figures are only slightly disguised portraits of actual persons. One of

Nathaniel Hawthorne's novels, *The Blithedale Romance,* has as its leading figure a man named Hollingsworth, who is a slightly disguised portrait of Herman Melville. A recent novel is reported to have a hero—if that's the word for it—closely resembling the late Errol Flynn.

rooftree

When I refer to my wife as "the lady who shares my *rooftree,*" don't misunderstand me. We have not decamped from our abode to live in a tree house.

No, *rooftree* here is used to symbolize the house as a whole. The *rooftree,* you see, is not a tree at all, but the ridgepole supporting the roof. Thus, it is one of the most vital members in the support of a house and, by extension, is often referred to as symbolic of the roof and, indeed, of the house itself.

roorback. *See* political slang.

rose, under the. *See* under the rose.

rostrum

Writing at home has its hazards, as I realized one day when I was seated in front of my typewriter, faced with an imminent deadline. In burst ebullient, vivacious sixteen-year-old Sue—certainly not likely to be a source of inspiration at this trying moment.

And the question she blurted at me wasn't, at first hearing, very constructive. "Know what *rostrum* comes from, Pop?" she queried in characteristically unmodulated teen-age tones. "Why, sure," replied the resident authority on words, reaching for a brace of etymological handbooks and racking a weary brain for Latin roots.

"Relax, Pop," said Sue. "Here's the pitch—and its strictly on the level. Our Latin teacher spent fifteen minutes on it today. Originally *rostrum* meant the beak of a bird and, way back, it came from *rodo,* "to gnaw"— which is the same root that *rodent* came from. Did you know rats and squirrels are called *rodents* because they can only gnaw—they can't chew because they only have incisor teeth, not canine teeth?

"Well, anyway, *rostrum* came to be used for the prow of a ship, which they used to carve in very fancy ways back in Roman times. So when the Romans beat the Carthaginians, they took the prows of the enemy ships back to Rome with them and used them to decorate the great Forum in the center of that city. And since the *rostrums* came to be used as platforms for public speakers in the Forum, that's how the word got the meaning it has today.

"Seems to me, too, Pop," added Sue, "that you have had some pretty

unkind things to say about Mussolini and his role in the war. I've seen
some old picture of him speaking to crowds in the middle of Rome. Guess
you could have made a classical sort of pun by calling him the *'rodent* of the
rostrum.' Good gag, hey, Pop?"

round robin

The *robin* in this expression has nothing whatever to do with the bird
of the same name. This *robin* is derived from the French *ruban* or "ribbon."
And here's the story of how this ribbon became a robin. During the seventeenth and eighteenth centuries in France, it was a brave man indeed who
had the courage to petition the Crown, even when he had a just grievance,
because more than one monarch followed the practice of ordering be-
headed the man whose signature came first on any petition distasteful to
the King. Finally, some clever officers devised a *round robin,* which was
attached to the document bearing their grievances. After each petitioner
had signed the ribbon, it was joined into a circle in such a fashion that no
one name headed the list—and thus no heads would roll.

Another way of signing *round robins* is for the signers to affix their
names at the foot of the document like the spokes of a wheel. This method,
one authority reports, originated in the British Navy where, in the days of
Lord Nelson and earlier, a ship's captain had the right to order hanged the
man first signing a petition of grievance. The fact of his signature being at
the top of the list was considered prima facie evidence that he was the
instigator of mutiny.

Nowadays, of course, *round robin* is a term widely used in sporting
circles to designate a tournament in which each contestant plays every
other contestant. *Round-robin golf* and tennis tournaments are common.

rout of wolves. *See* clowder, kindle and cowardice.

Rube Goldberg, a

For many years Rube Goldberg's "inventions" were part of the household lore of all America. In essence each invention consisted of a pre-
posterously complicated (but seemingly logical) method of performing
a very simple operation. The diagrams illustrating his weird and wonderful
contraptions were always ingeniously intricate and great good fun to
follow.

Rube swore off "inventions" a number of years ago and has, for most
of the past two decades, confined his artistic activities to the field of political cartooning, where he has won two Pulitzer Prizes. But he himself
ruefully admits that the public still associates *Rube Goldberg* primarily
with needlessly complicated gadgets—what the *Century Cyclopedia* calls
"fantastic inventions."

rule of thumb

The expression *rule of thumb* means a rough or guesswork estimate, based more upon experience than on precise measurement. An example of its use might like this: "According to the supermarket manager, three out of every four shoppers, as a general *rule of thumb,* leave their shopping carts in the parking lot."

There are two theories about the origin of this expression. The more logical theory is that it comes from the frequent use of the lower part of the thumb (roughly equal to one inch in the average adult male) as a crude measuring device.

However, some authorities trace the phrase to a practice once common among brewmasters. In the days when beer was truly beer, not the pasteurized soft drink that passes for beer today, the chief brewer sometimes tested the temperature of a batch of brew by dipping in his thumb. This technique was neither so accurate nor so hygienic as a thermometer check would be but, based on the brewmaster's long experience, this *rule of thumb* would tell him how well the brewing was proceeding.

ruminate

Ruminate (pronounced ROO-mih-nayt) comes directly from the Latin verb *ruminare* (to chew the cud) and carries the same meaning to the present day. An animal which chews its cud is a *ruminant. Ruminate* is most commonly used today, however, in the sense of contemplating a matter for some time, turning it over and over in the mind, meditating on it.

The act of *ruminating* is *rumination;* one who does so is a *ruminator.* The adjective form is *ruminative;* the adverbial form, *ruminatively.*

rummage sale

The *rummage* in *rummage sale* comes from a Middle French word *arrumage,* meaning to stow cargo in the hold of a ship. Since freighters usually carry a very varied cargo, considerable searching through—or *rummaging*—is often required before the desired lot is found. So a *rummage sale* is a sale of varied items of merchandise through which the prospective purchaser searches.

run-down. *See* baseball jargon.

rushing the growler

The origin of this phrase may shed a little light on the social customs of our land in the years before Prohibition.

In the old days it was the custom of laborers at lunch hour or the paterfamilias in the heat of a summer evening to dispatch someone to the corner saloon for a "bucket of suds." The person performing the errand was said to be *rushing the growler* and the *growler,* of course, was the pail itself. According to my informants—older, sager and more experienced folks than I—the typical *growler* held a half-gallon when filled to capacity and the average price for the contents was 25 cents, with a nickel tip for the *rusher* unless he was one of the family, in which case he got nothing.

Naturally the barkeep didn't expect to provide a full 64-ounce half-gallon for this relatively modest price, so the common practice was for him to put plenty of "head" on the beer—a technique not unknown to economy-minded bartenders today. The customers were not above matching guile with guile, though, and I'm told that it was a common practice for some *growler-rushers* to wipe the inside lip of the can with bit of bacon or salt-pork rind before bringing it in for refill.

The thin film of grease thus deposited on the rim of the *growler* prevented the formation of the bubbles which made up the head, thereby frustrating the bartender and guaranteeing the thirsty patron full measure.

rustler. *See* **cowboy jargon.**

S

sabbatical year

According to ancient Hebrew tradition, each seventh year the fields were allowed to lie fallow for a twelve-month period to "rest" the soil. *Sabbath* and *sabbatical* both come from the Hebrew word *shabath,* "to rest." Nowadays the term applies to the year or half-year leave of absence granted at seven-year intervals to college and university teachers for travel and study.

sabotage

The word *sabotage* comes from the French word *sabot,* meaning "shoe" or "boot," and derives its meaning of deliberate delay or obstruction of work from some use of *sabots* for this purpose. I have never been much persuaded, however, by the story that workers threw their wooden shoes into factory machinery to cause damaging delays. You see, wooden shoes have traditionally been worn by peasants, rather than by city-dwelling factory workers. So it seems more likely that the first instances of *sabotage* were peasant revolts against oppressive landowners—rebellions or "strikes," if you will, that might well have taken the form of workers trampling down the landowner's crops.

In any event, the word appeared in English around 1910 and attained its first popularity during World War I when it acquired its other chief meaning—the calculated hindrance of an enemy nation's war efforts by destruction of bridges, machinery and railroads through the efforts of secret agents.

saddler of Bawtry

During the eighteenth century it was the practice of a well-known tavern in York, England, to provide a farewell drink for all criminals condemned to death. The custom was for the condemned man and his guards to stop by the public house for this parting potion.

But one man, the *saddler of Bawtry,* refused to stop for the drink and quickly was hanged. The irony of the tale lies in the fact that, if he had tarried only a few minutes at the tavern, a reprieve en route from the king would have reached the gallows in time to spare his life.

sadism

There is no connection whatever between "sad" and *sadism*. The adjective "sad" comes from the Anglo-Saxon word *saed,* meaning "full" or "sated." At first it described the feeling of being overfull of food. Now, of course, it means mournful or unhappy.

Sadism and *sadistic* come from the name of Count Donatien de Sade, whose writings first brought to public attention the psychic aberration whereby one person derives pleasure from mistreating or hurting others.

saga

Today this means any long, involved narrative, especially one chronicling deeds of bravery. Originally, it was a medieval Norse legend celebrating the heroic exploits of one family. The most notable use of the elements of the *saga* in modern times is Richard Wagner's *Ring of the Nibelungs* which draws heavily on the Old Norse Volsunga Saga. Notable also, perhaps, is the comment of comedian Groucho Marx, paraphrasing the famous statement of Vice-President Thomas R. Marshall: "What this country really needs is a good five-cent *saga*."

sail under false colors

This phrase comes from the days of pirate ships and commerce raiders when it was common practice for the maurauder to fly the flag of a friendly nation until he was close by to make his surprise attack. At the moment of onslaught the pirate ship would "show its true colors" by hoisting the skull and crossbones. Today the expression means to pretend to be someone other than your true self.

St. Valentine's Day

St. Valentine's Day is the day when lovers traditionally exchange symbols of their mutual affection. It's a tradition at least as old as the English language for Chaucer mentions it, but originally it was thought of as the day on which birds chose their mates for the year to come.

St. Valentine himself had no direct connection with the romantic traditions we observe today. He was a priest in ancient Rome who was first jailed and eventually clubbed to death for his part in the rescue of early Christian martyrs.

But, thanks to the coincidence that the feast of the birds, with its romantic implications, fell on his birthday, the saint has been immortalized and become part of our common tongue in the word *valentine*.

St. Veronica

St. Veronica's name is a blend of two Latin words, *sudare* (to sweat) and *inconicus* (image). According to legend, the cloth which she gave Christ on His way to the Crucifixion was left with His features miraculously impressed upon it. The name St. Veronica was taken by her to indicate her faith that the cloth, which is one of the relics preserved at St. Peter's, Rome, is the "true image" of Christ's face.

salad days

Salad days are the days of youth, when lack of experience and general naïveté make you appear "green" to mature oldsters. The phrase comes from Shakespeare's *Anthony and Cleopatra* where, in Act I, Scene 5, Cleopatra speaks of "my *salad days,* when I was green in judgment, cold in blood."

salary. *See* salt, worth his.

salmagundi

Originally a dish of chopped meat and eggs, highly seasoned and served with lemon juice and olive oil. Its name supposedly came from the name of a French noble lady who either concocted it or popularized it during the reign of Henri IV. A more prosaic theory of the word's origin is that it is derived from the Italian phrase *salame conditi,* "pickled meat." Anyhow it gradually came to mean any kind of mishmash and, in the early 1800's, was used by Washington Irving as the name for a periodical he edited. Today it is also the name of a club whose membership is made up chiefly of noted New York artists and writers.

saloon. *See* automobile slang, British.

salt, above the

Some four or five centuries ago the ruling families of Britain began the custom which now is reflected in the phrase *above the salt.* In those medieval times the most important feature of the table setting was the *saler,* a word derived from the Latin *salarius,* meaning "pertaining to salt."

The *saler* established the social order at those medieval feasts. The guests seated *above the saler* were nearer to the host and were thus the more honored of the guests. The people seated *below the salt* were lesser fry or family dependents.

The *saler,* also gave us the word "salt *cellar,*" which, if you stop to think about it, is as redundant as "pizza pie."

salt of the earth

Anyone regarded as the finest of his kind is the *salt of the earth.* The expression comes from Matthew 5:13, where Jesus speaking to his disciples says: "Ye are the salt of the earth. . . . Ye are the light of the world."

salt, spilled

From earliest times salt has played a part in religious ceremonies. Even today it is used in the Roman Catholic baptismal service as a symbol of purity. So it has long been considered "bad luck" to spill salt accidentally. An elaborate ritual, familiar to most of us, has been passed down through the centuries to exorcise evil spirits allegedly set loose when salt is spilled. One must take a pinch of salt between the thumb and first finger of the right hand and cast it over the left shoulder.

salt, with a grain of

If you take something *with a grain of salt,* you are viewing it with considerable skepticism. The phrase, a direct translation of the Latin *cum grano salis,* indicates that, just as you would anticipate a very small quantity of salt in a dish served you, so you look for little truth in the statement made.

salt, worth his

Quite literally an employee who is not *worth his salt* is not worth his salary, for the two words have the same Latin root, *sal,* meaning "salt." Here's how it came about. The Romans realized that most foods are unappetizing without salt, so part of the wages of their soldiers was paid in salt. Later this was changed to a monetary allowance for the purchase of salt and, in time, the word *salarium*—"of salt"—came to mean payment for services rendered or "salary" as we use it today.

samurai

Pronounced SAM-oo-rye and spelled the same in both singular and plural, this Japanese word refers to members of the military class in feudal times. A *samurai* was usually the retainer of a noble, somewhat like the squires and equerries of European chivalry. Theoretically abolished in 1871 with the end of the Japanese feudal system, the code of the *samurai* continued to hold the allegiance of many military officers through World War II.

sandhog

A *sandhog* is a tunnel worker, one who works under air pressure in the early stages of excavation for tunnels and bridge foundations. His is dangerous work indeed, faced with the obvious immediate hazards of drowning and "the bends," and the long-range threat of death from silicosis, the disease caused by inhalation of stone dust.

sanguinary—sanguine

Sanguinary (pronounced SANG-gwin-nehr-ee) is an adjective meaning "bloody, murderous or bloodthirsty," a meaning which may seem highly illogical to those familiar with the word *sanguine,* which means "confident, cheerful and warm." The reason, if not the logic, lies in the fact that both words come from the Latin *sanguis* (blood).

Sanguine originally meant "of the color of blood," hence ruddy, particularly as applied to the complexion. It acquired its present-day meaning in medieval physiology when four fluids were held to be responsible for a person's disposition and health. Since a cheerful disposition and ruddy complexion were attributed to the strength of the blood, *sanguine* by extension means "warm, cheerful, confident and optimistic."

sandwich

Over the centuries, British nobility has made many contributions to the language. Perhaps the most famous was the invention of John Montague, nicknamed "Jemmy Twitcher," one of the most inveterate gamblers in the court of George III. Famous for his round-the-clock sessions at the gaming boards, "Jemmy" used to order his servant to bring him pieces of meat between slices of bread, so that he could continue gambling without loss of time. Very soon the bread-and-meat combination was given the name it retains to this day, the *sandwich*. "Jemmy Twitcher," you see, was more formally known as the fourth Earl of Sandwich.

sans-culotte

This French phrase meaning "without knee breeches" was originally applied by French aristocrats to the revolutionaries, who wore pantaloons instead of breeches. In time it came to refer to the extreme "red" republicans of the French Revolution and now it may be loosely used to describe any radical.

Santa Claus

This is a contraction of the Dutch "Sant Nikolaas," patron saint of children. His feast day is December 6 and originally gifts were given to children on the eve of that day. For more than a century, however, the celebration has been associated with the Christmas season in Western Europe and North America and Santa Claus is now believed by children to bring gifts to them on the eve of Christmas day. The much quoted "Night Before Christmas," incidentally, was originally titled "A Visit from St. Nicholas."

Satan

This word comes direct from the Hebrew *satan,* meaning "enemy" or "adversary." It has long been used as the name of the great enemy of mankind, Lucifer, the archangel who was cast out of heaven by Michael.

sauce Caruso. *See* food from the opera.

sawbuck

A *sawbuck* is a ten-dollar bill. The name has been current in American slang since before 1850, having been especially popular on the Western frontier. The *sawbuck* originally was a kind of sawhorse with the legs also projecting above the crossbar, so that they formed X's at each end of the sawhorse. The X, of course, is also the Roman numeral for "ten"—and that, in theory at least, is how the ten-dollar-bill came to be called a *sawbuck*.

sawed off, sawn off

In a recent issue of the *Times* of London appeared a story about three miners from Nottingham who were sentenced to prison for bank robbery. The story ran: "They were charged that, being armed with a *sawn-off* shotgun and a starting pistol, they robbed the Sherwood branch of the Nottingham Trustee Savings Bank of 91 pounds." The words *sawn off* interested me, accustomed to saying and writing *sawed-off* shotgun. Could the British be correct—and are we guilty of a corruption of the term?

Quite the contrary. The expression, like the shotgun, is an American invention. It did not quite survive intact the sea change involved in a trip to Britain.

The form *sawn* is simply an alternative past participle of the verb "to saw." *Sawn* is common enough in England, but it is nearly obsolete in America, though sometimes heard in certain regional dialects.

The shotgun itself was an American invention and the word first appeared in print in 1828. Unless memory fails, the *sawed-off* version made its first appearance as a handy, readily concealed firearm favored by bootleggers during the great drought of the twenties.

With characteristic British ingenuity, their phrase-borrowers have "just missed" on this one, with the result that *sawed off* turns up in Blighty as *sawn off*. And you know something? It takes real skill to miss anything with a shotgun—especially a sitting pigeon like this phrase which has been recorded in its original version in thousands of whodunits and gangster movies.

Perhaps, subconsciously, the writer of this piece is rebelling at the obvious impropriety of modern gangster firearms in the forest of Sherwood and the town of Nottingham, legendary homes of that prince of rogues, Robin Hood.

scab. *See* labor's lost lexicon.

scarlet letter

The letter *A* which a woman convicted of adultery was required to wear during the Puritan days of early New England. Hawthorne's novel (1850) of this title tells the story of its heroine, Hester Prynne, doomed to wear the letter as penalty for adultery with her pastor.

Scheherazade

In *The Arabian Nights,* the sultan plans to have a new bride every night, having her put to death at dawn. *Scheherazade* outwits him when she becomes his bride by telling such intriguing and suspenseful tales that, after one thousand and one nights, he changes his mind, takes her permanently to wife and declares her the liberator of her sex.

schlemiel

Schlemiel is a very common word in the German and Yiddish languages. It refers to a man or person who is in bad luck all the time, for whom nothing is successful and everything goes wrong. The word comes from the Bible, the Book of Numbers, Chapter 2. Shelumiel the son of Zurishaddai was the leader of the tribe of Simeon and it is said that whereas all other leaders were successful in battle, he was the only one who lost all the time. Hence the term *schlemiel.*

It's a long way from the pages of the Bible to the argot of the borax furniture peddlers who use the word to describe a naïve, trusting buyer but the word seems to have had an assist along the way. Back in 1814 a part-French, part-German poet with the name of Adelbert von Chamisso wrote a novel called *Peter Schlemihls Wundebare Geschichte,* a Faust-like tale of a man who sold his soul to the devil. The book was widely popular in Europe and *schlemihl* (it's spelled that way, too) became a synonym for a person who made a silly bargain.

It's in this sense that the furniture salesmen use it to describe a trusting customer. The general sense of *schlemiel* as a luckless fool of fortune is probably more widely recognized and is closer to the Biblical meaning.

schlock

Schlock means spurious, fake or worthless. It's a term which originally was part of the slang of criminals, but, in recent years, it has become more and more common in the jargon of some areas of commerce, notably in the clothing and furniture businesses. The term *schlock shop* is also heard, meaning a store specializing in worthless or nearly worthless merchandise.

schmier. *See* payola.

schmoozing

The term *schmoozing,* meaning to loaf about and talk shop, comes from the Yiddish word *schmus,* meaning "talk." It's not widely heard outside metropolitan areas.

scissorbill. *See* labor's lost lexicon.

scorched earth

This is an age-old practice of invaded countries of stripping and pillaging their own land in the path of an invader, leaving him nothing to sustain his troops. Most recently this practice was followed by Chinese troops at the time of the Japanese invasion during the 1930's and by Russian armies when the Nazis invaded their homeland in World War II.

Scotch verdict

A *Scotch verdict,* as it is commonly called, is a verdict of "not proven." Although in English and American law a jury in a criminal case is required to bring in a verdict of "guilty" or "not guilty," Scottish law allows this third alternative. In effect it says that while the jury strongly suspects that the defendant is guilty as charged, the prosecution has not adduced evidence sufficiently conclusive to justify a vote for conviction.

scot-free

Scot-free has nothing to do with Scotland or the Scottish people. In Shakespeare's day and before, a *scot* (or *sceot,* as it was originally spelled) was a municipal tax, one paid to the local bailiff or sheriff. Thus the present-day meaning of "without payment of a just penalty" can be traced directly back to the *scot-free* varlets of Elizabethan England who managed successfully to dodge paying their taxes. The Scotsman, though he has well earned his reputation for canniness and frugality, has equally well earned his reputation for facing up to his just obligations and hence is in no way libeled by the phrase *scot-free.*

Scourge of God

Attila, leader of the Huns, earned the title *Flagellum Dei* (*Scourge of God*) during the Middle Ages because of his relentless pillaging of most of Europe between A.D. 433 and 453. Ironically his name "Attila" is a baby-talk diminutive of *atta* the Gothic word for "father." So it literally means "little father." There is quite a difference between the name his followers used and the one given him by his victims!

scrambled eggs

Here is a highly descriptive, if somewhat disrespectful, term of the enlisted man in the armed services for the gold braid adorning the hats of top-ranking officers. See also BRASS.

Scratch, Old

Nickname for the devil. This has nothing to do with scratching to remedy an itch. The *Scratch* is derived from the Old Norse word *scratti,* meaning "devil" or "sorcerer."

scratching. *See* cowboy jargon

Scrooge

Ebennezer Scrooge, leading character in Dickens' *Christmas Carol,* has come to embody the traits of miserliness and greed so completely that his name has come into the language as a generic term for a very stingy person.

scrutiny

Coming from the Latin *scrutari* (to search into carefully), *scrutiny* has the built-in meaning of close examination. Hence the common phrase "close scrutiny" is obviously redundant. See also INSCRUTABLE.

scuttle butt

Scuttle butt means "gossip" but originally it meant the lidded cask ("scuttled butt") from which the ship's company obtained drinking water. Just as personnel in offices and factories today gather round the drinking fountain to exchange the latest rumors, so sailors since the days of John Paul Jones have clustered at the *scuttle butt* to pass on the latest rumor about whether or not the skipper will grant liberty at the next port. See also PAINTERS.

Scylla and Charybdis, between

One sailing *between Scylla and Charybdis* is traveling a very perilous course indeed. The reference is to the Straits of Messina where, according to Greek and Roman mythology, a monster dwelt on the rock *Scylla.* A steersman seeking to avoid this danger might well go too far in the other direction, thereby falling prey to the giant whirlpools of *Charybdis.*

sea lawyer

A *sea lawyer* is a know-it-all, especially a sailor of an argumentative turn of mind. His volubility is usually exceeded only by his ignorance.

sea, old man of

Originally the creature who, incubus-like, crawled on the back of Sinbad the Sailor (in *The Arabian Nights*) and refused to be cast loose. Nowadays the phrase is sometimes used figuratively to designate an evil person or habits that cannot be gotten rid of. Ernest Hemingway used the phrase as the title of a novel (1952), *The Old Man and the Sea.*

seas, high

This term applies to the oceans of the world beyond the three-mile jurisdictional limit allowed each coastal nation under international law. The *high seas* form the free waterways of the world.

seasons, four

These are the four arbitrary divisions of the year: spring, starting with the vernal equinox (March 21); summer, with the summer solstice (June 22); autumn, with the autumn equinox (September 23); and winter from the winter solstice (December 21).

sedulous ape, play the

This phrase is used to describe people, especially writers, who slavishly imitate their betters. It was coined by Robert Louis Stevenson, who, in a reminiscent essay once wrote: "I have played the sedulous ape to Hazlitt, to Lamb, to Wordsworth, to Sir Thomas Browne, to Defoe, to Hawthorne, to Montaigne, to Baudelaire, and to Obermann. . . . That, like it or not, is the way to learn to write."

seeded

The special meaning of *seed* in sports has to do with the scattering (*seeding*) of the names of superior players in a tournament in such a way as to insure that they will not meet each other in an early round. No tournament sponsor wants his stars to eliminate each other in the early rounds.

see red, to

The expression *see red* probably comes from the old belief that a bull seeing a red flag or garment will become enraged and run amuck. Scientific researchers—those perennial killjoys—have now proven that a bull will rush at any brightly colored cloth that is waved at him. In fact, there is some evidence indicating that a simple white cloth will attract, and enrage, a bull more quickly than a red one. And thus dies another cherished illusion—cherished, that is, by everyone but the bull.

segue

Segue (pronounced SEG-way) is a term common in the jargon of musicians. It means to move from one musical selection to another without modulation or interruption. *Segue* comes from the Italian and originally meant "to follow."

senator. *See* **candidate.**

send up salt river. *See* **political language.**

Sepoy Mutiny

A famous mutiny of native (*Sepoy*) Indian troops against their British overlords in 1857–58. It was touched off by the issuance to the troops of a new kind of musket requiring an application of grease to the cartridge. Since the soldiers were forbidden by their religion to touch beef fat, they rebelled and widespread massacres resulted. In the end, India became a crown colony, the East India Company was dissolved and many reforms of lands and laws were effected.

serendipity

Serendipity is the faculty of making happy and unexpected discoveries by accident. It was coined by the British author Horace Walpole, who based it on the title of an old fairy tale, "The Three Princes of Serendip." The princes in the story, he noted, were "always making discoveries of things they were not in quest of."

seven hills of Rome

The walled city of ancient Rome included these seven hills: Palatine, Capitoline, Quirinal, Aventine, Caelian, Esquiline and Viminal. As hills they never amounted to much, the tallest (Quirinal) being only 226 feet above sea level.

shady side, on the

A person *on the shady side* of a date is on the far side of it. Thus a person "*on the shady side* of thirty-nine" may be presumed to be in his forties.

shakes of a lamb's tail, in two

"In no time at all." Just why a lamb's tail should be chosen as more readily shaken than, say, a dog's tail, deponent knoweth not. In any event, the expression has been popular in America since shortly after the Revolution.

shampoo

Shampoo comes direct from the Hindu *champo*, meaning "press, knead or shampoo." While washing and massaging of the hair was not the only meaning of the original Hindu word, it was one of its meanings.

shanks' mare, going by

So far as I know, there never was any Mr. Shanks connected with the phrase. The *shanks* referred to are simply a person's legs. Just how the *mare* got into the expression is not known, but chances are that, since mares generally are more slow-paced than stallions, their pace would more nearly resemble walking.

Shavian

The correct meaning of such words as "Shakespearean" and "Wagnerian" are "concerning or like the works of this author." There is certainly nothing more "Shakespearean" than a play or sonnet by Will himself.

An adjective of this sort that I have always relished is *Shavian,* coined to refer to works by or in the style of Bernard Shaw. "Shawian" apparently sounded awkward or clumsy to this self-confessed genius, so he went to some pains to create his own adjective, inventing first the word *Shavius* as the Latinized form of "Shaw" and then deriving the adjective *Shavian* from it. Somehow this seems quite in character with this most Olympian, nay Jovian, of our twentieth-century wits.

Shaw's linguistic legacy

Newspapers and magazines have given much attention to the efforts in British courts to overthrow the will of George Bernard Shaw—that talented, cantankerous Irishman who, in death as well as life, defied convention and tried to effect his own personal, private revolution in language. The provisions of his legacy to a language reform movement are rather intricate but, in essence, he wanted to foster a move to add several new letters to our alphabet, eliminate some he felt are unnecessary, and establish new and phonetically more logical patterns of English spelling.

Surprisingly enough, most comment on Shaw's proposals treated them as something new. Actually Shaw is only the latest in a long line of language reformers, of whom one of the first was Dr. Samuel Johnson and one of the most effective was our own Noah Webster. For many years these dictators of language wielded great influence on the development of British and American orthography, but in recent years dictionary editors have changed their role from legislators of language to recorders of language.

During most of the last century, however, language reformers made many efforts to persuade the American people to accept simplified or "phonetic" spelling. Following in Webster's path, many of the nation's leading linguists spent countless man-hours of effort in a generally fruitless attempt to convert the nation and its press from such "wasteful" and "unscientific" spellings as *neighbor, thorough, philosophy* and *phonograph.*

Indeed, it has only been within the past few years that one of the country's major newspapers finally abandoned its long and futile effort to persuade the people of Chicago to adopt such spellings as *fonograf, filosofy* and *nabor*.

At one point Theodore Roosevelt brought all the prestige of the Presidency behind the movement and decreed that the Government Printing Office use "simplified spelling." One of the nation's great unabridged dictionaries entered hundreds of these revised spellings. Yet, on the whole, the movement was an utter failure.

Why? Simply because our language is a living, growing thing, the heritage and the creation of millions of Americans and English-speaking peoples throughout the world. No one person, no matter how highly placed or influential, is likely to succeed in imposing any substantial revision on our vocabulary. And that applies even to the efforts of as talented and brilliant a man as G. B. Shaw.

shebang

The most logical explanation of this word is that it is a variant of the Irish word *shebeen*. At any rate, its first recorded appearance in this country roughly coincides with the first major influx of Irish immigrants early in the nineteenth century.

A *shebeen* in Ireland was a very lowly public house, one where drinks were sold without a license. Indeed, a *shebeen* was very little better than the sort of establishment Americans of a generation back used to call a *blind pig*.

This being the case, a *shebeen* was regarded as a relatively valueless piece of real estate and the expression, "I'll give you so much for the whole *shebeen*" became current. Gradually the original reference to the lowly public house was lost and *shebeen*—now *shebang* after the trip across the Atlantic—came to mean any kind of trifling business affair or piece of property.

sheep, black

"There's a *black sheep* in every family," goes the old expression, meaning that there's sure to be one disreputable chap in every assemblage.

sheets in the wind

As colorful a special vocabulary as any in our language is that dealing with liquor and drinking. Why this should be so, why indulgence in the various forms of brews and spirits should lead to such inventiveness in language is a question whose answer lies beyond the scope of this book. But the fact remains that one scholar alone has chronicled more than a thousand synonyms for the word "liquor" in American slang. *Panther sweat, coffin varnish, mountain dew* and *red-eye* are only four of the seemingly infinite number of coinages.

And then there are the synonyms for "intoxicated"—*pifflicated, sozzled, plastered* and *stuccoed*—well, almost anyone can reel off a dozen more without half-trying—and still leave many hundreds to go.

The item which led to these ruminations was a request from a reader for an explanation of the origin of the colorful term *three sheets in the wind*. This comes from the vocabulary of sailors back in the days of "wooden ships and iron men."

The *sheet* referred to is not the common household bedcovering; it is the line or chain attached to the lower corner of a sail. By tightening up on this line or by slacking it off, the set of the sail is controlled. When the sheet is allowed to run quite free, the sail is said to be *in the wind.*

Thus, when all three sheets are *in the wind,* the sails are fluttering without control and the ship wallows and staggers like a person drunk. Hence the meaning of "very drunk" for *three sheets in the wind.*

As a matter of fact, old-time sailors used to observe a rather nice distinction between a person who had *one sheet in the wind*—slightly intoxicated—and one who had *three sheets in the wind*—completely sozzled, pifflicated, stuccoed and plastered.

shenanigans

Shenanigans—meaning "mischief," and pronounced exactly as written —may or may not be of Irish origin. According to one theory, it comes from the old Irish word *sionnachuighim,* meaning "I play the fox." But there's another theory, this one more farfetched, that *shenanigans* comes from a German dialect word, *schinageln,* meaning to "work at hard labor." The idea here is that scamps who used trickery to avoid hard work succeeded over the years in bringing to the word a meaning exactly the opposite of its original sense.

Well, this can happen. Words can change meaning radically. "Silly," for example, once meant "happy and innocent"; now it means "stupid." But a complete reversal in sense from "hard work" to carefree *shenanigans* hardly seems probable. So let's give credit to Ireland and agree that *shenanigan* once meant "I play the fox."

shibboleth

Only a comparative handful of words have come direct from ancient Hebrew to English and of these perhaps the most interesting is *shibboleth,* the Hebraic word for "ear of corn." In our language today, *shibboleth* has the very different meaning of "test word" or "watchword," and behind that change of meaning lies an intriguing bit of Biblical history.

During a battle between the Gileadites and the Ephraimites at the Jordan fords, the men of Gilead took command of the fords and, when any of the fugitives of the army of Ephraim asked to pass, they would be asked, "Are you an Ephraimite?"

If the answer was no, then—in the words of *Judges* 12:6—"They said to him, 'Say now *Shibboleth,*' and he said '*Sibboleth,*' for he could not frame to pronounce it right. Then they took him and slew him at the passages of the Jordan."

Thus the inability to pronounce correctly the Hebrew word for "ear of corn" was the distinguishing characteristic of the Ephraimites and one which the sons of Gilead were shrewd enough to use as their watchword, giving the word *shibboleth* the meaning it has today.

It is interesting to note that such *shibboleths* are still part of the equipment of the intelligence sections of most modern armies in the world today. During World War II, for example, our interrogating officers were careful to insist that each suspected Japanese spy read aloud several sentences containing words like *mellifluous, unintelligible* and *lollapalooza.*

The reason? Well, the Japanese have great difficulty pronouncing our letter *l.* It comes out usually sounding much like *r.* So a prisoner who talked of *rorraparoozas* was Japanese for a certainty—not the friendly Chinese he pretended to be. The Chinese, you see, have no trouble at all pronouncing the letter *l.* In fact their weakness is just the opposite of the Japanese failing—they cannot pronounce *r.* And that's why generations of cartoonists have used with every picture of a Chinese the stereotyped phrase, *"Velly, velly solly!"*

I suspect that our intelligence officers devised some sentences with lots of *r*'s to trap infiltrating Communist China spies during the Korean War but, to the best of my knowledge, no official information has been released on that point.

shill

A shill is a swindler's assistant. Most commonly he mingles with the crowd on sidewalk or carnival midway while the pitchman or peddler is making his sales talk to the crowd. By bidding or enthusiastic buying, he lures the unwary into the purchase of inferior merchandise or into fixed games of chance.

shillelagh

Shillelagh, pronounced shih-LAY-lee, originally meant a "club" or "cudgel" and takes its name from the village of Shillelagh in County Wicklow, Ireland, a region noted for its oaks and blackthorns. These cudgels became somewhat domesticated in the New World and did duty as walking sticks as well.

shindig

Shindig is thought to be a variation on *shindy,* an Old English slang term for a rousing party. Another theory, and this a pretty farfetched one, is that it is an abbreviation of "shin-dig," meaning a playful kick in the shins. To this I say only that he who kicks my shins had better expect a more violent retort than a merry laugh. Indeed, I can't offhand think of a worse way of starting a party than a kick in the shins.

ship. *See* boat, ship.

ship comes in, when my

This expression, meaning "when I'm a wealthy man," comes from the days when merchant commerce dominated the seas of the world. Then a wife waiting at home for her seafaring husband would literally be far better off when her ship came in, as would tradespeople receiving payment for a cargo shipped on the outbound voyage.

shopkeepers, nation of

This is Great Britain, so labeled in derision by Napoleon. He took the epithet from Adam Smith who wrote in his *Wealth of Nations:* "To found a great empire for the sole purpose of raising up a people of customers may at first sight appear a project fit only for a *nation of shopkeepers.*" Napoleon, like Kaiser Wilhelm and Adolf Hitler after him, might well have had occasion to paraphrase a famous remark of Winston Churchill: "Some shopkeepers!"

short-lived. *See* lived.

shoulder, cold

When we "turn the *cold shoulder"* to anyone, we treat him with disdain bordering on contempt. This is an especially appropriate phrase if the person was once on friendly terms with us.

shrewdness of apes. *See* clowder, kindle and cowardice.

shrift, give short

This interesting expression, meaning "to give very little attention" to a person or thing, comes from the medieval practice of allowing a condemned person a few seconds on the scaffold for confession of sins before execution. *Shrift* comes from the Anglo-Saxon *scrifan,* "to receive confession." It's closely related to the now archaic word "shriving," the act of hearing confession of sins and pronouncing absolution of them. So, when we *give short shrift* to a person who is bothering us, we're giving him about as much time as a criminal once had for a gallows confession.

Shrove Tuesday. *See* Pancake Tuesday.

shun-pike

A *shun-pike* is a detour around a toll-collecting point on a turnpike. A couple of centuries ago when the first American toll roads were built, *shun-pikes* were the essence of simplicity. The owner of a farm paralleling the road where the toll station was established would arrange for vehicles to pass around the gate and over his property for a fee substantially cheaper than that charged by the owners of the toll road. Today, with most of our states crisscrossed by hundreds of well-paved roads, ingenious autoists frequently find that it saves them money to plot a route which will parallel the new toll turnpikes for part of their trip.

shut-out. *See* baseball jargon.

sibling

The word *sibling* actually goes back to Anglo-Saxon times, though it had been very little used for centuries until psychologists and psychiatrists revived it in recent years as part of their trade jargon. Originally a *sib* was any relative. Indeed, in medieval times a *sib* was not even necessarily a blood relative. A *god-sib* (from which we get our word "gossip") was simply a godparent, a child's sponsor at baptism.

Nowadays, however, a *sibling* is one of two or more children having the same parents. More simply put, a *sibling* is simply a brother or a sister.

"*Sibling* rivalry" is the normal contention between children in a family, the sort of squabbling that is an inevitable part of growing up in a family of any size.

sideburns

Sideburns got their name from an illustrious American. He was General Ambrose Everett Burnside, onetime commander of the Army of the Potomac and the general in command when the Union forces suffered one of their most catastrophic defeats at the Battle of Petersburg.

Burnside was nearly drummed out of the Army after a court of inquiry found his leadership deficient, but he went on to business success and served as Governor of Rhode Island and Senator from that state. His mutton-chop whiskers were a readily identifiable trade-mark and were widely imitated during the latter part of the nineteenth century. They were first called *burnsides,* but later, through a curious semantic shift, became *sideburns.*

side of the angels, on the

Disraeli first used this phrase in the course of a speech on the Darwinian theory of *The Origin of the Species:* "The question is this," he said. "Is man an ape or an angel? I, my lord, am *on the side of the angels."*

Silence gives consent.

This axiom comes direct from Roman law: *Qui tacet consentire videtur* —"He who is silent seems to consent."

Silence is golden.

This aphorism, which surely gives the lie to the seemingly impeccable statement above, surely indicates that there are occasions—though possibly not in courts of law—when it's wise to remain silent. The full maxim reads: "Speech is silver; *silence is golden."*

silo drippings

Silo drippings is one of the innumerable slang terms that have been created as substitutes for the word "liquor"; specifically, it is corn liquor or "white lightning."

simplified spelling. *See* Shaw's linguistic legacy.

sincere. *See* infracaninophile.

sinecure

Pronounced sy-nih-kyoor, this word comes straight from the Latin phrase *sine cure* (without case). Originally an ecclesiastical term, it meant a church position which paid a salary but did not require its holder to concern himself with the care of souls. Nowadays a *sinecure* is any job requiring little or no work, especially one obtained by political pressure.

sine qua non

"That which is indispensable." Literally, "without which nothing." The original Latin phrase was: *Sine qua non potest esse*—"Without which it is not possible to exist."

sing. *See* recant.

Sing Sing

Sing Sing was originally the name of the town where the prison is located. It was the white man's version of the Delaware Indian name for the spot, *assinesink,* meaning "at the small stone."

By the end of the nineteenth century, the "small stone" had become "The Rock" and Sing Sing Prison was known as the toughest, cruelest penitentiary in the country. The townspeople were understandably unhappy that their charming community was regarded with such disfavor by the outer world, so in 1901 they officially changed their town's name to "Ossining."

sinister

Sinister, which comes from the Latin word of identical spelling, is one of the several words in the English language which reflect an unreasoning prejudice against left-handed persons. The Latin *sinister* simply meant "left," but over the years the word has acquired a meaning of "ominous" or "evil." See also GAUCHE.

sirloin

A legend that dies hard has it that King James I drew his sword and knighted a piece of beef "Sir Loin." This particular flight of fancy has been debunked so many times that one might expect people to know it for what it is—a word-play hoax that has amused Britons for more than three centuries.

Actually *sirloin* came into English from French at the time of the Norman Conquest—long centuries before James I or any of the other monarchs who are credited with knighting this cut of beef. The word, in Old French, was *surlonge,* from *sur* (upon or above) and *longe* (loin).

The transition from *surlonge* to *sirloin* evolved gradually, though one authority still stoutly maintains that *sirloin* is a "mistaken" spelling. Among the illustrious writers of the past who have accepted the fanciful legend of *sirloin*'s origin are Thomas Fuller, whose *Church History* (1655) credits Henry VIII with coining the word, and Jonathan Swift, who gave the honor to James I.

sit-down strike

A strike of workers who sit down at their machines in their place of employment, thereby making it impossible for management to put new workers in their places. This form of strike originated in the United States during the 1930's.

sit-in

A technique of nonviolent resistance whereby victims of discrimination "sit in" at lunch counters, schools and churches to manifest their displeasure. Widely practiced by Negroes and Negro sympathizers in the U.S., it is modeled upon the teachings of Mohandas K. Gandhi, Indian social reformer (1869–1948).

SK to O.K.

The controversy about the origin of the phrase *O.K.* has continued for more than a half-century by now and it shows no sign of abating. As we noted under o.k., at least two Presidents of the United States were involved in this matter—President Wilson when he tried to insist on the spelling *okeh* and President Van Buren from whose "Old Kinderhook" political club the initials probably originally came.

But even though Allen Walker Read's researches, first published in 1941, pretty definitely prove that Van Buren's *O.K.* Club first brought the phrase to the popular fancy, other theories still are circulated, including this one from C. W. Foss of Toledo. "Way back years ago," he wrote, "when radio telegraphers began receiving orders by sound, it became necessary to acknowledge receipt of such orders and 'all correct' was the signal given for the purpose. Soon it shifted to *O* for 'all' and *k* for 'correct.' So *O.K.* came into use and has been so used ever since."

Now there's at least one flaw in this particular word history, and that's the fact that *O.K.* was in widespread use long before 1890, when Mr. Foss says railroad telegraphers first started using it. Quite possibly the telegraphers picked it up then, but it had been widely used by others before.

My correspondent went on to report an interesting and rather more plausible story behind another common expression. "The designation *ham operator* always indicated a slow, sluggish Morse sender, one whose transmission would at times be unreadable. When called a *ham,* he could be induced to wake up and send clearly, because he would realize that all the other operators would be laughing at him. It's a peculiar fact that nowadays all amateur operators seem to have adopted the name of *ham*— probably not knowing these facts."

Well, that's an interesting theory. Now, from one retired telegrapher (radio, in my case) to another—*SK*. And, for the benefit of the uninitiated, *SK* is telegraphic symbol for "end of transmission."

skewgee

Skewgee is one of a number of dialect terms used to describe something that is askew. See also KITTY-CORNERED.

skiddoo, twenty-three

Here are two possible explanations of the old slang expression *twenty-three skiddoo*. The first is that a character in a play adapted from Dickens' *Tale of Two Cities* counted off the number of people being guillotined in the final scene. The hero was number twenty-three—and the expression became a favorite of theater folk to indicate the time to leave, especially with *skiddoo* added.

Another version dates back to the 1890's when the Flatiron Building at Twenty-third Street and Broadway in New York was the town's first skyscraper and its most glamorous building. The corner was also considered the city's windiest, so gallant blades of the day used to hang out on Twenty-third Street waiting for the breezes to lift the skirts of passing ladies. But policemen, then as always, disapproved of such unseemly loitering. Hence their order: *"Twenty-three skiddoo."*

In his syndicated column, your author has dipped from time to time into mild controversy ("argument" would be much too strong a word) about the origins of such phrases as "twenty-three skiddoo." Here is a letter from Floyd Montgomery of Washington, D.C., setting me and the other controversialists to rights on the subject:

"It appears that old-time telegraphers do not read your column," he wrote. "Some time ago when you were checking the derivation of *twenty-three skiddoo* I was tempted to fill in a little background from my own experience but decided that others would beat me to it. They didn't.

"I can only go back to 1904 when, as a messenger boy at the Western Union in Muncie, Indiana, and learning telegraphy, I soon became acquainted with *twenty-three* and felt that it was an old, old term even then. Operators at various stations, to relieve loneliness (and perhaps to keep awake during late hours), were in the habit of carrying on conversations in Morse code. One 'brass pounder' in Peoria played checkers nightly by wire with another.

"When the dispatcher wanted to come in with an order he would interrupt by tapping out *twenty-three*—meaning 'get off the wire.' This was an accepted signal, well understood in those days.

skid row, skid road

Each section of the country has its regional peculiarities of speech, expressions and pronunciations which the local residents cling to and know to be correct, even though those of us in the rest of the country may differ. Down Boston way, for example, anyone who pronounces the town name Quincy with anything other than a *zee* for the last syllable is regarded with the same suspicion afforded outlanders who desecrate clam chowder by adding tomatoes. In the same fashion, St. Louisans incline to take a dim view of people who pronounce their city's name LOO-ee rather than LOO-iss. And, of course, natives of San Francisco regard with withering scorn barbarians who call their fair city "Frisco."

Similar passions seem to beat in the breast of the average resident of the Pacific Northwest when he hears the phrase *skid row*. The term, you are told politely but very firmly, is *skid road*. The first *skid road,* a hanging-out place for human derelicts, was in Seattle and was so named because it was made of greased logs over which lumbermen used to skid logs to the mills. Indeed, one editor of a respected lexicon of slang flatly labels *skid row* a "perversion" of *skid road*.

Nevertheless, the expression heard in the greater part of the country is *skid row* and this is the formulation found in the newer dictionaries. What, then, does the conscientious word student do—adopt what was apparently the original term or go along with the rest of the country? The best answer seems to be: "When in Rome, do as the Romans do."

In the words of the program director of a radio station in the Pacific Northwest: "Not being a native but being a word purveyor to many native Washingtonians, I feel obliged to conform. However, my argument is this: Perhaps *skid road* did originate in Seattle. Therefore, Seattle, Tacoma, Olympia, Longview and other northwest lumbering camps had their *skid roads*. However, Chicago, San Diego and many other cities which have had no logs to skid, in my opinion, have their *skid rows*—which term derives from the fact that they are frequented by men 'on the skids.' Am I right or wrong?"

Well, it's an interesting theory and, as I said above, "When in Rome . . ."

skirl

Skirl, the shrill, piercing sound made by a bagpipe, comes from the Old Norse word *skrylla* (to scream). With the possible exception of native-born Scotsmen, who hold the bagpipes in high regard, most people will agree that that derivation is highly appropriate.

skirmish and scaramouche

Skirmish meaning a trifling and unimportant conflict, is one of the many words of chivalric warfare brought to England by the Norman conquerors. In Middle English it was often spelled *skrymishe,* the word from which the common football term "scrimmage" comes. In turn, the French had taken their word *escarmuche* from the Italian *scaramuccia* —and that's a word which should ring a bell of memory for many readers. For from *scaramuccia* comes the proper name *Scaramouche* (skar-uh-MOOSH) which was the title of Raphael Sabatini's best-selling novel of the 1920's and the source of one of the most popular motion pictures ever filmed. *Scaramouche* was originally a stock character in Italian farce, a boastful braggart always skirmishing on the fringes of danger, but too cowardly ever to become involved in serious battle.

skirt

Skirt came into English from Old Norse as the Anglo-Saxon word *scyrte,* which originally meant any short garment and, indeed, was more likely to mean a shirt than a skirt in those days.

skittles. *See* beer and skittles.

skulk of foxes. *See* clowder, kindle and cowardice.

sky pilot

Sky pilot originally was a slang term for "minister" or "preacher." The allusion, of course, was to a minister's ability to pilot an errant soul to an eventual home in heaven, symbolized by the sky. One of the best known and loved Canadian novels is *The Sky Pilot* by Ralph Connor, himself a onetime missionary to the lumbermen and miners in the Canadian Rockies.

During World War II the term was used by servicemen first as a slang term for "chaplain," later as a synonym for "aviator." Both meanings are now current, but only as slang terms.

slang

Slang began as a slang term itself and its ultimate origin is in dispute. It is first recorded in print in 1756 but was probably common in the argot of the underworld before that date. One authority credits its origin to a Norwegian word *slengjeord,* meaning "slang word" but, in the next breath, suggests it may be related to the English word "sling." From the way some people sling slang around, that last might be as good a theory as any.

Slang, incidentally, consists of two kinds of words: words regarded as "substandard," that is inadmissible into polite and proper use (*cop, ain't, scram*) and words coined for a fresh, often humorous, and usually transient purpose (*Chinese home run* or the now forgotten *whoopee*).

slaunchways. *See* kitty-cornered.

sleeper. *See* **philatelic jargon.**

slogan

One of the chief ingredients in the success of an advertising campaign, as any adman can tell you, is a catchy *slogan.* Through the years of the past half-century—from "Ask the man who owns one," through "Blow some my way," to the ubiquitous chant about the weed that "tastes good like a cigarette should"—many a product has been lifted into the best-seller category by insistent repetition of a *slogan.*

So complete has been the identification of the word *slogan* with contemporary advertising that many people think of it as a word recently coined. Here is an example of the queries regarding it: *"Slogan* is a word that has puzzled me for a long time," wrote a reader of my newspaper column. "I read in a book that, before the Battle of Lake Erie, Commodore Perry told his men to print the words of Captain James Lawrence, 'Don't Give Up the Ship,' on a pennant attached to the truck of the topmost mast of the *Lawrence.* In the book, Perry is quoted as saying, 'The cry, "Don't Give Up the Ship," will be our *slogan.'* I am wondering whether the word *slogan* was in use back in 1813. Please tell me when the word entered our language and how and why."

Yes, indeed, the word was in our language in 1813. In fact, the great *Oxford English Dictionary* records its first appearance in print as 1513 —exactly three centuries earlier. What's more, Commodore Perry was using the word in its earliest sense—that of a war cry.

For, amusingly enough, the *slogans* with which today's advertising geniuses do battle for a share of the consumer pocketbook are the direct lineal descendants of the war cries with which Scottish chieftains did battle. The word *slogan* comes from the Gaelic words *slaugh* (army) and *gairm* (a shout). The two were blended as a *slaughgairm,* meaning "battle cry," from which the present spelling was evolved.

Perhaps it is not to be wondered at that Scotch and soda remains the tribal drink of the gray-flanneled warriors of Madison Avenue as they create the war cries of today's battle for front rank in America's marketplace.

sloid

Sloid is a perfectly good, though now little-used, term from the educational jargon of a half-century ago. It's one of the comparative handful of words we have taken from Swedish—in this instance from *slojd,* meaning "skill." *Sloid* or *sloyd,* as it was often spelled, was a method of training boys in what used to be called the manual arts—wood carving, carpentry and the like. Nowadays "shop" classes have made the kind of instruction an older generation received in *sloid* as obsolete as the Mercer runabout, the air-cooled Franklin and the Stutz Bearcat.

slothful, sloth

Slothful (pronounced SLOTH-f'l) is an adjective which ascribes to a person the characteristics of the lazy, slow-moving animal which hangs by its feet from trees in most zoos of the country. *Sloth,* as a noun, is not only the name of the animal but is defined as sluggishness, laziness and a disinclination to work. *Sloth* comes to us from the Middle English *slou,* meaning "slow."

sloth of bears. *See* clowder, kindle and cowardice.

slug

While it's true that *slug* in sense of a great number or quantity is enjoying considerable vogue among our smart-talking young businessmen, the word is not at all new in this sense. Berry and Van den Bark's *American Thesaurus of Slang* gives *slug* along with dozens of other colloquial synonyms for "large amount." *Slew, scads, stacks, wads, hunk* and *oodles* are only a few of the expressions cited along with it.

It remains a slang expression, however, despite its momentary vogue among the brainy boys of the advertising and merchandising fraternities. No careful speaker or writer would use it except under most informal circumstances.

slum burner. *See* Old Army slang.

slush funds

The first *slush funds* were found aboard merchant ships of the last century. Money raised by the sale of surplus fats (*slush* in sailors' jargon) was put into a general fund for the purchase of luxuries the jack-tars could not otherwise afford. Before long the term became part of political slang, meaning money used for bribes which in turn provided the person taking the bribe with luxuries he could not otherwise obtain.

small beer

Something that is *very small beer* is a matter of very little consequence. The expression has been commonplace in Britain for centuries. In *Othello,* Iago speaking to Desdemona says: "She was a wight if ever such wight were—to suckle fools and chronicle *small beer.*" To which Desdemona replies: "O most lame and impotent conclusion!"

Conversely, a person who "does not think *small beer* of himself" is a conceited chap indeed.

smog, smust, smaze and sneet

Los Angelenos, the denizens of Los Angeles, have been hard pressed in recent years to find words to describe their disgust with the atmospheric conditions prevailing thereabouts. *Smog,* a blend of "smoke" and "fog," which had served Pittsburgh and St. Louis well enough—until protests of irate citizens brought reform of the conditions which caused it—was obviously too humdrum for this city of magnificent superlatives. So, they coined their own special vocabulary to describe the various degrees of nastiness to which they were being subjected. *Smust,* for instance, is a blend of "smoke" and "dust." *Snoud* is a combination of "snow" and low-hanging "clouds." (Snow in Los Angeles! What will the Chamber of Commerce say to all this?) And then there's *smaze*—"smoke" and "haze." But the worst of all would seem to be *sneet.* You guessed it—"snow" and "sleet"!

snake in the grass

A hidden enemy, especially one who pretends friendship in order to betray you. The phrase comes from Vergil's *Eclogues: "Latet anguis in herba"*—"A snake lurks in the grass."

snarky

A new word—and this is such a delight that it seems impossible that it is completely new, though unrecorded by the dictionaries—comes from Harriet Van Horne. After quoting a British critic of commercial TV as saying, "A nation fed on this pap for one generation might as well scrap its educational system and spend the money on asylums," she remarks, "Now this is a pretty *snarky* comment."

The snark, as all Lewis Carroll enthusiasts well know, is the mythical creature—a combination of "snake" and "shark"—hymned in *The Hunting of the Snark.* It seems to me that Miss Van Horne has given us in *snarky* a very felicitous new adjective which falls somewhere between *sneering* and *snide* (see below) in meaning and serves as an admirable and useful running mate for those worthy terms.

sneet. *See* smog, smust, snaze and sneet.

snide

Snide has been current for some twenty-five years as a slang term meaning "sly" or "subtly derogatory." Amazingly, it escaped the attention of lexicographers until a few years ago when it finally was entered in one of the leading "college" dictionaries. Without any question it will be listed in all the standard works as new editions are issued.

Incidentally, no one knows for certain where the word—most often heard in the phrase *"snide* remark"—came from. One theory is that it entered the language as a term of underworld slang derived from the German word *schneiden* meaning "to cut" or "to make cutting or sarcastic remarks."

snob

Incredible as it seems, a *snob* was originally a low-born dolt, a not-very-bright member of the lowest class. Nowadays, perhaps because of the analogy between *snob* and "snub," the word means a person of no particular social background who pretends to be a member of the upper class, scorns ("snubs") all those he regards as his inferiors, and tries to associate only with people he privately considers to be his superiors.

snollygoster

When ex-President Truman used the word *snollygoster* and defined it as "a man born out of wedlock," newspaper wire services were correct in pointing out that his definition didn't jibe with definitions found in the standard dictionaries. After quoting H. L. Mencken's *The American Language,* the wire service dispatches concluded that a *snollygoster* is "a fellow who wants office, regardless of party, platform or principles" and noted that the word was first recorded in a Georgia paper about 1895. For the record—and with no intent of supplying ammunition for either the pro- or anti-*snollygoster* faction—it should be noted that Wentworth's *American Dialect Dictionary* records its use as early as 1865 and defines *snollygoster* in a single word—"a shyster." And, to complete the record, Funk & Wagnalls defines *shyster* as "a lawyer who practices in an unscrupulous or tricky manner."

soapy Sam

A *soapy Sam* is a suave, unctuous public speaker. The first *soapy Sam* was Samuel Wilberforce, Bishop of Oxford midway through the Victorian era. He got his nickname from his unctuous manner of speaking. Once when he was asked about the sobriquet, he smilingly assured his questioner that he was called *soapy Sam* because "I am often in hot water but always come out with clean hands."

sockdolager

Sockdolager (pronounced sok-DOL-uh-jer) is from the frontier vocabulary of more than a century ago. It seems to be a combination of *sock,* meaning "a strong blow," of course, and *dolager,* a corruption of "doxology," the brief hymn sung toward the end of many church services. Thus it means anything that is truly decisive—the ultimate of its kind.

Though it's not often heard today, it's a word with the tang and color of the early settlements of the American West. Such words form a part of our linguistic heritage, a salty part, to be sure. But life and language would both be dull without a little salt on the side.

socked in

Socked in goes back to an earlier day in aviation, a day when such aids to pilots as radar and Ground Controlled Approach were undreamed of. Early pilots had to rely for information about wind direction on a conical wind *sock* hung from a mast atop the biggest hangar. In a rough way, the sock also would give them an idea as to the wind's velocity. Naturally when fog hung heavily over the airfield, the air *sock* would be invisible. Since planes would neither take off nor land under such "ceiling zero" conditions, the field was said to be *socked in.*

soda

Anywhere in the Eastern U.S., *soda* means a flavorless sparkling beverage, unless some flavor name is prefixed, such as "raspberry *soda,*" "cherry *soda*" and the like. In and around St. Louis, Missouri, though, *soda* invariably is a sweetish lemon-flavored beverage. And what New York calls *soda,* St. Louis calls "seltzer."

solecism

The Greek colony of Soloi, far removed from Athens, developed a dialect of its own, much as Americans did when removed from the mother country, England. The Athenians, like the English, were shocked by what they called the colony's *soloikismos,* "speaking incorrectly," from which comes our word *solecism,* meaning an error in grammar or the use of words.

solicitors. *See* barristers, solicitors.

Solon

Solon, a statesman who lived in Athens, Greece, five hundred years before Christ, might be called the headline writer's friend, for his name has joined the host of words that are virtually indispensable to the newspaper copyreader because of their brevity. The words "representative," "Congressman," "legislator" and "lawmaker" are all long words and, often as not, none will fit into a headline. So the name of *Solon,* used without the capital *S,* comes in very handily to mean any lawmaker.

This general use of Solon's name wasn't invented by the men on the newspaper copy desks, but they certainly have kept it alive. In the headlines the wise old Athenian often finds himself in rather violent company. This is not because men who write headlines are bloodthirsty—it's just that most of the milder words are too long. For example, "to criticize" becomes, depending on the severity of the criticism and the space available, *to hit, blast, flail, score* or *lash.* These shorter action words usually find their way into the reporter's stories because they liven things up.

sonorous

Sonorous (pronounced suh-NOH-russ) describes that which is resonant, vibrating or full-toned. Derived from the Latin *sonor* (a sound), it applies also to high-sounding speech, as in poetry or sermons. "The minister rambled on in *sonorous* platitudes."

sooney-sawney

Sawney was originally a British term, used derisively, meaning "Scotsman." In time, and this perhaps reflects the low state of British-Scottish relations during the Eighteenth Century, it came to mean "simpleton." Later, through the process known to language students as "reduplication," the adjective *sooney-sawney* was created, meaning simply "foolish."

sophisticated

A word which troubles some readers is *sophisticated* as used in phrases like *"sophisticated* missiles" or *"sophisticated* machines." Most of us think of something *sophisticated* as being "worldly, urbane and polished." The original meaning (from the Greek *sophos,* meaning "wise") was "worldly-wise." But *sophisticated* has also had the meaning, in Webster's words, of "made artificial, or, more narrowly, highly complicated, refined, subtilized." It is in this sense that missile-makers apply it to their intricate mechanisms.

sophophobia

An aversion to wisdom or learning is *sophophobia,* from the Greek *sophia* (wisdom) and *phobos* (fear).

sop to Cerberus, give a

Cerberus in ancient mythology was the three-headed dog who watched the gates to Hades. In order to guarantee easy passage, the ancients used to put a cake soaked in honey and poppy juice in the hands of a dead person. Nowadays the expression means giving a bribe to ease one's way out of an awkward or dangerous plight.

sord of mallards. *See* clowder, kindle and cowardice.

SOS

Many people believe *SOS* stands for "Save Our Ship," "Save Our Souls," "Stop Other Signals." Actually the letters have no significance whatever. The first distress call used by the early Marconi Company was *CQD*—*CQ* being the general call to alert other ships that a message is coming and *D* standing for "danger" or "distress." For various technical reasons this proved unsatisfactory and in 1908 by international agreement a signal made up of three dits, three dahs, and three dits was adopted as the one most easily transmitted and understood. By coincidence this signal is translatable as *SOS.*

During World War II a new distress signal *SSS* was devised for use only when the cause of the distress was a submarine torpedoing.

sounder of boars. *See* clowder, kindle and cowardice.

sourdough

The young man or woman who goes to Alaska will find that the language spoken there differs only very slightly from what he has heard all his life at home. Students of regional dialect find that there are remarkably few expressions that can be labeled "Alaskan." Indeed, even the best-known label for Alaskan old-timers, *sourdoughs,* was known on our Western frontier long before the Yukon and Klondike gold rushes. The *sourdough* got his name from the practice of early prospectors of carrying over a lump of sour dough from each biscuit baking to start fermentation of the next batch. It wasn't a very sanitary technique, but it worked.

Others of the scattered few native Alaskan terms are *mush,* to travel on foot over snow—usually with a dog sled—and the recent coinage *no-see-um.* This is a biting insect too small to be seen. There's also the *mukluk,* a heavy boot with leather bottoms and canvas tops. But, for the most part, the new arrival will find less to confuse him in the language spoken by Alaskans than, say, a New Yorker freshly deposited in London.

southpaw. *See* baseball jargon.

sow's ear, make a silk purse out of a

Just who first said, "You can't make a silk purse out of a sow's ear" is unknown. Like many proverbs, this has been used so often over the centuries—and in so many slightly varying forms—that the fellow who first uttered this homely truth has long been forgotten.

In Laurence Sterne's *Tristram Shandy* the phrase turns up in this form: "As certainly as you can make a velvet cap out of a sow's ear." At about the same time—the second half of the eighteenth century—a British versifier, John Walcott, who wrote under the name of "Peter Pindar," said it this way: "You cannot make, my Lord, I fear, a velvet purse of a sow's ear."

Just when the velvet turned to silk would be anyone's guess, but the fundamental moral—that you cannot make a first-quality product from inferior material—remains as sound as the day it was first uttered.

space jargon

Here is a sampling of the vocabulary of spacemen—or "astronauts" as they are properly called. It includes new uses of old words, together with a sampling of the new space age jargon.

Auntie, for example, has nothing to do with your relative of that name; now it's astronautical slanguage for the antimissile missile. And *lox* no longer is merely the smoked salmon which, with cheese and bagels, is a staple of menus in New York's garment district. In the argot of missile engineers, *lox* means "liquid oxygen, explosive."

Shortly after the end of World War II, when man first began to think about traveling faster than the speed of sound, scientists realized that the traditional miles-per-hour measurement of speed was no longer adequate to their needs. So they evolved a new term to express the ratio between the velocity of a moving object and the speed of sound. The word they chose—*mach* from the name of a noted Austrian physicist, Ernst Mach—is now a part of the everyday language of astronauts. A plane or missile traveling a *Mach 1* is going at exactly the speed of sound, which is figured at 760 mph at sea level. Thus a piston-powered airliner traveling at 3,800 mph is making *Mach 5,* while a military jet flying 1,520 mph is making *Mach 2.*

Stol is not a misprint for "stole." Actually it's engineer's shorthand for "short take-off and landing." And a *moon suit?* That's a special, inflatable flight uniform, covering the whole body and worn by the astronauts. And then there is that painfully punning concoction *dynasoar*—the name for a boost-glide, orbital space craft—a contraction of "dynamic" and "soaring."

Relaxation time is common enough in industry—the coffee break has certainly become standard operating procedure in most businesses—but in the wonderful world of space *relaxation time* means the period of time necessary for material to reach its normal state after being subjected to the unnatural stresses of space flight.

The *exosphere* is the outer fringe of the atmosphere—out past the stratosphere and the ionosphere. All three of these "spheres" are beyond the *troposphere,* which is where we earth beings normally dwell.

If you're going beyond the *exosphere,* you'd better be equipped with a *satelloid.* Now this is admittedly a science-fiction term, but the astronauts argue that it's so close to reality we might as well use this word to describe the first manned vehicle designed to reach the moon, then return to earth.

Wonders obviously will never cease, especially if you consider *inertial guidance.* This, according to *Space Talk,* a glossary of astronautical terms issued by the Republic Aviation people, "is a sophisticated automatic navigation system for high speed aircraft, missiles and spaceships which absorbs and interprets such data as speed and position and automatically adjusts the missile or spacecraft to a predetermined flight path. Essentially it knows where it is going and where it is by knowing where it came from and how it got there." That is a lot more than many humans know. But then a lot of us are just not "sophisticated," either in the standard or in the engineering sense of the word.

spade a spade, to call a

The first *spade-caller* is lost in antiquity, for the coiner of the Latin proverb *"Ficus ficus, ligonem ligonem vocat"* is unknown, though Menander and Plutarch are both credited with it. As long ago as the early part of the sixteenth century, John Knox, Scottish Protestant reformer, gave an English version: "I have learned to call wickedness by its own terms: a fig a fig, and *a spade a spade."*

Words you use when you don't want *to call a spade a spade* are "euphemisms." The heyday of the euphemism in our language and culture was undoubtedly the Victorian era. When the names of many items of wearing apparel were inadmissible in polite society, the mention of shirt, trousers or—worse yet—breeches was a symptom of utmost depravity. As one versifier noted:

> I've heard that breeches, petticoat and smock,
> Give to thy modest mind a grievous shock
> And that thy brain (so lucky its device)
> Christened them "inexpressibles," so nice.

In those days, of course, the word "leg" was entirely inadmissible in polite society and even piano "limbs" were decorated with frilled trousers—or "inexpressibles."

Though these particular euphemisms have long since been laughed into oblivion, the euphemism is still very much with us, and nowhere more prominently than in advertising copy. For example, how long has it been since you saw a printed reference to a "second-hand" automobile? Or a "ready-made" suit? Today all such cars are *reconditioned* and suits are *ready-to-wear* or even *custom-fitted*—by which a clothier merely means that sleeves will be shortened and cuffs attached.

Something like the ultimate in euphemistic labeling was reached recently by a major automobile manufacturer who labeled his cheapest line of stock cars *custom*—a word which, if it means anything any more, means "created to the customer's specifications." At precisely this point, it seems to me, "euphemism" becomes "misrepresentation"—and less a matter for the word experts than for the Federal Trade Commission.

spaniel. *See* cocker spaniel.

spanking, spanking new

In this case we are dealing with a pair of homonyms, words with the same sound, and, in this case, spelling but of different origin and meaning. *Spank,* meaning to strike with an open hand, is a word formed in imitation of the sound it represents, an "echoic" word. "Blast," "slap" and "thump" are other words which probably originated in attempts to echo the sounds represented.

Spanking as in *spanking new,* however, is thought to come from one of the Scandinavian tongues. Originally it was used to describe a fresh, lively breeze. Indeed it probably was first a sailor's term, since it surely is related to the *spanker,* a fore-and-aft sail. Eventually *spanking* came to its present meaning—anything remarkable or outstanding of its kind. Incidentally, it seems to be gradually falling into disuse. A generation ago one often heard of a *"spanking* team of horses." I have yet to hear anyone speak of his *"spanking new* convertible!"

spectacular, fantastic

A few years ago Sylvester J. "Pat" Weaver, then president of NBC, coined the noun *spectacular* to describe a television show of unusual length and importance. Weaver has since left NBC and the word *spectacular* has never officially been used in press handouts from that network since his departure, though shows of the type he devised are still occasionally seen.

A worthy contender for Weaver's labeling honors is Richard Dorso, whose contribution to the language is *fantastic*—and if it occurs to you that this is scarcely a new word, hold on a minute until you have the whole story.

Fantastic has done duty as an adjective at least since 1632, according to the *Oxford English Dictionary*. Many centuries before that it was the Latin word *fantasticus,* also an adjective. But now, thanks to Mr. Dorso, it has become a noun.

A fantastic is a television program dealing with unbelievable phenomena, a sort of nonscience fiction. To give you an idea, the hero of Mr. Dorso's brain child is an undercover agent of the conventional "Foreign Intrigue" type, except for one detail—he is only six inches tall.

speleologist

Here is a word which was buried in the dictionaries for many, many years until the atomic bomb snatched it—still dazed and blinking—into the glare of front-page publicity. You may have never seen it before, nor its parent word *speleology* (pronounced spee-lee-OL-uh-jee), but the chances are a thousand to one that you will be frantically searching for a *speleologist* if an atom bomb ever hits your part of the country.

Your *speleologist* will be a good man to know if that terrible day ever comes, for he is the person who will be able to guide you to safe underground shelter. He spends his time exploring caves, most recently with an eye to finding some suitable for human habitation.

A story is told of a high-ranking Army officer watching the bomb tests in Nevada. Asked what he thought the most effective missiles would be in the next war, he replied, "I really can't say. But I know what weapons they'll be using in the war after next—bows and arrows!"

And so it is literally quite true that the research now being carried on by these fascinating but little-known scientists, the *speleologists,* may one day be responsible for saving whatever remains of our civilization if a future holocaust drives us back thousands of years to the epoch of the cave dwellers. For all the seriousness of their study and research, *speleologists* display a disarming sense of humor in the casually irreverent name that they have chosen for intramural references to each other and their chosen work. They call each other not *speleologists* but *spelunkers!*

spelunker

A *spelunker* is a cave explorer, more correctly called a *speleologist,* from the name of the science of cave exploration, "speleology." Though *spelunker* has a disarmingly casual air about it—with more than a hint of an echo of "dunking"—it can trace its origin back more than two thousand years to the Latin word for "cave," *spelunca. Spelunkers* are becoming more numerous these days as people learn the fascinations of exploring underground. See also SPELEOLOGIST.

spencer jacket

The short wool jacket known as the *spencer* and designed for wear by either men or women was first created by the second Earl of Spencer, whose chief claim to fame in his lifetime was the fact that he, as First Lord of the Admiralty, chose Horatio Nelson to command the fleet in the Mediterranean.

spick-and-span

This is a shortened form of *spick-and-span-new,* a term originally used in the shipbuilding trade. A *spik* was a "spike" and a *span* was a "chip or shaving." Thus anything *spik-and-span-new* would be sparkling new.

As an example of how fashions in language change, note that Dr. Samuel Johnson entered this term very reluctantly in his dictionary (1755) for he felt that it was one that he "should not have expected to have found authorized by a polite writer." Although he had to admit that writers as distinguished as Dean Swift and Samuel Butler had used it, Dr. Sam still growled that *"spick-and-span* is, however, a low word."

spitting image

There is no agreement between linguistic experts on whether the *spit* in *spitting image* comes from the same root (the Anglo-Saxon *spittan*) as the common word meaning to eject from the mouth. One authority, claiming the phrase means a "speaking likeness," quotes a source as far back as 1602 in support of his case that the two words are the same.

I incline to favor the explanation given by my good friend Harold Wentworth in the *American Dialect Dictionary*. He observes that the phrase "He's the very *spit* of his father" is widely heard in the South and suggests that *spit* in this sense is probably derived from "spirit," noting that the Negro pronunciation of the letter *r* is often indistinct. In other words, the phrase originally was "He's the very spirit and image of his father."

split the ticket. *See* political language.

spoils of war

The earliest kind of *spoil* (in its Latin form *spolium*) was the hide stripped from an animal. Later *spoils* came to mean any kind of plunder or booty, especially arms surrendered by a conquered enemy, the *spoils of war*. The idea of *spoil* meaning to damage a thing so that it becomes virtually useless developed centuries later, obviously from the fact that the stripped carcass of an animal is worthless.

sponge, throw in the

This phrase, meaning "to surrender or give up the struggle," is from the vernacular of the prize ring. When a boxer is so badly beaten that he is on the verge of a knockout, his manager or second will sometimes literally *throw in the sponge* as a signal to the referee that the fracas should be ended.

spoof

The word *spoof* was created by a British comedian Arthur Roberts as the name of a game he invented about 1890. The invention which earned him a footnote in the dictionaries seems to have been a card game blended, as one might expect of a comedian's creation, with elements of pretense and humor. In the words of the *Oxford Dictionary, "Spoof* is a game of hoaxing and nonsensical character—a round game of cards in which certain cards when appearing together are termed *spoof.*"

There seems little evidence that this game which delighted our Victorian forebears and contributed such a charming word to the language is still much played.

spoon, by the great horned

The earliest known appearance of *by the great horned spoon*—an imprecation about as powerful as "Great Caesar's ghost!"—is in a song popular around 1840. Spoons were, of course, made from the horns of cattle in centuries past, just as the original shoehorns were.

But just how any horn spoon became "great" is the point that has puzzled researchers. One ingenious scholar suggests that the phrase is really a translation of *gros cornes* (great horns), which was the name given to Rocky Mountain bighorn sheep by the early explorers. And Francis Parkman, great historian of the opening of the West, noted that Indians made spoons capable of holding more than a quart from the horns of these sheep. So perhaps this theory of the origin of this frontier expression is not so farfetched after all.

spoonerism

The transposition of initial sounds, making "one swell foop" out of "one fell swoop" is called a *spoonerism* after the late William A. Spooner of Oxford, who made many of them in his time. One of his most celebrated *spoonerisms* came at the close of a wedding ceremony at which he officiated. Noticing that the groom was so nervous that he had overlooked an important part of the ceremony, the minister told him, "Son, it is kisstomery to cuss the bride."

These hilarious transpositions have been called *spoonerisms* ever since the memorable Sunday some seventy-five years ago when he approached one of his parishioners with this query: "Marden me, padam, aren't you occupewing the wrong pie?"

The good doctor also once chided one of his pupils for having "hissed my mystery lecture" and on another occasion startled clergy and laity alike by announcing that the next hymn would be "When Kinquering Congs Their Titles Take."

Spooner lived to the ripe old age of eighty-six, though quite a few of his auditors would not have gambled much on his life expectancy when, at the height of Queen Victoria's reign, he referred to "our dear old queen" as "our queer old dean"!

Incidentally, Spooner was not, of course, the first victim of these accidental slips of the tongue which now bear his name. The grammarians had a name for them long before Spooner was born. In the turgid lexicon of grammatical terms, this was known as "metathesis," derived from the Greek word meaning "to place differently," and it described any form of transposition of syllables or letters of words whether the effect was humorous or not.

sprouts, course of. *See* course of sprouts.

squalid

Squalid (pronounced SKWOL-id) pertains to that which is filthy, foul, wretched and unkempt and is used most commonly to describe dwellings and environment. From the Latin *squalere* (to be foul or filthy), the condition it describes is *squalor*. For example, "The *squalor* in which the Tobacco Roaders lived reflected the force of a poverty that had made them cease to care."

square. *See* jazzmen's jargon.

squash. *See* succotash.

squaw

Here's an interesting problem raised by a reader of my column: "I am a member of a discussion group and at the next meeting I plan to present the word *squaw*—the Indian name for woman. Originally I came here from the Middle West where the word was commonly used, especially among the underprivileged or less-educated. I regard it as derogatory, like certain other racial labels. Would I be correct in labeling it 'substandard'?"

While it's true that the word *squaw* is often used humorously as a synonym for "wife," I see in it none of the deliberately derogatory implications to be found in such racial epithets as *mick* and *wop*. *Squaw* is taken direct from the Algonquian Indian dialect and means any Indian woman or wife. I should label it perfectly good Standard American.

Incidentally, our twelve-year-old has been regaling her classmates with her current favorite anecdote about a squaw whose husband was a great Indian chief, Shortcake. When he died, the medicine men were setting about the ritual of burial when the widow appeared on the scene, insisting in no uncertain terms that she would take charge of the service. As she put it: "Squaw bury Shortcake."

squawk

Lewis Carroll, creator of *Alice in Wonderland,* gave to the English language many new words, each a blend of the sounds and the meanings of two words. Among these was *squawk*. See BLEND WORDS.

SS Corps

The SS were the *Schutzstaffel*, "Black Shirts," the elite corps of the Nazi Army, so named because they wore black shirts as part of their uniforms.

stamp collecting. *See* philatelic jargon.

stand. *See* political language.

starboard and larboard

For centuries these two terms were used to indicate the right and left sides of a boat, facing the bow. The *starboard* term—still very much in use —has nothing whatever to do with the stars. Rather it comes from the fact that an oarsman sculling and steering a small boat usually stood on the right side near the stern. *Star* in this instance, then, comes from the Anglo-Saxon word *steor,* meaning "to steer." *Larboard* came from the Anglo-Saxon *leere* "empty," referring to the fact that the steersman was not there. Because of the similarity of sounds in *starboard* and *larboard*—which some thought led to serious collisions—*larboard* is now obsolete and has been entirely supplanted by "port."

stash

Meaning to hide something away for future use, *stash* is probably a corruption of *cache* (pronounced KASH), which comes from the French *cacher,* "to hide away or conceal." It has been traced back to the mid-1920's and was widely used in the Midwest during the 1930's. Originally underworld, or at best hobo, jargon, it came into general use through its popularity among jazz musicians. At least two current dictionaries enter *stash,* though both label it "slang."

steal one's thunder

This phrase *steal my thunder,* meaning to appropriate for one's own use something created by another person, has been traced back to John Dennis, a playwright in Restoration England. It seems Mr. Dennis was a better sound-effects man than dramatist for the most impressive thing about his production of *Appius and Virginia* was a new method of creating realistic-sounding thunder. A few weeks after his play closed, Dennis attended a performance of *Macbeth* at a rival theater. As the curtain rose on the Witches' Scene, he heard thunder remarkably similar to the effects he himself had originally devised. Clapping his hand to his forehead, he cried: "See how the rascals use me. They will not let my play run—yet they *steal my thunder!*"

stenophobia

A morbid fear of narrow places or things is *stenophobia,* made from the Greek *stenos* (narrow) and *phobos* (fear).

Stetson

Stetson or *John B.* (both from the John B. Stetson hat manufacturing company) are the accepted terms for the cowpuncher's ten-gallon hat among working cowboys.

stevedore. *See* longshoreman.

sticks, in the

The phrase was originally used in the latter part of the nineteenth century by loggers to designate timberlands. Gradually it has come to mean any rural district, especially, but not necessarily, a backwoods area.

still, small voice

A *still, small voice* is a phrase from the Bible (I Kings 19:12): "And after the earthquake a fire; but the Lord was not in the fire; and after the fire a *still small voice.*" As to how a voice can be still and yet be heard —for the Lord, anything is possible.

stirrup cup

A phrase which Sir Harry Lauder often used is "wee doch an' dorris" —meaning a small *stirrup-cup* or "one for the road." A *stirrup cup* was literally a drink given a guest as he sat, feet in stirrups, on the horse which, quite unlike the mechanical monsters that are today's automobiles, could be counted on to bear him safely home, *stirrup cup* or no *stirrup cup*.

stoned, to get

To get stoned is show business slang for "to get drunk." For some reason this particular human activity calls forth all the creative talents of our popular wordsmiths. Berry and Van den Bark in their excellent *American Thesaurus of Slang* list more than nine hundred synonyms for "intoxicated"—and they haven't caught up with *stoned* yet.

Stoner, Lucy. *See* Lucy Stoner.

stooge

One of the phenomenons of the television and night club circuit is the amazing popularity of a comedy trio known as the Three Stooges. No newcomers in show business, they had been playing to steadily diminishing audiences, had been dropped by the studio which made their movie shorts and seemed just about ready for retirement. Then, with the appearance of some of their old films on TV, their popularity soared—and the word *stooge* became once again a household word.

"Where did *stooge* come from?" is the question asked by a number of readers—and the answer isn't easy because this is one word so new to the popular tongue that dictionary editors haven't yet come up with any final theories about its origin.

But, though *stooge* is a recent addition to our general language, it has been part of show business talk for at least half a century and, in the opinion of *Variety*'s Frank Scully may go all the way back to Shakespeare's day.

One of the most famous *stooges* of this century was Dave Chasen, now an eminent Hollywood restaurateur, who served as foil for the late and beloved Joe Cook. Accordionist Phil Baker also employed a *stooge* who heckled him from a balcony box. And, of course, Jack Benny has used many *stooges,* of whom the most notable surely is Rochester, his butler.

Thus a *stooge*—which probably originated as a variation of "student" —first meant a person who serves as foil for a comedian. Now, in general speech, it means any underling, especially an assistant held in low regard by the boss.

But, as Moe Howard of the Three Stooges notes with pardonable pride, "The *stooge* may be the low man on the totem pole, but without him there is nothing to hold up the pole."

strain at a gnat, and swallow a camel

This refers to the often prevalent custom of becoming greatly exercised over minor sins but overlooking really major offenses. It comes from the Bible (Matthew 23:24) when Jesus, rebuking the scribes and Pharisees for their hypocrisy, says: "Ye blind guides, which *strain at a gnat, and swallow a camel.*"

strangler. *See* automobile slang, British.

stump, to

This particular use of the word *stump* in "take to the *stump*" and "*stump* the district" dates back to the earliest days of our nation. Specifically, the first recorded use of the word is in the *Memoirs of a Huguenot Family* by Ann Maury and the story it tells occurred in 1716. "I went down to the Saponey Indian town," runs the narrative. "There is in the center of the circle a great stump of a tree. I asked the reason they left it standing, and they informed me that it was for one of their head men to stand upon when he had anything of consequence to relate to them, so that being raised, he might the better be heard."

The tradition, then, dates back to an Indian custom, but it was one quickly adopted by the politicians among the colonists. As early as 1775 a popular patriotic song referred to the father of our country in these words:

> Upon a stump he placed himself,
> Great Washington, did he.

Campaigners for political preferment have been placing themselves upon stumps ever since, though today's stump usually is accoutered with lectern, bunting and the inevitable microphones and loudspeakers and, sometimes, TV cameras.

stump liquor. *See* mountain dew.

sturm und drang

A German phrase meaning "storm and stress." It was first applied to the cultural awakening of Germany under the inspiration of Goethe late in the eighteenth century; it has been called the early phase of German romanticism.

suasion, persuasion, dissuasion

Suasion (pronounced SWAY-zh'n) is the act of persuasion or convincing. *Suasion, persuasion* and *dissuasion* all stem from the Latin verb *suadere* (to persuade). Unlike the other two words, however, *suasion* has no verb form but becomes *suasive* as an adjective and *suasively* as an adverb. Like *persuasion,* it means convincing someone to do something he would not otherwise do; *dissuasion* is convincing him that he should not do what he intended.

subordination

Subordination comes from the Latin word *subordinaire* which means "to order under"—hence, to put a person under the power of another person or group. See also SUBORNATION.

subornation

Subornation comes from *sub* (under) plus *ornare* (to furnish) and means "to supply or incite secretly." Thus the meaning of inducing a person to perform an illegal act by bribing him has been implicit in the word *subornation* since its earliest use in the courts and temples of ancient Rome.

sub rosa. *See* under the rose.

succotash

Succotash is the way the early Pilgrim settlers approximated the Narragansett Indian word *misickquatash*. The word originally meant "ear of corn" but in time came to mean the succulent dish, corn and beans cooked together, that we know today. Similarly, our earliest American forebears took the Algonquian Indian word *askutasquash* and converted it into plain, everyday *squash.*

sudarium, sudary

Both words come, of course, from the Latin verb *sudare* (to sweat). They are pronounced, respectively, soo-DAIR-ee-um and soo-duh-ree.

Nowadays these words are seldom encountered outside religious commentaries, since they are now used chiefly to describe the cloth given to Christ by St. Veronica on his way to the Crucifixion. According to tradition, His features were miraculously impressed upon the handkerchief—or *sudarium.*

Incidentally, St. Veronica's name is a blend of two Latin words *verus* (true) and *iconicus* (image). The name was taken by the saint to indicate her faith that the cloth, which is one of the relics preserved at St. Peter's, Rome, is the "true image" of Christ's face.

sundae

The origin of the word *sundae,* according to H. L. Mencken, who devotes several pages of *The American Language* to the topic, belongs to the town of Two Rivers, Wisconsin. Here, in the early 1890's, was located an ice cream parlor run by E. C. Berners. One evening a customer named Hallauer was being served a portion of vanilla ice cream when he suggested that the proprietor pour over it some chocolate syrup ordinarily used in the making of sodas. Berners protested that the syrup would ruin the taste of the ice cream, but his customer insisted and thus the dish was born.

It didn't, however, acquire its name at once. That developed in nearby Manitowoc where George Giffy ran an ice cream parlor. Since he charged extra for the ice cream with syrup, he regarded it as a special item and sold it only on Sundays. One weekday a little girl demanded a dish of the new concoction. "I sell it only on Sundays," said Giffy. "Then this must be Sunday," replied the girl, "because that's the kind of ice cream I want." Thus inspired, Giffy decided to name the concoction a *Sunday.* Just how the spelling came to be changed to *sundae* is not known. Presumably the reasons were two: to avoid confusion with "Sunday," the day of the week, and to add a touch of elegance to the word.

sun field. *See* baseball jargon.

sui generis

One of a kind, with a unique character. The Latin phrase, meaning literally "of its own kind," is usually rendered in English as soo-eye-JEN-er-is.

supercilious

Highfalutin, hoity-toity, condescending, disdainful, contemptuous and arrogant—all these are synonyms for *supercilious,* which, in its literal Latin derivation, means "with lifted eyebrow." It comes from *super* (over) and *cilium* (eyelid or brow).

supplicatory, supplicate, supplication, supplicant

Supplicatory (pronounced sup-lih-kuh-tor-ee) is the adjective form of the verb *supplicate* which means "to implore, beseech or entreat; to request in a humble and earnest manner." It comes from the Latin verb *supplicare* (to kneel down, to pray) which in turn is made up of *sub* (under) and *plicare* (to fold). All forms of the word *supplicate* retain the accent on the first syllable except *supplication* (sup-lik-KAY-shun). A *supplicant* is one who humbly and earnestly seeks.

suspenders

Suspenders, in Britain, is the proper term for what we call *garters.* In turn, *braces* is the British term for what we call *suspenders.* See ENGLISH ENGLISH.

supposititious

Derived from the Latin *suppositicius*—"something that has been substituted"—our word may mean either "hypothetical" or, more commonly, "spurious" or "substituted with intent to defraud."

It's a word not commonly met with outside of legal briefs, perhaps, but it's calculated to make quite an impression on family and friends if you toss it trippingly from the tongue in the course of casual conversation. Better practice up on it first, though. It's pronounced suh-poz-uh-TISH-us.

sutler

Sutlers since the time of Queen Elizabeth have been merchants who followed armies, selling food and liquor to the soldiers. That they were not an especially admirable group is indicated by the origin of their name which comes from the Dutch *soetaler,* "one who performs menial or dirty work."

swallow doesn't make a summer, one

The meaning of this phrase is simply that you mustn't think all your troubles are over simply because things have begun to improve. It originated with Aristotle, whose version was only slightly different from the one we use today: "One swallow doesn't make a spring."

swan song

The legend that every swan sings one glorious song just before death is about as old as recorded legend goeth. The fact of the matter is, of course, that a swan doesn't sing ever. But a romantic legend dies hard, especially when poets such as Shakespeare, Coleridge and Spenser hymn it in verse. Nowadays we often refer to the last great work of a creative artist, be he poet, writer, painter or musician, as his *swan song.*

swashbuckler

A *swashbuckler* today means a swaggering, romantic doer of deeds of daring. In American movies the two Douglas Fairbankses, Errol Flynn and Tyrone Power specialized in the type of role called *swashbuckling*.

Originally the word came from *swash* (to dash against) and *buckler* (shield). It referred to the swordsmen's practice of tapping their shields before attacking. As long ago as Shakespeare's time, though, *swashbucklers* had a bad reputation. John Florio in 1598 defined them as "braves that for money and good cheer will follow any man to defend him; but if any danger come, they run away the first and leave him in the lurch."

switch hitter. *See* baseball jargon.

swoop, one fell

One fell swoop simply means one fierce, sudden onslaught, of the kind a hawk might make when swooping down on a defenseless small animal. *Fell* is a word rarely met outside of this particular phrase. It has no connection with "fall," by the way. This *fell* comes from the Anglo-Saxon word *fel,* from which we also get *felon,* a person guilty of a major crime.

sword of Damocles

A peril or danger hanging over one. The reference is to the legend that Damocles, a courtier of ancient Syracuse, used to try to curry favor with his king by talking about the wondrous ease of the kingly life. In order to teach him the lesson that perils and responsibilities also accompany the privileges of kingship, King Dionysius invited him to a banquet where he was seated under a sword hanging by a single thread. Damocles was so distraught with his peril that he could not enjoy any of the sumptuous repast set before him.

syzygy

Syzygy (pronounced sɪz-uh-jee) is a term used in several sciences but most commonly in astronomy to indicate the precise conjunction or opposition of two heavenly bodies.

T

table, under the. *See* **drunk as a lord.**

tacks, brass. *See* **brass tacks.**

tailgating

A word relatively new to the vocabulary of the average motorist is *tailgating,* to describe the practice of one car's following too closely behind another, especially when traveling at a high rate of speed. A survey of highway traffic in North Carolina indicated that this practice is fairly common among drivers of interstate trailer trucks who deliberately crowd as close as possible to passenger cars on a downgrade, forcing the passenger car driver to accelerate beyond the speed limit to maintain a safe distance.

The trailer truck driver does this for two reasons. First, if anyone is stopped for speeding, chances are it will be the fellow in the passenger car. Second, the truck driver, by getting well above the maximum permissible speed for trucks, will reduce his chances of having to downshift on the next grade. From the standpoint of the hapless motorist, it's a vicious practice.

The Motor Vehicle Bureau of New York State, which has a law prohibiting *tailgating,* was called on to define the "reasonable and prudent" distance ordered by the law. The Bureau's advice is to allow one car length's distance for each ten miles an hour of your driving speed. Thus if you're traveling thirty miles per hour, you should be three car lengths behind the car ahead; fifty miles, five car lengths, and so on.

If all motorists would observe this rule, the word *tailgating,* so newly added to the lexicon of motoring, would quickly drop into oblivion.

take down a peg, to

The term comes from British Navy jargon of the eighteenth century. In those days a ship's colors were raised by a system of pegs; the higher the peg, the higher the honor. Conversely, if the flag was lowered a peg, the honor conferred was correspondingly reduced. So *to take him down a peg* meant to reduce the honor or esteem in which a person is held—even by himself.

take, on the. *See* payola.

take to the stump. *See* stump.

talk turkey

Chances are you have used this phrase all your life to mean "talk serious business." Yet the odds are equally good that you don't know the rather charming story behind this expression.

Back in early Colonial days a white hunter and a friendly Indian made a pact before they started out for the day's hunt. Whatever they bagged was to be divided equally between them. At the end of the day the white man undertook to divide the spoils, three crows and two turkeys.

He first handed a crow to the Indian, then gave a turkey to himself; then another crow to the Indian and the second turkey to himself. At this point, the noble redskin complained, "You *talk all turkey* for you. Only talk crow for Indian."

tanbark

Tanbark is simply the bark of trees—usually oak trees—which is rich in tannin, a substance used in tanning hides into leather. After the bark has been used for this purpose, it is used to provide ground covering for circuses.

tar

There's certainly nothing very glamorous about *tar* as a name for a sailor, for it's only a shortened form of "tarpaulin," a tar-impregnated cloth. In Lord Nelson's time sailors wore broad-brimmed hats made of this material. First the hats, then the sailors, were called "tarpaulins"—which gradually was shortened to *tars*.

tarantella

This Italian dance may loosely be said to have been named after the poisonous spider called "tarantula." Actually, this is an oversimplification, what is called a "folk etymology."

During the fifteenth and sixteenth centuries, Southern Europe and especially Italy were the scenes of dreadful epidemics of a disease called *tarantism,* named after the town of Taranto, Italy, where the first epidemics occurred. *Tarantism* was a nervous disease characterized by extreme lethargy at the start and in later stages by a hysterical mania for dancing.

For centuries people believed that this disease resulted from the bite of a poisonous spider which they called "tarantula," also from the name of the town. And, in time, they evolved a lively folk dance which—from its resemblance to the actions of victims of the disease *tarantism*—they called the *tarantella*.

So, while it is not strictly accurate to say that the dance is named after the spider, both derive their names from the common source, Taranto.

tarheel

In the *National Geographic Magazine* the author of an article on North Carolina stated: "North Carolina was nicknamed the '*Tarheel* State' because the long-leaf pine forests of the coastal plains produced such an abundance of rosin, turpentine and tar." This is a fine explanation of the *Tar* element but where does the *heel* come in?

Much study has been given to this question—with no completely satisfactory solution. Apparently the term dates from the Civil War period and was originally a derogatory reference. The earliest account of the origin (1869) records that "A brigade of North Carolinians . . . failed to hold a certain hill, and were laughed at by the Mississippians for having forgotten to *tar* their *heels* that morning."

Before long, though, the epithet was accepted by North Carolinians with no thought to its unhappy origin. In 1864 Governor Zebulon B. Vance, visited some North Carolina troops serving with the Army of Northern Virginia. "I don't know what to call you fellows," he said. "I cannot call you fellow soldiers, because I am not now a soldier, nor fellow citizens because we do not live in this state. So I have concluded to call you 'Fellow *Tarheels*.' "

According to reports, "There was a slight pause before the applause came, and from that time *Tarheel* has been honored as an epithet worthy to be offered to a gallant North Carolina soldier."

Henry L. Mencken, to whose *The American Language* I am indebted for this account, goes on to say: "Whatever the truth of all this, the fact remains that *tarheel* has now lost all its derogatory significance in North Carolina."

taste. *See* jazzmen's jargon.

tattoo, military

A *military tattoo* is an elaborately formal and enormously impressive ceremony involving massed bands and marching by torchlight. It had a more common origin, though, for it started with pub-crawling by British soldiers in the Netherlands around 1700.

In those days of relatively civilized warfare, it was common practice for both armies to withdraw at sundown to previously prepared rest areas. During the early evening hours the soldiers would hie themselves to nearby pubs—with the result that many of them would not hear or would choose to ignore the 9:30 P.M. summons back to camp (First Post). So searching parties, bearing torches, were sent out to round up the stragglers. Dutch barkeeps seeing the torchlights would call: "Tap toe"—meaning "Shut the bar" or "Turn off the taps."

In time, "tap toe" became *tattoo* and the ceremony became a formalized spectacle, in considerable contrast to the pub-crawling of the original *tattoos*.

teachers college. *See* normal school.

Teddy Boy. *See* Borstal Boy.

teleran

This is an electronic device for transmitting pilot charts and other navigation data by television to planes in flight. *Teleran* (pronounced TEL-uh-ran) is made up from the first two syllables of Television plus the first letters of Radar, Air and Navigation.

television language

Some of the more advanced of the TV directors have learned the lesson that Lewis Milestone projected brilliantly in the final scenes of the early talking picture, *All Quiet on the Western Front*. The lesson simply is that in a "sound" medium like the talkies and TV, dramatic tension can sometimes be greatly heightened by playing a scene in complete silence. Today, when a TV director calls for a soundless scene, it's labeled on the script *MOS*—short for "mitout-sound."

Television's cameramen, likewise, have their own special lingo. For instance, there are *BCU's, MCU's* and *pocket shots. BCU's* are "big close-ups"—those shots which show an actor, usually under the stress of great emotion, in a picture so greatly magnified that only his face shows. An *MCU* is a "medium close-up" showing the actor plus some background, and the *pocket shot* falls somewhere between the *BCU* and the *MCU*. It usually shows a male actor from the breast or handkerchief pocket upward.

There is also a trade term for that stage in every program when the star, seemingly overcome with regret at leaving your living room, starts his spiel about "Now we're going to have to say so long. . . ." That's the *bye-bye* in TV parlance.

Next comes that interminable list of credits to cast, director, costumer, makeup man and even, occasionally, the writer. This listing, appropriately enough, is called the *play off*.

Kinescope is a filmed recording of a television show. In the trade it is generally shortened to *kine* and pronounced kinny. For a long time, though, one of the major networks had a standing rule that the word *Kinescope* must not be used by any of the network personnel. The reason? Well, Kinescope is a trade-mark owned by an affiliate of another major network. So all of Network One's employees had to use the phrase "television recordings," which they quickly shortened to *TVR's*. The living language has never been any respecter of dictators, though, and at last report the banned word was being rather freely used in all network studios.

A *wipe* is, in the words of *Sponsor Magazine*'s interesting new *Television Dictionary:* "a transition from one scene or image to another in which a new scene slowly replaces the old one in some gradually increasing geometric pattern, such as a circle, square, fan or roll wipe. In a horizontal wipe the action is from the side of the picture. In a fan wipe it is semi-circular." And a *push-over wipe?* Well, that's just a more graphic term for horizontal wipe.

When a director wants a group of extras to "talk it up," make noise suggestive of a crowd, he calls for "*Wallawalla.*"

And then there is the one menace all sound men must be alert for—the pair of bit players who, all unaware, are carrying on trivial conversation within range of an open mike. Their crime—and a grievous one it is—is called *quonking*.

And that, as the conductor says when he signals for the end of the musical portion of a TV program, *puts a button on it*.

tell it to the Marines. *See* **Marines, tell it to the.**

temporize

Temporize (pronounced TEM-per-yze) is to compromise or seem to yield but always with thought of the time element involved. Derived from the Latin *tempus* (time), it may mean to avoid action at the given moment, to stall for time, to procrastinate, or to suit action to the time and place. It is easy to see its kinship to the word *temporary;* however, the noun form of *temporize* is *temporization* and that of *temporary* is *temporariness*.

Tenderloin, the

A now almost forgotten district of Manhattan, extending from Madison Square (Twenty-third Street) to Longacre Square (Forty-second Street), the *Tenderloin* in the 1880's was the "wide-open" section of the big town.

Indeed, some authorities say that every other building in the *Tenderloin* was devoted to vice of one form or another.

Gambling was rife and the graft—what we now would call *payola*—was very substantial. So one police captain, being transferred there from a Wall Street precinct, remarked in eager anticipation: "I've had nothing but chuck for a long time but now I'm going to get some *tenderloin*." And thus the district got its name.

The character of the district has completely changed in the past half-century, of course. Where once were saloons and gambling dens, now stand modern department stores, business office buildings and an occasional theater or hotel. Now the *Tenderloin* name is now known only to antiquarians and musical comedy devotees.

Another New York district name which even today has about it the air of disrepute that was associated with *Tenderloin* in its heyday is *The Bowery*. Now known chiefly as the final refuge of drunken riffraff, it was once the sunniest, healthiest part of the city. Indeed, its name came from the Dutch word for "farm" (*bouwerij*) and in the early days of New Amsterdam the *bowery* was a place of open fields, grazing cattle and frolicking, happy-faced children.

tenterhooks

A *tenter* is a framework on which newly woven cloth is stretched, and a *tenterhook* is one of the hooks on the frame which holds the material taut. Thus, a person *on tenterhooks* is in a state of great tension or suspense. His anxiety or curiosity is "stretched" to the utmost.

tenuous, tenuity, tenuousness

Tenuous (pronounced TEN-yoo-us) is from the Latin *tenuis* (thin) and can be used to mean thin in either a physical or figurative sense. In the physical sense it is applied to a thing slender and delicate, like a strand of a spider's web. More generally, though, it is used in such statements as "His was a very *tenuous* argument," in that it had no substance, was flimsy. *Tenuity* or *tenuousness* is the state or quality of being *tenuous*.

Texas leaguer. *See* baseball jargon.

thin red line of heroes

In the poem "Tommy," Kipling's hero says: "We aren't no *thin red 'eroes*"—but that was not the first version of this famous line. In reporting the Battle of Balaclava for the London *Times,* W. H. Russell, the greatest war correspondent of his era, wrote: "The Russians dashed on towards that *thin red-line* streak tipped with a line of steel."

30

In many newspaper offices the symbol *30* is used to mark the end of a piece of copy. There are several theories of the origin of the symbol. The most common is that *30* was simply taken over from the slang of old-time telegraph operators who used that symbol to indicate the end of a day's or night's transmission. As one old-timer wrote: "*30* meant 'Good Night (GN), we are closing up the office and going home.' Another numerical sign that is still used by the telegraphic fraternity is 73. Its accepted meaning is 'Best regards and God bless you.' "

A typesetter disagrees with this theory, however, as witness this comment from Patrick Driscoll of Alexandria, Virginia: "May I suggest that the origin of the term *30* as a symbol at the end of newspaper copy is not, as stated in your column recently, from telegraphy but of more ancient lineage. The maximum line or length of slug on such composing machines as Linotype or Intertype is 30 picas, approximately 5 inches. When the operator reaches 30 picas, he has gone as far as he can.

"The close association of journalists and printers has carried over into their terminology. I trust an old 'iron printer's' background will be of some use to you and your readers."

However that may be, some of the romance seems to have gone out of telegraphy, for today's wireless operator when ending a transmission uses the symbol *SK* (dit-dit-dit-dah-dit-dah), which is utterly and absolutely meaningless. See also SK TO O.K.

Thomas, doubting. *See* **doubting Thomas.**

threads, set of. *See* **jazzmen's jargon.**

three cheers. *See* **Old Army slang.**

three sheets in the wind. *See* **sheets in the wind, three.**

thruway

Many communities and the homes in them have been affected by the building of vast *thruways*—modern versions of the King's Highway. Where did this new word come from? Well, its origin is attributed to the original sponsor of the bill which authorized the recently completed New York Thruway.

The story goes that State Assemblyman Abbot Low Moffat and his wife were out for a Sunday drive along one of New York's parkways and fell to discussing the name "parkway" as applied to the network of roads leading out of the city. Mr. Moffat objected to the name, feeling that it no longer suited roads which, originally intended for leisurely pleasure driving, had now become clogged with fast-moving through traffic.

Searching for a name for the new superhighways he was to propose to the State Legislature, he sought one which would express the primary function of the road—a two-way express artery uninterrupted by grade crossings. At that time (more than a score of years ago) the Queen Elizabeth Way, a four-lane limited-access highway, had just been opened in Canada.

Mr. Moffat took *thoroughfare,* modified it to *throughway,* shortened that to *thruway* and had his name for the new highways.

thug, thuggee

Thug, which, because of its brief and ugly sound, would seem to many readers to be American underworld slang, actually comes from the Hindustani.

The East Indian *thags* or *thugs* were not very different from their latter-day counterparts, though they cloaked their violence and thievery in the guise of religious fanaticism. Members of a sect honoring the goddess Kali, they would follow lone and wealthy travelers, waiting their chance to strangle and rob them.

Theoretically a portion of the loot was assigned to devotion of the goddess—but in time the procedure came to bear all the earmarks of a modern underworld "syndicate" operation.

Another word, seldom used in America though fairly common in England, coming from this same sect, is *thuggee,* meaning the crime of strangulation—favorite method of the Indian *thugs.*

Nearly a century ago the sect was wiped out—but not before contributing to the language a word which, perhaps because of its admirable conciseness, is in daily use by headline writers on newspapers the country over.

tick, on

On tick is British slang for "on credit." Originally when a person took on a credit obligation he signed a contract known as a "ticket." In time this was shortened to *tick* and today in England as well as in America countless families are "living *on tick.*"

t.i.d. *See* b.i.d.

timbromania

Timbromania is another name for "philately"—stamp collecting. This hobby is barely more than a hundred years old and when it first started, no one quite knew what to call it. Just "stamp collecting" sounded too matter-of-fact. So a variety of high-sounding names were proposed, including *timbromania* and *timbrophily,* both based on the French word for "stamp," *timbre.* Neither one caught on, though, and throughout the English-speaking world the name for this engrossing pastime today is philately.

tinhorn gambler, tinhorn sport

The question of the origin of these phrases is one that has engaged the attention of many erudite dictionary editors. You see, the terms *tinhorn gambler* and *tinhorn sport* are so much a part of our language that they have to appear in any reasonably comprehensive dictionary and some account of their origin must be given.

Most of the word books content themselves with saying that the phrases get their meaning from "the flashy appearance and cheap quality of tinhorns." Since a *tinhorn sport* is a pretentious fraud and an actual tin horn is a cheap imitation of the real thing, there is a certain plausibility to this theory of the term's origin.

But why, when hundreds of items were made of tin in order to pass for gold, should the *horn* have been the only one immortalized in our language? Well, George Willison, the Pulitzer Prize-winning historian, found the answer to that when he reported on the gambling ethics of the early West in his book *Here They Found Gold.* "Chuck-a-luck operators," reports Willison, "shake their dice in a small churn-like affair of metal—hence the expression 'tinhorn gambler,' for the game is rather looked down on as one for 'chubbers' and chuck-a-luck gamblers are never admitted within the aristocratic circle of faro-dealers." It follows that a *tinhorn sport,* pretty obviously, would be one who patronized the *tinhorn gamblers.*

tinker's dam (damn)

This expression is used to refer to something utterly without value. There are two theories about its origin. The first is that tinkers were itinerant menders of pots and pans who were generally held in low repute. Their speech was often profane—so it follows that a tinker would utter *damn* so frequently that it finally became meaningless. The other theory is that the word is actually *dam* and refers to a tiny pellet of bread used by old-time tinkers to keep patching solder from running through the holes in pans being mended. When the patch was completed, the *dam* would be thrown away and hence was shown to be something utterly without value.

tipping

Most dictionaries dodge behind the label "uncertain" as far as this common word is concerned. A popular theory is that it is made from the first letters of the signs TO INSURE PROMPTNESS posted on coin boxes of tables in the coffeehouses of Dr. Johnson's day. This is one of those derivations that is just a bit too pat to be believable. More probably *tip* is a corruption of *stipend,* a small payment of money, from the Latin word *stips,* meaning "gift."

toady, to

Toadying means being unnecessarily flattering and obsequious. The verb *to toady* originally was "to toadeat" and refers to a custom common among traveling medicine men of a century or more ago. In those days the toad was popularly considered violently poisonous. So the mountebank would set up his pitch, displaying an obsequious assistant—usually a half-witted boy—who would swallow or pretend to swallow a toad. The medicine man then would purge the lad with some of his nostrums and, on the strength of this dramatic "cure," peddle his wares.

toast, toastmaster

One of the pleasanter and more civilized of our customs is *toasting* the continued good health of a friend. There is nothing new about the practice, for in all likelihood it began in ancient times, long before the Christian era.

In those days the common practice was to pour a bit of the guest's wine into the host's glass and vice versa before either drank. The reason? Simply that few people trusted anyone outside the immediate circle of their family and one way to be sure the host hadn't poisoned your cup was to see to it that he drank some himself.

With the passage of time and, presumably, the growth of goodwill among men, the practice of mixing the wine was abandoned and a ceremonial clicking of glasses took its place. The spoken wish "To your good health!" would logically accompany this ceremonial gesture.

The word *toast* itself seems incongruous these days, although the serving of beverages today is often accompanied by varieties of toasted tidbits. In the time of Shakespeare and before, however, a piece of toasted bread was put in the bottom of the tankard or cup before the ale or wine was poured in. Chroniclers of the period say this was done to "improve the taste," but this scrivener suspects its chief purpose was to clarify the drink by collecting all sediment and impurities at the bottom of the cup. Thus the drink itself became a *toast*.

A person who attained great popularity, so that his health was often toasted, soon became known himself as a *toast*—a usage that survives today in the phrase *toast of the town*.

Logically, also, the man in charge of introducing speakers at festive occasions was usually called upon to say felicitous words *toasting* each new speaker—and thus became known as the *toastmaster*.

Incidentally, though the practice of *toasting* one's fellows is usually associated with alcoholic beverages, members of many temperance groups pledge each other's health with water or, as it's sometimes called, "Adam's Ale."

tomato. *See* love apple.

tomfoolery

Tomfoolery nowadays simply means nonsense, silly behavior. But back in medieval times it was considered great sport to watch the antics of insane people in asylums like Bedlam in London. The nicknames "Tom o' Bedlam" and "Tom Fool" were often used for mate inmates who were favorites of the audience. Over the centuries the word *tomfoolery* evolved, eventually acquiring the relatively innocuous meaning it has today.

tonic. *See* moxie.

top brass

Brass in this phrase originated in the Army and refers to the gold braid on the hats of military officers. Carried over into civilian life, *top brass* refers to top-ranking executives in the business, as well as the military, world. See BRASS.

top mounter

Part of the language of the circus world, a *top mounter* is the man at the peak of a human pyramid. He is also known, logically enough, as *high man*. See CIRCUS JARGON.

trade-marks. *See* brands and trade-marks.

transistor

The *transistor* gets its name from the first syllable of "transfer" and the last two syllables of "resistor." Its function is to control and amplify an electron current in a manner similar to that of a vacuum tube but without the use of a vacuum and with much lower power consumption. However, what makes the transistor the modern miracle of electronic science is its almost infinitesimally minute size. Scarcely any larger than a phonograph needle, it is less than one-thousandth the size of the vacuum tube whose functions it performs. Thus the designer of electronic equipment can produce models far more compact than would have been dreamed possible only a few years ago.

Trojan, works like a

Trojan originally referred to the inhabitants of Troy, the ancient city besieged by the Greeks in their efforts to return their Queen, Helen, who had been abducted by the son of the King of Troy. According to legend, as recorded both in Vergil's *Aeneid* and Homer's *Iliad,* the Trojans were a hard-working, determined, industrious people. Hence: "He worked like a *Trojan.*"

troop of monkeys. *See* clowder, kindle and cowardice.

trousers. *See* pants.

truck farm

Many people share the notion that a *truck farm* is a farm close enough to urban centers that its produce may be transported by truck to the city. However, there is no connection whatever between truck farms and motor transportation. Long before motor trucks were even dreamed of—at least as far back as 1785—the word *truck* was used to mean garden vegetables intended for sale in the markets.

In fact, we have here an excellent example of the confusion that can develop from "homonyms"—words which are identical in spelling and pronunciation but very different in meaning. Often, to unravel the complexities, one has to go back to the root of each word. In this case the *truck* which means a vehicle for transportation of freight comes from the Greek word *trochos,* meaning "wheel." However, *truck,* meaning originally any commodities for sale and, later, garden produce for market, comes from an entirely different root, *troque,* meaning the Old French word for "barter."

So you see, the truck farmer can move his produce by any means of transportation available to him. What marks him off from the general run of farmers is not that he uses trucks but that he specializes in growing vegetables—usually on a relatively small scale.

trumped-up charges

The *trump* in this phrase comes from the same root as the word *trumpet,* in that both owe their origin to the French word *tromper,* which once meant "to play on the trumpet" and now means "to deceive." Gradually—and perhaps by analogy to the card-game use of *trump* (from the French *triomphe*)—the word came to mean "cheat or deceive." Thus *trumped-up charges* are spurious, deceitful charges concocted out of whole cloth.

try out

Trying out, in the sense of extracting oil or fat from a substance by heating it, is not commonly heard these days but actually goes back to the Elizabethans.

Perhaps the commonest use of the term in this country was in the whaling industry. As all readers of *Moby Dick* will recall, great *trying* vats were carried on some of the whaling vessels to reduce whale blubber to valuable and more readily transportable whale oil.

I heard the expression fairly commonly in the New England of a generation ago, on Cape Cod and around Gloucester particularly. No doubt it was as commonplace as *pilot crackers* and *quahogs* to the descendants of early sailing men.

tube, on the. *See* jazzmen's jargon.

tulipomania

Any collector of racial stereotypes can tell you that the Dutch are phlegmatic, unemotional and assuredly not a race given to mass displays of frenzied excitement. But the stereotype—like nearly all such—is far from the truth. A few years ago dispatches from the Netherlands told of the wild frenzy induced in an audience at Amsterdam's hallowed hall of music, the Concertgebouw, when American jazzman Lionel Hampton led his men into his theme song, "Flying Home."

As Hampton remarked after the police forcibly quieted some of the noisiest demonstrators, "There's a big epidemic going on over here for our jazz. They go for our heavy beat. It's just an epidemic. You can't explain it."

More than three centuries ago, however, the Dutch had induced an "epidemic" which swept all over Europe—and contributed a word to our language.

Tulipomania started in the 1630's when the acquisition of beautiful tulips suddenly became a mad passion with Dutchmen. As they bid against each other for the choicest specimens, prices began to soar and speculators all over the continent and in Britain became involved. About 1636, when the rage reached its peak, a single bulb was sold at more than £500— and that, even at the most conservative estimate, would be at least five thousand of today's dollars.

Soon brokers were selling "futures" in tulips and eager investors were buying prodigiously on margin. It couldn't last, of course, and when the market finally broke, disaster was widespread. That was the end of history's only recorded botanical boom and bust.

turkey talk

Guinea fowl with *fenberry sauce* and a choice of *askutasquash* or *misickquatash* sounds like a bizarre menu, doesn't it? Yet the chances are that some or all of these foods appear on your table at least once a year. For these are the original names for the staples of the Thanksgiving Day feast: turkey, cranberry sauce, squash and succotash.

The original settlers did not, of course, bring turkeys with them. They found a wild fowl somewhat similar in appearance to the guinea fowl they had known in England—a fowl that had acquired the common name *turkey* from the fact that it was at one time imported to Europe by way of Turkey. Thus a native American wild fowl acquired the truly exotic and rather inappropriate name of *turkey*.

But the early explorers had already set a pattern of blundering in the application of names to their discoveries. Amerigo Vespucci, the same who gave his name to our country, and Columbus himself were half a world away when they named the natives *Indians,* mistakenly thinking that our continent was Asia and that the inhabitants were natives of India.

So the Pilgrim fathers can be forgiven a goof or two in their choice of names for the viands that grace our tables today. And surely they did us all a favor by shortening *askutasquash* to just plain "squash" and *misickquatash*—both "Indian" names—to "succotash."

And the *fenberry sauce?* Well, the cranberry was known in England as "fenberry." Not until the Dutch settlers came over many years later did the name "cranberry" come into English from their *kranbeere*.

So it seems entirely appropriate that America, long called the "melting pot of nations," should celebrate its most traditional feast with food whose origins span most of the world known at the time America was discovered —from Turkey to India by way of Holland and Great Britain.

turnpike

The pike, in olden days, was a pole, set on a vertical post, so as to bar movement along a road. When the fee was paid, the pike was turned and the traveler passed through and along his way.

Because early toll roads were, as again they are today, the most important highways, the term *turnpike* (often shortened to *pike*) came in time to be applied to any important road. In my youth in New England, for example, the most important highway north of Boston was called the Newburyport Turnpike, though no tolls of any kind were levied on it at that time.

tuxedo

While many of the youth of today are more apt to say "dinner jacket" than *tuxedo,* the word is still in common use. The origin of *tuxedo* is a fairly recent one as word origins go.

Tuxedo Park, about forty miles north of New York City on the west bank of the Hudson River, was a famous and very exclusive residential community late in the nineteenth century. Astors, Goulds, Harrimans and the like were to be found there and lavish were the formal parties they gave. One dandy among the socialites—his name is lost to history—became irked with the awkward tails on his formal full-dress coat and had his tailor run up the first tailless dinner coat. It was an immediate sensation and, because of its greater convenience, soon replaced the tail coat on all but the most formal occasions. The new jacket, which *Harper's Magazine* described in 1894 as a "hybrid garment," quickly became known as the Tuxedo coat and, by the turn of the century, was simply called a *tuxedo.*

Wilfred Funk carried the research a step further and reported that *tuxedo* comes from an Algonquian Indian word *p' tuksit* meaning the "animal with the round foot"—or the wolf.

So, ladies, the next time a tuxedo-clad gay blade exceeds the limits of social propriety, you'll know him for what he is—a wolf in wolf's clothing.

TV's superscientific cure-alls

Have you noticed that practically every cosmetic or medicine advertised on radio and TV is touted as having some supersecret scientific ingredient that makes it infinitely superior to every other similar product? Have your ears become weary of the fantastic claims made for "miracle factors," each of which sounds like something out of a twenty-first-century science-fiction story?

One of the indefatigable researchers for *Variety,* the weekly magazine of show business, came up with a list of these high-sounding, though usually meaningless, secret ingredients. After noting that "the average viewer is floored by the mumbo jumbo of scientific phrases in the sales pitch for deodorants," *Variety* listed the following "technically jargoned gems": Gardol, Estron, Lurex, Lumium, Vionate, Byo-dyne, Liquifix, Purscent, Opaquelon—and about a dozen more.

Well, they all seem pretty silly to these eyes and ears. One wonders whether anyone—any single person—ever bought a product because it was alleged to contain a miracle-working ingredient which no one but the advertiser ever heard of. My guess would be no—but the ad agencies could surely marshal reams of impressive statistics to prove how wrong I am.

Of one thing, though, we may be certain: none of these elaborately fabricated terms will ever be admitted to the pages of the nation's general-use dictionaries. They are all what dictionary editors call "nonce words" —words coined for a single purpose and forgotten as soon as that purpose has been served.

twin bill and twi-night double header. *See* baseball jargon.

U

unabridged dictionary

Taking the word *unabridged* in its most literal sense (without restriction or limit), there can be no such thing as an *unabridged dictionary,* for no single book can possibly list and define the millions of words that make up our common language.

However, as a matter of practical convenience, the label *unabridged* is customarily applied (in the words of Webster) to "the dictionary most complete in its class."

Some years ago the U.S. Bureau of Federal Supply (then called the Procurement Division) set up standards of completeness for dictionaries. Roughly speaking, they state that an *unabridged dictionary* must contain at least 400,000 entries and a "desk" dictionary in the neighborhood of 100,000 entries.

Note that I said "entries," not "words." According to the federal specifications, an "entry" was not only a word and its definitions; an entry could also be an undefined form of a verb (principal parts, for example) or an adverb which needed no definition because its meaning was obvious from the adjective definition preceding it.

And that, dear friends, is why so many dictionaries have long, long lists of undefined "entries" beginning with "un-" or "non-." By counting each one of these tiny-type words, the publishers arrive at those stupendous multi-thousand figures that they proudly proclaim on the book jackets. And it is all quite legal.

Leaving aside the "numbers of entries" game, though, there are now only three American dictionaries which merit the label *unabridged* in the sense used by the general public: the Funk & Wagnalls *New Standard Dictionary,* the Merriam-Webster *New International,* Second Edition, and the Webster's *Third New International*. Of the three, much the best is the Merriam-Webster *New International,* Second Edition.

under the rose

Rather a romantic tale lies behind this expression, which is, incidentally, a direct translation of the Latin phrase *sub rosa*. According to ancient legend, the Greek god of silence, Harpocrates, stumbled upon Venus, the goddess of love, in the course of one of her amorous adventures. Cupid, Venus' son, happened along at an opportune moment and, by making a gift of a rose to Harpocrates, bought his pledge of secrecy.

Since that time, the rose has been the symbol of silence. During the Renaissance and later during the reigns of the pre-Revolutionary kings of France, the rose was a favorite architectural motif and often was sculptured on ceilings of dining and drawing rooms where diplomats gathered. The obvious implication was that matters discussed *under the rose* were considered to be held in confidence.

A phrase often whispered at such diplomatic gatherings was: *Sub vino sub rosa est*—"What one says under the influence of wine is secret." The belated revelations of conversations of some of our topmost representatives —notably at Yalta, Potsdam and Geneva—would seem to indicate that this phrase might well be updated to read: *Sub vodka sub rosa est!*

understander

Not the most spectacular but certainly the sturdiest one in the act, the *understander,* in circus slang, is the one whose shoulders carry the full weight of the acrobatic team. See CIRCUS JARGON.

unusual words

Ten somewhat out-of-the-ordinary words were used as elements in the cover design of the paperback edition of one of my books, *It's Easy to Increase Your Vocabulary*. The words seem to have been chosen because they lie just on the outer fringes of the average vocabulary, representative of words you would like to have in your working vocabulary but may not quite have mastered. Let's look at the ten words.

Ameliorate (pronounced uh-MEEL-yor-ayt)—To make better, to improve. This comes direct from the Latin *ad* (to) and *melior* (better).

Culpable (KUL-puh-b'l)—Blameworthy, deserving of censure. Again, this comes from the Latin: *culpa* (blame).

Equivocate (ih-KWIV-uh-kayt)—To hedge; to use double-talk in an effort to mislead or deceive. Again from the Latin, this word literally means to speak with two voices: *aequi* (equal) and *vocare* (to call). So you see, our idea of "double-talk" is anything but new.

Esoteric (es-oh-TEHR-ik)—Intended for a chosen few, the insiders. This comes from the Greek *esoteros* (inner).

Extirpate (EK-ster-payt)—To root out, destroy completely, from the Latin *ex* (out) and *stirps* (root).

Incipient (in-SIP-ee-unt)—Just beginning to exist, from the Latin *in* (in or on) and *capere* (take).

Inveterate (in-VET-er-it)—Firmly established, deep-rooted. Again this is from Latin: *in* (in) and *vetus* (old).

Jocose (joh-KOHSS)—Humorous, facetious, from the Latin *jocus* (a joke).

Mitigate (MIT-ih-gayt)—Make less severe, from the Latin *mitis* (mild) and *agere* (do).

Reprehensible (rep-rih-HEN-sih-b'l)—Deserving to be censured or rebuked. Again our source is Latin: *re* (back) and *prehendere* (take).

Well, there are ten words that struck my editors as being enough out of the ordinary to be interesting. Whether you agree with them or not, you must agree that this is a striking indication of the debt our English language owes to the classical languages of Greece and Rome.

upcoming, up-and-coming

Upcoming is a journalistic version of "coming up" and indicates futurity. Instead of "The Yankees have two big games coming up," you may find "The Yankees' two big *upcoming* games are with . . ." This kind of verbal shorthand is commonly used in *cablese,* a style of writing notable for its compounded words and often used by newsmen to economize on cable charges for foreign dispatches.

Up-and-coming is a well-established colloquial phrase meaning "enterprising, ambitious and promising." You'll hear it in sentences like: "That new salesman certainly seems to be an *up-and-coming* chap."

U.S.S.

These three letters stand for "United States Ship," and may be used only with the names of ships of the U.S. Navy. The abbreviation S.S. (as in *S.S. America*) means "steamship" and is generally used for ships of all nationalities.

Worth noting, perhaps, is that the initials *H.M.S.* appear only on ships in the British service and stand for His or (as in the current instance) Her Majesty's Service. The initials *M.S.* designate a motor (rather than steam) ship.

V

vagary

Vagary (pronounced vuh-GAIR-ee) like the word *vagabond* is derived from the Latin *vagari* (to wander) and means "a whim or a wild fancy." In earlier use *vagary* still meant "to wander" or "to ramble" but it is no longer used in this way. "Shelley's verse captured many of the fleeting *vagaries* of his fancy-free inspiration."

vamoose

This word came into our language from a source many hundreds of miles away from the habitat of the *moose*. Specifically, it is a word that early Texan cowboys picked up from their Mexican counterparts, the *vaqueros*. The word comes from the Spanish *vamos*, meaning "let's go." Most commonly it was used by cowhands when there was some pressing reason for a hasty departure. Something along the lines of, *"Vamoose, boys, here comes the law!"*

van, in the

This *van* is short for "vanguard," which in turn is the English equivalent of the French term *avant-garde*—the advance guard. It originally meant that part of an army which moved into battle ahead of the main forces. Nowadays it means any person or group of persons that has moved well to the forefront of a mass movement.

vet, to

This rather odd verb has recently enjoyed a vogue among editors and teachers, in such phrases as "credit for *vetting* the manuscript" and "the plans may be *vetted* by your attorney." It is actually nothing more than a verb formed from the noun "veterinarian" and originally meant "to examine or treat as a veterinarian does." More recently it has come to be used—as the dictionaries say, "jocosely"—to mean any careful inspection of a document or manuscript.

I first came upon the word some years ago when the editor of one of our major dictionaries asked me to *vet* a certain portion of a revision of his word book—the section dealing with words new to the language. He was somewhat taken aback when I pointed out that among the new usages he had overlooked was the word he himself had just used—*to vet*.

The word was promptly added to the manuscript and now appears, with the label "colloquial," in the dictionary. But the name of the dictionary and the name of the distinguished editor will remain my secret. We are all fallible—even dictionary editors—and, as Dr. Johnson once remarked: "Dictionaries are like watches; the worst is better than none, and the best cannot be expected to go quite true."

vicissitude

Vicissitude (pronounced vih-SISS-ih-tood) is constantly occurring change, especially in fortune or condition. It is derived from the Latin *vicis* (a turn, change). "Through life's many *vicissitudes,* he never lost his faith in the basic decency of his fellow humans."

victuals, vittles

The word *victuals*—from the Latin *victualia,* meaning "food" or "provisions"—is pronounced VIT-t'ls, which has led to the erroneous spelling *vittles*. In the nineteenth century when the word was much more common in America than it is today, such humorists as Petroleum V. Nasby and Bill Nye used to affect all sorts of deliberate misspellings in an effort to represent what they considered to be the dialects of farmers and frontiersmen. As a result, incidentally, their writings are all but unreadable today.

One of the favorite misspellings of this school of humor was *vittles* for *victuals* and, since the word is rarely seen in print today, some people simply don't know the correct spelling of the word.

videot. *See* kidult.

vituperate

Vituperate (pronounced vy-TOO-per-ayt) is a verb meaning "to berate, to revile, to speak to or about in abusive language." From the Latin *vituperate* (to blame), it has the variant forms *vituperation, vituperative* and *vituperator*. "Bowing his head to the torrent of shrill abuse, he commented only, 'There stands a truly *vituperative* shrew.' "

vol au vent

Vol au vent in French means "flight in the wind." It is a pastry shell made of puff pastry, filled with creamed meat or fish. The name refers, of course, to the pastry. Properly made, it is so light that a puff of wind will make it take flight. But don't order it if you're on a diet.

volt

Three terms, *volt, ampere* and *ohm,* commonly used in electricity are derived from the names of the scientists who first established their functions. *Volt* is from Alessandro Volta, an Italian physicist. *Ampere* was named for André Marie Ampère, a Frenchman. And *ohm* comes from the noted German scientist, G. S. Ohm, who has also achieved a curiously inverted fame through the word *mho.* A *mho* is the electrical unit of conductance—the opposite of *ohm,* the unit of resistance. As you have doubtless noticed, scientists in an unwonted burst of whimsy created the designation for the opposite of *ohm* by reversing letters in that word.

voracious

Voracious (pronounced voh-RAY-shus) is an adjective meaning "greedy, gluttonous or rapacious." It stems from the Latin *vorare* (to devour) and is used not only in reference to eating but in the sense of being insatiable in other matters. The noun form is either *voraciousness* or *voracity;* the adverb, *voraciously.* "After a day of fasting on the march, the scouts fell on the simple meal with *voracious* appetites."

vulgar

Vulgar comes from Latin also, from *vulgus,* "the mob" or "the common people." A word labeled *vulgar* need not be obscene, although all obscene words are *vulgar.* A *vulgarism* is simply a coarse expression, characteristic of the lowest levels of society, culturally speaking.

W

WAC. *See* **acronyms.**

WAE. *See* **WOC.**

War Between the States

Exactly who first used *War Between the States,* meaning the American Civil War, is not known for certain. However, one of the first to give the expression world-wide currency was the British government, which used the term in recognizing a state of "belligerency" in May, 1861. This act was a great disappointment to the Confederate States, which had hoped to be recognized as an independent nation with the probability of overt support from Britain in the struggle.

warden

Among many not especially flattering terms teensters reserve for their elders are *warden,* which applies to parents and teachers, and *prehistoric,* meaning anyone and everyone over twenty-one years old.

warm the cockles of one's heart. *See* cockles of the heart.

warranty, guaranty

Warranty and *guaranty* are known to linguists as "doublets"—words derived from the same original source but traveling to today's English by different routes. Both can be traced to the Old French word *garantie* and thence, via *warant,* to the Old High German *werento,* meaning "protector." The meanings of the two words are today quite similar, but not by any means interchangeable. *Warranty* has several special legal meanings that *guaranty* lacks. Check a reliable dictionary for the various shadings of meaning.

watch of nightingales. *See* clowder, kindle and cowardice.

weather vane

In ancient days, before even such relatively simple meteorological devices as barometers were perfected, wind direction was one of the most important elements in the art of telling the weather in advance.

So the *weathercock,* as the *weather vane* was originally called, has been in standard use for more than eight centuries. Chaucer wrote "as a wedercock that turneth his face with every wind." A usage so well established need not be scoffed at today. *Weathercock* or *weather vane* remains, even if the wind is the only part of the weather that it records.

wee doch an' dorris. *See* stirrup cup.

weeds. *See* widow's weeds.

weigh anchor

To *weigh anchor* merely means to haul it up, so that a ship may sail from the spot where it has been moored. This nautical use of *weigh* can be traced to its early Anglo-Saxon origin in the word *wegan* which meant "to carry, bear or move."

The concept of lifting or balancing objects in the hands to determine their weight came later and represents a somewhat more sophisticated sense of the original word.

Incidentally, this matter of *weighing anchor* has led to confusion among sailors, many of whom use the phrase *under weigh* to indicate that their boats or ships are in motion. This is a variation of "under way," which most authorities regard as the simpler and more correct expression. Indeed, at least one British authority labels *under weigh* a "solecism"—a distinctly substandard use of words.

weird words

Ankh, bleb, crambo, fyke, grigri, hoicks, phat, skua, titi and *xylyl*— weird-looking words, aren't they? Or, you may ask, are they words at all or just scrambled assortments of letters like the puzzle groups set before an anagram player?

Well, they are words all right. Furthermore, each is duly entered in American unabridged dictionaries as a word perfectly correct for use in every-day conversation. Yet I'll wager not one in a thousand has ever seen them before.

What use are they then? Not very much use, in truth—unless you're an avid word-game player. In that case one of these odd words might mean the difference between winning and losing a hotly contested game of Scrabble or Ghosts. These particular words, indeed, were chosen by the authors of *The Scrabble Word Guide* as among the most unusual they had come across in their years of play at that fascinating game.

Let's look at the meanings of these verbal oddities. *Ankh* (which is pronounced like "tank" without the *t*) is an ancient Egyptian symbol of life, a cross with a loop at the top. A *bleb* (and surely you need no help in pronouncing that) is a blister. *Crambo* (to rhyme with "hambo") is a word-rhyming game. There are two kinds of *fyke*. It can mean either a kind of fish trap made of a series of conical nets with open mouths, or fidgetiness.

Grigri sounds like the name of a Polynesian dance; actually it is the name of an African witch doctor's fetish or talisman. *Hoicks* is a variant of the better-known "yoicks"—a call to hounds in fox hunting. *Phat* is a term used in printing. It means "profitable" and is used for advertising or other layouts that have an unusually large proportion of open space or illustrations. It is also, and more logically, spelled "fat."

Skua is a gull-like bird. A *titi* (pronounced TEE-tee) may be either an evergreen shrub or a small South American monkey. And *xylyl* is the univalent radical, not to be confused with "xylylene," the bivalent radical.

What do you make of *rynd, ryot, rotl, rotche, leet, lehr, kudu* and *kibe?*

Rynd, which has nothing to do with skin of citrus or other fruit, is (brace yourself; this will take some time): "an iron fitting supporting an upper millstone, having a central hollow bearing which rests on the upper pointed end of the mill spindle." Just in case you want to drop *rynd* into your lunchtime conversation, it's pronounced either to rhyme with "wind" or "mind." Take your choice.

Ryot looks as though it might mean a sort of upper-class scrimmage, the kind college boys indulge in every spring. But don't be misled. Actually a *ryot* is, in India, a peasant or tiller of the soil.

Rotl—it rhymes with "bottle"—is an Oriental unit of weight. It varies from one to five pounds depending on locality and, perhaps, on the gullibility of the purchaser.

Rotche (pronounced, surprisingly, with a long *o* sound) is the little short-billed auk of the Arctic regions.

A *leet* was, in earlier times, a British court of minor jurisdiction, handling only petty cases. *Lehr* has no connection with the late comedian Lew Lehr. This crossword-puzzle *lehr* is a nearly obsolete word meaning "cheek" or "complexion."

Kudu is a large, striped African antelope, grayish-brown in color, while a *kibe* is a crack in the flesh or a sore on a sheep's foot.

welkin

Welkin, a word now archaic except in the phrase, "making the *welkin* ring," literally means the heavens, the vault of the sky where clouds float, and it comes from the Anglo-Saxon word *wolcen,* meaning "cloud." So, whether you raise Ned, Cain or the roof, you will be making enough noise to make the *welkin* ring—though not, we trust, enough to attract the local constabulary.

Wellingtons. *See* English English.

welsh, to

I'm afraid this expression comes from just where you would expect—from the word "Welshman." Most dictionaries label the word *welsh,* in the sense of cheating on a bet, "origin obscure." But any editor who uses that label is either trying to spare the feelings of the Welsh people or grossly ignorant of a tradition older even than the traditional nursery rhyme: "Taffy was a Welshman; Taffy was a thief." *Taffy,* incidentally, is the generic name for Welshman, a corruption of "David," the patron saint of Wales.

How did *welsh* acquire such a derogatory meaning? Well, the Welshman has shared for centuries with the Scotsman a reputation for being a canny trader, one who may even resort to subterfuge to get the better end of a bargain. This, incidentally, is not an uncommon trait, nor necessarily a bad one. Our own Yankee traders are legendary for trickery and even Abe Lincoln is remembered as one of the canniest horse-traders of his time.

In Britain during the eighteenth and early nineteenth centuries the term *welsher* became common in the argot of racing bettors, to describe a person who made a bet and then reneged on payment. The term was very definitely a derogatory racial label, but it received wide circulation and, eventually, was shortened into the verb form as we know it today: *to welsh*. Welshmen may not be happy about the origin of this word (I am of part-Welsh extraction myself) but it's a fact. And it's the duty of scholarship to deal in facts, not to gloss them over with labels like "origin obscure."

And, after all, the Dutchman is much worse off. See DUTCH COURAGE, DUTCH TREAT, IN DUTCH, ETC.

Welsh rabbit (rarebit)

A widely held misconception is that *Welsh rabbit* is a vulgar form of *Welsh rarebit*. Actually the opposite is true, for *Welsh rarebit* is merely a mannered and affected corruption of a phrase that dates back nearly to Shakespeare's time.

In those days only the wealthy in Wales could afford game from the royal preserves. So, since rabbit itself was such a rarity, melted cheese on toast became known semihumorously as *Welsh rabbit*. In similar fashion, scrambled eggs on toast spread with anchovy butter came to be called *Scotch woodcock*. Up in New England even today, you may occasionally hear codfish called *Cape Cod turkey*.

It's unfortunate that the editors of some cookbooks have helped to spread the nice-nellyism, *rarebit*. Perhaps it's because the term has long been a favorite of restaurant menu writers—a curious breed who seem never able to say anything simply.

H. W. Fowler, as usual, has a brusque and trenchant comment on the matter. "*Welsh rabbit*," he writes, "is amusing and right, and *Welsh rarebit* stupid and wrong."

west, young man, go. *See* go west, young man.

wetback

Wetback is the slang term designating illegal immigrant farm laborers who enter California and Texas from Mexico. So called because most of them wade or swim across the Rio Grande under cover of darkness to escape detection by Border Patrol officers, they have been the subject of considerable legal hocus-pocus. First, the Department of Justice announced its intention of deporting all such *wetback* aliens found in U.S. territory and proceeded with a program which resulted in the deportation of nearly 100,000 per month. Considering that official estimates place the number of *wetbacks* entering the country illegally each year at 1,000,000, this program would in time have sharply reduced the supply of wetback laborers, who, because of their extralegal status, have to work for wages considerably below prevailing wages for native farm labor.

This action by the Justice Department led to sharp protests from Southern California farmers, who reported severe shortages of labor and who contended that some *wetback* labor is essential to get in the crops on schedule. In addition, of course, large numbers of migrant laborers are brought across the border legally under a contract system which guarantees the workers certain minimum wages and living conditions and provides for their return to Mexico when the harvest season is finished.

whipping boy

This expression used in the sense of a person who is a scapegoat—a person punished for mistakes committed by someone else—comes to us from a practice common to European royalty four or five centuries ago.

Each young princeling or royal personage was educated along with a boy of common birth—and the commoner was flogged whenever the young prince committed an act deemed worthy of punishment. So today when an office underling has to stand by and take the reprimand properly due his superior, he may at least take comfort in the thought that he is merely enacting a role once played by commoners at the courts of kings.

whiskey

The word *whiskey* comes from the Gaelic word *uisgebeatha,* meaning "water of life." This has been a favorite phrase for potent spirits ever since ancient Romans downed their *aqua vitae.* The Swedish brand of liquid lightning is called *akavit,* while the French often refer to a choice brandy as *eau de vie.*

Both Scotsmen and Irishmen—but not the English—can claim credit for inventing whiskey and yours truly surely is not audacious enough to mediate their respective claims. It seems clear, though, that whiskey first became widely popular during the reign of Henry VIII—a stalwart trencherman and two-fisted devotee of what, in his day, was called *whiskeybaugh.*

white elephant

Many centuries ago in Siam, now Thailand, the white or albino elephant was so rare that each one born became automatically the property of the king and none were permitted to work.

So, if the king took a dislike to one of his courtiers, the punishment was swift, simple and devastating. The king simply gave a white elephant to the victim of his displeasure—and waited for time and the enormous appetite of the elephant to reduce the courtier to ruin.

white horses

The white peaks of waves may be called *whitecaps* in America but in Britain they are known as *white horses*. See ENGLISH ENGLISH.

white mule. *See* mountain dew.

whoopee, making

Neither Walter Winchell nor Eddie Cantor invented the phrase *making whoopee,* though both did much to popularize it. Simply as a shout of exuberance or rejoicing, *whoopee* has been commonplace since midway through the nineteenth century. Scholars have even traced the form *whoope* back to 1450. Best research, however, indicates that the *e* on *whoope* was silent—which leaves us with the simple "whoop."

In 1927, or perhaps a year or two earlier, Winchell began to use the phrase *making whoopee* to describe the speakeasy revels of the gay blades of the period. The term caught on so quickly that within a very few years Eddie Cantor was starring in a musical comedy titled *Whoopee,* whose best-known tune was certainly "Making Whoopee," which Eddie sang for years afterward.

widow's peak

A *widow's peak* is the point formed by hair growing down in the middle of the forehead. According to old superstition, a woman having such a growth was slated for early widowhood.

widow's weeds

Originally *weeds* were any kind of clothing. The Anglo-Saxon word for garment was *waede*. Thus Spenser wrote of: "A goodly lady clad in hunter's *weed*." Over the centuries, though, its use has become chiefly restricted to mourning garments worn by widows.

wild and wooly West

Nobody is quite sure how *wooly* got into this phrase—though the alliteration of the three *w*'s is doubtless why it stayed there.

One theory is that the wool of sheep allowed to graze on the open range grows coarse and rough—thus furnishing a parallel to the rough, coarse life of the frontier. The chief trouble with this theory is that the cattlemen who opened up the West held sheep herders in the same low esteem that Kentucky moonshiners reserve for "revenooers." So it's hardly likely that Western cattlemen would have rejoiced in a description which involved their pet hate, the sheep.

More plausible is the theory that *wooly* refers to a kind of minor tornado, so-called because the winds "beat the water into a wool-white foam" —according to a nineteenth-century authority. The trouble with this theory is that there wasn't much water around those parts of the West that were wildest and wooliest.

So we come to my own surmise—that the word comes from the angora chaps worn by many cowpokes, the kind they themselves now call "hair pants." These angora chaps certainly qualify for the adjective *wooly* and were popular garb when the hands "duded up" for some special occasion like the trip to town after roundup.

Another logical explanation—though one your young son may not be happy to accept if he's thinking of clean-shaven television cowboys—is that the cowhands themselves looked quite *wooly* after long weeks of riding the range or herding cattle along one of the early trails. After all, the safety razor was unknown in those days—and any kind of shaving facilities were hard to come by. So the *wild and wooly West* expression may well have originated with wild and wooly-faced cowboys!

wild oats, to sow

Wild oats are tall weeds similar in appearance to oats but relatively worthless. So a person *sowing wild oats* would be planting a worthless crop, just as a young man does when he fritters away his time in fruitless dissipation.

wings. *See* automobile slang, British.

wisp of snipe. *See* clowder, kindle and cowardice.

wisteria

When you admire the blossoms on a wisteria tree, you may not be aware of the fact that it is named after a famous American botanist of the nineteenth century, Caspar Wistar.

A few years ago Joshua Logan, famed producer-director-playwright, embarked on a fruitless attempt to change the spelling of *wisteria* to *wistaria* on the ground that this spelling is closer to the botanist's name. In spite of the fact that his play, *The Wistaria Trees,* had a fair run on Broadway, Logan's quixotic attempt to bring belated fame to Wistar failed.

wobblies. *See* labor's lost lexicon.

WOC, WAE

Investigations by various scandal-hunting Congressional committees a few years ago taught the general public the meaning of at least one of the cabalistic items in the jargon of governmentese. A *WOC,* we learned, was a person who donated his services to the government—usually, though not always, from altruistic motives—"without compensation." The name, of course, came from the key letters in that last phrase.

Thanks to Adlai Stevenson's 1957 tour of duty with the State Department, we learned another item from the private language of our bureaucrats. According to a departmental release, the two-time Democratic nominee was first classified as a *WAE*—a person who received pay "When Actually Employed." In fact, Stevenson refused any remuneration except his travel expenses, so he was later reclassified from a *WAE* to a *WOC.*

woman

Woman, appropriately enough, is one of the more perplexing and unusually formed words in our language. It all starts with *mann,* the Anglo-Saxon word for "human being," to which was prefixed *wif-* for "female." (That's the same *wif-,* by the way, from which "wife" comes.)

That gave us *wifmann* which gradually became *wimman* and eventually *woman,* with the plural form *women.* But the pronunciation WIM-'n carried over from the earlier phase when the plural of *wimman* was *wimmen.*

Incidentally, both these words form plurals in accordance with an Old English form *-en* which survives in very few other words today. Three that come readily to mind are "oxen," "brethren" and, of course, "children."

wood, knock on

There are many different theories, none entirely provable, as to where the expression *to knock on wood* came from. Here are three of the more popular. Take your pick.

In the Bible (Galatians, Sixth Chapter) appears this statement: "God forbid that I should glory save in the cross of our Lord Jesus Christ." The idea is that your boast will be forgiven if you turn your thoughts at once to the wooden cross of Christ.

More ancient even than this theory is that *knocking on wood* goes back to antiquity, when druids and other spirits were thought to live in trees. Thus you might rap on a tree trunk to call up the spirit of the tree as protection against impending harm.

A less spiritual theory is that the superstition goes back to a form of the children's game of "tag." The child who succeeds in tagging a tree (touching wood) is free from capture.

wool over his eyes, pulling the

This expression goes back to the days when all gentlemen wore powdered wigs similar to the ones still worn by the judges in British courts. The word *wool* was then a popular, joking term for hair—as it still is in some areas today, especially when referring to very curly hair. The expression *pulling the wool over his eyes* came from the practice of jokingly tilting a man's wig over his eyes, so that he'd be unable to see what was going on. From this came, of course, today's meaning of "to deceive or hoodwink" a person.

world does move, the

One theory of the origin of the phrase *The world does move* ascribes it to Galileo. In 1633 he was hauled before the Inquisition and made to recant his belief in the Copernican theory of the rotation of the earth on its axis. As he completed his recantation, he is supposed to have murmured, *Eppur si muove!*—an Italian phrase meaning "And yet it does move!" This is an interesting fable, but probably no more than that.

worsted cloth

Worsted came first from the town of Worsted, now Worstead, England. I must say I prefer the warm rich sound of such a centuries-old fabric to brisk but evanescent names like Dynel, chromespun and the other synthetics we see so widely advertised today.

worth his salt. *See* salt, worth his.

wowser

Wowser, meaning a puritanical person, was originally Australian slang but became fairly widely used in America during H. L. Mencken's heyday when he and George Jean Nathan were valiantly battling the bluenoses through the medium of the old *American Mercury* magazine. It is supposed to be based on the initial letters of an Australian reform group's motto: "We Only Want Social Evils Righted."

wreak, wreck

There is a fairly close kinship between these two words and, in the opinion of some word authorities, both come from the same Icelandic word *rek*. However that may be, there is a clear distinction between the two today. *Wreak* (pronounced REEK) means to inflict or to execute. Thus a hurricane wreaks (inflicts) havoc (destruction and devastation) along the New England shore.

Wreck (pronounced REK) means to destroy or badly damage. Thus, "A tidal wave *wrecked* the ship."

X

xenophobia

Meaning fear or hatred of strangers or foreigners, *xenophobia* comes from the Greek *xenos* (stranger) and *phobos* (fear).

xylography

From the Greek *xylon* (wood) and *graphia* (writing), *xylography* is the art of engraving on wood or the making of prints from wood engraving.

Y

Yale University

Yale University took its name from an early British colonial governor of Madras, India. It seems old Elihu Yale heard of the struggling little school in Connecticut and he sent three trunks of madras as his contribution to Yale's first of many fund-raising drives. He also sent some books and about $4,000. See also BORN WITH THE GIFT OF LAUGHTER AND A SENSE THAT THE WORLD WAS MAD.

yellow dog. *See* labor's lost lexicon.

yes man

Like *hot dog,* this is one of the creations of the great sports cartoonist TAD (T. A. Dorgan). *Yes man* first appeared in a cartoon in 1913. The

[375]

cartoon was labeled "Giving the First Edition the Once Over" and showed a newspaper editor with his assistants looking over sheets fresh from the press. The assistants were all praising the edition—and each bore the label *yes-man.*

A few years ago the late Fred Allen added a phrase to the language which deserves to be better known. Describing the reaction with which smart young sycophants greet the boss' attempts at joke-making, Allen coined the phrase *loyalty laughter.* Both *yes-men* and *loyalty laughter* are very much a part of the business scene today—but never so funny in real life as when spoofed by Bobby Morse and Rudy Vallee in *How to Succeed in Business Without Really Trying.*

Yuletide. *See* **Christmas words.**

Z

zoophobia

Zoophobia victims experience a morbid fear of all animals. The prefix "zoo-" comes from the German *zoion,* which means a single animal. It is in the plural sense that "zoo-" is used in *zoophobia*—intense distaste for all animals. The American word *zoo,* meaning a collection of wild animals or menagerie, is actually an abbreviation of "zoological gardens."

Bailey Bridge

After the disastrous Connecticut Valley floods a few years ago, a woman from Middletown, Connecticut, wrote me: "Since the flood has struck our Naugatuck Valley, I've been hearing about the Army's *Bailey Bridge*. Several are supposed to be installed in this area, although I haven't seen one due to the ban on sightseeing. For whom and when was this piece of engineering named?"

The *Bailey Bridge* is a portable bridge made of prefabricated steel sections in the form of lattices. It was named for its inventor, Donald Coleman Bailey of the British Ministry of Supply in World War II. So successful was his invention that he was knighted in 1945 for his contribution to the victorious war effort.

bake. *See* jazzmen's jargon.

baker's dozen

There are many theories about the origin of this phrase. The most commonly accepted theory dates back to fifteenth-century England. It seems that bakers had long had a reputation—whether deserved or not—for short-weighting their bread. As a result, very strict laws were passed, regulating the weight of the various breads, muffins and cakes. But, as every cook knows, it's not possible—especially when cooking with the primitive ovens then available—to have the loaves absolutely uniform in weight.

So the practice developed of giving thirteen loaves on every order for twelve, thereby guaranteeing that there would be no penalty for shortages.

Another theory is that the phrase developed by analogy from *printer's dozen*, for in the early days of publishing it was the custom of printers to supply the retailer with thirteen copies of a book on each order of twelve. Since the retailer was billed at list price, the return on the thirteenth book represented his profit on the transaction. As a sidelight on this medieval selling technique, by the way, we may note that today one of the most prevalent practices of the book trade is for the publisher to offer retailers "one-for-ten" or one free book with every ten ordered, thereby increasing the retailer's margin of profit and, of course, the number of books sold by the publisher.

Then there's still another theory. It seems that the bakers of the medieval period had such a bad name that the words *baker* and *devil* were sometimes used interchangeably. Thus, the term *baker's dozen* may have evolved from *devil's dozen,* which was a common folk phrase meaning thirteen. And thirteen was the number of witches usually present at meetings summoned by Old Nick.

balk

The word *balk* comes from the Anglo-Saxon *balca,* a wooden beam, and refers to the huge timbers used to bar outer doors, thus *balking* an enemy's onslaught. See also BILK.

balletomane

This is the name for an enthusiast for ballets. The word, which was coined fairly recently in France, is from the words *ballet* and *manie* (mania). Thus a *balletomane* (pronounced bal-LET-uh-mayn) is one whose devotion to the dance is roughly equal to a Milwaukee baseball fan's enthusiasm for the Braves in mid-August and *fan,* in case you have forgotten is often thought to be a shortened form of *"fanatic."* See also LABANOTATION.

balling the jack

This is a phrase from the jargon of railroadmen and simply means going at top speed. It also has acquired the meaning in gambling circles of risking everything on a single throw of the dice or turn of a card.

ballistophobia

If you suffer from fear of bullets, you are a victim of ballistophobia. Root words for this unusual word are the Latin *ballista* (to throw) and the Greek *phobos* (fear). See also PHOBIAS.

Baltimore chop. *See* baseball jargon.

bankrupt

In medieval Italy moneylenders operated from *bancas*—benches or shelves. When a moneylender was forced to suspend his business from lack of funds, his *banka* was broken up and he was given the name *bancarotto.* From this beginning the word *bankrupt* eventually came to mean any insolvent person, especially anyone who had been legally declared unable to pay his debts.

banns, posting of the

Banns are a series of announcements of the intent of a couple to wed. Today's common meaning of "ban"—to forbid or prohibit—is nowhere involved in the *banns* of marriage. Yet the two words come from the same Anglo-Saxon root, *bannan* (to proclaim or to summon).

What has happened is that the word, which in the times of Robin Hood merely meant to announce, has acquired through the centuries the specialized meaning of to proclaim a prohibition. This probably resulted from the use of *bann* and later *ban* by church authorities to proclaim the excommunication of sinners. This most serious form of ecclesiastical disapproval soon diverted the word from its general meaning to the special sense of prohibition in which it is most commonly used today.

banshee

Most of us associate *banshee* with the unearthly wails of a female spirit foretelling a death in the family. But in the original Gaelic, the *banshee* was usually depicted as a beautiful woman, not a hag.

barley duck

It is a comparatively easy matter to trace down *barley duck* and discover that it is a tangy preserve made of gooseberries or currants, frequently served as an accompaniment to the main roast meat course at dinner. But where did the strange name come from? It's what the language experts call a "corrupted" pronunciation of *Bar-le-Duc* (pronounced bar-luh-DYOOK), which is the name of the French town where this preserve is thought to have originated.

barnstorming

This term, though now almost exclusively a political word meaning to travel rapidly about the country making speeches wherever people will gather, was originally a theatrical term. It described itinerant stock companies whose repertory and talent were not topflight and who in consequence had to appear in second-rate auditoriums and even occasionally in barns. Since such itineraries as they had were usually hastily improvised, they gave the impression of *storming* (moving impetuously) around the country.

barristers, solicitors

Generally speaking, *barristers* are lawyers who practice in the superior courts in England. Indeed, there are two classes: the simple *barrister,* an attorney admitted to the bar and a higher order known as "King's Counsel." The latter are said to *take silk* when appointed "K.C." because they thenceforth wear silk gowns while junior counsel (barristers) wear gowns of ordinary cloth.

Solicitors are lawyers who are not members of the bar and do not plead cases in higher courts.

baseball jargon

The sport pages are a daily reminder that no American activity has developed so colorful and extensive a vocabulary as baseball. Ever since the days of Abner Doubleday, sports writers and the players themselves have coined graphic and picturesque phrases to describe all aspects of the National Game.

We assume that everyone knows the difference between a base hit and an out, so we'll pass over the standard terms and concentrate on the colorful "slanguage" of baseball reporters and sportscasters.

Aboard—On base. When there are three men on base, the bases are *loaded* and there are *three men aboard.*

Bad ball—A ball pitched well outside of the strike zone. A batter who habitually "goes after" such pitches is known as a *"bad ball* hitter."

Baltimore chop—A ball that hits the ground just in front of the plate and takes a long, high bounce, slow enough to enable the batter to reach first base. This term is now almost obsolete. In fact, it's so far out it may soon be "in" again.

Bases loaded—The situation when there are runners on first, second and third bases.

Bean ball—A ball pitched directly at the batter's head, to force him back from the plate. Technically illegal, it is resorted to fairly frequently, though not so often as indignant batters would have you believe.

Bench jockey—A player or coach who taunts members of the opposing team from his place on the bench. Most notable *bench jockey* in recent years has been Leo "The Lip" Durocher.

Bleeder—Kissing cousin of the *blooper* (which see) except that it spends most of its time on the ground. Usually it's a weak grounder that takes a bad bounce just outside the reach of an infielder. It's also called a *scratch hit.*

Blooper—A weak fly which falls beyond the infield and short of the outfield. It's also called a *banjo hit* and, in the old days, was named a *Texas leaguer.*

Change-up or *change of pace*—A slow ball pitched after one or more fast balls, but with the same motions of delivery. What used to be called a "slow ball" is now referred to by most sportscasters as a *change-up,* even when the pitch is the first one delivered to the batter.

Clutch hitter—The kind of hitter who can be counted on to deliver a hit when it is most needed.

Cousin—A pitcher whom a batter finds consistently easy to hit. Even very great pitchers sometimes find an occasional opposition batter who can fathom their trickiest deliveries.

Cripple—Ball pitched when the count on the batter is three balls and